THE HUMANITIES THROUGH THE ARTS

Tenth Edition

Lee A. Jacobus

Professor of English Emeritus
University of Connecticut

F. David Martin

Professor of Philosophy Emeritus
Bucknell University

Mc
Graw
Hill
Education

THE HUMANITIES THROUGH THE ARTS, TENTH EDITION

Published by McGraw-Hill Education, 2 Penn Plaza, New York, NY 10121. Copyright © 2019 by McGraw-Hill Education. All rights reserved. Printed in the United States of America. Previous editions © 2015, 2011, and 2008. No part of this publication may be reproduced or distributed in any form or by any means, or stored in a database or retrieval system, without the prior written consent of McGraw-Hill Education, including, but not limited to, in any network or other electronic storage or transmission, or broadcast for distance learning.

Some ancillaries, including electronic and print components, may not be available to customers outside the United States.

This book is printed on acid-free paper.

2 3 4 5 6 7 8 9 LCR 21 20 19 18

Bound:
ISBN 978-1-259-91687-8
MHID 1-259-91687-1

Looseleaf:
ISBN 978-1-260-15418-4
MHID 1-260-15418-1

Portfolio Manager: *Sarah Remington*
Product Developers: *Beth Tripmacher, Bruce Cantley*
Content Project Managers: *Mary E. Powers (Core), Emily Windelborn (Assessment)*
Buyer: *Susan K. Culbertson*
Design: *Tara McDermott*
Content Licensing Specialist: *Carrie Burger*
Compositor: *MPS Limited*
Cover Image: **(background):** *LACMA - Los Angeles County Museum of Art;* **(back cover (left) to front cover (right));** *(door): ©Lee A. Jacobus; (wall carving): ©Lee A. Jacobus; (cave painting): ©siloto/Shutterstock RF; (amphitheater): ©Inu/Shutterstock RF; (Taj Mahal): ©Seb c'est bien/Shutterstock RF; (dancer): ©Fuse/Getty Images RF; (Shakespeare): ©duncan1890/Getty Images RF; (sculpture): National Gallery of Art, Washington; (graffiti): ©Lee A. Jacobus; (church): National Archives Catalog; (violin): ©Comstock Images/SuperStock RF.*

All credits appearing on page or at the end of the book are considered to be an extension of the copyright page.

Library of Congress Cataloging-in-Publication Data

Martin, F. David, 1920- author. | Jacobus, Lee A., author.
  The humanities through the arts/F. David Martin, Professor of
  Philosophy Emeritus, Bucknell University; Lee A. Jacobus, Professor of
  English Emeritus, University of Connecticut.
  Tenth edition. | New York : McGraw-Hill Education, 2018. | Includes index.
  LCCN 2017051530 | ISBN 9781259916878 (alk. paper)
  LCSH: Arts–Psychological aspects. | Art appreciation.
  LCC NX165 .M37 2018 | DDC 701/.18–dc23 LC record available
  at https://lccn.loc.gov/2017051530

The Internet addresses listed in the text were accurate at the time of publication. The inclusion of a website does not indicate an endorsement by the authors or McGraw-Hill Education, and McGraw-Hill Education does not guarantee the accuracy of the information presented at these sites.

mheducation.com/highered

ABOUT THE AUTHORS

Lee A. Jacobus (PhD, Claremont Graduate University) taught at Western Connecticut State University and then at the University of Connecticut (Storrs) until he retired in 2001. He held a Danforth Teachers Grant while earning his doctorate. His publications include *Shakespeare and the Dialectic of Certainty* (St. Martin's Press, 1992); *Sudden Apprehension: Aspects of Knowledge in Paradise Lost* (Mouton, 1976); *John Cleveland: A Critical Study* (G. K. Hall, 1975); *Aesthetics and the Arts* (McGraw-Hill, 1968); *The Bedford Introduction to Drama* (Bedford/St. Martin's, 2018); and *A World of Ideas* (Bedford/St. Martin's, 2017).

F. David Martin (PhD, University of Chicago) taught at the University of Chicago and then at Bucknell University until his retirement in 1983. He was a Fulbright Research Scholar in Florence and Rome from 1957 through 1959 and received seven other major research grants during his career, as well as the Christian Lindback Award for Distinguished Teaching. Dr. Martin's publications include *Art and the Religious Experience* (Associated University Presses, 1972); *Sculpture and the Enlivened Space* (The University Press of Kentucky, 1981); and *Facing Death: Theme and Variations* (Associated University Presses, 2006). Professor Martin died in 2014.

We dedicate this study to
teachers and students of the humanities.

Source: The Michael C. Rockefeller Memorial Collection, Bequest of Nelson A. Rockefeller, 1979/The Metropolitan Museum of Art

BRIEF CONTENTS

Photo: Kira Perov. Courtesy Bill Viola Studio

CONTENTS

16 The Interrelationships of the Humanities   397

©ArenaPal/Topham/The Image Works

PREFACE

OVERVIEW

The Humanities through the Arts, tenth edition, explores the humanities with an emphasis on the arts. Examining the relationship of the humanities to values, objects, and events important to people is central to this book. We make a distinction between artists and other humanists: Artists reveal values, while other humanists examine or reflect on values. We study how values are revealed in the arts while keeping in mind a basic question: "What is art?" Judging by the existence of ancient artifacts, we see that artistic expression is one of the most fundamental human activities. It binds us together as a people by revealing the most important values of our culture.

Our genre-based approach offers students the opportunity to understand the relationship of the arts to human values by examining, in-depth, each of the major artistic media. Subject matter, form, and content in each of the arts supply the framework for careful analysis. Painting and photography focus our eyes on the visual appearance of things. Sculpture reveals the textures, densities, and shapes of things. Architecture sharpens our perception of spatial relationships, both inside and out. Literature, theater, cinema, and video explore values and make us more aware of the human condition. Our understanding of feelings is deepened by music. Our sensitivity to movement, especially of the human body, is enhanced by dance. The wide range of opportunities for criticism and analysis helps the reader synthesize the complexities of the arts and their interaction with values of many kinds. All of this is achieved with an exceptionally vivid and complete illustration program alongside detailed discussion and interactive responses to the problems inherent in a close study of the arts and values of our time.

ORGANIZATION

This edition, as with previous editions, is organized into three parts, offering considerable flexibility in the classroom:

Part 1, "Fundamentals," includes the first three introductory chapters. In Chapter 1, *The Humanities: An Introduction*, we distinguish the humanities from the sciences, and the arts from other humanities. In Chapter 2, *What Is a Work of Art?*, we raise the question of definition in art and the ways in which we distinguish art from other objects and experiences. Chapter 3, *Being a Critic of the Arts*, introduces the vital role of criticism in art appreciation and evaluation.

Part 2, "The Arts," includes individual chapters on each of the basic arts. The structure of this section permits complete flexibility: The chapters may be used in their present order or in any order one wishes. We begin with the individual chapters *Painting, Sculpture,* and *Architecture;* follow with *Literature, Theater, Music,* and *Dance;* and continue with *Photography, Cinema,* and *Television and Video Art.* Instructors may reorder or omit chapters as needed. The chapter *Photography* logically precedes the chapters *Cinema* and *Television and Video Art* for the convenience of instructors who prefer to teach the chapters in the order presented.

Part 3, "Interrelationships," begins with Chapter 14, *Is It Art or Something Like It?* We study illustration, folk art, propaganda, and kitsch while raising the question "What is art?" We also examine the avant-garde as it pushes us to the edge of definition. Chapter 15, *The Interrelationships of the Arts,* explores the ways in which the arts work together, as in how a film interprets E. M. Forster's novel *Howards End,* how literature and a musical interpretation of a Beaumarchais play result in Mozart's opera *The Marriage of Figaro,* how Walt Whitman's poetry inspires van Gogh's painting *The Starry Night,* how a passage from Ovid's epic poem "The Metamorphoses" inspires the Bernini sculpture *Apollo and Daphne,* and more. Chapter 16, *The Interrelationships of the Humanities,* addresses the ways in which the arts reveal values shared by the other humanities—particularly history, philosophy, and theology.

KEY CHANGES IN THE TENTH EDITION

NEW Expanded Connect course with SmartBook.   Connect is a highly reliable, easy-to-use homework and learning management solution that embeds learning science and award-winning adaptive tools to improve student results.

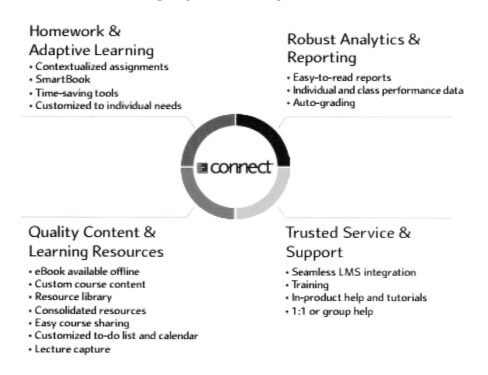

Homework & Adaptive Learning
- Contextualized assignments
- SmartBook
- Time-saving tools
- Customized to individual needs

Robust Analytics & Reporting
- Easy-to-read reports
- Individual and class performance data
- Auto-grading

Quality Content & Learning Resources
- eBook available offline
- Custom course content
- Resource library
- Consolidated resources
- Easy course sharing
- Customized to-do list and calendar
- Lecture capture

Trusted Service & Support
- Seamless LMS integration
- Training
- In-product help and tutorials
- 1:1 or group help

LearnSmart is an adaptive learning program designed to help students learn faster, study smarter, and retain more knowledge for greater success. Distinguishing what students know from what they don't, and focusing on concepts they are most likely to forget, LearnSmart continuously adapts to each student's needs by building a personalized learning path. An intelligent adaptive study tool, LearnSmart is proven to strengthen memory recall, keep students in class, and boost grades.

The Humanities Through the Arts now offers two reading experiences for students and instructors: SmartBook and eBook. Fueled by LearnSmart, SmartBook is the first and only adaptive reading experience currently available. SmartBook™ creates a personalized reading experience by highlighting the most impactful concepts a student needs to learn at that moment in time. The reading experience continuously adapts by highlighting content based on what the student knows and doesn't know. Real-time reports quickly identify the concepts that require more attention from individual students—or the entire class. eBook provides a simple, elegant reading experience, available for offline reading.

SmartBook

DESIGNED FOR

- Preparing for class
- Practice and study
- Focusing on key topics
- Reports and analytics

SUPPORTS

- Adaptive, personalized learning
- Assignable content
- Smartphone and tablet via iOS and Android apps

eBook

DESIGNED FOR

- Reading in class
- Reference
- Offline reading
- Accessibility

SUPPORTS

- Simple, elegant reading
- Basic annotations
- Smartphone and tablet via iOS and Android apps

Updated illustration program and contextual discussions. More than 30 percent of the images in this edition are new or have been updated to include fresh classic and contemporary works. New discussions of these works appear near the illustrations. The 200-plus images throughout the book have been carefully chosen and reproduced in full color when possible, resulting in a beautifully illustrated text. Newly added visual artists represented include painters Artemisia Gentileschi, Diego Velasquez, Frederic Lord Leighton, Amedeo Modigliani, Winslow Homer, Morris Louis, Hokusai, Willem de Kooning, Jean-Honore Fragonard, Arshile Gorky, Henry Wallis, Dante Gabriel Rossetti, Arthur Hughes, William Holman Hunt, and John Waterhouse; sculptors Edgar Degas, Kara Walker, Magdalena Abakanowicz, and Naum Gabo; photographers Berenice Abbott, Nan Goldin, Paul Strand, Bruce Davidson, Carrie Mae Weems, Tina Barney, Wang Quinsong, and Bill Gekas; and video artists Pipilotti Riist and Bill Viola. Newly added film and television stills represent Michael Curtiz's classic film *Casablanca*, the popular television shows *Game of Thrones* and *The Americans*, Orson Wells's *The Lady from Shanghai*, Jonathan Demme's *The Silence of the Lambs*, Steven Spielberg's *Saving Private Ryan*, Alejandro Inarritu's *The Revenant*, and more.

Along with the many new illustrations and contextual discussions of the visual arts, film, and television, new works and images in the literary, dance, theatrical, and musical arts have been added and contextualized. These include works by Robert Herrick, John Masefield, Amy Lowell, Alfred Lord Tennyson, John Donne, Wang Chang-Ling, Po Chu'i, John Millington Synge, Lin-Manuel Miranda, Frederic Chopin, Tupac Shakur, and the Batsheva Dance Company.

Increased focus on non-Western art and art by minority and female artists. This edition contains numerous new examples, including paintings (Artemesia Gentileschi's *Self-portrait as the Allegory of Painting* and Hokusai's *The Wave*), sculpture (Kara Walker's *A Subtlety, or The Marvelous Sugar Baby* and Magdalena Abakanowicz's *Bronze Crowd*), architecture (the Mortuary Temple of Hatshepsut, Egypt), literature (Amy Lowell's "Venus Transiens" and Po Chu'i's T'ang dynasty poetry), theater (Lin-Manual Miranda's *Hamilton*), dance (the Batsheva Dance Company), photography (Berenice Abbott, Nan Goldin, Carrie Mae Weems, Tina Barney, and Wang Quinsong), film (*The Revenant*), and television and video art (Pipilotti Riist).

PEDAGOGICAL FEATURES

Four major pedagogical boxed features enhance student understanding of the genres and of individual works within the genres: Perception Key, Conception Key, Experiencing, and Focus On.

- The **Perception Key** boxes are designed to sharpen readers' responses to the arts. These boxes raise important questions about specific works of art in a way that respects the complexities of the works and of our responses to them. The questions raised are usually open-ended and thereby avoid any doctrinaire views or dogmatic opinions. The emphasis is on perception and awareness, and how a heightened awareness will produce a fuller and more meaningful understanding of the work at hand. In a few cases our own interpretations and analyses follow the keys and are offered not as *the* way to perceive a given work of art but, rather, as one *possible* way. Our primary interest is in exciting our readers to perceive the splendid singularity of the work of art in question.

PERCEPTION KEY Chartres Cathedral

1. Form and function usually work together in classic architecture. What visible exterior architectural details indicate that Chartres Cathedral functions as a church? Are there any visible details that conflict with its function as a church?
2. The two spires of the church were built at different times. Should they have been made symmetrical? What might be some reasons for their not being symmetrical?
3. What seem to be the primary values revealed by the rose window of Chartres?
4. How did the builders satisfy the fourth requirement of architecture: that the building be revelatory? What values does the exterior of the building reveal?
5. What is implied by the fact that the cathedral dwarfs all the buildings near it?

- We use **Conception Key** boxes, rather than Perception Key boxes, in certain instances throughout the book where we focus on thought and conception rather than observation and perception. Again, these are open-ended questions that involve reflection and understanding. There is no single way of responding to these keys, just as there is no simple way to answer the questions.

CONCEPTION KEY Theories

Our theory of art as revelatory, as giving insight into values, may appear to be mired in a tradition that cannot account for the amazing developments of the avant-garde. Is the theory inadequate? As you proceed with this chapter, ask yourself whether the distinction between art and artlike is valid. How about useful? If not, what theory would you propose? Or would you be inclined to dismiss theories altogether?

- Each chapter provides an **Experiencing** box that gives the reader the opportunity to approach a specific work of art in more detail than the Perception Key boxes. Analysis of the work begins by answering a few preliminary questions to make it accessible to students. Follow-up questions ask students to think critically about the work and guide them to their own interpretations. In every case we raise major issues concerning the genre of the work, the background of the work, and the artistic issues that make the work demanding and important.

EXPERIENCING Bernini's *Apollo and Daphne* and Ovid's *The Metamorphoses*

1. If you had not read Ovid's *The Metamorphoses*, what would you believe to be the subject matter of Bernini's *Apollo and Daphne*? Do you believe it is a less interesting work if you do not know Ovid?

   One obvious issue in looking at this sculpture and considering Ovid's treatment of Apollo and Daphne is that today very few people will have read Ovid before seeing the sculpture. In the era in which Bernini created the work, he expected it to be seen primarily by well-educated people, and in the seventeenth century, most educated people would have been steeped in Ovid from a young age. Consequently, Bernini worked in a classical tradition that he could easily rely on to inform his audience.

- In each chapter of "The Arts" and "Interrelationships" sections of the book, we include a **Focus On** box, which provides an opportunity to deal in-depth with a group of artworks in context, the work of a single artist, or a single work of art. Many of the Focus On boxes are new to this edition, including those discussing the pre-Raphaelite Brotherhood, the Alhambra, Chinese poet Po Chu'i, the popular musical play *Hamilton*, the classic film *Casablanca,* and the critically acclaimed television series *The Americans*. Each of these opportunities encourages in-depth and comparative study.

FOCUS ON The Alhambra

The Alhambra (Figure 6-33) is one of the world's most dazzling works of architecture. Its beginnings in the Middle Ages were modest, a fortress on a hilly flatland above Granada built by Arab invaders—Moors—who controlled much of Spain. In time, the fortress was added to, and by the fourteenth century the Nasrid dynasty demanded a sumptuous palace and King Yusuf I (1333–1352) began construction. After his death it was continued by his son Muhammad V (1353–1391).

While the needs of a fortress were still evident, including the plain massive exterior walls, the Nasrids wanted the interior to be luxurious, magnificent, and beautiful. The Alhambra is one of the world's most astounding examples of beautifully decorated architecture. The builders created a structure that was different from any that had been built in Islam. But at the same time, they depended on many historical traditions for interior decoration, such as the Seljuk, Mughal, and Fatimid styles. Because Islam forbade the reproduction in art of the human form, we see representations of flowers, plants, vines, and other natural objects in the midst of elaborate designs, including Arabic script.

The aerial view (Figure 6-34) reveals the siting of the Alhambra rising above trees surrounding it. The large square structure was added much later by Charles V, after the Nasrid dynasty collapsed and the Moors were driven from Spain.

FIGURE 6-33
The Alhambra, Granada, Spain. Circa 1370–1380. "Alhambra" may be translated as red, possibly a reference to the color of the bricks of its outer walls. It sits on high ground above the town.

©Daniel Viñé Garcia/Getty Images RF

Image Bank

Instructors can access a database of images from select McGraw-Hill Education art and humanities titles, including *The Humanities through the Arts.* Connect Image Bank includes all images for which McGraw-Hill Education has secured electronic permissions. Instructors can access a text's images by browsing its chapters, style/period, medium, and culture or by searching on key terms.

Instructors can also search for images from other McGraw-Hill Education titles included in the database. Images can easily be downloaded for use in presentations and in PowerPoints. The download includes a text file with image captions and information.

You can access *Connect Image Bank* under the library tab in Connect.

McGraw-Hill Create

create™ Easily rearrange chapters, combine material from other content sources, and quickly upload content you have written, such as your course syllabus or teaching notes, using McGraw-Hill Education's Create. Find the content you need by searching through thousands of leading McGraw-Hill textbooks. Arrange your book to fit your teaching style. Create even allows you to personalize your book's appearance by selecting the cover and adding your name, school, and course information. Order a Create book and you'll receive a complimentary print review copy in three to five business days or a complimentary electronic review copy (eComp) via e-mail in about an hour. Experience how McGraw-Hill Education empowers *you* to teach your students your way. http://www.mcgrawhillcreate.com/

Question Bank

The Humanities through the Arts, tenth edition, includes a number of resources to assist instructors with planning and teaching their courses: an instructor's manual, which offers learning objectives, chapter outlines, possible discussion and lecture topics, and more; a test bank with multiple-choice and essay questions; and a chapter-by-chapter PowerPoint presentation.

ACKNOWLEDGMENTS

This book is indebted to more people than we can truly credit. We are deeply grateful to the following survey respondents for their help on this edition:

Micheal Jay Adamek, *Ozarks Technical Community College*; Larry Atkins, *Ozarks Technical Community College*; Michael Bajuk, *Western Washington University*; Michael Berberich, *Galveston College*; Bill Burrows, *Lane Community College*; Aaron

Butler, *Warner Pacific College Adult Degree Program*; Linda Carpenter, *Coastline Community College*; Jordan Chilton, *Ozarks Technical Community College*; Patricia Dodd, *Houston Community College*; Laura Early, *Highland Community College*; Kristin Edford, *Amarillo College*; Jeremy R. Franklin, *Colorado Mesa University*; Diane Gaston, *Cuyahoga Community College*; Donna Graham, *Ozarks Technical Community College*; Daniel Hieber, *Ozarks Technical Community College*; Jennifer Keefe, *Valencia College*; Donny Leveston, *Houston Community College*; Susanna Lundgren, *Warner Pacific College*; Jimidene Murphey, *Wharton County Junior College*; Sven Pearsall, *Alpena Community College*; Debbi Richard, *Dallas Baptist University*; Matthew Scott, *Ozarks Technical Community College*; Timothy Soulis, *Transylvania University*; Peter C. Surace, *Cuyahoga Community College*; Normand Theriault, *Houston Community College*; Peter Utgaard, *Cuyamaca College*; Dawn Hamm Walsh, *Dallas Baptist University*; and Adrian S. Windsor, *Coastline Community College*

We also thank the following reviewers for their help shaping previous editions:

Addell Austin Anderson, *Wayne County Community College District*; David Avalos, *California State University San Marcos*; Bruce Bellingham, *University of Connecticut*; Eugene Bender, *Richard J. Daley College*; Michael Berberich, *Galveston College*; Barbara Brickman, *Howard Community College*; Peggy Brown, *Collin County Community College*; Lance Brunner, *University of Kentucky*; Alexandra Burns, *Bay Path College*; Bill Burrows, *Lane Community College*; Glen Bush, *Heartland Community College*; Sara Cardona, *Richland College*; Brandon Cesmat, *California State University San Marcos*; Selma Jean Cohen, *editor of* Dance Perspectives; Karen Conn, *Valencia Community College*; Harrison Davis, *Brigham Young University*; Jim Doan, *Nova University*; Jill Domoney, *Johnson County Community College*; Gerald Eager, *Bucknell University*; Kristin Edford, *Amarillo College*; D. Layne Ehlers, *Bacone College*; Jane Ferencz, *University of Wisconsin–Whitewater*; Roberta Ferrell, *SUNY Empire State*; Michael Flanagan, *University of Wisconsin–Whitewater*; Kathy Ford, *Lake Land College*; Andy Friedlander, *Skagit Valley College*; Harry Garvin, *Bucknell University*; Susan K. de Ghizee, *University of Denver*; Amber Gillis, *El Camino College–Compton Center*; Michael Gos, *Lee College*; M. Scott Grabau, *Irvine Valley College*; Lee Hartman, *Howard Community College*; Jeffrey T. Hopper, *Harding University*; James Housefield, *Texas State University–San Marcos*; Stephen Husarik, *University of Arkansas–Fort Smith*; Ramona Ilea, *Pacific University Oregon*; Joanna Jacobus, *choreographer*; Lee Jones, *Georgia Perimeter College–Lawrenceville*; Deborah Jowitt, *Village Voice*; Nadene A. Keene, *Indiana University–Kokomo*; Marsha Keller, *Oklahoma City University*; Paul Kessel, *Mohave Community College*; Edward Kies, *College of DuPage*; John Kinkade, *Centre College*; Gordon Lee, *Lee College*; Tracy L. McAfee, *North Central State College*; L. Timothy Myers, *Butler Community College*; Marceau Myers, *North Texas State University*; Martha Myers, *Connecticut College*; William E. Parker, *University of Connecticut*; Seamus Pender, *Franklin Pierce College*; Ellen Rosewall, *University of Wisconsin–Green Bay*; Susan Shmeling, *Vincennes University*; Ed Simone, *St. Bonaventure University*; C. Edward Spann, *Dallas Baptist University*; Mark Stewart, *San Joaquin Delta College*; Robert Streeter, *University of Chicago*; Peter C. Surace, *Cuyahoga Community College*; Robert Tynes, *University of North Carolina at Asheville*; Walter Wehner, *University of North Carolina at Greensboro*; and Keith West, *Butler Community College*.

We want to thank the editorial team at McGraw-Hill for their smart and generous support for this edition. Lead Product Developer Beth Tripmacher, along with Brand Manager Sarah Remington, oversaw the revision from inception through production. Product Developer Bruce Cantley guided us carefully through the process of establishing a revision plan and incorporating new material into the text. In all things he was a major sounding board as we thought about how to improve the book. We also owe thanks to Lead Content Project Manager Mary Powers, who oversaw the book smoothly through the production process; Tara McDermott, who oversaw the interior design in both the print and online versions of the text as well as the cover; Deb DeBord, who was an exceptionally good copyeditor; Content Licensing Specialist Carrie Burger, who oversaw the permissions process, along with Julie De Adder and Danny Meldung, who did a wonderful job researching and obtaining reprint rights for images; and Isabel Saraiva, who likewise did excellent work researching and clearing the rights for text reprints. All the wonderful people who worked on this book made our job easier and helped make this book distinctive and artistic.

A Note from the Authors

Our own commitment to the arts and the humanities has been lifelong. One purpose of this book is to help instill a love of all the arts in its readers. We have faced many of the issues and problems that are considered in this book and, to an extent, we are still undecided about certain important questions concerning the arts and their relationship to the humanities. Clearly, we grow and change our thinking as we grow. Our engagement with the arts at any age will reflect our own abilities and commitments. But as we grow, we deepen our understanding of the arts we love as well as deepen our understanding of our own nature, our inner selves. We believe that the arts and the humanities function together to make life more intense, more significant, and more wonderful. A lifetime of work unrelieved by a deep commitment to the arts would be stultifying and perhaps destructive to one's soul. The arts and humanities make us one with our fellow human beings. They help us understand each other, just as they help us admire the beauty that is the product of the human imagination. As the philosopher Susanne K. Langer once said, the arts are the primary avenues to the education of our emotional lives. By our efforts in understanding the arts, we are indelibly enriched.

©RMN-Grand Palais/Art Resource, NY

Chapter 1

THE HUMANITIES: AN INTRODUCTION

THE HUMANITIES: A STUDY OF VALUES

Today we think of the *humanities* as those broad areas of human creativity and study, such as philosophy, history, social sciences, the arts, and literature, that are distinct from mathematics and the "hard" *sciences,* mainly because in the humanities, strictly objective or scientific standards are not usually dominant.

The current separation between the humanities and the sciences reveals itself in a number of contemporary controversies. For example, the cloning of animals has been greeted by many people as a possible benefit for domestic livestock farmers. Genetically altered wheat, soybeans, and other cereals have been heralded by many scientists as a breakthrough that will produce disease-resistant crops and therefore permit us to continue to increase the world food supply. On the other hand, some people resist such modifications and purchase food identified as not being genetically altered. Scientific research into the human genome has identified certain genes for inherited diseases, such as breast cancer or Alzheimer's disease, that could be modified to protect individuals or their offspring. Genetic research also suggests that in a few years individuals may be able to "design" their children's intelligence, body shape, height, general appearance, and physical ability.

Scientists provide the tools for these choices. Their values are centered in science in that they value the nature of their research and their capacity to make it work in a positive way. However, the impact on humanity of such a series of dramatic changes to life brings to the fore values that clash with one another. For example, is it a positive social value for couples to decide the sex of their offspring rather than following nature's own direction? In this case who should decide if "designing" one's offspring is a positive value, the scientist or the humanist?

Even more profound is the question of cloning a human being. Once a sheep had been cloned successfully, it was clear that this science would lead directly to the possibility of a cloned human being. Some proponents of cloning support the process because we could clone a child who has died in infancy or clone a genius who has given great gifts to the world. For these people, cloning is a positive value. For others, the very thought of cloning a person is repugnant on the basis of religious belief. For still others, the idea of human cloning is objectionable because it echoes the creation of an unnatural monster, and for them it is a negative value. Because this is a worldwide problem, local laws will have limited effect on establishing a clear position on the value of cloning of all sorts. The question of how we decide on such a controversial issue is at the heart of the humanities, and some observers have pointed to Mary Wollstonecraft Shelley's famous novel *Frankenstein, Or the Modern Prometheus*, which in some ways enacts the conflict among these values.

These examples demonstrate that the discoveries of scientists often have tremendous impact on the values of society. Yet some scientists have declared that they merely make the discoveries and that others—presumably politicians—must decide how the discoveries are to be used. It is this last statement that brings us closest to the importance of the humanities. If many scientists believe they cannot judge how their discoveries are to be used, then we must try to understand why they give that responsibility to others. This is not to say that scientists uniformly turn such decisions over to others, for many of them are humanists as well as scientists. But the fact remains that many governments have made use of great scientific achievements without pausing to ask the "achievers" if they approved of the way their discoveries were being used. The questions are, Who decides how to use such discoveries? On what grounds should their judgments be based?

Studying the behavior of neutrinos or string theory will not help us get closer to the answer. Such study is not related to the nature of humankind but to the nature of nature. What we need is a study that will get us closer to ourselves. It should be a study that explores the reaches of human feeling in relation to *values*—not only our own individual feelings and values but also the feelings and values of others. We need a study that will increase our sensitivity to ourselves, others, and the values in our world. To be sensitive is to perceive with insight. To be sensitive is also to feel and believe that things make a difference. Furthermore,

FIGURE 1-1
Cave painting from Chauvet Caves, France. Discovered in 1994, the Chauvet Caves have yielded some of the most astonishing examples of prehistoric art the world has seen. These aurochs may have lived as many as 35,000 years ago, while the painting itself seems as modern as a contemporary work.

©Javier Trueba/MSF/Science Source

it involves an awareness of those aspects of values that cannot be measured by objective standards. To be sensitive is to respect the humanities, because, among other reasons, they help develop our sensitivity to values, to what is important to us as individuals.

There are numerous ways to approach the humanities. The way we have chosen here is the way of the arts. One of the contentions of this book is that values are clarified in enduring ways in the arts. Human beings have had the impulse to express their values since the earliest times. Ancient tools recovered from the most recent Ice Age, for example, have features designed to express an affection for beauty as well as to provide utility.

The concept of progress in the arts is problematic. Who is to say whether the cave paintings (Figure 1-1) of 30,000 years ago that were discovered in present-day France are less excellent than the work of Picasso (Figure 1-4)? Cave paintings were probably not made as works of art to be contemplated. Getting to them in the caves is almost always difficult, and they are very hard to see. They seem to have been made for a practical purpose, such as improving the prospects for the hunt. Yet the work reveals something about the power, grace, and beauty of all the animals it portrayed. These cave paintings function now as works of art. From the beginning, our species instinctively had an interest in making revealing forms.

Among the numerous ways to approach the humanities, we have chosen the way of the arts because, as we shall try to elucidate, the arts clarify or reveal values. As we deepen our understanding of the arts, we necessarily deepen our understanding of values. We will study our experience with works of art as well as the values others associate with them, and in this process we will also educate ourselves about our own values.

Because a value is something that matters, engagement with art—the illumination of values—enriches the quality of our lives significantly. Moreover, the *subject matter* of art—what it is about—is not limited to the beautiful and the pleasant, the bright sides of life. Art may also include and help us understand the dark sides—the ugly, the painful, and the tragic. And when it does and when we get it, we are better able to come to grips with those dark sides of life.

Art brings us into direct communication with others. As Carlos Fuentes wrote in *The Buried Mirror,* "People and their cultures perish in isolation, but they are born or reborn in contact with other men and women of another culture, another creed, another race. If we do not recognize our humanity in others, we shall not recognize it in ourselves." Art reveals the essence of our existence.

ART, COMMERCE, AND TASTE

When the great paintings of the Italian Renaissance were being made, their ultimate value hinged on how good they were, how fully they expressed the values—usually religious but sometimes political—that the culture expected. Michelangelo's great, heroic-sized statue of David in Florence was admired for its representation of the values of self-government by the small city-state as well as for its simple beauty of proportion. No dollar figure was attached to the great works of this period—except for the price paid to the artists. Once these works were in place, no one expressed admiration for them because they would cost a great deal in the marketplace.

Today the art world has changed profoundly and is sometimes thought to be art of an essentially commercial enterprise. Great paintings today change hands for tens of millions of dollars. Moreover, the taste of the public shifts constantly. Movies, for example, survive or fail on the basis of the number of people they appeal to. Therefore, a film is often thought good only if it makes money. As a result, film producers make every effort to cash in on current popular tastes, often by making sequels until the public's taste changes—for example, the *Batman* series (1989 to 2017). The *Star Wars* series (1977 to 2019 [projected]) cashed in on the needs of science-fiction fans whose taste in films is excited by the futuristic details and the narrative of danger and excitement of space travel. These are good films despite the emphasis on commercial success. But in some ways they are also limited by the demands of the marketplace.

Our study of the humanities emphasizes that commercial success is not the most important guide to excellence in the arts. The long-term success of works of art depends on their ability to interpret human experience at a level of complexity that warrants examination and reexamination. Many commercially successful works give us what we think we want rather than what we really need with reference to insight and understanding. By satisfying us in an immediate and superficial way, commercial art can dull us to the possibilities of complex, more deeply satisfying art.

Everyone has limitations as a perceiver of art. Sometimes we assume that we have developed our taste and that any effort to change it is bad form. The saying "Matters of taste are not disputable" can be credited with making many of us feel righteous about our own taste. What the saying means is that there is no accounting for what people like in the arts, for beauty is in the eye of the beholder. Thus, there is no use in trying to educate anyone about the arts. Obviously we disagree. We believe that all of us can and should be educated about the arts and should learn to respond to as wide a variety of the arts as possible: from jazz to string quartets, from Charlie Chaplin to Steven Spielberg, from Lewis Carroll to T. S. Eliot, from folk art to Picasso. Most of us defend our taste because anyone who challenges it challenges our deep feelings. Anyone who tries to change our responses to art is really trying to get inside our minds. If we fail to understand its purpose, this kind of persuasion naturally arouses resistance.

For us, the study of the arts penetrates beyond facts to the values that evoke our feelings—the way a succession of Eric Clapton's guitar chords playing the blues can be electrifying, or the way song lyrics can give us a chill. In other words, we want to go beyond the facts about a work of art and get to the values revealed in the work. How many times have we found ourselves liking something that, months or years before, we could not stand? And how often do we find ourselves now disliking what we previously judged a masterpiece? Generally we can say the work of art remains the same. It is we who change. We learn to recognize the values illuminated in such works as well as to understand the ways they are expressed. Such development is the meaning of "education" in the sense in which we have been using the term.

RESPONSES TO ART

Our responses to art usually involve processes so complex that they can never be fully tracked down or analyzed. At first they can only be hinted at when we talk about them. However, further education in the arts permits us to observe more closely and thereby respond more intensely to the content of the work. This is true, we believe, even with "easy" art, such as exceptionally beautiful works—for example, those by Giorgione (Figure 2-9), Cézanne (Figure 2-4), and O'Keeffe (Figure 4-12). Such gorgeous works generally are responded to with immediate satisfaction. What more needs to be done? If art were only of the beautiful, textbooks such as this would never find many users. But we think more needs to be done, even with the beautiful. We will begin, however, with three works that obviously are not beautiful.

The Mexican painter David Alfaro Siqueiros's *Echo of a Scream* (Figure 1-2) is a highly emotional painting, in the sense that the work seems to demand a strong emotional response. What we see is the huge head of a baby crying and, then, as if issuing from its own mouth, the baby himself. What kinds of *emotions* do you find stirring in yourself as you look at this painting? What kinds of emotions do you feel are expressed in the painting? Your own emotional responses—such as shock; pity for the child; irritation at a destructive, mechanical society; or any other nameable emotion—do not sum up the painting. However, they are an important starting point, since Siqueiros paints in such a way as to evoke emotion, and our understanding of the painting increases as we examine the means by which this evocation is achieved.

FIGURE 1-2
David Alfaro Siqueiros, Mexican, 1896–1974, *Echo of a Scream.* **1937. Enamel on wood, 48 × 36 inches (121.9 × 91.4 cm). Gift of Edward M. M. Warburg. Museum of Modern Art, New York.** Siqueiros, a famous Mexican muralist, fought during the Mexican Revolution and possessed a powerful political sensibility, much of which found its way into his art. He painted some of his works in prison, held there for his political convictions. In the 1930s he centered his attention on the Spanish Civil War, represented here.

PERCEPTION KEY *Echo of a Scream*

1. What are the important distortions in the painting?
2. What effect does the distortion of the baby's head have on you?
3. Why is the scream described as an echo?
4. What are the objects on the ground around the baby? How do they relate to the baby?
5. How does the red cloth on the baby intensify your emotional response to the painting?

FIGURE 1-3
Peter Blume, 1906–1992, *The Eternal City.* 1934–1937. Dated on painting 1937. Oil on composition board, 34 × 47⅞ inches. Museum of Modern Art, New York. Mrs. Simon Guggenheim Fund. Born in Russia, Blume came to America when he was six. His paintings are marked by a strong interest in what is now known as magic realism, interleaving time and place and the dead and the living in an emotional space that confronts the viewer as a challenge. He condemned the tyrant dictators of the first half of the twentieth century.

Art ©The Education Alliance, Inc./Estate of Peter Blume/Licensed by VAGA, New York, NY. Photo: ©The Museum of Modern Art/Licensed by SCALA/Art Resource, NY

Study another work, very close in temperament to Siqueiros's painting: *The Eternal City* by the American painter Peter Blume (Figure 1-3). After attending carefully to the kinds of responses awakened by *The Eternal City,* take note of some background information about the painting that you may not know. The year of this painting is the same as that of *Echo of a Scream*: 1937. *The Eternal City* is a name reserved for only one city in the world—Rome. In 1937 the world was on the verge of world war: Fascists were in power in Italy and the Nazis in Germany. In the center of the painting is the Roman Forum, close to where Julius Caesar, the alleged tyrant, was murdered by Brutus. But here we see fascist Blackshirts, the modern tyrants, beating people. In a niche at the left is a figure of Christ, and beneath him (hard to see) is a crippled beggar woman. Near her are ruins of Roman statuary. The enlarged and distorted head, wriggling out like a jack-in-the-box, is that of Mussolini, the man who invented fascism and the Blackshirts. Study the painting closely again. Has your response to the painting changed?

PERCEPTION KEY Siqueiros and Blume

1. What common ingredients do you find in the Blume and Siqueiros paintings?
2. Is your reaction to the Blume similar to or distinct from your reaction to the Siqueiros?
3. Is the effect of the distortions similar or different?
4. How are colors used in each painting? Are the colors those of the natural world, or do they suggest an artificial environment? Are they distorted for effect?
5. With reference to the objects and events represented in each painting, do you think the paintings are comparable? If so, in what ways?
6. With the Blume, are there any natural objects in the painting that suggest the vitality of the Eternal City?
7. What political values are revealed in these two paintings?

Before going on to the next painting, which is quite different in character, we will make some observations about what we have said, however briefly, about the Blume. With added knowledge about its cultural and political implications—what we shall call the background of the painting—your responses to *The Eternal City* may have changed. Ideally they should have become more focused, intense, and certain. Why? The painting is surely the same physical object you looked at originally. Nothing has changed in that object. Therefore, something has changed because something has been added to you, information that the general viewer of the painting in 1937 would have known and would have responded to more emotionally than viewers do now. Consider how a Fascist, on the one hand, or an Italian humanist and lover of Roman culture, on the other hand, would have reacted to this painting in 1937.

A full experience of this painting is not unidimensional but multidimensional. Moreover, "knowledge about" a work of art can lead to "knowledge of" the work of art, which implies a richer experience. This is important as a basic principle, since it means that we can be educated about what is in a work of art, such as its shapes, objects, and **structure**, as well as what is external to a work, such as its political references. It means we can learn to respond more completely. It also means that artists such as Blume sometimes produce works that demand background information if we are to appreciate them fully. This is particularly true of art that refers to historical circumstances and personages. Sometimes we may find ourselves unable to respond successfully to a work of art because we lack the background knowledge the artist presupposes.

Picasso's *Guernica* (Figure 1-4), one of the most famous paintings of the twentieth century, is also dated 1937. Its title comes from the name of an old Spanish town that was bombed during the Spanish Civil War—the first aerial bombing of noncombatant civilians in modern warfare. Examine this painting carefully.

FIGURE 1-4
Pablo Picasso, *Guernica.* **1937. Oil on canvas, 11 feet 6 inches × 25 feet 8 inches. Museo Nacional Centro de Arte Reina Sofia, Madrid, Spain.** Ordinarily Picasso was not a political painter. During World War II he was a citizen of Spain, a neutral country. But the Spanish Civil War excited him to create one of the world's greatest modern paintings, a record of the German bombing of a small Spanish town, Guernica. When a Nazi officer saw the painting he said to Picasso, "Did you do this?" Picasso answered scornfully, "No, you did."

PERCEPTION KEY *Guernica*

1. Distortion is powerfully evident in this painting. How does its function differ from that of the distortion in Blume's *The Eternal City* or Siqueiros's *Echo of a Scream*?
2. What are the most prominent objects in the painting? What seems to be the relationship of the animals to the humans?
3. The figures in the painting are organized by underlying geometric forms. What are they and how do they focus your attention? Is the formal organization strong or weak?
4. How does your eye move across the painting? Do you begin at the left, the right, or the middle? This is a gigantic painting, over twenty-five feet long. How must one view it to take it all in? Why is it so large?
5. Some viewers have considered the organization of the images to be chaotic. Do you agree? If so, what would be the function of chaos in this painting?
6. We know from history that *Guernica* memorializes the Nazi bombing of the town of Guernica in the Spanish Civil War in 1937. What is the subject matter of *Guernica*—what the work is about: War? Death? Horror? Suffering? Fascism? Or something else?
7. Which of these paintings by Blume, Siqueiros, and Picasso makes the most powerful statement about the human condition?

The next painting (Figure 1-5), featured in "Experiencing: The *Mona Lisa*," is by Leonardo da Vinci, arguably one of the greatest painters of the Italian Renaissance. Da Vinci is a household name in part because of this painting. Despite the lack of a political or historically relevant subject matter, the *Mona Lisa,* with its tense pose and enigmatic expression, has become possibly the most famous work of art in the West.

EXPERIENCING The *Mona Lisa*

1. Leonardo da Vinci's *Mona Lisa* is one of the most famous paintings in the history of art. What, in your opinion, makes this painting noteworthy?
2. Because this painting is so familiar, it has sometimes been treated as if it were a cliché, an overworked image. In several cases it has been treated with satirical scorn. Why would any artist want to make fun of this painting? Is it a cliché, or are you able to look at it as if for the first time?
3. Unlike the works of Siqueiros, Blume, and Picasso, this painting has no obvious connections to historical circumstances that might intrude on your responses to its formal qualities. How does a lack of context affect your understanding of the painting?
4. It has been pointed out that the landscape on the left and the landscape on the right are totally different. If that judgment is correct, why do you think Leonardo made such a decision? What moods do the landscapes suggest?
5. The woman portrayed may be Lisa Gherardini del Giocondo, the wife of a local businessman, and the painting has long been known in Italy as *La Gioconda*. Is it necessary to our sense of participation that we know who the sitter is, or that we know that Leonardo kept this painting with him throughout his life and took it wherever he went?

FIGURE 1-5
Leonardo da Vinci, *Mona Lisa.* **Circa 1503–1506. Oil on panel, 30¼ × 21 inches. Musée du Louvre, Paris.** Leonardo's most personal picture has sometimes been hailed as a psychologically powerful painting because of the power of Mona Lisa's gaze, which virtually rivets the viewer to the spot. The painting is now protected under glass and, while always surrounded by a crowd of viewers, its small size proportional to its reputation has sometimes disappointed viewers because it is so hard to see. And in a crowd it is impossible to contemplate.

©RMN-Grand Palais/Art Resource, NY

Experiencing a painting as frequently reproduced as *Mona Lisa,* which is visited by millions of people every year at the Louvre in Paris, takes most of us some special effort. Unless we study the painting as if it were new to us, we will simply see it as an icon of high culture rather than as a painting with a formal power and a lasting value. Because it is used in advertisements and on mouse pads, playing cards, jigsaw puzzles, and a host of other banal locations, we might see this as a cliché.

However, we are also fortunate in that we see the painting as itself, apart from any social or historical events, and in a location that is almost magical or mythical. The landscape may be unreal, fantastic, and suggestive of a world of mystical opportunity. Certainly it emphasizes mystery. Whoever this woman is, she is concentrating in an unusual fashion on the viewer, whether we imagine it is us or it is Leonardo whom she contemplates. A study of her expression reminds us that for generations the "Gioconda smile" has teased authors and critics with its mystery. Is she making an erotic suggestion in that smile, or is it a smile of self-satisfaction? Or is it a smile of tolerance, suggesting that she is just waiting for this sitting to be done? Her expression has been the most intriguing of virtually any portrait subject in any museum in the world. It is no surprise, then, that Leonardo kept this for himself, although we must wonder whether he was commissioned for the painting and for some reason did not want to deliver it.

The arresting quality of the painting is in part because of the enigmatic expression on Mona Lisa's face, but the form of the painting is also arresting. Leonardo has posed her so that her head is the top of an isosceles triangle in which her face glows in contrast with her dark clothing. Her hands, expressive and radiant, create a strong diagonal, leading to the base of the triangle. Her shoulders are turned at a significant angle so that her pose is not really comfortable, not easy to maintain for a long time. However, her position is visually arresting because it imparts a tension to the entire painting that contributes to our response to it as a powerful object.

The most savage satirical treatment of this painting is the Dadaist Marcel Duchamp's *L.H.O.O.Q.* (see Figure 14-15). By parodying this work, Duchamp thumbed his nose at high culture in 1919, after World War I, and after the *Mona Lisa* had assumed its role as an epitome of high art. His work was an expression of disgust at the middle and upper classes, which had gone so enthusiastically into a war of attrition that brought Europe to the verge of self-destruction.

Structure and Artistic Form

Your responses to the *Mona Lisa* are probably different from those you have when viewing the other paintings in this chapter, but why? You might reply that the *Mona Lisa* is hypnotizing, a carefully structured painting depending on a subtle but basic geometric form, the triangle. Such structures, while operating subconsciously, are obvious on analysis. Like all structural elements of the artistic form of a painting, they affect us deeply even when we are not aware of them. We have the capacity to respond to pure form even in paintings in which objects and events are portrayed. Thus, responding to *The Eternal City* will involve responding not just to an interpretation of fascism taking hold in Italy but also to the ***sensuous*** surface of the painting. This is certainly true of *Echo of a Scream*; if you look again at that painting, you will see not only that its sensuous surface is interesting intrinsically but also that it deepens your response to what is represented. Because we often respond to artistic form without being conscious that it is affecting us, the painter must make the structure interesting. Consider the contrast between the simplicity of the structure of the *Mona Lisa* and the urgent complexity of the structures of the Siqueiros and the Blume.

The composition of any painting can be analyzed because any painting has to be organized: Parts have to be interrelated. Moreover, it is important to think carefully about the composition of individual paintings. This is particularly true of paintings one does not respond to immediately—of "difficult" or apparently uninteresting paintings. Often the analysis of structure can help us gain access to such paintings so that they become genuinely exciting.

PERCEPTION KEY *The Eternal City*

1. Sketch the basic geometric shapes of the painting.
2. Do these shapes relate to one another in such a way as to help reveal the obscenity of fascism? If so, how?

Artistic form is a composition or structure that makes something—a subject matter—more meaningful. The Siqueiros, Blume, and Picasso reveal something about the horrors of war and fascism. But what does the *Mona Lisa* reveal? Perhaps just the form and structure? For us, structures or forms that do not give us insight are not artistic forms. Some critics will argue the point. This major question will be pursued throughout the text.

Perception

We are not likely to respond sensitively to a work of art that we do not perceive properly. What is less obvious is what we referred to previously—the fact that we can often give our attention to a work of art and still not perceive very much. The reason for this should be clear from our previous discussion. Frequently we need to know something about the background of a work of art that would aid our perception. Anyone who did not know something about the history of Rome, or who Christ was, or what fascism was, or what Mussolini meant to the world would have a difficult time making sense of *The Eternal City*. But it is also true that anyone who could not perceive Blume's composition might have a completely superficial response to the painting. Such a person could indeed know all about the background and understand the symbolic statements made by the painting, but that is only part of the painting. From seeing what da Vinci can do with form, structure, pose, and expression, you can understand that the formal qualities of a painting are neither accidental nor unimportant. In Blume's painting, the form focuses attention and organizes our perceptions by establishing the relationships between the parts.

Abstract Ideas and Concrete Images

Composition is basic in all the arts. Artistic form is essential to the success of any art object. To perceive any work of art adequately, we must perceive its structure. Examine the following poem by Robert Herrick (1591-1674) and consider the purpose of its shape. This is one of many shaped poems designed to have a visual formal structure that somehow illuminates its subject matter.

THE PILLAR OF FAME

Fame's pillar here at last we set,
Out-during marble, brass or jet;
Charmed and enchanted so
As to withstand the blow
Of   overthrow;
Nor shall the seas,
Or   OUTRAGES
Of storms, o'erbear
What we uprear;
Tho' Kingdoms fall,
This pillar never shall
Decline or waste at all;
But stand forever by his own
Firm and well-fixed foundation.

PERCEPTION KEY "The Pillar of Fame"

1. What is a pillar and in what art form are pillars used?
2. In what sense is fame the subject matter of the poem?
3. Herrick is using a number of metaphors in this poem. How many can you identify? What seems to be their purpose?
4. In what sense is the shape of the poem a metaphor?
5. To whom does the word "his" in the last line refer?
6. The poem includes abstract ideas and concrete things. What is abstract here? And what is the function of the concrete references?

Robert Herrick, a seventeenth-century poet, valued both honor and fame. During the English Civil War he lost his job as a clergyman because he honored his faith and refused to abandon his king. He hoped to achieve fame as a poet, in imitation of the great Roman poets. His "outrages" and "storms" refer to the war and the decade following, in which he stayed in self-exile after the "overthrow" of King Charles I. He portrayed fame as a pillar because pillars hold up buildings, and when the buildings become ruins pillars often survive as testimony to greatness. Herrick hoped his poem would endure longer than physical objects, such as marble, brass, and jet (a black precious jewel made of coal), because fame is an abstraction and cannot wear or erode. Shaping the poem to resemble a pillar with a capital and a stylobate (foundation) is an example of wit. When he wrote poetry, one of Herrick's greatest achievements was the expression of wit, a poetic expression of intelligence and understanding. This poem achieves the blending of ideas and objects, of the abstract and the concrete, through its structure. The poem is a concrete expression of an abstract idea.

In *Paradise Lost,* John Milton describes hell as a place with "Rocks, Caves, Lakes, Fens, Bogs, Dens, and shades of death." Now, neither you nor the poet has ever seen "shades of death," although the idea is in Psalm 23, "the valley of the shadow of death." Milton gets away with describing hell this way because he has linked the abstract idea of shades of death to so many concrete images in this single line. He is giving us images that suggest the mood of hell just as much as they describe the landscape, and we realize that he gives us so many topographic details in order to get us ready for the last detail—the abstract idea of shades of death.

There is much more to be said about poetry, of course, but on a preliminary level poetry worked in much the same way in the seventeenth-century England of Milton as it does in contemporary America. The same principles are at work: Described objects or events are used as a means of bringing abstract ideas to life. The descriptions take on a wider and deeper significance—wider in the sense that the descriptions are connected with the larger scope of abstract ideas, deeper in the sense that because of these descriptions the abstract ideas become vividly focused and more meaningful.

The following poem is highly complex: the memory of an older culture (simplicity, in this poem) and the consideration of a newer culture (complexity). It is an African poem by the contemporary Nigerian poet Gabriel Okara; and knowing that it is African, we can begin to appreciate the extreme complexity of Okara's feelings about the clash of the old and new cultures. He symbolizes the clash in terms of music, and he opposes two musical instruments: the drum and the piano. They stand, respectively, for the African and the European cultures. But even beyond the musical images that abound in this poem, look closely at the images of nature, the pictures of the panther and leopard, and see how Okara imagines them.

PIANO AND DRUMS

When at break of day at a riverside
I hear jungle drums telegraphing
the mystic rhythm, urgent, raw
like bleeding flesh, speaking of
primal youth and the beginning,
I see the panther ready to pounce,
the leopard snarling about to leap
and the hunters crouch with spears poised;
And my blood ripples, turns torrent,
topples the years and at once I'm
in my mother's lap a suckling;
at once I'm walking simple
paths with no innovations,
rugged, fashioned with the naked
warmth of hurrying feet and groping hearts

in green leaves and wild flowers pulsing.
Then I hear a wailing piano
solo speaking of complex ways
in tear-furrowed concerto;
of far-away lands
and new horizons with
coaxing diminuendo, counterpoint,
crescendo. But lost in the labyrinth
of its complexities, it ends in the middle
of a phrase at a daggerpoint.
And I lost in the morning mist
of an age at a riverside keep
wandering in the mystic rhythm
of jungle drums and the concerto.

PERCEPTION KEY "Piano and Drums"

1. What are the most important physical objects in the poem? What cultural significance do they have?
2. Why do you think Okara chose the drum and the piano to help reveal the clash between the two cultures? Where are his allegiances?

Such a poem speaks directly to legions of the current generation of Africans. But consider some points in light of what we have said earlier. In order to perceive the kind of emotional struggle that Okara talks about—the subject matter of the poem—we need to know something about Africa and the struggle African nations have in modernizing themselves along the lines of more technologically advanced nations. We also need to know something of the history of Africa and the fact that European nations, such as Britain in the case of Nigeria, once controlled much of Africa. Knowing these things, we know, then, that there is no thought of the "I" of the poem accepting the "complex ways" of the new culture without qualification. The "I" does not think of the culture of the piano as manifestly superior to the culture of the drum. That is why the labyrinth of complexities ends at a "daggerpoint." The new culture is a mixed blessing.

We have argued that the perception of a work of art is aided by background information and that sensitive perception must be aware of form, at least implicitly. But we believe there is much more to sensitive perception. Somehow the form of a work of art is an artistic form that clarifies or reveals values, and our response is intensified by our awareness of those revealed values. But how does artistic form do this? And how does this awareness come to us? In the next chapter we shall consider these questions, and in doing so we will also raise that most important question, What is a work of art? Once we have examined each of the arts, it will be clear, we hope, that the principles developed in these opening chapters are equally applicable to all the arts.

Participate, analyze, and participate again with Edward Hopper's *Early Sunday Morning* (Figure 1-6).

FIGURE 1-6
Edward Hopper, *Early Sunday Morning*. 1930. Oil on canvas, 35 × 60 inches. When the Whitney Museum of American Art purchased *Early Sunday Morning* in 1930, it was their most expensive acquisition. Hopper's work, centered in New York's Greenwich Village, revealed the character of city life. His colors—vibrant, intense—and the early morning light—strong and unyielding—created indelible images of the city during the Great Depression.

©Whitney Museum of American Art/akg-images

PERCEPTION KEY *Early Sunday Morning*

1. If you did not know the title of the painting, what emotions might it excite in you?
2. How does Hopper's title, *Early Sunday Morning*, direct or enrich your emotional response?
3. What are the concrete objects represented in the painting? Which are most obvious and visually demanding? Which provide you with the most information about the scene?
4. What abstract ideas are suggested by the painting?
5. Is this an urban or rural scene? Why is no one present in the painting?
6. Would the painting be any different if it were titled *Early Wednesday Morning*?
7. What is the subject matter of the painting?

On one level the subject matter is a city street scene. Packed human habitation is portrayed, but no human being is in sight (incidentally but noteworthy, a human figure originally placed behind one of the windows was painted out). We seem to be at the scene alone on New York's Seventh Avenue. We seem to be strangely located across the street at about the level of the second-story windows. We see storefronts, concrete examples of business activity. But above the storefronts are windows, some with curtains, some open, some closed, implying the presence of people in their homes. The barber pole suggests a particular neighborhood. What is missing is people to make the street active. Are they at church? Or is the painting portraying loneliness of the kind that is sometimes associated with living in a city? Loneliness is usually accompanied by anxiety. And anxiety is expressed by the silent windows, especially the ominous dark storefronts, the mysterious translucent lighting, and the strange dark rectangle (what is it?) on the upper right. The street and buildings, despite their rectilinear format, seem to lean slightly downhill to the left, pushed by the shadows, especially the unexplainable, weird, flaglike one wrapping over the second window on the left of the second story. Even the bright barber pole is tilted to the left, the tilt accentuated by the uprightness of the door and window frames in the background and the wonderfully painted, toadlike fire hydrant. These subtle oddities of the scene accent our separateness.

SUMMARY

Unlike scientists, humanists generally do not use strictly objective standards. The arts reveal values; other humanities study values. "Artistic form" refers to the structure or organization of a work of art. Values are clarified or revealed by a work of art. Judging from the most ancient efforts to make things, we can assert that the arts represent one of the most basic human activities. They satisfy a need to explore and express the values that link us together. By observing our responses to a work of art and examining the means by which the artist evokes those responses, we can deepen our understanding of art. Our approach to the humanities is through the arts, and our taste in art connects with our deep feelings. Yet our taste is continually improved by experience and education. Background information about a work of art and increased sensitivity to its artistic form intensify our responses.

Chapter 2

WHAT IS A WORK OF ART?

No definition for a *work of art* seems completely adequate, and none is universally accepted. We shall not propose a definition here, therefore, but rather attempt to clarify some criteria or distinctions that can help us identify works of art. Since the term "work of art" implies the concept of "making" in two of its words—"work" and "art" (short for "artifice")—a work of art is usually said to be something made by a person. Hence, sunsets, beautiful trees, "found" natural objects such as grained driftwood, "paintings" by insects or songs by birds, and a host of other natural phenomena are not considered works of art, despite their beauty. You may not wish to accept the proposal that a work of art must be of human origin, but if you do accept it, consider the construction shown in Figure 2-1, Jim Dine's *Shovel*.

Shovel is part of a valuable collection and was first shown at an art gallery in New York City. Furthermore, Dine is considered an important American artist. However, he did not make the shovel himself. Like most shovels, the one in his construction, although designed by a person, was mass-produced. Dine mounted the shovel in front of a painted panel and presented this construction for serious consideration. The construction is described as "mixed media," meaning it consists of several materials: paint, wood, a cord, and metal. Is *Shovel* a work of art?

We can hardly discredit the construction as a work of art simply because Dine did not make the shovel; after all, we often accept objects manufactured to specification by factories as genuine works of sculpture (see the Calder construction,

FIGURE 2-1
Jim Dine, *Shovel.* **1962.**
Mixed media. Using off-
the-shelf products, Dine
makes a statement about
the possibilities of art.

©2017 Jim Dine/Artists Rights
Society (ARS), New York. Photo:
Courtesy of Sonnabend Gallery

Figure 5-10). *Collages* by Picasso and Braque, which include objects such as paper and nails mounted on a panel, are generally accepted as works of art. Museums have even accepted objects such as a signed urinal by Marcel Duchamp, one of the *Dadaist* artists of the early twentieth century, which in many ways anticipated the works of Dine, Warhol, and others in the *Pop Art* movement of the 1950s and 1960s.

IDENTIFYING ART CONCEPTUALLY

Three criteria for determining whether something is a work of art are that (1) the object or event is made by an artist, (2) the object or event is intended to be a work of art by its maker, and (3) recognized experts agree that it is a work of art. Unfortunately, one cannot always determine whether a work meets these criteria only by perceiving it. In many cases, for instance, we may confront an object such as *Shovel* (Figure 2-1) and not know whether Dine constructed the shovel, thus not satisfying the first criterion that the object be made by an artist; or whether Dine intended it to be a work of art; or whether experts agree that it is a work of art. In fact, Dine did not make this particular shovel, but because this fact cannot be established by perception, one has to be told.

PERCEPTION KEY Identifying a Work of Art

1. Why not simply identify a work of art as what an artist makes?
2. If Dine actually made the shovel, would *Shovel* then unquestionably be a work of art?
3. Suppose Dine made the shovel, and it was absolutely perfect in the sense that it could not be readily distinguished from a mass-produced shovel. Would that kind of perfection make the piece more a work of art or less a work of art? Suppose Dine did not make the shovel but did make the panel and the box. Then would it seem easier to identify *Shovel* as a work of art?
4. Find people who hold opposing views about whether *Shovel* is a work of art. Ask them to point out what it is about the object itself that qualifies it for or disqualifies it from being identified as a work of art.

Identifying art conceptually seems to us as not very useful. Because someone intends to make a work of art tells us little. It is the *made* rather than the *making* that counts. The third criterion—the judgment of experts—is important but debatable.

IDENTIFYING ART PERCEPTUALLY

Perception, what we can observe, and *conception*, what we know or think we know, are closely related. We often recognize an object because it conforms to our conception of it. For example, in architecture we recognize churches and office buildings as distinct because of our conception of what churches and office buildings are supposed to look like. The ways of identifying a work of art mentioned in the previous section depend on the conceptions of the artist and experts on art and not enough on our perceptions of the work itself.

We suggest an approach here that is simple and flexible and that depends largely on perception. The distinctions of this approach will not lead us necessarily to a definition of art, but they will offer us a way to examine objects and events with reference to whether they possess artistically perceivable qualities. And in some cases at least, it should bring us to reasonable grounds for distinguishing certain objects or events as art. We will consider four basic terms related primarily to the perceptual nature of a work of art:

"Artistic form": the organization of a medium that results in clarifying some subject matter

"Participation": sustained attention and loss of self-awareness

"Subject matter": some value expressed in the work of art

"Content": the interpretation of subject matter

Understanding any one of these terms requires an understanding of the others. Thus, we will follow what may appear to be an illogical order: artistic form; participation; participation and artistic form; content; subject matter; subject matter and artistic form; and, finally, participation, artistic form, and content.

ARTISTIC FORM

All objects and events have form. They are bounded by limits of time and space, and they have parts with distinguishable relationships to one another. Form is the interrelationships of part to part and part to whole. To say that some object or event has form means it has some degree of perceptible unity. To say that something has ***artistic form***, however, usually implies a strong degree of perceptible unity. It is artistic form that distinguishes a work of art from objects or events that are not works of art.

Artistic form implies that the parts we perceive—for example, line, color, texture, shape, and space in a painting—have been unified for the most profound effect possible. That effect is revelatory. Artistic form reveals, clarifies, enlightens, and gives fresh meaning to something valuable in life, some subject matter. A form that lacks a significant degree of unity is unlikely to accomplish this. Our daily experiences usually are characterized more by disunity than by unity. Consider, for instance, the order of your experiences during a typical day or even a segment of that day. Compare that order with the order most novelists give to the experiences of their characters. One impulse for reading novels is to experience the tight unity that artistic form usually imposes, a unity almost none of us comes close to achieving in our daily lives. Much the same is true of music. Noises and random tones in everyday experience lack the order that most composers impose.

Since strong, perceptible unity appears so infrequently in nature, we tend to value the perceptible unity of artistic form. Works of art differ in the power of their unity. If that power is weak, then the question arises: Is this a work of art? Consider Mondrian's *Broadway Boogie Woogie* (Figure 4-10) with reference to its artistic form. If its parts were not carefully proportioned in the overall structure of the painting, the tight balance that produces a strong unity would be lost. Mondrian was so concerned with this balance that he often measured the areas of lines and rectangles in his works to be sure they had a clear, almost mathematical, relationship to the totality. Of course, disunity or playing against expectations of unity can also be artistically useful at times. Some artists realize how strong the impulse toward unity is in those who have perceived many works of art. For some people, the contemporary attitude toward the loose organization of formal elements is a norm, and the highly unified work of art is thought of as old-fashioned. However, it seems that the effects achieved by a lesser degree of unity succeed only because we recognize them as departures from our well-known, highly organized forms.

Artistic form, we have suggested, is likely to involve a high degree of perceptible unity. But how do we determine what is a high degree? And if we cannot be clear about this, how can this distinction be helpful in distinguishing works of art from things that are not works of art? A very strong unity does not *necessarily* identify a work of art. That formal unity must give us insight into something important.

Consider the news photograph—taken on one of the main streets of Saigon in February 1968 by Eddie Adams, an Associated Press photographer—showing Brigadier General Nguyen Ngoc Loan, then South Vietnam's national police chief, killing a Vietcong captive (Figure 2-2). Adams stated that his picture was an accident, that his hand moved the camera reflexively as he saw the general raise the revolver. The lens of the camera was set in such a way that the background was thrown out of focus. The blurring of the background helped bring out the drama of the foreground scene. Does this photograph have a high degree of perceptible unity? Certainly the experience of the photographer is evident. Not many amateur photographers would have had enough skill to catch such a fleeting event with such stark clarity. If an amateur

FIGURE 2-2
Eddie Adams, *Execution in Saigon*.
1968. Silver halide. Adams captured General Loan's execution of a Vietcong captive. He said later, "The general killed the Vietcong; I killed the general with my camera. Still photographs are the most powerful weapon in the world."

©Eddie Adams/AP Photo

FIGURE 2-3
Francisco Goya, *May 3, 1808*. 1814–
1815. Oil on canvas, 8 feet 9 inches ×
13 feet 4 inches. The Prado, Madrid.
Goya's painting of Napoleonic
soldiers executing Spanish guerrillas
the day after the Madrid insurrection
portrays the faces of the victims, but
not of the killers.

©Copyright of the image Museo Nacional
del Prado/Art Resource, NY

had accomplished this, we would be inclined to believe that it was more luck than skill. Adams's skill in catching the scene is even more evident, and he risked his life to get it. But do we admire this work the way we admire Siqueiros's *Echo of a Scream* (Figure 1-2)? Do we experience these two works in the same basic way?

Compare a painting of a somewhat similar subject matter—Goya's *May 3, 1808* (Figure 2-3). Goya chose the most terrible moment, that split second before the crash of the guns. There is no doubt that the executions will go on. The desolate mountain pushing down from the left blocks escape, while from the right the firing squad relentlessly hunches forward. The soldiers' thick legs—planted wide apart and parallel—support like sturdy pillars the blind, pressing wall formed by their backs. These are men of a military machine. Their rifles, flashing in the bleak light of the ghastly lantern, thrust out as if they belonged to their bodies. It is unimaginable that any of these men would defy the command of their superiors. In the dead of night, the doomed are backed up against the mountain like animals ready for slaughter. One man flings up his arms in a gesture of utter despair—or is it defiance? The uncertainty increases the intensity of our attention. Most of the rest of the men bury their faces, while a few, with eyes staring out of their sockets, glance out at what they cannot help seeing—the sprawling dead smeared in blood.

With the photograph of the execution in Vietnam, despite its immediate and powerful attraction, it takes only a glance or two to grasp what is presented. Undivided attention, perhaps, is necessary to become aware of the significance of the event, but not sustained attention. In fact, to take careful notice of all the details—such as the patterns on the prisoner's shirt—does not add to our awareness of the significance of the photograph. If anything, our awareness will be sharper and more productive if we avoid such detailed examination. Is such the case with the Goya? We believe not. Indeed, without sustained attention to the details of this work, we would miss most of what is revealed. For example, block out everything but the dark shadow at the bottom right. Note how different that shadow appears when it is isolated. We must see the details individually and collectively, as they work together. Unless we are aware of their collaboration, we are not going to grasp fully the total form.

Close examination of the Adams photograph reveals several efforts to increase the unity and thus the power of the print. For example, the flak jacket of General Loan has been darkened so as to remove distracting details. The buildings in the background have been "dodged out" (held back in printing so that they are not fully visible). The shadows of trees on the road have been softened so as to lead the eye inexorably to the hand that holds the gun. The space around the head of the victim is also dodged out so that it appears that something like a halo surrounds the head. All this has been done in the act of printing sometime after the picture was taken. Careful printing helps achieve the photograph's artistic formal unity.

Yet we are suggesting that the Goya has a higher degree of perceptible unity than Adams's photograph, that perhaps only the Goya has artistic form. We base these conclusions on what is given for us to perceive: the fact that the part-to-part and the part-to-whole relationships are much stronger in the Goya. Now, of course, you may disagree. No judgment about such matters is indisputable. Indeed, that is part of the fun of talking about whether something is or is not a work of art—we can learn how to perceive from one another.

PERCEPTION KEY Adams and Goya

1. How is the painting different from Adams's photograph in the way the details work together?
2. Could any detail in the painting be changed or removed without weakening the unity of the total design? What about the photograph?
3. Does the photograph or the painting more powerfully reveal human barbarity?
4. Do you find yourself participating more with the Adams photograph or the Goya painting?
5. How does blurring out the buildings in the background of the photograph improve its visual impact? Compare the effect of the looming architecture in the painting.
6. What do the shadows on the street add to the significance of the photograph? Compare the shadows on the ground in the painting.
7. Does it make any significant difference that the Vietcong prisoner's shirt is checkered? Compare the white shirt on the gesturing man in the painting.
8. Is the expression on the soldier's face, along the left edge of the photograph, appropriate to the situation? Compare the facial expressions in the painting.
9. Can these works be fairly compared when one is in black and white and the other is in full color? Why or why not?
10. What are some basic differences between viewing a photograph of a real man being killed and viewing a painting of such an event? Does that distinction alone qualify or disqualify either work as a work of art?

Both Adams's photograph (Figure 2-2) and the Goya (Figure 2-3) tend to grasp our attention. Initially for most of us, probably, the photograph has more pulling power than the painting, especially as the two works are illustrated here. In its setting in the Prado in Madrid, however, the great size of the Goya and its powerful lighting and color draw the eye like a magnet. But the term "participate" is more accurately descriptive of what we are likely to be doing in our experience of the painting. With the Goya, we must not only give but also sustain our undivided attention so that we lose our self-consciousness—our sense of being separate, of standing apart from the painting. We participate. And only by means of participation can we come close to a full awareness of what the painting is about.

Works of art are created, exhibited, and preserved for us to perceive with not only undivided but also sustained attention. Artists, critics, and philosophers of art (aestheticians) generally are in agreement about this. Thus, if a work requires our participation in order to understand and appreciate it fully, we have an indication that the work is art. Therefore—unless our analyses have been incorrect, and you should satisfy yourself about this—the Goya would seem to be a work of art. Conversely, the photograph is not as obviously a work of art as the painting, and this is the case despite the fascinating impact of the photograph. Yet these are highly tentative judgments. We are far from being clear about why the Goya requires our participation and the photograph may not. Until we are clear about these "whys," the grounds for these judgments remain shaky.

Goya's painting tends to draw us on until, ideally, we become aware of all the details and their interrelationships. For example, the long, dark shadow at the bottom right underlines the line of the firing squad, and the line of the firing squad helps bring out the shadow. Moreover, this shadow is the darkest and most opaque part of the painting. It has a forbidding, blind, fateful quality, which in turn reinforces the ominous appearance of the firing squad. The dark shadow on the street just below the forearm of General Loan seems less powerful. Sustained attention or participation cannot be achieved by acts of will. The splendid singularity of what we are attending to must fascinate and control us to the point that we no longer need to will our attention. We can make up our minds to give our undivided attention to something. But if that something lacks the pulling power that grasps our attention, we cannot participate with it.

The ultimate test for recognizing a work of art, then, is how it works in us, what it does to us. *Participative experiences* of works of art are communions—experiences so full and fruitful that they enrich our lives. Such experiences are life-enhancing not just because of the great satisfaction they may give us at the moment but also because they make more or less permanent contributions to our future lives. Does da Vinci's *Mona Lisa* (Figure 1-5) heighten your perception of a painting's underlying structure, the power of simplicity of form, and the importance of a figure's pose? Does Robert Herrick's "The Pillar of Fame" (Chapter 1) affect your concept of fame? Do you see shovels differently, perhaps, after experiencing *Shovel* by Dine (Figure 2-1)? If not, presumably they are not works of art. But this assumes that we have really participated with these works, that we have allowed them to work fully in our experience, so that if the meaning or content were present, it had a chance to reveal itself to our awareness. Of the four basic distinctions—subject matter, artistic form, content, and participation—the most fundamental is participation. We must not only understand what it means to participate but also be able to participate. Otherwise, the other basic distinctions, even if they make good theoretical sense, will not be of much practical help in making art more important in our lives. The central importance of participation requires further elaboration.

As participators, we do not think of the work of art with reference to categories applicable to objects—such as what kind of thing it is. We grasp the work of art directly. When, for example, we participate with Cézanne's *Mont Sainte-Victoire* (Figure 2-4), we are not making geographical or geological observations. We are not thinking of the mountain as an object. If we were, Mont Sainte-Victoire would pale into a mere instance of the appropriate scientific categories. We might judge that the mountain is a certain type. But in that process, the vivid impact of Cézanne's mountain would be lessened as the focus of our attention shifted beyond in the direction of generality. This is the natural thing to do with mountains if you are a geologist.

When we are participators, our thoughts are dominated so much by something that we are unaware of our separation from that something. Thus, the artistic form initiates and controls thought and feeling. We see the Cézanne—name it, identify its maker, classify its style, recall its background information—but this approach will not lead us into the Cézanne as a work of art. Of course, such knowledge can be very helpful, but only when it is under the control of our experience of participating with the painting. Otherwise, the painting will fade away. Its splendid specificity will be sacrificed for some generality. Its content or meaning will be missed.

FIGURE 2-4
Paul Cézanne, *Mont Sainte-Victoire.* **1886–1887. Oil on canvas, 23½ × 28½ inches. The Phillips Collection, Washington, D.C.** Cézanne painted Mont Sainte-Victoire in Aix, France, throughout his life. Local legend is that the mountain was home to a god and therefore a holy place.

©Painting/Alamy

These are strong claims, and they may not be convincing. In any case, before concluding our search for what a work of art is, let us seek further clarification of our other basic distinctions—artistic form, content, and subject matter. Even if you disagree with the conclusions, clarification helps understanding. And understanding helps appreciation.

PARTICIPATION AND ARTISTIC FORM

The participative experience—the undivided and sustained attention to an object or event that makes us lose our sense of separation from that object or event—is induced by strong or artistic form. Participation is not likely to develop with weak form because weak form tends to allow our attention to wander. Therefore, one indication of a strong form is the fact that participation occurs. Another indication of artistic form is the way it clearly identifies a whole, or totality. In the visual arts, a whole is a visual field limited by boundaries that separate that field from its surroundings.

Both Adams's photograph (Figure 2-2) and Goya's painting (Figure 2-3) have visual fields with boundaries. No matter what wall these two pictures are placed on, the Goya will probably stand out more distinctly and sharply from its background. This is partly because the Goya is in vibrant color and on a large scale—eight feet nine inches by thirteen feet four inches—whereas the Adams photograph is normally exhibited as an eight by ten-inch print. However carefully such a photograph is printed, it will probably include some random details. No detail in the Goya, though, fails to play a part in the total structure. To take one further instance, notice how the lines of the soldiers' sabers and their straps reinforce the ruthless forward push of the firing squad. The photograph, however, has a relatively weak form because a large number of details fail to cooperate with other details. For example, running down the right side of General Loan's body is a very erratic line that fails to tie in with anything else in the photograph. If this line were smoother, it would connect more closely with the lines formed by the Vietcong prisoner's body. The connection between killer and killed would be more vividly established.

Artistic form normally is a prerequisite if our attention is to be grasped and held. Artistic form makes our participation possible. Some philosophers of art, such as Clive Bell and Roger Fry, even go so far as to claim that the presence of artistic form—what they call "significant form"—is all that is necessary to identify a work of art. And by "significant form," in the case of painting, they mean the interrelationships of elements: line to line, line to color, color to color, color to shape, shape to shape, shape to texture, and so on. The elements make up the artistic medium, the "stuff" the form organizes. According to Bell and Fry, any reference of these elements and their interrelationships to actual objects or events should be basically irrelevant in our awareness.

According to the proponents of significant form, if we take explicit notice of the executions as an important part of Goya's painting, then we are not perceiving properly. We are experiencing the painting not as a work of art but rather as an illustration telling a story, thus reducing a painting that is a work of art to the level of commercial communications. When the lines, colors, and the like pull together tightly, independently of any objects or events they may represent, there is a significant form. That is what we should perceive when we are perceiving a work of art, not a portrayal of some object or event. Anything that has significant form is a work of art. If you ignore the objects and events represented in the Goya, significant form is evident. All the details depend on one another and jell, creating a strong structure. Therefore, the Goya is a work of art. If you ignore the objects and events represented in the Adams photograph, significant form is not evident. The organization of the parts is too loose, creating a weak structure. Therefore, the photograph, according to Bell and Fry, would not be a work of art. "To appreciate a work of art," according to Bell, "we need bring with us nothing from life, no knowledge of its ideas and affairs, no familiarity with its emotions."

Does this theory of how to identify a work of art satisfy you? Do you find that in ignoring the representation of objects and events in the Goya, much of what is important in that painting is left out? For example, does the line of the firing squad carry a forbidding quality partly because you recognize that this is a line of men in the process of killing other men? In turn, does the close relationship of that line with the line of the long shadow at the bottom right depend to some degree on that forbidding quality? If you think so, then it follows that the artistic form of this work legitimately and relevantly refers to objects and events. Somehow artistic form goes beyond itself, referring to objects and events from the world beyond the form. Artistic form informs us about things outside itself. These things—as revealed by the artistic form—we shall call the "content" of a work of art. But how does the artistic form do this?

CONTENT

Let us begin to try to answer the question posed in the previous section by examining more closely the meanings of the Adams photograph (Figure 2-2) and the Goya painting (Figure 2-3). Both basically, although oversimply, are about the same abstract idea—barbarity. In the case of the photograph, we have an example of this barbarity. Since it is very close to any knowledgeable American's interests, this instance is likely to set off a lengthy chain of thoughts and feelings. These thoughts and feelings, furthermore, may seem to lie "beyond" the photograph. Suppose a debate developed over the meaning of this photograph. The photograph itself would play an important role primarily as a starting point in a discussion of man's inhumanity to man.

In the debate about the Goya, every detail and its interrelationships with other details become relevant. The meaning of the painting may seem to lie "within" the painting. And yet, paradoxically, this meaning, as in the case of the Adams photograph, involves ideas and feelings that lie beyond the painting. How can this be? Let us first consider some background information. On May 2, 1808, guerrilla warfare had flared up all over Spain. By the following day, Napoleon's men were completely back in control in Madrid and the surrounding area. Many of the guerrillas were executed. And, according to tradition, Goya portrayed the execution of forty-three of these guerrillas on May 3 near the hill of Principe Pio just outside Madrid. This background information is important if we are to understand and appreciate the painting fully.

The execution in Adams's photograph was of a man who had just murdered one of General Loan's best friends and had then knifed to death his wife and six children. The general was part of the Vietnamese army fighting with the assistance of the United States, and this photograph was widely disseminated with a caption describing the victim as a suspected terrorist. What shocked Americans who saw the photograph was the summary justice that Loan meted out. It was not until much later that the details of the victim's crimes were published.

With the Goya, the background information, although very helpful, is not as essential. Test this for yourself. Would your interest in Adams's photograph last very long if you completely lacked background information? In the case of the Goya, the background information helps us understand the where, when, and why of the scene. But even without this information, the painting probably would still grasp and hold the attention of most of us because it would still have significant meaning. We would still have a powerful image of barbarity, and the artistic form would hold us on that image. In the Prado Museum in Madrid, Goya's painting continually draws and holds the attention of innumerable viewers, many of whom know little or nothing about the rebellion of 1808. Adams's photograph is also a powerful image, of course—and probably initially more powerful than the Goya—but the form of the photograph is not strong enough to hold most of us on that image for very long.

With the Goya, the abstract idea (barbarity) and the concrete image (the firing squad in the process of killing) are tied tightly together because the form of the painting is tight. We see the barbarity in the lines, colors, masses, shapes, groupings, and lights and shadows of the painting itself. The details of the painting keep referring to other details and to the totality. They keep holding our attention. Thus, the ideas and feelings that the details and their organization awaken within us keep merging with the form. We are prevented from separating the meaning or content of the painting from its form because the form is so fascinating. The form constantly intrudes, however unobtrusively. It will not let us ignore it. We see the firing squad killing, and this evokes the idea of barbarity and the feeling of horror. But the lines, colors, mass, shapes, and shadowings of that firing squad form a pattern that keeps exciting and guiding our eyes. And then the pattern leads us to the pattern formed by the victims. Ideas of fatefulness and feelings of pathos are evoked but they, too, are fused with the form. The form of the Goya is like a powerful magnet that allows nothing within its range to escape its pull. Artistic form fuses or embodies its meaning with itself.

In addition to participation and artistic form, then, we have come upon another basic distinction—*content*. Unless a work has content—meaning that is fused or embodied with its form—we shall say that the work is not art. Content is the meaning of artistic form. If we are correct (for our view is by no means universally accepted), artistic form always informs—has meaning, or content. And that content, as we experience it when we participate, is always ingrained in the artistic form. We do not perceive an artistic form and then a content. We perceive them as inseparable. Of course, we can separate them analytically. But when we do so, we are not having a participative experience. Moreover, when the form is weak—that is, less than artistic—we experience the form and its meaning separately.

PERCEPTION KEY **Adams and Goya Revisited**

We have argued that the painting by Goya is a work of art and the photograph by Adams is questionable. Even if the three basic distinctions we have made so far—artistic form, participation, and content—are useful, we may have misapplied them. Bring out every possible argument against the view that the painting is a work of art and the photograph may not be a work of art.

SUBJECT MATTER

The content is the meaning of a work of art. The content is embedded in the artistic form. But what does the content interpret? We shall call it subject matter. Content is the interpretation—by means of an artistic form—of some subject matter. Thus, **subject matter** is the fourth basic distinction that helps identify a work of art. Since every work of art must have a content, every work of art must have a subject matter, and this may be any aspect of experience that is of human interest. Anything related to a human interest is a value. Some values are positive, such as pleasure and health. Other values are negative, such as pain and ill health. They are values because they are related to human interests. Negative values are the subject matter of both Adams's photograph (Figure 2-2) and Goya's painting. But the photograph, unlike the painting, has no content. The less-than-artistic form of the photograph simply *presents* its subject matter. The form does not transform the subject matter, does not enrich its significance. In comparison, the artistic form of the painting enriches or interprets its subject matter, says something significant about it. In the photograph, the subject matter is directly given. But the subject matter of the painting is not just there in the painting. It has been transformed by the form. What is directly given in the painting is the content.

The meaning, or content, of a work of art is what is revealed about a subject matter. But in that revelation you must infer or imagine the subject matter. If someone had taken a news photograph of the May 3 executions, that would be a record of Goya's subject matter. The content of the Goya is its interpretation of the barbarity of those executions. Adams's photograph lacks content because it merely shows us an example of this barbarity. That is not to disparage the photograph, for its purpose was news, not art. A similar kind of photograph—that is, one lacking artistic form—of the May 3 executions would also lack content. Now, of course, you may disagree with these conclusions for very good reasons. You may find more transformation of the subject matter in Adams's photograph than in Goya's painting. For example, you may believe that transforming the visual experience in black and white distances it from reality while intensifying its content. In any case, such disagreement can help the perception of both parties, provided the debate is focused. It is hoped that the basic distinctions we are making—subject matter, artistic form, content, and participation—will aid that focusing.

SUBJECT MATTER AND ARTISTIC FORM

Whereas a subject matter is a value—something of importance—that we may perceive before any artistic interpretation, the content is the significantly interpreted subject matter as revealed by the artistic form. Thus, the subject matter is never directly presented in a work of art, for the subject matter has been transformed by the form. Artistic form transforms and, in turn, informs about life. The conscious intentions of the artist may include magical, religious, political, economic, and other purposes; the conscious intentions may not include the purpose of clarifying values. Yet underlying the artist's activity—going back to cavework (Figure 1-1)—is always the creation of a form that illuminates something from life, some subject matter.

Artistic form draws from the chaotic state of life, which, as van Gogh describes it, is like "a sketch that didn't come off"—a distillation. In our interpretation, a work of art creates an illusion that illuminates reality. Thus, such paradoxical declarations as

Delacroix's are explained: "Those things which are most real are the illusions I create in my paintings." Or Edward Weston's "The photographer who is an artist reveals the essence of what lies before the lens with such clear insight that the beholder may find the recreated image more real and comprehensible than the actual object." Camus: "If the world were clear, art would not exist." Artistic form is an economy that produces a lucidity that enables us better to understand and, in turn, manage our lives. Hence, the informing of a work of art reveals a subject matter with value dimensions that go beyond the artist's idiosyncrasies and perversities. Whether or not Goya had idiosyncrasies and perversities, he did justice to his subject matter: He revealed it. The art of a period is the revelation of the collective soul of its time.

PARTICIPATION, ARTISTIC FORM, AND CONTENT

Participation is the necessary condition that makes possible our insightful perception of artistic form and content. Unless we participate with the Goya (Figure 2-3), we will fail to see the power of its artistic form. We will fail to see how the details work together to form a totality. We will also fail to grasp the content fully, for artistic form and content are inseparable. Thus, we will have failed to gain insight into the subject matter. We will have collected just one more instance of barbarity. The Goya will have basically the same effect on us as Adams's photograph except that it may be less important to us because it happened long ago. But if, on the contrary, we have participated with the Goya, we probably will never see such things as executions in quite the same way again. The insight that we have gained will tend to refocus our vision so that we will see similar subject matters with heightened awareness.

Look, for example, at the photograph by Kevin Carter (Figure 2-5), which was published in the *New York Times* on March 26, 1993, and which won the Pulitzer

FIGURE 2-5
Kevin Carter, *Vulture and Child in Sudan.* 1993. Silver halide. Carter saved this child but became so depressed by the terrible tragedies he had recorded in Sudan and South Africa that he committed suicide a year after taking this photograph.

©Kevin Carter/Sygma/Getty Images

Prize for photography in 1994. The form isolates two dramatic figures. The closest is a starving Sudanese child making her way to a feeding center. The other is a plump vulture waiting for the child to die. This powerful photograph raised a hue and cry, and the *New York Times* published a commentary explaining that Carter chased away the vulture and took the child to the feeding center. Carter committed suicide in July 1994.

PERCEPTION KEY Adams, Goya, and Carter

1. How does our discussion of the Adams photograph affect your response to Carter's photograph?
2. To what extent does Carter's photograph have artistic form?
3. Why are your answers to these questions fundamentally important in determining whether Adams's photograph, Carter's photograph, Goya's painting, or all of them are works of art?
4. Describe your experience regarding your participation with either Adams's or Carter's photograph or Goya's painting. Can you measure the intensity of your participation with each of them? Which work do you reflect upon most when you relax and are not thinking directly on the subject of art?
5. The intensity of your reactions to the Adams and Carter photographs may well be stronger than the intensity of your experience with the Goya. If so, should that back up the assertion that the photographs are works of art?

Artistic Form: Examples

Let us examine artistic form in two examples of work by an anonymous cartoonist and Roy Lichtenstein. In the late 1950s and early 1960s, Lichtenstein became interested in comic strips as subject matter. The story goes that his two young boys asked him to paint a Donald Duck "straight," without the encumbrances of art. But much more was involved. Born in 1923, Lichtenstein grew up before the invention of television. By the 1930s the comic strip had become one of the most important of the mass media. Adventure, romance, sentimentality, and terror found expression in the stories of Tarzan, Flash Gordon, Superman, Wonder Woman, Steve Roper, Winnie Winkle, Mickey Mouse, Donald Duck, Batman and Robin, and the like.

The purpose of the comic strip for its producers is strictly commercial. And because of the large market, a premium has always been put on making the processes of production as inexpensive as possible. And so generations of mostly unknown commercial artists, going far back into the nineteenth century, developed ways of quick, cheap color printing. They developed a technique that could turn out cartoons like the products of an assembly line. Moreover, because their market included a large number of children, they developed ways of producing images that were immediately understandable and striking.

Lichtenstein reports that he was attracted to the comic strip by its stark simplicity—the blatant primary colors, the ungainly black lines that encircle the shapes, the balloons that isolate the spoken words or thoughts of the characters.

He was struck by the apparent inconsistency between the strong emotions of the stories and the highly impersonal, mechanical style in which they were expressed. Despite the crudity of the comic strip, Lichtenstein saw power in the directness of the medium. Somehow the cartoons mirrored something about ourselves. Lichtenstein set out to clarify what that something was. At first people laughed, as was to be expected.

However, Lichtenstein saw how adaptable the style was for his work. He produced a considerable number of large oil paintings that, in some cases, referred specifically to popular cartoon strips. They were brash in much the same way cartoons are, and they used brilliant primary colors that were sensational and visually overwhelming. Much of his early work in this vein involved war planes, guns, and action scenes. For him the cartoon style permitted him to be serious in what he portrayed.

Examine Figures 2-6 and 2-7. Lichtenstein saw artistic potential for the anonymous cartoon panel with a woman tearing up in reaction to an unknown problem. Because these two representations of a sad woman are detached from the narrative in which the original cartoon appeared, we are left to respond only to the image we see. Lichtenstein did not expect that his painting would relate to any missing narrative: It was made to stand alone. However, the anonymous cartoon was created in greater haste partly because its significance would have been understood in a dramatic context.

FIGURE 2-6
Anonymous cartoon panel.

FIGURE 2-7
Roy Lichenstein, *Hopeless.* **1963. Magna on canvas.**

©Estate of Roy Lichtenstein

PERCEPTION KEY Cartoon Panel and Lichtenstein's Transformation

1. Begin by establishing which formal elements are similar or the same in both works. Consider the shape of the face and hair, the features of the woman.
2. Then establish what Lichtenstein removed from the original cartoon. What seems to you the most important omission? Does it strengthen or weaken the overall visual force of the work?
3. The power of the line makes cartoons distinct. Compare the strength of the line in each work. Which is more satisfying? Which is stronger?
4. What has Lichtenstein added to the composition? What has he changed from the original?
5. Is it fair to say one of these is a work of art and the other is not? Or would you say they are both works of art?
6. Is either of these works an example of artistic form? How would you describe artistic form?
7. Discuss with others who have seen these works what you and they think is their subject matter. Do they have the same content?

Hopeless treats an emotional moment that is familiar to everyone who has ever been involved in the breakup of a love affair. Comparing the two panels, it is clear that Lichtenstein has simplified the portrayal of the woman by making her hair light in color, thus changing the focal point of the image. In the cartoon the hair is the darkest form, taking up the most room and attention in the panel. Lichtenstein's revision shifts the viewer's attention to the face. By smoothing out the tone of the skin—by removing the mechanical "dots" in the cartoon version— he makes the face more visually prominent. The addition of the fingers gives the viewer the sense that the woman is holding on. By placing the balloon (with the dialogue) close to the woman's ear and removing the background—very prominent in the cartoon—Lichtenstein gives the woman's representation much more space in the panel. These are subtle differences, and while both panels treat the same subject matter, it seems to us that the content of the Lichtenstein is greater and more significant because his control of artistic form informs us more fully of the circumstances represented in the painting. Compare our analyses of these works. You may disagree with our view but, if so, make an effort to establish your own assessment of these two examples in terms of artistic form.

Examine Figure 2-8, Artemisia Gentileschi's *Self-portrait as the Allegory of Painting*.

PERCEPTION KEY Artemisia Gentileschi, *Self-portrait as the Allegory of Painting*

1. Compare the painter's arms. How effective is their contrast in terms of their movement and their pose?
2. How does the simplicity of the background help clarify the essential form of the painter? What are the most powerful colors in the compostion?
3. What is the figure actually doing? How does Gentileschi make us aware of her action?

4. Place yourself in the same pose as Gentileschi. How would you paint yourself in that position?
5. What forms in the painting work best to achieve a visual balance? Which forms best express a sense of energy in the painting?
6. How does Gentileschi achieve artistic form? If you think she does not achieve it, explain why.
7. The painting is titled *Allegory*. Allegory is a special kind of symbol; what is this painting a symbol for? Does it work for you as a symbol?
8. How does answering these questions affect your sense of participating with the painting?

FIGURE 2-8
Artemisia Gentileschi, Rome 1593–
Naples 1652, *Self-portrait as the
Allegory of Painting* (La Pittura). Circa
1638–1639.

©Fine Art Images/Superstock

We feel this is a particularly powerful example of artistic form. For one thing, Gentileschi's challenge of painting her own portrait likeness in this pose is extraordinary. It has been supposed that she may have needed at least two mirrors to permit her to position herself. Or her visual memory may have been unusually powerful. Artemisia Gentileschi was one of the most famous female artists of the seventeenth century. This painting was done in England for King Charles I and remains in the Royal Collection. The painting is an *allegory*, which is to say it represents the classical idea of the painter, which was expressed as female, Pittura. Because no male painter could do a self-portrait as Pittura, Gentileschi's painting is singular in many respects. The color of her clothing—silken, radiant—is rich and appropriate to the painter. Her right arm is strong in terms of its being brilliantly lighted as well as strong in reaching out dramatically in the act of painting. Her clothing and decolletage emphasize her femininity. Her straggly hair and the necklace containing a mask (a symbol of imitation) were required by the conventional allegorical representations of the time describing Pittura. The contrasting browns of the background simplify the visual space and give more power to the figure and the color of her garment. One powerful aspect of the painting is the light source. Gentileschi is looking directly at her painting, and the painting—impossibly—seems to be the source of that light.

The subject matter of the painting seems to be, on one level, the idea of painting. On another level, it is the act of painting by a woman painter. On yet another level, it is the act of Artemisia Gentileschi painting her self-portrait. The content of the painting may be simply painting itself. On the other hand, this was an age in which women rarely achieved professional status as royal painters. The power of the physical expression of the self-portrait implies a content expressing the power of woman, both allegorically and in reality. Artemisia is declaring herself as having achieved what was implied in having the allegory of painting expressed as a female deity.

As in the painting by Goya and the photograph by Adams, the arms are of great significance in this work. Instead of a representation of barbarity, the painting is a representation of art itself, and therefore of cultivated society. The richness of the garment, the beauty of Artemisia, and the vigor of her act of painting imply great beauty, strength, and power. We are virtually transfixed by the light and the urgency of the posture. Some viewers find themselves participating so deeply that they experience a kinesthetic response as they imagine themselves in that pose.

What significance does the artistic form of the painting reveal for you? How would you describe the content of the painting? Would the content of this painting be different for a woman than for a man? Would it be different for a painter than for a non-painter? What content does it have for you?

Subject Matter and Content

While the male nude was a common subject in Western art well into the **Renaissance**, images of the female body have since predominated. The variety of treatment of the female nude is bewildering, ranging from the Greek idealization of erotic love in the *Venus de Milo* to the radical reordering of Duchamp's *Nude Descending a Staircase, No. 2*. A number of female nude studies follow (Figures 2-9 through 2-18). Consider, as you look at them, how the form of the work interprets the female body. Does it reveal it in such a way that you have an increased understanding of and sensitivity to the female body? In other words, does it have content? Also ask yourself whether the content is different in the two paintings by women compared with those by men.

FIGURE 2-9
Giorgione, *Sleeping Venus*. 1508–1510. Oil on canvas, 43 × 69 inches. Gemaldegalerie, Dresden. Giorgione established a Renaissance ideal in his painting of the goddess Venus asleep in the Italian countryside.

FIGURE 2-10
Pierre-Auguste Renoir, *Bather Arranging Her Hair*. 1893. Oil on canvas, 36⅜ × 29⅛ inches. National Gallery of Art, Washington, D.C., Chester Dale Collection. Renoir's impressionist interpretation of the nude provides a late-nineteenth-century idealization of a real-life figure who is not a goddess.

Source: National Gallery of Art, Washington, D.C., Chester Dale Collection

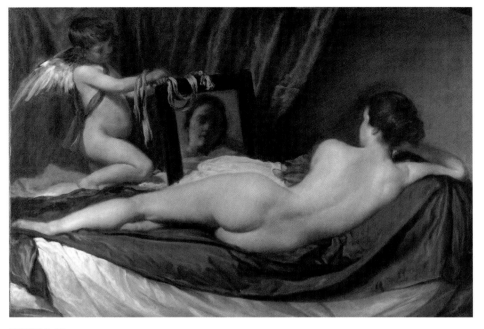

FIGURE 2-12
Rokeby Venus. Circa 1647–1651. 48 × 49.7 inches (122 × 177 cm). National Gallery, London. Velazquez's *Rokeby Venus (Toilet of Venus)* is an idealized figure of the goddess. Cupid holds a mirror for Venus to admire herself.

©VCG Wilson/Corbis/Getty Images

FIGURE 2-11
Venus de Milo. Greece. Circa 100 BCE. Marble, 5 feet ½ inch. Louvre, Paris. Since its discovery in 1820 on the island of Cyclades, the *Venus de Milo* has been thought to represent the Greek ideal in feminine beauty. It was originally decorated with jewelry and may have been polychromed.

©DeA Picture Library/Art Resource, NY

FIGURE 2-13
Tom Wesselmann, 1931–2004, *Study for Great American Nude.* 1975. Watercolor and pencil, 19½ × 54 inches. Private collection. Wesselmann's study leaves the face blank and emphasizes the telephone as a suggestion of this nude's availability in the modern world.

Art: ©Estate of Tom Wesselmann/Licensed by VAGA, New York, NY. Photo: ©Connaught Brown, London/Bridgeman Images

FIGURE 2-14
Marcel Duchamp, *Nude Descending a Staircase, No. 2*. 1912. Oil on canvas, 58 × 35 inches. Philadelphia Museum of Art. Louise and Walter Arensberg Collection. This painting provoked a riot in 1913 and made Duchamp famous as a chief proponent of the distortions of cubism and modern art at that time.

©Association Marcel Duchamp/ADAGP, Paris/ Artists Rights Society (ARS), New York 2017. Photo: ©Philadelphia Museum of Art, Philadelphia/Art Resource, NY

FIGURE 2-15
Standing Woman. Ivory Coast. Nineteenth or twentieth century. Wood and beads, 20⅜ × 7⅝ × 5⅜ inches. Detroit Institute of Arts. *Standing Woman* was once owned by Tristan Tzara, a friend of Picasso. Sculpture such as this influenced modern painters and sculptors in France and elsewhere in the early part of the twentieth century. It is marked by a direct simplicity, carefully modeled and polished.

©Detroit Institute of Arts/Bridgeman Images

FIGURE 2-16
Suzanne Valadon, *Reclining Nude*. 1928. Oil on canvas, 23⅝ × 30¹¹⁄₁₆ inches. Photo: Metropolitan Museum of Art, New York. Robert Lehman Collection, 1975. Valadon interprets the nude simply, directly. To what extent is the figure idealized?

Source: Robert Lehman Collection, 1975/ The Metropolitan Museum of Art

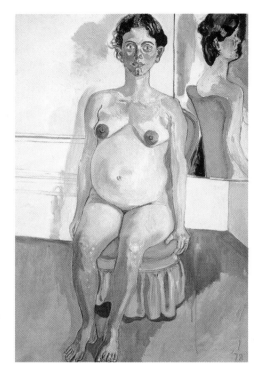

FIGURE 2-17
Alice Neel, *Margaret Evans Pregnant*. 1978. Oil on
canvas, 57¾ × 38 inches. Collection, John McEnroe
Gallery. Neel's *Margaret Evans Pregnant* is one of a
series of consciously anti-idealized nude portraits of
pregnant women.

Courtesy of David Zwirner, New York/London. ©The estate
of Alice Neel

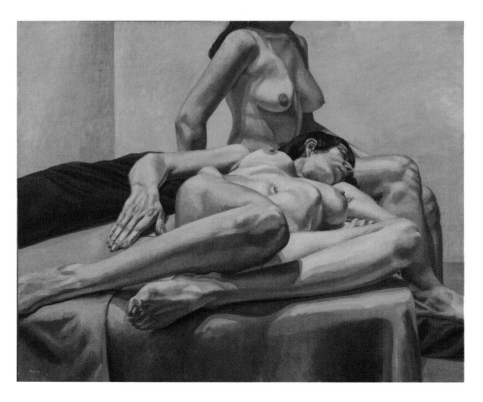

FIGURE 2-18
Philip Pearlstein, *Two Female
Models in the Studio*. 1967. Oil on
canvas, 50⅛ × 60¼ inches. Gift
of Mr. and Mrs. Stephen B. Booke.
Museum of Modern Art, New York.
Pearlstein's attention to anatomy,
his even lighting, and his unsensuous
surroundings seem to eliminate the
erotic content associated with the
traditional female nude.

Courtesy of the Artist and Betty Cuningham
Gallery. Photo: ©The Museum of Modern
Art/Licensed by Scala/Art Resource, NY

Most of these works are highly valued—some as masterpieces—because they are powerful interpretations of their subject matter, not just presentations of the human body as erotic objects. Notice how different the interpretations are. Any important subject matter has many different facets. That is why shovels and soup cans have limited utility as subject matter. They have very few facets to offer for interpretation. The female nude, however, is almost limitless. The next artist interprets something about the female nude that had never been interpreted before, because the female nude seems to be inexhaustible as a subject matter, more so perhaps than the male nude.

More precisely, these works all have somewhat different subject matters. All are about the nude, but the painting by Giorgione is about the nude as idealized, as a goddess, as Venus. Now there is a great deal that all of us could say in trying to describe Giorgione's interpretation. We see not just a nude but an idealization that presents the nude as Venus, the goddess who the Romans felt best expressed the ideal of woman. She represents a form of beautiful perfection that humans can only strive toward. A description of the subject matter can help us perceive the content if we have missed it. In understanding what the form worked on—that is, the subject matter—our perceptive apparatus is better prepared to perceive the *form-content*, the work of art's structure and meaning.

The subject matter of Renoir's painting is the nude more as an earth mother. In the *Venus de Milo,* the subject matter is the erotic ideal, the goddess of love. In the Duchamp, it is a mechanized dissection of the female form in action. In the Wesselmann, it is the nude as exploited. In the Velazquez, the nude is idealized; however, with Cupid holding the mirror for Venus to admire herself, we sense a bit of coyness, perhaps a touch of narcissism. This painting is the only surviving nude by Velazquez. Because the Spanish Inquisition was in power when he painted, it was dangerous to have and display this work in Spain. In 1813 it was purchased by an English aristocrat and taken to Rokeby Park. In all eight paintings by men, the subject matter is the female nude—but qualified in relation to what the artistic form focuses upon and makes lucid.

The two paintings by Suzanne Valadon and Alice Neel treat the female nude somewhat differently than those painted by men. Neel's painting emphasizes an aspect of femaleness that the men usually ignore—pregnancy. Her painting does not show the alluring female but the female who is beyond allure. Valadon's nude is more traditional, but a comparison with Renoir and Giorgione should demonstrate that she is far from their ideal.

PERCEPTION KEY Ten Female Nudes

1. Which of these nudes is most clearly idealized? What visual qualities contribute to that idealization?
2. Which of these nudes seem to be aware of being seen? How does their awareness affect your interpretation of the form of the nude?
3. *Nude Descending a Staircase* caused a great uproar when it was exhibited in New York in 1913. Do you feel it is still a controversial painting? How does it interpret the female nude in comparison with the other paintings in this group? Could the nude be male? Why not? Suppose the title were *Male Descending* or *Body Descending*. Isn't the sense of human movement the essential subject matter?

continued

4. If you were not told that Suzanne Valadon and Alice Neel painted, would you have known they were painted by women? What are the principal differences in the treatment of the nude figure on the part of all these artists? Does their work surprise you?
5. Decide whether *Standing Woman* is the work of a male artist or a female artist. What criteria do you use in your decision?

EXPERIENCING Interpretations of the Female Nude

1. Is there an obvious difference between the representations of the female nude by male and female artists?
2. Does distortion of the human figure help distance the viewer from the subject?
3. To what extent does the represented figure become a potential sexual object?

Following are some suggestions for analysis.

First, working backward, we can see that the question of the figure being a sexual object is to a large extent parodied by Tom Wesselmann's *Study for Great American Nude*. The style and approach to painting are couched in careful design, including familiar objects—the telephone, the rose, the perfume bottle, the sofa cushions, the partial portrait—all of which imply the boudoir and the commodification of women and sex. The figure's face is totally anonymous, implying that this is not a painting of a woman but of the idea of the modern American woman, with her nipple carefully exposed to accommodate advertising's breast fetish as a means of selling goods.

Even Velazquez's *Rokeby Venus*, a painting whose subject is more sensual than ideal, is less a sexual object than Wesselmann's. For one thing, her body is less revealed than Wesselmann's, and her face, shown to us in a mirror, is looking at her reflection, suggesting that she is in command of herself and is not to be taken lightly. The colors in the painting are sumptuous and sensuous—rich red fabrics, an inviting bed, and a delighted boy-god Cupid. Since Cupid is the archer who causes people to fall in love, could it be that some of the subject matter is Venus loving herself? What does the form of the painting reveal to you in terms of its content?

Then, the question of the distortion of the subject is powerfully handled by Duchamp's *Nude Descending a Staircase, No. 2*. This painting provoked a riot in 1913 because it seemed to be a contemptuous portrait of the nude at a time when the nude aesthetic was still academic in style. Duchamp was taunting the audience for art while also finding a modern technological representation of the nude on canvas that mimed the cinema of his time. Philip Pearlstein's study of two nudes moves toward a de-idealization of the nude. He asks us to look at the nudes without desire, yet with careful attention to form and color.

Finally, we may partly answer the question of whether women paint nude females differently by looking at Suzanne Valadon's and Alice Neel's paintings. Neel represents Margaret Evans in a manner emphasizing her womanness, not her sexual desirability. Hers is the only pregnant female figure—emphasizing the power of women to create life. Valadon's nude makes an effort to cover herself while looking at the viewer. She is relaxed yet apprehensive. There is no attempt at commodification of either of these figures, which means we must look at them very differently than the rest of the paintings represented here.

Artistic form is an organized structure, a design, but it is also a window opening on and focusing our world, helping us to perceive and understand what is important. This is the function of artistic form. The artist uses form as a means to understanding some subject matter, and in this process the subject matter exerts its own imperative. A subject matter has, as Edmund Husserl puts it, a "structure of determination," which to some significant degree is independent of the artist. Even when the ideas of the artist are the subject matter, they challenge and resist, forcing the artist to discover their significance by discarding irrelevancies.

Subject matter is friendly, for it assists interpretation, but subject matter is also hostile, for it resists interpretation. Otherwise, there would be no fundamental stimulus or challenge to the creativity of the artist. Only subject matter with interesting latent or uninterpreted values can challenge the artist, and the artist discovers these values through form. If the maker of a work takes the line of least resistance by ignoring the challenge of the subject matter—pushing the subject matter around for entertaining or escapist effects instead of trying to uncover its significance—the maker functions as a decorator rather than an artist.

Whereas decorative form merely pleases, artistic form informs about subject matter embedded in values that to an overwhelming extent are produced independently of the artist. By revealing those values, the artist helps us understand ourselves and our world, provided we participate with the work and understand the way artistic form produces content. The artist reveals the content in the work—the content is revealed to us through the act of participation and close attention to artistic form.

Participation is a flowing experience. One thought, image, or sensation merges into another, and we don't know where we are going for certain, except that what we are feeling is moving and controlling the flow, and clock time is irrelevant.

Participation is often interrupted—someone moves in front of the painting, the telephone call breaks the reading of the poem, someone goes into a coughing fit at the concert—but as long as we keep coming back to the work as dominant over distraction, we have something of the wonder of participation.

SUMMARY

A work of art is a form-content. An artistic form is a form-content. An artistic form is more than just an organization of the elements of an artistic medium, such as the lines and colors of painting. The artistic form interprets or clarifies some subject matter. The subject matter, strictly speaking, is not in a work of art. When participating with a work of art, one can only imagine the subject matter, not perceive it. The subject matter is only suggested by the work of art. The interpretation of the subject matter is the content, or meaning, of the work of art. Content is embodied in the form. The content, unlike the subject matter, is in the work of art, fused with the form. We can separate content from form only by analysis. The ultimate justification of any analysis is whether it enriches our participation with that work, whether it helps that work "work" in us. Good analysis or criticism does just that. But, conversely, any analysis not based on participation is unlikely to be helpful. Participation is the only way to get into direct contact with the form-content, so any analysis that is not based upon a participative experience inevitably misses the work of art. Participation and good analysis, although necessarily occurring at different times, end up hand in hand.

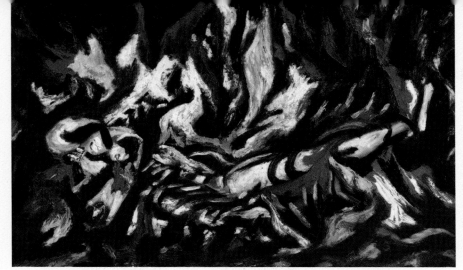

Chapter 3

BEING A CRITIC OF THE ARTS

The goals of responsible *criticism* aim for the fullest understanding and participation possible. Being a responsible critic demands being at the height of awareness while examining a work of art in detail, establishing its context, and clarifying its achievement. It is not to be confused with popular journalism, which can sidetrack the critic into being flashy, negative, and cute. The critic aims at a full understanding of a work of art.

YOU ARE ALREADY AN ART CRITIC

On a practical level, everyday criticism is an act of choice. You decide to change from one program to another on television because you have made a critical choice. When you find that certain programs please you more than others, that, too, is a matter of expressing choices. If you decide that Albert Inaurrato's film *Revenant* is better than John Ford's film *The Searchers*, you have made a critical choice. When you stop to admire a powerful piece of architecture while ignoring a nearby building, you have again made a critical choice. You are active every day in art criticism of one kind or another. Most of the time it is low-level criticism, almost instinctive, establishing your preferences in music, literature, painting, sculpture, architecture, film, and video art. You have made such judgments since you were young. The question now is how to move on to a higher-level criticism that accounts for the subtlest distinctions in the arts and therefore the most-complex choices.

What qualifies us to make critical distinctions when we are young and uninformed about art? Usually it is a matter of simple pleasure. Art is designed to give us pleasure, and for most children the most pleasurable art is simple: representational painting, lyrical and tuneful melodies, recognizable sculpture, light verse, action stories, and animated videos. It is another thing to move from that pleasurable beginning to account for what may be higher-level pleasures, such as those in Cézanne's still lifes, Beethoven's symphonies, Jean Arp's sculpture *Growth,* Amy Lowell's poem "Venus Transiens," Sophocles's tragedy *Oedipus Rex,* or David Simon's video triumph *The Wire.* One of the purposes of this chapter is to point to the kinds of critical acts that help us expand our repertoire of responses to the arts.

Participation and Criticism

Participation with a work of art is complex but also sometimes immediate. Participation is an essential act that makes art significant in our lives. We have described it as a loss of self, by which we mean that when contemplating, or experiencing, a work of art we tend to become one with the experience. As in films such as *Citizen Kane, Thelma and Louise,* or *Dunkirk,* we become one with the narrative and lose a sense of our physical space. We can also achieve a sense of participation with painting, music, and the other arts. The question is not so much how we become outside ourselves in relation to the arts, but why we may not achieve that condition in the face of art that we know has great power but does not yet speak to us. Developing critical skills will help bridge that gap and allow participation with art that may not be immediately appealing. In essence, that is the purpose of an education in the arts.

Patience and perception are the keys to beginning high-level criticism. Using painting as an example, it is clear that careful perceptions of color, rhythm, line, form, and balance are useful in understanding the artistic form and its resultant content. Our discussion of Goya's *May 3, 1808* (Figure 2-3) in terms of the emphasis of the line at the bottom of the painting and the power of the lines formed by the soldiers' rifles, while in contrast with the white blouse of one of the men being executed, helps us perceive the painting's artistic form. Coming to such a huge and demanding painting with enough patience to stand and perceive the underlying formal structures, while seeing the power of the color and details designed to heighten our awareness of the significance of the action, makes it possible to achieve participation. From there it is possible to go back to the Eddie Adams photograph *Execution in Saigon* (Figure 2-2) and decide whether the same kind of participation is possible and whether the formal significance of the photograph is comparable. Any decision we make in this context is an act of art criticism.

Three Kinds of Criticism

We point to three kinds of criticism that aim toward increasing our ability to participate with works of art. In Chapter 2, we argued that a work of art is a form-content and that good criticism, which involves careful examination and thoughtful analysis, will sharpen our perception and deepen our understanding. Descriptive criticism aims at a careful accounting of the formal elements in the work. As its name implies, this stage of criticism is marked by an examination of the large formal elements as well as the details in the composition. Interpretive criticism focuses on the content of the work, the discovery of which requires reflection on how the formal elements transform the subject matter. Evaluative criticism, on the other hand, is an effort to qualify the relative merits of a work.

CONCEPTION KEY **Kinds of Criticism**

1. In Chapter 2, which portions of the discussion of Goya's *May 3, 1808* (Figure 2-3) and Adams's *Execution in Saigon* (Figure 2-2) are descriptive criticism? How do they help you better perceive the formal elements of the works?
2. Comment on the usefulness of the descriptive criticism of Robert Herrick's poem "The Pillar of Fame" in Chapter 1. When does that discussion become interpretive criticism?
3. "Experiencing: Interpretations of the Female Nude" (Figures 2-9 through 2-18) introduces a series of interpretive criticisms of some of the paintings in the chapter. Which of these interpretations, in your opinion, is most successful in sharpening your awareness of the content of the painting? What are the most useful interpretive techniques used in the discussion of the paintings of female nudes?
4. Evaluative criticism is used in Chapters 1 and 2. To what extent are you most enlightened by this form of criticism in our discussion of the Goya painting and the Adams photograph?
5. In what other discussions in this book do you find evaluative criticism? How often do you practice it on your own while examining the works in this book?

Descriptive Criticism

Descriptive criticism concentrates on the form of a work of art, describing, sometimes exhaustively, the important characteristics of that form in order to improve our understanding of the part-to-part and part-to-whole interrelationships. At first glance this kind of criticism may seem unnecessary. After all, the form is all there, completely given—all we have to do is observe. Yet we can spend time attending to a work we are very much interested in and still not perceive all there is to perceive. We miss things, often things that are right there for us to observe.

Good descriptive critics call our attention to what we otherwise might miss in an artistic form. And more important, they help us learn how to do their work when they are not around. We can, if we carefully attend to descriptive criticism, develop and enhance our own powers of observation. Descriptive criticism, more than any other type, is most likely to improve our participation with a work of art, for such criticism turns us directly to the work itself.

Study Leonardo da Vinci's *Last Supper* (Figure 3-1), damaged by repeated restorations. Leonardo unfortunately experimented with dry fresco, which, as in this case, deteriorates rapidly. Still, even in its present condition, this painting can be overwhelming.

FIGURE 3-1
Leonardo da Vinci, *Last Supper*.
Circa 1495–1498. Oil and tempera
on plaster, 15 feet 1⅛ inches ×
28 feet 10½ inches. Refectory of
Santa Maria delle Grazie, Milan.
Leonardo's painting was one of many
on this subject, but his is the first
to represent recognizably human
figures with understandable facial
expressions. This is the dramatic
moment when Jesus tells his disciples
that one of them will betray him.

©Erich Lessing/Art Resource, NY

PERCEPTION KEY *Last Supper*

Descriptively criticize the *Last Supper*. Point out every facet of form that seems important. Look for shapes that relate to each other, including shapes formed by groupings of figures. Do any shapes stand out as unique—for example, the shapes of Christ and Judas, who leans back, fourth from the left? Describe the color relationships. Describe the symmetry, if any. Describe how the lines tend to meet in the landscape behind Christ's head.

Leonardo planned the fresco so that the perspectival vanishing point would reside in the head of Jesus, the central figure in the painting (Figure 3-2). He also used the concept of the trinity, in the number 3, as he grouped each of the disciples in threes, two groups on each side of the painting. Were you to diagram them, you would see they form the basis of triangles. The three windows in the back wall also repeat the idea of three. The figure of Jesus is itself a perfect isosceles triangle, while the red and blue garment centers the eye. In some paintings, this kind of architectonic organization might be much too static, but because Leonardo gathers the figures in dramatic poses, with facial expressions that reveal apparent emotions, the viewer is distracted from the formal organization while being subliminally affected by its perfection. It seems that perfection—appropriate to his subject matter—was what Leonardo aimed at in creating the underlying structure of the fresco. Judas, the disciple who will betray Jesus, is the fourth figure from the left, his face in shadow, pulling back in shock.

FIGURE 3-2
The *Last Supper* is geometrically arranged with the single-point vanishing perspective centered on the head of Jesus. The basic organizing form for the figures in the painting is the triangle. Leonardo aimed at geometric perfection.

©Erich Lessing/Art Resource, NY

Detail and Structural Relationships When we address a painting we concern ourselves both with the **structural relationships** and the **detail** that control our visual attention. For example, the dominant structures in the *Last Supper* are the white rectangular table cloth contrasting with the high receding white walls that create the single-point vanishing perspective ending in the head of Jesus. These dynamic lines of force imply a dramatic moment. As you examine the painting and consider the following discussion, decide whether the relationship of structural elements or detail elements is dominant in how you see this painting.

When we talk about details, we are concerned with how the smaller elements of the work function together. For example, in the *Last Supper*, we see that the figure of Jesus at the center is a geometric shape, an isosceles triangle. Within this painting, this triangle constitutes a detail. Moreover, when examining the painting for more details, we see that all the apostles are grouped in patterns of three. However, their triangular shapes are not as perfect as the center triangle. If you draw the implied triangle for any other group of three, you will see that it is not isosceles, but somewhat misshapen. Perfection in this painting is reserved for only one figure.

In examining other details in the painting we see that the three open windows in the rear are details that replicate the idea of three, echoing the three lines of the triangle. The four tapestries on each wall act as background, but may refer to the traditional "perfect" number, eight, which signifies the new beginning. (The eight white keys on a piano illustrate that idea: C-D-E-F-G-A-B-C.)

The triangular figure of Jesus, with red and blue garments, in the center of the *Last Supper* is a dominant settling force for the eye, but it contrasts immediately with the other triangular arrangements of the apostles. Among other contrasting details are the colors of the garments of the apostles. They are paler complementary

FIGURE 3-3
Jackson Pollock, *The Flame* (1934–1938). Oil on canvas mounted on fiberboard, 20½ × 30 inches (51.1 × 76.2 cm). Enid A. Haupt Fund. The Metropolitan Museum of Art, New York, NY.

colors of red, blue, and ochre, competing with the dominant darkness of the rear wall and the tapestries on the left and right walls. Observing the apostles's colored garments and their less than equilateral triangular grouping is important for interpreting their relationship to the main figure in the painting and its main dramatic moment.

In Jackson Pollock's *The Flame* (Figure 3-3), the details of the flames, in the brilliant reds, the orange-whites, and the deep contrasts in the blacks of the composition, are so vigorous that on first inspection it is difficult to see the forms that begin to appear. If we did not know the name of the painting, we might have no idea whether something is being represented or if the painting is an example of abstraction, a style for which Pollock was usually known. But closer examination shows the formal order in the center of the painting, creating a triangular structure controlled by the angular red flames rising to the top center. The central flame in orange-white seems to rise from two angular forms in white (possibly parts of a skeleton?) that angle down in the middle, the base for the central flames. All the detailed shapes angle upward, as we expect fire to do. The subject matter of the painting is flame, but the intensity of the colors and the power of the contrasts of black, white, and red reveal an energy in the flame that suggests something dreadful. If this were a painting made in the Middle Ages, we would assume it an allusion to the pits of hell. However, Pollock was influenced in 1936 by the work of José Clemente Orozco portraying war in Mexico and threats to civilization. Destruction and skeletons figure in much of Orozco's work in the 1930s. Could the content of the painting point to an apocalypse?

Picasso's *Guernica* (Figure 1-4) is more or less balanced with respect to detail and structure. The detail relationships are organized into three major regions: the great triangle—with the apex at the candle and two sides sloping down to the lower corners—and the two large rectangles, vertically oriented, running down along the left and right borders. Moreover, these regions are hierarchically ordered. The triangular region takes precedence in both size and interest, and the left rectangle, mainly because of the fascination of the impassive bull (what is he doing here?), dominates the right rectangle, even though both are about the same size. Despite the complexity of the detail relationships in *Guernica,* we gradually perceive the power of a very strong, clear structure.

The basic formal element in Leonardo's *Mona Lisa* (Figure 1-5) is the isosceles triangle, but in this portrait the roundness of the three points of the triangle soften the impact of the form. We are drawn to the hands, which are crossed in such a way as to create an "upside down" triangle with the elbows and the other points. The flesh of her neck and bosom creates another triangle, while her oval face dominates the composition. Naturally her smile has been an enigma because it implies an understanding between the painter and the model. Its enigmatic quality is echoed slightly by the strange landscapes in the background—they carefully avoid any stable geometric figure as a way of contrast. Return to the discussion of this painting in "Experiencing: The *Mona Lisa*" in Chapter 1 and consider the descriptive criticism offered there.

PERCEPTION KEY Detail and Structural Dominance

1. In the *Last Supper*, do you find that detail or structural relationships dominate—or are equal? Which analysis, of structure or detail, yields the most understanding of the painting's content?
2. Whether detail or structural relationships dominate—or are equal—often varies widely from work to work. Compare Pollock's *The Flame*, Picasso's *Guernica* (Figure 1-4), and Leonardo's *Mona Lisa* (Figure 1-5). In which painting or paintings, if any, do detail relationships dominate? Structural relationships?

Interpretive Criticism

Interpretive criticism explicates the content of a work of art. It helps us understand how form transforms subject matter into content: what has been revealed about some subject matter and how that has been accomplished. The content of any work of art will become clearer when the structure is perceived in relation to the details and regions. The Le Corbusier and Sullivan examples (Figures 3-4 and 3-5) demonstrate that the same principle holds for architecture as for painting. The subject matter of a building—or at least an important component of it—is traditionally the practical function the building serves. We have no difficulty telling which of these buildings was meant to serve as a bank and which was meant to serve as a church.

FIGURE 3-4
Le Corbusier, Notre Dame-du-Haut, Ronchamps, France. 1950–1955. The chapel is built on a hill where a pilgrimage chapel was destroyed during the Second World War. Le Corbusier used soaring lines to lift the viewer's eyes to the heavens and the surrounding horizon, visible on all four sides.

PERCEPTION KEY Le Corbusier and Sullivan

1. If you had not been told, would you know that Le Corbusier's building is a church? Now, having been told, which structural details help identify it as a church?
2. Which of these buildings better uses its basic structure to suggest solidity? Which better uses formal patterns to suggest flight and motion?
3. In which of these buildings does detail better complement the overall structure?
4. Comment on how the formal values of these buildings contribute to their content as serving their established functions as bank and church.
5. One of these buildings is symmetrical and one is not. Symmetry is often praised in nature as a constituent of beauty. How important is symmetry in evaluating these buildings?

Form-Content   The interpretive critic's job is to find out as much about an artistic form as possible in order to explain its meaning. This is a particularly useful task for the critic—which is to say, for us as critics—since the forms of numerous works of art seem important but are not immediately understandable. When we look at the examples of the bank and the church, we ought to realize that the significance of these buildings is expressed by means of the ***form-content***. It is true that without knowing the functions of these buildings we could appreciate them as structures without special functions, but knowing about their functions deepens our appreciation. Thus, the lofty arc of Le Corbusier's roof soars heavenward more mightily when we recognize the building as a church. The form moves our eyes upward. For a Christian church, such a reference is perfect. The bank, however, looks like a pile of square coins or banknotes and moves our eyes downward. Certainly the form "amasses"

FIGURE 3-5
Louis Henry Sullivan, Guaranty (Prudential) Building, Buffalo, New York. 1894. Sullivan's building, among the first high-rise structures, was made possible by the use of mass-produced steel girders supporting the weight of each floor.

something, an appropriate suggestion for a bank. We will not belabor these examples, since it should be fun for you to do this kind of critical job yourself. Observe how much more you get out of these examples of architecture when you consider each form in relation to its meaning—that is, the form as form-content. Furthermore, such analyses should convince you that interpretive criticism operates in a vacuum unless it is based on descriptive criticism. Unless we perceive the form with sensitivity—and this means that we have the basis for good descriptive criticism—we simply cannot understand the content. In turn, any interpretive criticism will be useless.

Participate with a poem by William Butler Yeats:

THE LAKE ISLE OF INNISFREE

I will arise and go now, and go to Innisfree,
    And a small cabin build there, of clay and wattles made;
Nine bean rows will I have there, a hive for the honey bee,
    And live alone in the bee-loud glade.

And I shall have some peace there, for peace comes dropping slow,
    Dropping from the veils of the morning to where the cricket sings;
There midnight's all a glimmer, and noon a purple glow,
    And evening full of the linnet's wings.

I will arise and go now, for always night and day
    I hear lake water lapping with low sounds by the shore;
While I stand on the roadway, or on the pavements gray,
    I hear it in the deep heart's core.

> Source: William Butler Yeats, "The Lake Isle of Innisfree," *The Collected Works in the Verse and Prose of William Butler Yeats, Volume 8 (of 8)*. Project Gutenberg.

PERCEPTION KEY   Yeats's Poem

1. Offer a brief description of the poem, concentrating on the nature of the rhyme-words, the contrasting imagery, the rhythms of the lines.
2. What does the poet say he intends to do? Do you think he will actually do it?

"The Lake Isle of Innisfree" is a lyric written from the first person, "I." Its three stanzas of four lines each rhyme in simple fashion with full vowel sounds, and as a result, the poem lends itself to being sung, as indeed it has often been set to music. The poet portrays himself as a simple person preferring the simple life. The descriptive critic will notice the basic formal qualities of the poem: simple rhyme, steady meter, the familiar quatrain stanza structure. But the critic will also move further to talk about the imagery in the poem: the image of the simply built cabin, the small garden with bean rows, the bee hive, the sounds of the linnet's wings and the lake water lapping the shore, the look of noon's purple glow. The interpretive critic will address the entire project of the poet, who is standing "on the roadway, or on the pavements gray," longing to return to the distant country and the simple life. The poet "hears" the lake waters "in the deep heart's core," which is to say that the simple life is absolutely basic to the poet. The last three words actually repeat the same idea. The heart is always at the core of a person, and it is always deep in that core. Such emphasis helps produce in the reader a sense of completion and significance. In a sense the triangular shape of the heart is replicated in the three words applied to it, as if the idea of the number 3 were a stabilizing "shape" similar to the visually stabilizing shape of the triangles in the paintings we have been describing.

Yeats later commented on this poem and said it was the first poem of his career to have a real sense of music. He also said that the imagery came to him when he was stepping off a curb near the British Museum in the heart of London and heard the sound of splashing water. The sounds immediately brought to mind the imagery of the island, which is in the west of Ireland.

It is important that we grasp the relative nature of explanations about the content of works of art. Even descriptive critics, who try to tell us about what is really there, will perceive things in a way that is relative to their own perspective. An amusing story in Cervantes's *Don Quixote* illustrates the point. Sancho Panza had two cousins who were expert wine tasters. However, on occasion, they disagreed. One found the wine excellent except for an iron taste; the other found the wine excellent except for a leather taste. When the barrel of wine was emptied, an iron key with a leather thong was found. As N. J. Berrill points out in *Man's Emerging Mind,*

> The statement you often hear that seeing is believing is one of the most misleading ones a man has ever made, for you are more likely to see what you believe than believe what you see. To see anything as it really exists is about as hard an exercise of mind and eyes as it is possible to perform.[1]

Two descriptive critics can often "see" quite different things in an artistic form. This is not only to be expected but also desirable; it is one of the reasons great works of art keep us intrigued for centuries. But even though they may see quite different aspects when they look independently at a work of art, when they talk it over, the critics will usually come to some kind of agreement about the aspects each of them sees. The work being described, after all, has verifiable, objective qualities each of us can perceive and talk about. But it has subjective qualities as well, in the sense that the qualities are observed only by "subjects."

In the case of interpretive criticism, the subjectivity and, in turn, the relativity of explanations are more obvious than in the case of descriptive criticism. The content is "there" in the form, and yet, unlike the form, it is not there in a directly perceivable way. It must be interpreted.

Interpretive critics, more than descriptive critics, must be familiar with the subject matter. Interpretive critics often make the subject matter more explicit for us at the first stage of their criticism, bringing us closer to the work. Perhaps the best way initially to get at Picasso's *Guernica* (Figure 1-4) is to discover its subject matter. Is it about a fire in a building or something else? If we are not clear about this, perception of the painting is obscured. But after the subject matter has been elucidated, good interpretive critics go much further: exploring and discovering meanings about the subject matter as revealed by the form. Now they are concerned with helping us grasp the content directly, in all of its complexities and subtleties. This final stage of interpretive criticism is the most demanding of all criticism.

---

[1]N. J. Berrill, *Man's Emerging Mind* (New York: Dodd, Mead, 1955), p. 147.

Evaluative Criticism

To evaluate a work of art is to judge its merits. At first this seems to suggest that *evaluative criticism* is prescriptive criticism, which prescribes what is good as if it were a medicine and tells us that this work is superior to that work. However, our approach is somewhat different. Evaluative criticism functions to establish the quality and excellence of the work. To some extent, our discussion will include comparisons that inevitably urge us to make quality decisions. Those decisions are best made after descriptive and interpretive criticism have taken part in examining the work of art.

> **PERCEPTION KEY** Evaluative Criticism
>
> 1. Suppose you are a judge of an exhibition of painting, and in Chapter 2 (Figures 2-9 through 2-18) have been placed into competition. You are to award first, second, and third prizes. What would your decisions be? Why?
> 2. Suppose, further, that you are asked to judge which is the best work of art from the following selection: Le Corbusier's church, Yeats's "The Lake Isle of Innisfree," and Cézanne's *Mont Sainte-Victoire* (Figure 2-4). What would your decision be? Why?

It may be that this kind of evaluative criticism makes you uncomfortable. If so, we think your reaction is based on good instincts. First, each work of art is unique, so a relative merit ranking of several of them seems arbitrary. This is especially the case when the works are in different media and have different subject matters, as in the second question of the Perception Key. Second, it is not clear how such judging helps us in our basic critical purpose—to learn from our reflections about works of art how to participate with these works more intensely and enjoyably.

Nevertheless, evaluative criticism of some kind is generally necessary. As authors, we have been making such judgments continually in this book—in the selections for illustrations, for example. You make such judgments when, as you enter a museum, you decide to spend your time with this painting rather than that. Obviously directors of museums must also make evaluative criticisms, because usually they cannot display every work owned by the museum. If a van Gogh is on sale—and one of his paintings, *Vase with Fifteen Sunflowers,* was bought in 1997 for $90 million—someone has to decide its worth. Evaluative criticism, then, is always functioning, at least implicitly.

The problem, then, is how to use evaluative criticism as constructively as possible. How can we use such criticism to help our participation with works of art? Whether Giorgione's painting (Figure 2-9) or Pearlstein's (Figure 2-18) deserves first prize seems trivial. But if almost all critics agree that Shakespeare's poetry is far superior to Edward Guest's, and if we have been thinking Guest's poetry is better, we should do some reevaluating. Or if we hear a music critic whom we respect state that the music of Duke Ellington is worth listening to—and up to this time we have dismissed it—then we should make an effort to listen. Perhaps the basic importance of evaluative criticism lies in its commendation of works that we might otherwise dismiss. This may lead us to delightful experiences. Such criticism may also make us more skeptical about our own judgments.

Evaluative criticism presupposes three fundamental standards: perfection, insight, and inexhaustibility. When the evaluation centers on the form, it usually values a form highly only if the detail and regional relationships are organically related. If they fail to cohere with the structure, the result is distracting and thus inhibits participation. An artistic form in which everything works together may be called perfect. A work may have perfect organization, however, and still be evaluated as poor unless it satisfies the standard of insight. If the form fails to inform us about some subject matter—if it just pleases, interests, or excites us but doesn't make some significant difference in our lives—then, for us, that form is not artistic. Such a form may be valued below artistic form because the participation it evokes, if it evokes any at all, is not lastingly significant. Incidentally, a work lacking representation of objects and events may possess artistic form. Abstract art has a definite subject matter—the sensuous. Who is to say that the Pollock is a lesser work of art because it informs only about the sensuous? The sensuous is with us all the time, and to be sensitive to it is exceptionally life-enhancing.

Finally, works of art may differ greatly in the breadth and depth of their content. The subject matter of Pollock's *The Flame*—the sensuous—is not as broad as the subject of Cézanne's *Mont Sainte-Victoire* (Figure 2-4). Yet it does not follow necessarily that the Cézanne is a superior work. The stronger the content—that is, the richer the insight into the subject matter—the more intense our participation, because we have more to keep us involved in the work. Such works apparently are inexhaustible, and evaluative critics usually will rate only those kinds of works as masterpieces.

The sensuous was central to the British art show titled Sensation, which showed controversial works that caused the Royal Academy of Art to restrict entry to those over age eighteen. Some of the works were perceived as repugnant by some churchmen and politicians in New York. Ron Mueck's four-foot-long *Mask II: Self-portrait* (Figure 3-6) was a sensation because of its hugeness and its hyper-real style. The Saatchi Gallery commissioned this work for the Sensation show in London.

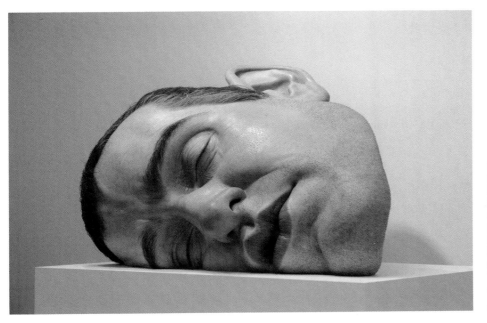

FIGURE 3-6
Ron Mueck, *Mask II*. 2001–2002. Mixed media, 30⅜ × 46½ × 33½ inches (77.2 × 118.1 × 85.1 cm). Collection of the Art Supporting Foundation to the San Francisco Museum of Modern Art. Mueck's huge sculptures were part of the original Sensation show in London. Their effect on the viewer is one of surprise and, ultimately, delight.

©MaxPPP/Annie Viannet/Newscom

FIGURE 3-7
Chris Ofili, *Holy Virgin Mary*. 1996. Mixed media,
96 × 72 inches. Victoria Miro Gallery, London. This
is another example of shock art, by Ofili, a British
artist noted for works referencing his African
heritage. Audiences were alarmed when they
discovered one of the media was elephant dung,
a substance common in African art but not easily
accepted by Western audiences.

Courtesy of Chris Ofili/Afroco and David Zwirner

Rudolph Giuliani, mayor of New York at the time, did not see the show but was horrified by complaints from William Donahue, president of the Catholic League, and cut off funding to the museum. He later restored it, but not until protesters accused him of censorship. Churchmen and politicians thought the most shocking work of art was by Chris Ofili, a young black painter whose *Holy Virgin Mary* (Figure 3-7) alarmed religious New Yorkers because images of naked female bottoms and elephant dung were part of the mixed media that went into the painting.

PERCEPTION KEY The Sensation Show

1. David Bowie said Sensation was the most important show since the 1913 New York Armory show in which Duchamp's *Nude Descending a Staircase, No. 2* (Figure 2-14) created a scandal, protest, and intense controversy. Most art that was once shocking seems tame a few years later. To what extent do any of these works of art still have shock value?

2. Should politicians, like the mayor of New York, punish major museums for showing art that the politicians feel is offensive? Does such an act constitute a legitimate form of evaluative art criticism? Does it constitute art criticism if, like ex-mayor Giuliani, the politician has not seen and experienced the art?

3. The Sensation show was described as shock art. Ofili's use of naked female bottoms and dung in a portrait of the Madonna shocked many people. Why would it have been shocking? To what extent is shock an important value in art? Would you agree with those who said Chris Ofili's work was not art? What would be the basis for such a position?

4. Would Chris Ofili's painting be shocking if people were unaware that he painted some of it with elephant dung? Would people be less alarmed if they knew that in Africa such a practice in art is relatively common? Does any of this matter in making a judgment about the painting's success as a work of art? What matters most for you in evaluating this painting?

The Polish Rider (Figure 3-8), featured in "Experiencing: *The Polish Rider*," was originally attributed to Rembrandt. But in 1982 a group of five scholars, members of the Rembrandt Research Project, "disattributed" the painting. Studying subtleties such as brushwork, color transitions, transparency, shadowing, and structuring, they concluded that Willem Drost, a student of Rembrandt, was probably the artist. In the Frick Museum in New York City, *The Polish Rider* no longer draws crowds. Another work, presumably by Rembrandt, had been expected to sell for at least $15 million. It, too, was disattributed and was sold for *only* $800,000!

EXPERIENCING *The Polish Rider*

1. Does knowing *The Polish Rider* was probably painted by Willem Drost instead of Rembrandt van Rijn diminish your participation with the painting? Does the fact that it was painted by a student negatively affect your evaluation of the painting?
2. Should a work of art be evaluated completely without reference to its creator?
3. How should our critical judgment of the painting be affected by knowing it was once valued at millions of dollars and is now worth vastly less?

One of the authors, as a young adult, saw this painting in the Frick Museum and listened to a discussion of its merits when it was thought to be by Rembrandt. Although today the painting is neglected, it is no less excellent than it was.

One school of thought holds that paintings are to be evaluated wholly on their own merit without reference to the artist who created it. *The Polish Rider*, for instance, would still be held in great esteem if it had not been assumed to be by Rembrandt. But another school of thought holds that a

FIGURE 3-8
Willem Drost, *The Polish Rider*. 1655. Oil on canvas, 46 × 53⅛ inches. Frick Collection, New York.
Long thought to be a painting by Rembrandt, *The Polish Rider* is now credited to one of his gifted students. The Frick removed it from a prominent place after Julius Held determined that it is probably the work of Willem Drost.

©Fine Art Images/Heritage/The Image Works

continued

painting is best evaluated when seen in the context of other paintings by the same artists, or even in the context of other paintings with similar style and subject matter.

Because in modern times artworks have sometimes been investment opportunities for wealthy people, the question of value has become a financial question even more than an aesthetic question. The result is that some works of art have been grossly overvalued by art critics who are swayed by the dollar value, not the artistic value. We believe art must be valued for its capacity to provide us with insight and to promote our participation, not for its likelihood to be worth a fortune.

FIGURE 3-9
Amedeo Modigliani, *Nu Couché* (*Sleeping Nude*). 1917–1918. Via Christies.

©Christie's Images/Bridgeman Images

4. Which school of thought do you belong to: those who evaluate a painting on its own merits or those who consider the reputation of the artist?
5. Prices for art soared enormously beginning in the 1980s. The highest recent price paid at auction for a work of art was $170 million for Amedeo Modigliani's nude, *Nu Couché* (*Sleeping Nude*) (Figure 3-9). How does its money value affect its artistic value?

This painting surprised the art world by selling for $170 million to a Chinese collector, a taxi driver who became a billionaire. It took nine minutes to sell this painting via an international telephone call. Examine this painting in terms of descriptive, interpretive, and evaluative criticism. How does it compare with the nudes in Chapter 2? Why would any information regarding its sale or the price paid for it affect our sense of the artistic value of the painting? What is your judgment of *Nu Couché*'s artistic value?

Summary

Being a responsible critic demands being at the height of awareness while examining a work of art in detail, establishing its subject matter, and clarifying its achievement. There are three main types of criticism: Descriptive criticism focuses on form, interpretive criticism focuses on content, and evaluative criticism focuses on the relative merits of a work.

Good critics can help us understand works of art while giving us the means or techniques that will help us become good critics ourselves. They can teach us about what kinds of questions to ask. Each of the following chapters on the individual arts is designed to do just that—to give some help about what kinds of questions a serious viewer should ask in order to come to a clearer perception and deeper understanding of any specific work. With the arts, unlike many other areas of human concern, the questions are often more important than the answers. The real lover of the arts will often not be the person with all the answers but rather the one who asks the best questions. This is not because the answers are worthless but because the questions, when properly applied, lead us to a new awareness, a more exalted consciousness of what works of art have to offer. Then when we get to the last chapter, this preparation will lead to a better understanding of how the arts are related to other branches of the humanities.

©Universal History Archive/Getty Images

Chapter 4

PAINTING

OUR VISUAL POWERS

Painting awakens our visual senses so as to make us see color, shape, light, and form in new ways. Painters such as Siqueiros, Goya, Cézanne, Gentileschi, Neel, and virtually all the painters illustrated in this book make demands on our sensitivity to the visual field, rewarding us with challenges and delights that only painting can provide. But at the same time, we are also often dulled by day-to-day experience or by distractions of business or study that make it difficult to look with the intensity that great art requires. Therefore, we sometimes need to refresh our awareness by sharpening our attention to the surfaces of paintings as well as to their overall power. For example, by referring to the following Perception Key we may prepare ourselves to look deeply and respond in new ways to some of the paintings we considered in earlier chapters.

PERCEPTION KEY Our Visual Powers

1. Jackson Pollock, *The Flame* (Figure 3-3). Identify the three major colors Pollock uses. How do these colors establish a sense of visual rhythm? Which of the colors is most intense? Which most surprising?
2. Suzanne Valadon, *Reclining Nude* (Figure 2-16). Examine the piece of furniture, the sofa, on which Valadon's nude reclines. What color is it? Why is it an effective

contrast to the nude? What are the designs on the sofa? What color are the lines of the designs? How do they relate to the subject matter of the painting?

3. Edward Hopper, *Early Sunday Morning* (Figure 1-6). What are the most important colors in the painting? How do they balance and complement each other? Why does Hopper limit the intensity of the colors as he does? What is the visual rhythmic effect of the patterns formed in the windows of the second floor? Are any two windows the same? How does Hopper use unexpected forms to break the rhythm of the first level of shops? What emotional qualities are excited by Hopper's control of the visual elements in the painting?

4. Paul Cézanne, *Mont Sainte-Victoire* (Figure 2-4). How many colors does Cézanne use in this painting? Which color is dominant? Which figure in the painting is most dominant? How do the most important lines in the painting direct your vision? Describe the way your eye moves through the painting. How does Cézanne use line and color to direct your attention?

Our point is that everyday life tends to dull our senses so that we do not observe our surroundings with the sensitivity that we might. For help we must go to the artists, especially the painter and the sculptor—those who are most sensitive to the visual appearances of things. Their works make things and their qualities much clearer than they usually appear. The artist purges from our sight the films of familiarity. Painting, with its "all-at-onceness," more than any other art, gives us the time to allow our vision to focus.

THE MEDIA OF PAINTING

Throughout this book we will be talking about the basic materials and *media* in each of the arts, because a clear understanding of their properties will help us understand what artists do and how they work. The most prominent media in Western painting—and most painting in the rest of the world—are tempera, fresco, oil, watercolor, and acrylic. In early paintings the *pigment*—the actual color—required a *binder* such as egg yolk, glue, or casein to keep it in solution and permit it to be applied to canvas, wood, plaster, and other substances.

Tempera

Tempera is pigment bound by egg yolk and applied to a carefully prepared surface like the wood panels of Cimabue's thirteenth-century *Madonna and Child Enthroned with Angels* (Figure 4-1). The colors of tempera sometimes look slightly flat and are difficult to change as the artist works, but the marvelous precision of detail and the subtlety of linear shaping are extraordinary. The purity of colors, notably in the lighter range, can be wondrous, as with the tinted white of the inner dress of Giotto's *Madonna Enthroned* (Figure 4-2). In the fourteenth century, Giotto achieves an astonishing level of detail in the gold ornamentation below and around the Madonna. At the same time, his control of the medium of tempera permitted him to represent figures with a high degree of individuality and realism, representing a profound change in the history of art.

FIGURE 4-1
Cimabue, *Madonna and Child Enthroned with Angels*. Circa 1285–1290. Tempera and gold on wood, 12 feet 7¾ inches × 7 feet 4 inches. Uffizi, Florence. Cimabue's painting is typical of Italian altarpieces in the thirteenth century. The use of tempera and gold leaf creates a radiance appropriate to a religious scene.

©Alinari/Art Resource, NY

FIGURE 4-2
Giotto, *Madonna Enthroned*. Circa 1310. Tempera and gold on wood, 10 feet 8³/₁₆ inches × 6 feet 8³/₈ inches. Uffizi, Florence. Giotto, credited with creating a realistic portrayal of figures from nature in religious art, lavishes his *Madonna Enthroned* with extraordinary detail permitted by the use of tempera and gold leaf. Giotto was one of Florence's greatest painters.

The power of these works, when one stands before them in Florence's Uffizi Galleries, is intense beyond what can be shown in a reproduction. Cimabue's painting is more than twelve feet tall and commands the space as few paintings of the period can. The brilliance of the colors and the detail of the expressions of all the figures in the painting demand a remarkable level of participation. By comparison, the Giotto, only a few years later, uses contrasting colors to affect us. But Giotto's faces are more realistic than Cimabue's, marking an important shift in Renaissance art. Giotto achieves an illusion of depth and a sense that the figures are distinct, as if they were portraits.

Fresco

Because many churches and other buildings required paintings directly on plaster walls, artists perfected the use of ***fresco***, pigment dissolved in lime water applied to wet plaster as it is drying. In the case of wet fresco, the color penetrates to about

one-eighth of an inch and is bound into the plaster. There is little room for error because the plaster dries relatively quickly, and the artist must understand how the colors will look when embedded in plaster and no longer wet. One advantage of this medium is that it will last as long as the wall itself. One of the greatest examples of the use of fresco is Michelangelo's Sistine Chapel, on the ceiling of which is the famous *Creation of Adam* (Figure 4-3).

Oil

Oil painting uses a mixture of pigment, linseed oil, varnish, and turpentine to produce either a thin or thick consistency, depending on the artist's desired effect. In the fifteenth century, oil painting dominated because of its flexibility, the richness of its colors, and the extraordinary durability and long-lasting qualities. Because oil paint dries slowly and can be put on in thin layers, it offers the artist remarkable control over the final product. No medium in painting offers a more flexible blending of colors or subtle portrayal of light and textures, as in Parmigianino's *The Madonna with the Long Neck* (Figure 4-4). Oil paint can be messy, and it takes sometimes months or years to dry completely, but it has been the dominant medium in easel painting since the Renaissance.

FIGURE 4-4
Parmigianino, *The Madonna with the
Long Neck*. Circa 1535. Oil on panel,
85 × 52 inches. Uffizi, Florence.
Humanistic values dominate the
painting, with recognizably distinct
faces, young people substituting
for angels, and physical distortions
designed to unsettle a conservative
audience. This style of oil painting,
with unresolved figures and
unanswered questions, is called
Mannerism—painting with an
attitude.

©Erich Lessing/Art Resource, NY

FIGURE 4-5
Winslow Homer, Sketch for *"Hound and Hunter*." 1892. Watercolor on wove paper. 13 5/16 × 19 5/16 inches. Gift of Ruth K. Henschel in memory of her husband, Charles R. Henschel. Accession No. 1975.92.7. National Gallery of Art, Washington, D.C. Although a mixed-media composition, *Sketch for "Hound and Hunter"* is dominated by watercolor. An apparently unfinished quality imparts a sense of energy, spontaneity, and intensity, typical of Homer's work.

Source: National Gallery of Art, Washington, D.C.

Watercolor

The pigments of **watercolor** are bound in a water-soluble adhesive, such as gum-arabic, a gummy plant substance. Usually watercolor is slightly translucent so that the whiteness of the paper shows through. Unlike artists working with tempera or oil painting, watercolorists work quickly, often with broad strokes and in broad washes. The color resources of the medium are limited in range, but often striking in effect. Modern watercolor usually does not aim for precise detail. In his *Sketch for "Hound and Hunter"* (Figure 4-5), Winslow Homer delights in the unfinished quality of the watercolor and uses it to communicate a sense of immediacy. He controls the range of colors as a way of giving us a sense of atmosphere and weather.

Acrylic

A modern synthetic polymer medium, **acrylic** is fundamentally a form of plastic resin that dries very quickly and is flexible for the artist to apply and use. One advantage of acrylic paints is that they do not fade, darken, or yellow as they age. They can support luminous colors and look sometimes very close to oil paints in their

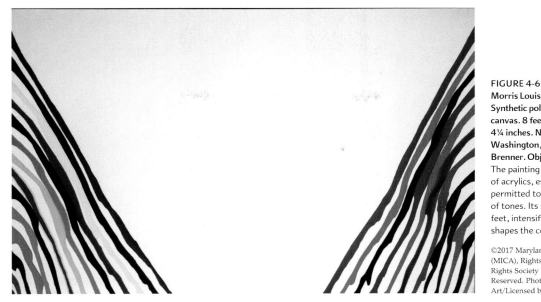

final effect. Many modern painters use this medium. Morris Louis's *Beta Lamda* (Figure 4-6) is a large abstract painting whose colors suggest a range of intensities similar to what we see in oil paintings.

The ease of using acrylic shows in the fluidity of the lines of stark colors balancing a huge open space of uncolored canvas. This painting was done in Louis's small dining room, but its size is such that only a few spaces can exhibit it. In viewing, one is captured by its gigantic presence. The triangular forms that dominate give the color a power that seems to radiate from the wall. Louis was a colorist experimenting with acrylic up to his death only a year after this painting was finished.

Other Media and Mixed Media

The great Japanese artist Hokusai was prominent in the first half of the nineteenth century in the medium of woodcuts, using ink for his color. The process is extremely complex, but he dominated in the Edo period, when many artists produced brilliantly colored prints that began to be seen in Europe, especially in France, where the painters found great inspiration in the brilliance of the work. *The Great Wave,* his most famous work (Figure 4-7), is from his project, *Thirty-Six Views of Mount Fuji.* Here the mountain is tiny in comparison with the roiling waves threatening even smaller figures in two boats. The power of nature is the subject matter, and the respect for nature may be part of its content.

The dominant medium for Chinese artists has been ink, as in Wang Yuanqi's *Landscape after Wu Zhen* (Figure 4-8). Modern painters often employ *mixed media*, using duco and aluminum paint, house paint, oils, even grit and sand. Andy Warhol used acrylic and silk-screen ink in his famous *Marilyn Monroe* series. Some basic kinds of *prints* are produced by methods including woodcut, engraving, linocut, etching, drypoint, lithography, and aquatint.

FIGURE 4-7
Katsushika Hokusai (Japanese, 1760–1849). *Under the Wave off Kanagawa (Kanagawa oki nami ura)*, also known as *The Great Wave, from the series* Thirty-Six Views of Mount Fuji (Fugaku sanjurokkei). Circa 1830–1832. Polychrome woodblock print; ink and color on paper; 10¹/₈ × 14¹⁵/₁₆ inches (25.7 × 37.9 cm). The Metropolitan Museum of Art, New York, H. O. Havemeyer Collection, Bequest of Mrs. H. O. Havemeyer, 1929.

Source: Robert Lehman Collection, 1975/The Metropolitan Museum of Art

PERCEPTION KEY The Media of Painting

1. Compare the detail of tempera in Giotto's *Madonna Enthroned* with the radiance of color in Parmigianino's oil painting *The Madonna with the Long Neck*. What differences do you see in the quality of detail in each painting and in the quality of the color?
2. Compare the color effects of Hokusai's *The Great Wave* woodblock print with the colors in Winslow Homer's *Sketch for "Hound and Hunter."* What seem to be the differences in the treatment of color?
3. Contrast the effect of Homer's watercolor approach to nature with Wang Yuanqi's use of ink. Which communicates a sense of nature more readily? In which is nature the most evident subject matter? Compare the formal structure of each painting.
4. Compare the traditional fresco of Michelangelo's *Creation of Adam* with Leonardo's experimental fresco of the *Last Supper* (Figure 3-1). To what extent does Michelangelo's use of the medium help you imagine what Leonardo's fresco would have looked like if he had used Michelangelo's technique?

FIGURE 4-8
Wang Yuanqi, *Landscape after*
Wu Zhen. **1695. Hanging scroll;**
ink on paper, 42¾ × 20¼ inches.
Metropolitan Museum of Art. Bequest
of John M. Crawford Jr. Typical of
many of the great Chinese landscape
scrolls, Wang Yuanqi uses his
brush and ink prodigiously, finding
a powerful energy in shaping the
rising mountains and their trees.
The presence of tiny houses and
rising pathways to the heights places
humanity in a secondary role in
relation to nature and to the visual
power of the mountain itself.

Source: Bequest of John M. Crawford Jr.,
1988/The Metropolitan Museum of Art

ELEMENTS OF PAINTING

The *elements* are the basic building blocks of a medium. For painting they are line, color, texture, and composition.* Before we discuss the elements of painting, consider the issues raised by the Perception Key associated with Frederic, Lord Leighton's painting *Flaming June* (Figure 4-9).

PERCEPTION KEY *Flaming June*

The subject matter of this painting is sleep itself. But it is also a painting with intense sensuous content. We respond to it partly because it is so vivid in color.

1. What powerful ideas does sleep imply?
2. What does the painting tell us about the pleasures of watching a beautiful woman sleeping? How difficult is it for you to imagine this a nymph rather than a living woman?
3. Comment on the color in this painting. In most visions of sleeping figures the tones are dampened, sometimes dark, as one would expect in a nighttime vision. In what ways does the astounding contrast between sleep and the brilliance of the color affect your sense of what the subject matter is? How does it contribute to your efforts to decide on the content of the painting?
4. How does the clarity of the line in this painting help you understand its significance?
5. Compare *Flaming June* with the paintings by Giorgione (Figure 2-9), Tom Wesselmann (Figure 2-13), and Philip Pearlstein (Figure 2-18). All are slumbering women. What makes the concerns of Leighton different from those of the other painters?

Line

Line is a continuous marking made by a moving point on a surface. Line outlines shapes and can contour areas within those outlines. Sometimes contour or internal lines dominate the outlines, as with the robe of Cimabue's *Madonna* (Figure 4-1). *Closed line* most characteristically is hard and sharp, as in Lichtenstein's *Hopeless* (Figure 2-7). In the Cimabue and in Leighton's *Flaming June,* the line is also closed but somewhat softer. *Open line* most characteristically is soft and blurry, as in Renoir's *Bather Arranging Her Hair* (Figure 2-10).

PERCEPTION KEY Goya, Leighton, and Cézanne

1. Goya used both closed and open lines in his *May 3, 1808* (Figure 2-3). Locate these lines. Why did Goya use both kinds?
2. Does Leighton use both closed and open lines in *Flaming June*?
3. Identify outlines in Cézanne's *Mont Sainte-Victoire* (Figure 2-4). There seem to be no outlines drawn around the small bushes in the foreground. Yet we see these bushes as separate objects. How can this be?

---

*Light, shape, volume, and space are often referred to as elements, but strictly speaking, they are compounds.

FIGURE 4-9
Frederic, Lord Leighton, *Flaming June*. Circa 1895. Museo de Arte Ponce, Puerto Rico. Oil on canvas. 47½ × 47½ inches. *Leighton was near the end of his career when he did this painting. He was an admirer of classical figures, such as Michelangelo's sculpture of* Night *in the Medici Tombs, which inspired the pose in this painting. He is said to have compared this figure with the sleeping naiads and mythic nymphs of classical literature. He aimed at a perfection of the figure as well as of the clothing.*

Line can suggest movement. Up-and-down movement may be indicated by the vertical, as in Parmigianino's *The Madonna with the Long Neck* (Figure 4-4). Lateral movement may be indicated by the horizontal and tends to stress stability, as in the same Parmigianino. Depending on the context, however, vertical and horizontal lines may appear static, as in Wesselmann's *Study for Great American Nude* and Lichtenstein's *Hopeless*. Generally, diagonal lines, as in Cézanne's *Mont Sainte-Victoire*, express more tension and movement than verticals and horizontals. Curving lines usually appear softer and more flowing, as in Leighton's *Flaming June*.

Line in Mondrian's *Broadway Boogie Woogie* (Figure 4-10) can also suggest rhythm and movement, especially when used with vibrant colors, which in this painting are intended to echo the neon lights of 1940s Broadway. Mondrian lived and worked for twenty years in Paris, but in 1938, with Nazis threatening war, he moved to London. In 1940, with the war under way, he went to New York. He was particularly attracted to American jazz music. He arrived in New York when the swing bands reached their height of popularity and he used his signature grid style in *Broadway Boogie Woogie* to interpret jazz visually. The basic structure is a grid of vertical and

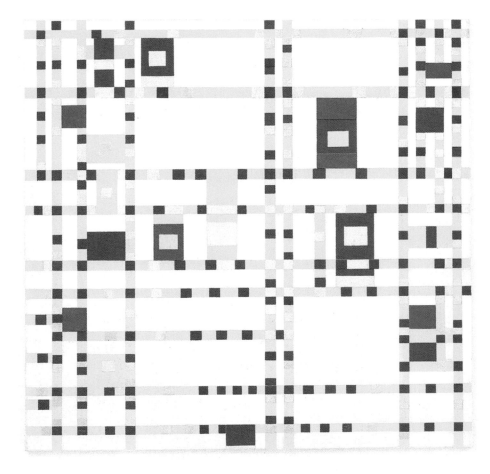

FIGURE 4-10
Piet Mondrian, *Broadway Boogie Woogie*, 1942–1943. Oil on canvas, 50 × 50 inches (127 × 127 cm). Given anonymously. Museum of Modern Art, New York.

©The Museum of Modern Art/Licensed by SCALA/Art Resource, NY

horizontal yellow lines—and only vertical and horizontal lines. On these lines, and between these lines, Mondrian places patterns of intense blocks of color to suggest the powerful jazz rhythms he loved so much. Even the large "silent" blocks of white imply musical rests.

An ***axis line*** is an imaginary line that helps determine the basic visual directions of a painting. In Goya's *May 3, 1808*, for example, two powerful axis lines move toward and intersect at the white shirt of the man about to be shot: Lines of the rifles appear to converge and go on, and the line of those to be executed moving out of the ravine seems to be inexorably continuing. Axis lines are invisible vectors of visual force. Every visual field is dynamic, a field of forces directing our vision, some visible and some invisible but controlled by the visible. Only when the invisible lines are basic to the structuring of the image, as in the Goya, are they axis lines.

Since line is usually the main determinant of shapes, and shapes are usually the main determinant of detail, regional, and structural relationships, line is usually fundamental in the overall composition—Willem de Kooning's *Woman I* (Figure 4-11) is an exception. Here lines and colors seem to perform the same kind of operation on the canvas.

FIGURE 4-11
Willem de Kooning, American, born in the Netherlands. 1904–1997. *Woman I*, 1950–1952. Oil on canvas, 6 feet 3⁷⁄₈ inches by 58 inches (192.7 x 147.3 cm). Museum of Modern Art, New York. At more than six feet high, *Woman I* has a huge physical impact on the viewer. De Kooning worked on this painting for quite a while, beginning with sketches, then reworking the canvas again and again. He is said to have drawn inspiration from female fertility goddesses as well as images of dark female figures in literature and myth.

Examine the lines in de Kooning's *Woman I*. Critics have commented on the vigor with which de Kooning attacked the canvas, suggesting that he was working out psychological issues that bordered on misogyny. We cannot know if that was the case, but we can see how the lines—vertical, horizontal, lateral—all intersect to produce an arresting power, completely opposite of the power of Leighton's *Flaming June*.

By way of contrast, Cézanne's small bushes in *Mont Sainte-Victoire* are formed by small, juxtaposed, greenish-blue planes that vary slightly in their tinting. These planes are hatched by brushstrokes that slightly vary the textures. And from the center of the planes to the perimeters there is usually a shading from light to dark. Thus emerges a strong sense of volume with density. We see those small bushes as somehow distinct objects, and yet we see no separating outlines. Colors and textures meet and create impressions of line. As with axis lines, the visible suggests the invisible—we project the outlines.

In the Asian tradition, the expressive power of line is achieved generally in a very different way from the Western tradition. The stroke—made by flexible brushes of varying sizes and hairs—is intended to communicate the spirit and feelings of the artist, directly and spontaneously. The sensitivity of the inked brush is extraordinary. The ink offers a wide range of nuances: texture, shine, depth, pallor, thickness, and wetness. The brush functions as a seismograph of the painter's mind.

The brushwork in Wang Yuanqi's painting (Figure 4-8) varies with the tone of the ink. The rising forms of the mountains are made with a broad brush, almost translucent ink-tone, with intense, dark dots implying the vegetation defining the top of each ridge. The manmade structures in the painting are made with a smaller brush, as in the curved bridge at the lower right of the painting. The rooftops and buildings in the mid portion of the painting on both the left and right use a small brush with strong lines, like those of the trees in the mid foreground. The leaves of the nearest trees and bushes are deep-tone dark ink produced by chopping strokes, sometimes known as the ax-cut. The painting demands that our eyes begin with the trees in the foreground, then rise inexorably upward following the rising nearby mountains, leading us to the smooth, distant higher mountains that have no vegetation.

PERCEPTION KEY Line

1. Which of the paintings in this chapter have the most vigorous line? How does the line in these paintings interact with color?
2. When does the color in the painting actually constitute line? How can color do the work of line?
3. Try drawing a copy of one of these paintings using only the line of your pencil or pen. What do you learn about how the artist used line to clarify his subject matter?
4. Compare the brushwork of Cézanne and Wang Yuanqi with the brushwork of Frederic Leighton and Willem de Kooning.

Color

Color is composed of three distinct qualities: hue, saturation, and value. *Hue* is simply the name of a color. Red, yellow, and blue are the *primary colors*. Their mixtures produce the *secondary colors*: green, orange, and purple. Further mixing produces six more, the *tertiary colors*. Thus, the spectrum of the color wheel shows twelve hues. *Saturation* refers to the purity, vividness, or intensity of a hue. When we speak of the "redness of red," we mean its highest saturation. *Value*, or shading, refers to the lightness or darkness of a hue, the mixture in the hue of white or black. A high value of a color is obtained by mixing in white, and a low value is obtained by mixing in black. The highest value of red shows red at its lightest; the lowest value of red shows red at its darkest. *Complementary colors* are opposite each other—for example, red and green, orange and blue. When two complements are equally mixed, a neutral gray appears. An addition of a complement to a hue will lower its saturation. A red will look less red—will have less intensity—by even a small addition of green. And an addition of either white or black will change both the value and the saturation of the hue.

Texture

Texture is the surface "feel" of something. When the brushstrokes have been smoothed out, the surface is seen as smooth, as in Wesselmann's *Study for Great American Nude*. When the brushstrokes have been left rough, the surface is seen as rough, as in van Gogh's *The Starry Night* (Figure 15-4) and Pollock's *The Flame* (Figure 3-3). In these two examples, the textures are real, for if—heaven forbid!—you were to run your fingers over these paintings, you would feel them as rough.

Distinctive brushstrokes produce distinctive textures. Compare, for example, the soft hatchings of Valadon's *Reclining Nude* (Figure 2-16) with the grainy effect of most of the brushstrokes in Wang Yuanqi's painting (Figure 4-8). Sometimes the textural effect can be so dominant that the specific substance behind the textures is disguised, as in the background behind the head and shoulders of Renoir's *Bather Arranging Her Hair*.

PERCEPTION KEY Texture

1. In what ways are the renditions of textures an important part in Willem de Kooning's *Woman I*?
2. Suppose the ultra-smooth surfaces of Wesselmann's nude had been used by Neel. How would this have significantly changed the content of her picture?

Neel's nude would be greatly altered, we believe, if she had used textures such as Wesselmann's. A tender, vulnerable, motherly appearance would become harsh, confident, and brazen. With the de Kooning, the vigor of the painting would have lost power if the texture were smooth. De Kooning's constant attack at the canvas, and his overpainting, produces a unique texture.

The medium of a painting may have much to do with textural effects. Tempera usually has a dry feel. Watercolor naturally lends itself to a fluid feel. Because they can be built up in heavy layers, oil and acrylic are useful for depicting rough textures, but of course they can be made smooth. Fresco usually has a grainy, crystalline texture.

Composition

In painting or any other art, *composition* refers to the ordering of relationships: among details, among regions, among details and regions, and among these and the total structure. Deliberately or more usually instinctively, artists use organizing principles to create forms that inform.

Principles   Among the basic principles of traditional painting are balance, gradation, movement and rhythm, proportion, variety, and unity.

- *Balance* refers to the equilibrium of opposing visual forces. Leonardo's *Last Supper* (Figure 3-1) is an example of symmetrical balance. Details and regions are arranged on either side of a central axis. Goya's *May 3, 1808* (Figure 2-3) is an example of asymmetrical balance, for there is no central axis.
- *Gradation* refers to a continuum of changes in the details and regions, such as the gradual variations in shape, color value, and shadowing in Siqueiros's *Echo of a Scream* (Figure 1-2).
- *Movement and rhythm* refers to the way a painting controls the movement and pace of our vision. For example, in Michelangelo's *Creation of Adam* (Figure 4-3), the implied movement of God from right to left establishes a rhythm in contrast with Adam's indolence.
- *Proportion* refers to the emphasis achieved by the scaling of sizes of shapes—for example, the way the large Madonna in the Cimabue (Figure 4-1) contrasts with the tiny prophets.
- *Unity* refers to the togetherness, despite contrasts, of details and regions to the whole, as in Picasso's *Guernica* (Figure 1-4).
- *Variety* refers to the contrasts of details and regions—for example, the color and shape oppositions in O'Keeffe's *Rust Red Hills* (Figure 4-12).

FIGURE 4-12
Georgia O'Keeffe, 1930. *Rust Red Hills,* **1930. Oil on canvas, 16 x 30 inches. Sloan Fund Purchase. Brauer Museum of Art, Valparaiso University.** O'Keefe found the American West to be a refreshing environment after living for years in New York. This is a study of hills that fascinated her near her home in Abiqui, New Mexico, where she painted many landscapes such as this.

Space and Shapes   Perhaps the best way to understand ***space*** is to think of it as a hollow volume available for occupation by ***shapes***. Then that space can be described by referring to the distribution and relationships of those shapes in that space; for example, space can be described as crowded or open.

Shapes in painting are areas with distinguishable boundaries, created by colors, textures, and usually—and especially—lines. A painting is a two-dimensional surface with breadth and height. But three-dimensional simulation, even in the flattest of paintings, is almost always present, even in de Kooning's *Woman I*. Colors when juxtaposed invariably move forward or backward visually. And when shapes suggest mass—three-dimensional solids—depth is inevitably seen.

The illusion of depth—***perspective***—can be made by various techniques, including setting a single vanishing point, as in Leonardo's *Last Supper* (Figure 3-2), in which all lines in the painting seem to move toward Jesus's head. The vanishing point in Figure 4-17, Renoir's *Luncheon of the Boating Party*, is in the upper right corner, in which figures seem to recede into darkness. Many techniques, such as darkening and lightening colors, will help give the illusion of depth to a painting.

THE CLARITY OF PAINTING

The Swing (Figure 4-13), Fragonard's painting of young libertines, seems to be the picture of innocent pleasures, but the painter and his audience knew that he was portraying a liberal society that enjoyed riches, station, and erotic opportunity. This painting has been considered one of the Wallace Collection's masterpieces.

FIGURE 4-13
Jean-Honore Fragonard, *The Swing*. 1776. Oil on canvas, 35 × 32 inches. The Wallace Collection, London. This famous painting seems at first glance to be a picture of young people at play, emulating innocent children. But the eighteenth-century audience read this as a libertine and his mistress. The swing was a code for the sexual freedom of the privileged "playmates" in the painting.

©Lebrecht Music and Arts Photo Library/ Alamy

PERCEPTION KEY *The Swing*

1. What are the most contrasting colors in this painting? Which character is most highlighted by color? What does the color imply?
2. How is nature portrayed in the painting? What colors and contrasts seem most expressive of nature's powers?
3. Why is the richness of the garden the best locale for this scene? What do the lovers have in common with the garden?
4. One of the men on the ground is a clergyman. One is the woman's lover. Which is which? How does the use of color clarify the relationship?
5. The bough and leaves above the woman are mysteriously shaped. In what sense may it be a comment on the relationship of the woman and her lover?

This painting was commissioned by a French baron who explicitly asked Fragonard to paint the woman as a portrait of his mistress. The baron is himself highlighted by color at the lower left looking up the skirts of his mistress. The painting established a clarity of the relationships of the figures to the eighteenth-century viewer, and of course to the characters portrayed. The figure of the man in the lower right is a clergyman who may be hopeful that the baron will marry his mistress.

The small stone sculptures are classical figures, a Cupid on the left and putti in the lower center. The overabundance of the leaves and trees implies a fruitfulness and an erotic quotient illustrated by the castoff slipper and the baron's recumbent posture.

This painting has a special clarity because it is something of an allegorical representation of erotic play. Audiences today would not necessarily be aware of the specifics of the relationship of the man on the lower left with the woman on the swing. However, a careful analysis of the details of the painting—the pink dress, the man looking up her skirt, the overabundance of the vegetation, and the Cupid with his finger to his lips—and the richness of the coloration point to erotic play and erotic joy.

The "All-at-Onceness" of Painting

In addition to revealing the visually perceptible more clearly, paintings give us time for our vision to focus, hold, and participate. Of course, there are times when we can hold on a scene in nature. We are resting with no pressing worries and with time on our hands, and the sunset is so striking that we fix our attention on its redness. But then darkness descends and the mosquitoes begin to bite. In front of a painting, however, we find that things stand still, like the red in Siqueiros's *Echo of a Scream* (Figure 1-2). Here the red is peculiarly impervious and reliable, infallibly fixed and settled in its place. It can be surveyed and brought out again and again; it can be visualized with closed eyes and checked with open eyes. There is no hurry, for all of the painting is present, and under normal conditions it is going to stay present; it is not changing in any significant perceptual sense.

Moreover, we can hold on any detail or region or the totality as long as we like and follow any order of details or regions at our own pace. No region of a painting strictly presupposes another region temporally. The sequence is subject to no absolute constraint. Whereas there is only one route in listening to music, for example, there is a freedom of routes in seeing paintings. With *The Swing* (Figure 4-13), for example, we may focus on the overhanging trees, then on the figure on the lower left, and finally on the woman in her pink dress. The next time, we may reverse the order. "Paths are made," as the painter Paul Klee observed, "for the eye of the beholder which moves along from patch to patch like an animal grazing." There is a "rapt resting" on any part, an unhurried series, one after the other, of "nows," each of which has its own temporal spread.

Paintings make it possible for us to stop in the present and enjoy at our leisure the sensations provided by the show of the visible. That is the second reason paintings can help make our vision whole. They not only clarify our world but also may free us from worrying about the future and the past, because paintings are a framed context in which everything stands still. There is the "here-now" and relatively speaking nothing but the "here-now." Our vision, for once, has time to let the qualities of things and the things themselves unfold.

ABSTRACT PAINTING

Abstract, or *nonrepresentational, painting* may be difficult to appreciate if we are confused about its subject matter. Since no objects or events are depicted, abstract painting might seem to have no subject matter: pictures of nothing. But this is not the case. The subject matter is the sensuous. The sensuous is composed of visual qualities—line, color, texture, space, shape, light, shadow, volume, and mass. Any qualities that stimulate our vision are *sensa*. In representational painting, sensa are used to portray objects and events. In abstract painting, sensa are freed. They are depicted for their own sake. Abstract painting reveals sensa, liberating us from our habits of always identifying these qualities with specific objects and events. They make it easy for us to focus on sensa themselves, even though we are not artists. Then the radiant and vivid values of the sensuous are enjoyed for their own sake, satisfying a fundamental need. Abstractions can help fulfill this need to behold and treasure the images of the sensuous. Instead of our controlling the sensa, transforming them into signs that represent objects or events, the sensa control us, transforming us into participators.

Moreover, because references to objects and events are eliminated, there is a peculiar relief from the future and the past. Abstract painting, more than any other art, gives us an intensified sense of here-now, or *presentational immediacy*. When we perceive representational paintings such as *Mont Sainte-Victoire* (Figure 2-4), we may think about our chances of getting to southern France sometime in the future. Or when we perceive *May 3, 1808* (Figure 2-3), we may think about similar massacres. These suggestions bring the future and past into our participation, causing the here-now to be somewhat compromised. But with abstract painting—because there is no portrayal of objects or events that suggest the past or the future—the sense of presentational immediacy is more intense.

Although sensa appear everywhere we look, in paintings sensa shine forth. This is especially true with abstract paintings, because there is nothing to attend to but the sensa. What you see is what you see. In nature the light usually appears as external to the colors and surface of sensa. The light plays on the colors and surface. In paintings the light usually appears immanent in the colors and surface, seems to come—in part at least—through them, even in the flat, polished colors of a Mondrian.

In Arshile Gorky's *Untitled 1943* (Figure 4-14), the light seems to be absorbed into the colors and surfaces. There is a depth of luminosity about the sensa of paintings that rivals nature. Generally the colors of nature are more brilliant than the colors of painting, but usually in nature the sensa are either so glittering that our squints miss their inner luminosity or so changing that we lack the time to participate and penetrate. To ignore the allure of the sensa in a painting, and in turn in nature, is to miss one of the chief glories life provides. It is especially the abstract painter—the shepherd of sensa—who is most likely to call us back to our senses.

Study the Gorky. Then reflect on how you experienced a sense of the rhythms of your eyes as you moved across and through the painting, aware of the various shapes and their colors. The rhythmic durations are "spots of time"—ordered by the relationships between the regions of sensa. Compare your experience of this painting with listening to music. What music might be "illustrated" by this painting?

FIGURE 4-14
Arshile Gorky, *Untitled*, **1943–1948. Oil on canvas, 54½ × 64½ inches.** The power of Gorky's red is dominant in the painting. The interruptions of the indefinite dark-colored objects offer a contrast that makes the red even more powerful. A close look at the painting shows the levels of color in the brushstrokes that reveal layers of color beneath the surface. We see yellows and light blues and tints of gray, but they all make us aware of the sensa that clarify our understanding of Gorky's red.

INTENSITY AND RESTFULNESS IN ABSTRACT PAINTING

Abstract painting reveals sensa in their primitive but powerful state of innocence. This makes possible an extraordinary intensity of vision, renewing the spontaneity of our perception and enhancing the tone of our physical existence. We clothe our visual sensations in positive feelings, living in these sensations instead of using them as means to ends. And such sensuous activity—sight, for once minus anxiety and eyestrain—is sheer delight. Abstract painting offers us a complete rest from practical concerns. Abstract painting is, as Matisse in 1908 was beginning to see,

> an art of balance, of purity and serenity devoid of troubling or depressing subject matter, an art which might be for every mental worker, be he businessman or writer, like an appeasing influence, like a mental soother, something like a good armchair in which to rest from physical fatigue.[1]

PERCEPTION KEY de Kooning, Gorky, and O'Keeffe

1. De Kooning's *Woman I* (Figure 4-11) is, we think, an example of timelessness and the sensuous. O'Keeffe's *Rust Red Hills* (Figure 4-12) also emphasizes the sensuous, especially the rich reds, browns, and blue. What makes one painting presumably more timeless?
2. Examine the sensa in the O'Keeffe. Does the fact that the painting represents real things distract you from enjoying the sensa? How crucial are the sensa to your full appreciation of the painting?
3. What difference do you perceive in de Kooning's and Gorky's treatment of sensa?
4. Look at the Gorky upside down. Is the form weakened or strengthened? Does it make a difference? If so, what?

Gorky's *Untitled 1943* (Figure 4-14) is characterized by a color field that has been worked over and over. It is essentially red, but a close look will show that there are levels of red, layers of red. And the painting seems to have a range of floating objects that, when taken symbolically, seem to impersonate ideas or messages. All the symbols have been connected to what the Dallas Museum calls a special language of Gorky's own. In this way the expression is not of abstract ideas but of concrete color, of the sensa that Gorky moves through the painting's plane. Nothing specific is represented in this painting, but instead color is itself presented. It is for us to enjoy and to respond to in a fundamental way without the imposition of meaning or ideas. Ironically we call this abstract art as a way of contrasting it with representational art. But abstract art is not abstract—it presents to us the concrete material of sensory experience. We see concrete color and form, and that may be the most profound aesthetic purpose of painting.

---

[1]Source: Matisse, "Notes of a Painter," *La Grande Revue,* December 25, 1908.

In the participative experience with *representational paintings*, the sense of here-now, so overwhelming in the participative experience with abstractions, is somewhat weakened. Representational paintings situate the sensuous in objects and events. A representational painting, like an abstraction, is "all there" and "holds still." But past and future are more relevant than in our experience of abstract paintings because we are seeing representations of objects and events. Inevitably, we are at least vaguely aware of place and date; and, in turn, a sense of past and future is a part of that awareness. Our experience is more ordinary than it is when we feel the extraordinary isolation from objects and events that occurs in the perception of abstract paintings. Representational paintings always bring in some suggestion of "once upon a time." Moreover, we are kept closer to the experience of every day, because images that refer to objects and events usually lack something of the strangeness of the sensuous alone.

Representational painting furnishes the world of the sensuous with objects and events. The horizon is sketched out more closely and clearly, and the spaces of the sensuous are filled, more or less, with things. But even when these furnishings (subject matter) are the same, the interpretation (content) of every painting is always different.

COMPARISON OF FIVE IMPRESSIONIST PAINTINGS

From time to time, painters have grouped themselves into "schools" in which like-minded artists sometimes worked and exhibited together. The Barbizon school in France in the 1840s, a group of six or seven painters, attempted to paint outdoors so that their landscapes would have a natural feel in terms of color and light, unlike the studio landscapes that were popular at the time. Probably the most famous school of art of all time is the *Impressionist school*, which flourished between 1870 and 1905, especially in France. The Impressionists' approach to painting was dominated by a concentration on the impression light made on the surfaces of things.

PERCEPTION KEY Comparison of Five Impressionist Paintings

1. In which of the following paintings is color most dominant over line? In which is line most dominant over color? How important does line seem to be for the impressionist painter?
2. In terms of composition, which paintings seem to rely on diagonal lines or diagonal groups of objects or images?
3. Comment on the impressionist reliance on balance as seen in these paintings. In which painting is symmetry most effectively used? In which is asymmetry most effective? How is your response to the paintings affected by symmetry or asymmetry?
4. If you were to purchase one of these paintings, which would it be? Why?

FIGURE 4-15
Claude Monet, *Impression, Sunrise*. 1873. Oil on canvas, 19 × 24 inches. Musée Marmottan Monet, Paris. This painting gave the name to the French Impressionists and remains one of the most identifiable paintings of the age. Compared with paintings by Ingres or Giorgione, this seems to be a sketch, but that is the point. It is an impression of the way the brilliant light plays on the waters at sunrise.

©Erich Lessing/Art Resource, NY

Claude Monet's *Impression, Sunrise* (Figure 4-15) was shown at the first show of the impressionist painters in Paris in 1874, and it lent its name to the entire group. The scene in *Sunrise* has a spontaneous, sketchy effect, the sunlight breaking on glimmering water. Boats and ships lack mass and definition. The solidity of things is subordinated to shimmering surfaces. We sense that only a moment has been caught. Monet and the Impressionists painted, not so much objects they saw but the light that played on and around them.

Edouard Manet was considered the leader of the impressionist group. His striking painting *A Bar at the Folies-Bergère* (Figure 4-16) is more three-dimensional than Monet's, but the emphasis on color and light is similar. In this painting the Impressionists' preference for everyday scenes with ordinary people and objects is present. Details abound in this painting—some mysterious, such as the legs of the trapeze artist in the upper left corner.

Pierre-Auguste Renoir's joyful painting (Figure 4-17) also represents an ordinary scene of people dining on a warm afternoon, all blissfully unaware of the painter. The scene, like many impressionist scenes, could have been captured by a camera. The perspective is what we would expect in a photograph, while the cut-off elements of people and things are familiar from our experience with snapshots. The use of light tones and reds balances the darker greens and grays in the background. Again, color dominates in this painting.

Childe Hassam was well known for his cityscapes, particularly for his colorful views of New York and Paris. But he also spent summers in the New England countryside, capturing moments such as *Summer Evening* (Figure 4-18),

FIGURE 4-16
Edouard Manet, *A Bar at the Folies-Bergère*. 1881–1882. Oil on canvas, 37¾ × 51¼ inches. Courtauld Institute Galleries, London. Typical of impressionist paintings, this one has for its subject matter ordinary, everyday events. Viewers may also surmise a narrative embedded in the painting, given the character in the mirror, not to mention the feet of the trapeze artist in the upper left.

recollecting an ordinary evening in New Hampshire. The sharp, diagonal figure of a woman is presented in contrast to the strong, horizontal lines of the window. Hassam creates a relaxed moment, a sense of the ordinary in life, by avoiding any studied traditional composition. He seems to depend upon a photographer's "trick" called the "rule of thirds," by placing the figure in the right third of the composition and placing the lower horizontal of the window one-third of the way up from the bottom of the canvas. By avoiding traditional centrality of organization, Hassam produces a painting that echoes a photograph, as if doing little more than recording a simple moment.

Mary Cassatt's sister Lydia is also posed in a sharp diagonal in *Autumn* (Figure 4-19). Cassatt's intense autumn colors create a brilliance almost unexpected. For most

FIGURE 4-17
Pierre-Auguste Renoir, *Luncheon of the Boating Party*. 1881. Oil on canvas, 51 × 68 inches. The Phillips Collection, Washington, D.C. Renoir, one of the greatest of the Impressionists, portrays ordinary Parisians in *Luncheon of the Boating Party*. Earlier painters would have seen this as unfit for exhibition because its subject is not heroic or mythic. The Impressionists celebrated the ordinary.

©Album/Art Resource, NY

FIGURE 4-18
Childe Hassam, *Summer Evening*. 1886. Oil on canvas, 12¹⁄₈ × 20³⁄₈ inches. Florence Griswold Museum. The softness of both color and line implies a muted moment. Childe Hassam studied and painted in France and New York, but this scene commemorates a visit to New Hampshire. It has some of the influence of photography—an off-the-cuff pose, the figure and window both cut off—a characteristic of much impressionist painting. Hassam was considered an American Impressionist and famously connected with the Old Lyme, Connecticut, painters from the 1880s to the 1920s.

Courtesy of the Florence Griswold Museum, Old Lyme, CT

people autumn suggests a duller pallette and a more somber mood. Lydia is dressed very warmly in a bulky but cheerful coat, with a warm hat and gloves, and while her expression is calm and perhaps enigmatic, she is restful in the midst of an explosion of colors. In this painting, line may be less significant in terms of composition than the vitality of the brushstrokes that seem to attack the canvas. The deep, resonant colors suggest the ripening of autumn vegetables and fruits characteristic of harvest time.

FIGURE 4-19
Mary Cassatt, *Autumn* (Profile of Lydia Cassatt). 1880. Musée du Petit Palais, Paris. Mary Cassatt and her sister Lydia shared an apartment in Paris. Lydia frequently modeled for her. This scene is rich with autumn colors set in a Parisian garden.

FOCUS ON *The Pre-Raphaelite Brotherhood*

Historically, groups of painters have gathered together to form a "school" of painting. They are like-minded, often young and starting out, and usually disliked at first because they produce a new, unfamiliar style. The Impressionists in France faced a struggle against prevailing taste but eventually were accepted as innovative and marvelous. The Pre-Raphaelite Brotherhood is such a school. In 1848 in England, Henry Wallis (Figure 4-20), Dante Gabriel Rossetti (Figure 4-21), Arthur Hughes (Figure 4-22), and William Holman Hunt (Figure 4-23), along with a few other painters, began having monthly meetings to discuss their ideas. They felt that followers of Italian Renaissance painter Raphael (1483–1520) had moved painting in the wrong direction, toward a realistic portrayal of life. Instead, they vowed to return to some of the medieval styles, those characterized by Giotto's use of tempera (see Figure 4-2), although they used oil paint and watercolor. Much of their subject matter was spiritual and religious. 1848 was a year of revolutions in Europe, and the Pre-Raphaelites felt they were revolting against corruption and immorality in modern life.

The first paintings Rossetti and others exhibited included the letters "PRB," signaling their association, which at the time was a secret society. Their first

FIGURE 4-21
Dante Gabriel Rossetti, *Proserpine*. 1874. Oil on canvas, 49.3 × 24 inches. Tate Britain, London. Rossetti painted this many times in different tonalities. This version was the last he did, for a client, and soon after Rossetti died. The model was Jane Morris, a favorite of the Pre-Raphaelite Brotherhood. Proserpine was taken to Hades to be wife to Pluto. Her mother, Ceres, asked Jupiter to let her go and he agreed as long as she did not eat of the fruit of Hades. But she ate one pomegranate seed and was lost forever.

FIGURE 4-20
Henry Wallis, *The Death of Chatterton*. 1855–1856. Oil on canvas, 23¼ × 36 inches. Tate Gallery, London. Bequeathed by Charles Gent Clement 1899. Reference N01685. Thomas Chatterton (1752-1770) was a romantic figure. At age seventeen he committed suicide after having been rejected by critics. He had written a book of poems in a medieval style and passed them off as authentic relics. John Ruskin, a great writer and critic, praised the painting as "faultless and wonderful."

FIGURE 4-22
Arthur Hughes, *April Love*. 1855–1856. Oil on canvas, 35 × 19½ inches. Tate Gallery, London. The rich color of the young woman's gown contrasts with the green leaves (ivy?) and the bark of the trees. She looks down to the fallen petals, and the man behind her seems a vague presence. The scene is spring and the lovers have found a quiet grotto in which to talk. Hughes married the model for this painting, and it may be a tribute to their love.

©Tate, London/Art Resource, NY

FIGURE 4-23
William Holman Hunt, *Awakening Conscience*. 1853. Oil on canvas, 30 × 22 inches. Tate Gallery, London. This is another painting like Fragonard's *The Swing*, in that it needs to be "read" by the viewer. Because the standing woman has no wedding ring, it is clear that she is the young man's mistress. The awakening conscience is her becoming aware that she must change her ways and become "respectable." She is inspired by nature as she looks out the window to a brilliant spring garden—visible in the mirror behind her. The room is full of symbols: The music on the piano is a Tom Moore melody, "Oft in the Stilly Night"; the cat is toying with a bird; the man's tossed off glove on the floor suggests her future; the tangled skein of wool in the lower right implies disorder.

©Christophel Fine Art/UIG/Getty Images

paintings were not well received. Their purposes, however, were stated clearly by William Michael Rossetti, who explained the aims of the brotherhood: to have genuine ideas, to study nature very closely, to respond deeply to medieval and renaissance art, to produce excellent pictures.

The result of their efforts is a style that is deeply sensuous, with rich color; subject matter connected with religion, myth, and literature; and careful attention to the smallest details of nature. Their style is rich with the sensa that we see in abstract painting, but it includes a narrative that explores a moral issue.

continued

Typical of the Pre-Raphaelite Brotherhood's approach to nature, the details of the leaves and the fallen petals are extraordinary. But the young woman's gown is portrayed with a richness that, in the dark corner these two have found, radiates so powerfully that it seems to be a source of illumination. The detail of her scarf is also notable. Only the young man remains a mystery, although the bright floral opening in the distance implies a bright future.

These paintings have a wide variety, yet they all present a richness of sensa, profound colors that dominate the composition. Their narratives are romantic and their attention to detail roots us in the worlds they portray. They are fascinating in that they are often profoundly sensuous at the same time that they seem to reject sensuality and praise morality. We see this particularly in *The Awakening Conscience*. In the case of *The Death of Chatterton*, Wallis reminds us how fragile the life of the artist can be and pictures Chatterton as a victim of a world that did not appreciate his gifts. We are meant to be moved by the death of a youth, and most of Wallis's audience were indeed moved. In the case of Rossetti's *Proserpine*, the colors are deep and dark, suitable for a view of Hades, and the portrait of Proserpine is haunting.

The Pre-Raphaelite Brotherhood began with a small group of painters in the 1840s, but it left its mark on painting because its style was modern even as it declared that it was looking backward to the Renaissance. They achieved their success in part because of their subject matter and in part because they produced intense visions in brilliant color and appealed to our sense of emotional understanding.

PERCEPTION KEY The Pre-Raphaelite Brotherhood

1. Which of these paintings is most dominated by detail? How does color control the detail?
2. In which of the portraits is the facial expression most mysterious?
3. What do these paintings reveal about their subject matter? With which of the paintings do you find it easiest to participate?
4. In which painting does line play the most important role? In which does color play the most important role?
5. Which painting has the most complex composition? Which has the simplest?
6. Which painting tells you the most about the painter's personality? Which is most psychologically revealing?
7. Which of the paintings has the most original composition?
8. Using one of these paintings, block out the most important shapes and analyze the effectiveness of its composition.

FRAMES

Photographs of paintings, as in this book, usually do not include their frames, the exceptions being Figures 4-1, 4-2, and 4-10. In general, it seems obvious that a "good" or appropriate frame should harmonize and enhance rather than dominate the picture. For example, the frame of the Cimabue delicately picks up the colors and lines of the Madonna's throne. Furthermore, an appropriate frame usually should separate the picture from its surroundings, as again with the Cimabue. Sometimes the artist doesn't bother with a frame.

EXPERIENCING Frames

1. What importance does the frame have for our enjoyment of a painting?
2. Giotto's frame is plainer than Cimabue's. But would a more decorative frame be appropriate for the Giotto?
3. The fresco on the ceiling of the Sommaria Chapel in Castel Capuano (Figure 4-24) is an extreme example of the domination of frames. What is the relationship of the frames in this ceiling to the paintings they support?
4. If the frames in the Sommaria Chapel ceiling rise to the level of artifacts, what might be their artistic function? How do you react to them?

Sometimes a frame overwhelms a painting, and sometimes paintings have no frames, as in almost all of Mondrian's paintings. The consensus seems to be that a frame is valuable when it complements the painting, either by establishing its preciousness—as in the ordinary gold frame—or by establishing its shape and purpose, as in the case of the Giotto and Cimabue frames. Neither is very ornate; both are sufficient and useful. Clearly the fact that almost all the paintings illustrated in this book lack frames tells us something about the frame's ultimate worth. Yet all museums include frames for most of the paintings represented here. Frames stabilize the canvas, establish the period and value of a painting, and set it off from the wall. They also "finish" the painting—almost like the final chord of a great symphony or the closing of the final curtain on a play. They say "the end."

The fresco on the ceiling of the Sommaria Chapel in Naples is an example of frames that rise to the level of artifacts in themselves. The paintings in the center of the ceiling portray religious themes, as in the Ascension of Christ in the center. But the paintings themselves are overwhelmed by the frames. As a result, we look at the ceiling and respond to the astounding detail in the frames: their intersection and symmetry, their brilliance and harmony. One comes to the chapel not just to see the paintings, but to marvel at the decorative elements. The frames take on a value similar to architecture (of which they are clearly a part). In this case it would not be difficult to imagine the ceiling with no paintings at all, but merely frames. If that were the case, would we be correct in describing them as frames—since all they would frame is empty space? Or would we consider them as sculptural elements?

When you next go to a gallery or museum to see paintings, take time to examine the frames and decide what their value is to the paintings themselves. Find one example of a good relationship between painting and frame, and one poor relationship. What makes you decide one way or the other?

FIGURE 4-24
Fresco on the ceiling of the Sommaria Chapel, in Castel Capuano, Naples, Campania, Italy, 16th century.

©DeAgostini/Getty Images

Summary

Painting is the art that has most to do with revealing the sensuous and the visual appearance of objects and events. Painting shows the visually perceptible more clearly. Because a painting is usually presented to us as an entirety, with an all-at-onceness, it gives time for our vision to focus, hold, and participate. This makes possible a vision that is both extraordinarily intense and restful. Sensa are the qualities of objects or events that stimulate our sense organs. Sensa can be disassociated or abstracted from the objects or events in which they are usually joined. Sensa and the sensuous (the color field composed by the sensa) are the primary subject matter of abstract painting. Objects and events are the primary subject matter of representational painting.

Chapter 5

SCULPTURE

The concept of "all-at-onceness" that usually relates to painting does not relate to sculpture because in most cases sculpture is a ***mass*** extending into space inviting us to walk around and view it from several positions. While some sculpture seems best viewed from a single position, as in carved reliefs such as the *Temple Carving* (see Figure 5-2), most sculpture, such as Michelangelo's *David* (see Figure 5-8) or Rodin's *Danaïde* (see Figure 5-9), must be viewed from a number of positions. As we move around a sculpture, we build in our imagination's eye the whole, but at no instant in time can we conceive its wholeness.

Henry Moore, one of the most influential sculptors of the twentieth century, said that the sculptor "gets the solid shape, as it were, inside his head—he thinks of it, whatever its size, as if he were holding it completely enclosed in the hollow of his hand." Moore continues: The sculptor "mentally visualizes a complex form *all round itself*; he knows while he looks at one side what the other side is like; he identifies himself with its center of gravity, its mass, its weight; he realizes its volume, as the space that the shape displaces in the air."[1] In a sense, Moore tells us that sculpture is perceptible not only by sight, as with painting, but by our either real or imagined sense of touch. The ***tactile*** nature of sculpture is important for us to recognize, just as it is important to recognize imaginatively the density and weight of a piece of sculpture.

---

[1]Source: Henry Moore, "Notes on Sculpture," in *Sculpture and Drawings 1921–1948*, 4th rev. ed., David Sylvester ed. (New York: George Wittenborn, 1957), p. xxxiii ff.

SENSORY INTERCONNECTIONS

It is an oversimplification to distinguish the various arts on the basis of which sense organ is activated—for example, to claim that painting is experienced solely by sight and sculpture solely by touch. Our nervous systems are far more complicated than that. Generally no clear separation is made in experience between the faculties of sight and touch. The sensa of touch, for instance, are normally joined with other sensa—visual, aural, oral, and olfactory. Even if only one kind of sensum initiates a perception, a chain reaction triggers other sensations, either by sensory motor connections or by memory associations. We are constantly grasping and handling things as well as seeing, hearing, tasting, and smelling them. And so when we see a thing, we have a pretty good idea of what its surface would feel like, how it would sound if struck, how it would taste, and how it would smell if we approached. And if we grasp or handle a thing in the dark, we have some idea of what its shape looks like.

SCULPTURE AND PAINTING COMPARED

Compare Arshile Gorky's *Untitled 1943* (Figure 4-14) with Arp's *Growth* (Figure 5-1). Both works are abstract, we suggest, for neither has objects or events as its primary subject matter. Arp's sculpture has something to do with growth, of course, as confirmed by the title. But is it human, animal, or vegetable growth? Male or female? Clear-cut answers do not seem possible. Specificity of reference, just as in the Gorky, is missing. And yet, if you agree that the subject matter of the Gorky is the sensuous, would you say the same for the Arp? To affirm this may bother you, for Arp's marble is dense material. This substantiality of the marble is very much a part of its appearance as sculpture. Conversely, *Untitled 1943* as a painting—that is, as a work of art rather than as a physical canvas of such and such a weight—does not appear as a material thing. The weight of the canvas is irrelevant to our participation with *Untitled 1943* as a work of art.

Gorky has abstracted sensa, especially colors, from objects or things, whereas Arp has brought out the substantiality of a thing—the density of the marble. Figuration is not "in" Gorky's painting. Conversely, Arp has made the marble relevant to his sculpture. This kind of difference is perhaps the underlying reason the term "abstract painting" is used more frequently than the term "abstract sculpture." There is an awkwardness about describing as abstract something as material as most sculpture. Still, the distinction between abstract and representational sculpture is worth making, just as with painting, for being clear about the subject matter of a work of art is essential to all sensitive participation. It is the key to understanding the content, for the content is the subject matter interpreted by means of the form.

PERCEPTION KEY Gorky and Arp

1. Which work seems to invite you to touch it? Why?
2. Would you expect either the Gorky or the Arp to feel hot or cold to your touch?
3. Which work seems to require the more careful placement of lighting? Why?

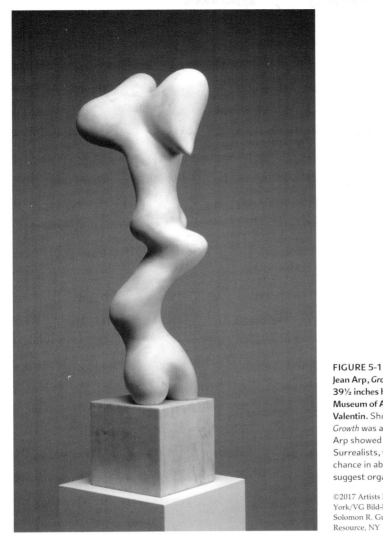

FIGURE 5-1
**Jean Arp, *Growth*. 1938. Marble,
39½ inches high. Philadelphia
Museum of Art. Gift of Curt
Valentin.** Shown here in marble,
Growth was also cast in bronze.
Arp showed his work with the
Surrealists, who often included
chance in abstract pieces that
suggest organic natural forms.

©2017 Artists Rights Society (ARS), New
York/VG Bild-Kunst, Bonn. Photo: ©The
Solomon R. Guggenheim Foundation/Art
Resource, NY

4. Which of the two works appears to be the more unchangeable in your perception?
5. Why do the authors claim that *Untitled 1943* is more abstract than *Growth*? Can you think of other reasons—for example, the shapes in the two works?

Most sculpture, whether abstract or representational, returns us to the voluminosity (bulk), density (mass), and tactile quality of things. Thus, sculpture has touch or tactile appeal. Most sculptures appear resistant, substantial. Hence, the primary subject matter of most abstract sculpture is the density of sensa. Sculpture is more than skin deep. Abstract painting can only represent density, whereas sculpture, whether abstract or representational, presents density. Abstract painters generally emphasize the surfaces of sensa, as in *Untitled 1943*. Their interest is in the vast ranges of color qualities, lines, and the play of light that bring out textural nuances. Abstract sculptors, on the other hand, generally restrict themselves to a minimal range of color, line, and textural qualities and emphasize light not only to play on these qualities but also to bring out the inherence of these qualities in things. Whereas abstract painters are shepherds of surface sensa, abstract sculptors are shepherds of depth sensa.

Sculpture and Space

A painting is usually set off by a frame, the painting space being imaginary, separate and distinct from real space. Between the painting and us, space is transparent. With sculpture, the space between is translucent, the space from the material body of a work of art to the participator we call "the between." With sculpture, even if we do not actually touch the material body, we can still sense the solidity of the material body permeating and animating the surrounding space. Shadows cast by a sculpture, for example, slant into the space between us and the material body of the sculpture, charging the between with energy, whereas shadows cast by the things represented in a painting stay within the painting. The convexities of a sculpture are actively outgoing into the between, and the between invades the concavities, whereas the convexities and concavities of a painting stay within the frame.

  With sculpture, however, in our view there is *also* a direct or physical impact. The space between us and any three-dimensional thing that we are perceiving comes forth into our perception, by literally pushing into our bodies. Sculpture transforms real space, making the between more perceptible and impacting. To put it awkwardly but succinctly, sculpture is a "more real world."

Sunken-Relief Sculpture

The *Temple Carving* (Figure 5-2) is incised in sandstone, representing the gods Horus and Hathor. These figures have weathered for millennia, yet they are sharp and distinct. For the ancient Egyptians they told a familiar story, reassuring them that the gods are supportive in the next world. Compare this **sunken-relief sculpture** with Jackson Pollock's *The Flame* (Figure 3-3). While their subject matters are very different, their surfaces are curiously similar. The *Temple Carving* does not project into space, as do most sculptures, but actually projects inward, into the surface of the stone. Pollock's painting, although considered essentially flat, is built up and, in some spots, projects slightly into space.

  The light helps clarify the tactile qualities of the *Temple Carving* by revealing the sharp edges of the sandstone. The density of the stone is evident. We virtually sense the weight of the object. Pollock's work lacks significant tactile appeal despite the projection of its thick paint. And while the *Temple Carving* makes us aware of its material texture and substance—perhaps even revealing essential qualities of the limestone—the painting remains an essentially two-dimensional image whose impact is much less tactile than visual.

FIGURE 5-2
Temple Carving at the Temple of Edfu.
Wall sculpture of ancient Egypt. The
gods Horus and Hathor greet royalty.

©Lee A. Jacobus

LOW-RELIEF SCULPTURE

Low-relief sculpture projects relatively slightly from its background plane, and so its depth dimension is very limited. Medium- and high-relief sculpture project farther from their backgrounds, their depth dimensions expanded. Sculpture in the round is freed from any background plane, and so its depth dimension is unrestricted. Frank Stella's *Giufà, the Moon, the Thieves, and the Guards* (Figure 5-3) is, we think, most usefully classified as sculpture of the medium-relief species. The materiality of the magnesium, the fiberglass, and especially the aluminum is brought out very powerfully by their juxtaposition. Unfortunately, this is difficult to perceive from a photograph. Because of its three-dimensionality, sculpture generally suffers even more than painting from being seen only in a photograph.

Relief sculpture, except sunken relief, allows its materials to stand out from a background plane. Thus, relief sculpture in at least one way reveals its materials simply by showing us—directly—their surface and something of their depth. By moving to a side of *Giufà, the Moon, the Thieves, and the Guards,* we can see that

95

FIGURE 5-3
Frank Stella, *Giufà, the Moon, the Thieves, and the Guards*. 1984. Synthetic polymer paint, oil, urethane enamel, fluorescent alkyd, and printing ink on canvas, and etched magnesium, aluminum, and fiberglass, 9 feet 7¼ inches × 16 feet 3¼ inches × 24 inches. **Museum of Modern Art.** This work was done after Stella spent two years at the American Academy at Rome. Giufà is a character out of Sicilian folklore, a trickster who gets into amusing situations. This work refers to a story called "Giufà and the Judge" in which the boy kills a fly on the nose of the judge, doing great damage to the judge. Stella's sculpture was influenced by Picasso's cubist experiments.

©2017 Frank Stella/Artists Rights Society (ARS), New York. Photo: ©The Museum of Modern Art/Licensed by SCALA/Art Resource, NY

FIGURE 5-4
Mithuna Couple. Twelfth to thirteenth century. Orissa, India. Stone, 83 inches high. **Metropolitan Museum of Art, New York.** Stone, high-relief sculpture like this, found on Indian temples built in the thirteenth and fourteenth centuries, represents figures combining the divine spirit with the erotic.

Source: Purchase, Florance Waterbury Bequest, 1970/The Metropolitan Museum of Art

the materials are of such and such thickness. However, this three-dimensionality in relief sculpture, this movement out into space, is not allowed to lose its ties to its background plane. Hence, relief sculpture, like painting, is usually best viewed from a frontal position.

HIGH-RELIEF SCULPTURE

The *high-relief sculpture* from a thirteenth-century temple in Orissa (Figure 5-4) was carved during a period of intense temple-building in that part of India. The tenderness of the two figures is emphasized by the roundness of the bodies as well as by the rhythms of the lines of the figures and the overarching swoop of the vegetation above them. This temple carving was made in a very rough stone, which emphasizes the bulk and mass of the man and woman, despite their association with religious practice. Almost a thousand years of weathering have increased its sense of texture. The happy expression on the faces is consistent with the great erotic religious sculpture of this period.

SCULPTURE IN THE ROUND

Edgar Degas's *The Little Fourteen-Year-Old Dancer* (Figure 5-5), one of several of his sculptures of dancers, was not universally approved by the critics at its first showing. A number of critics thought it grotesque and others were mystified by its subject matter, which they thought rather common. But some commentators saw immediately that it was one of the most modern of sculptures and its simplicity has helped it become one of the most admired modern sculptures.

PERCEPTION KEY *The Little Fourteen-Year-Old Dancer*

1. What details of the posture of the dancer help the sculpture seem to command its space?
2. What is the subject matter of the sculpture? What does the composition of the dancer tell us about the subject matter? What do you think the content of the work is?
3. Is this sculpture in the round? The viewer can walk around this work. But is *The Little Fourteen-Year-Old Dancer* in the round in the same way as Arp's *Growth* (Figure 5-1)?

FIGURE 5-5
Edgar Degas, *The Little Fourteen-Year-Old Dancer*, 1880, cast 1922. Bronze, partially tinted, with cotton skirt and satin hair ribbon; wood base. H. 38½ × W. 17¼ × D. 14⅜ inches. Metropolitan Museum of Art, New York. H. O. Havemeyer Collection, Bequest of Mrs. H. O. Havemeyer, 1929 Accession Number: 29.100.370. Degas was better known as a painter of dancers, but *The Little Fourteen-Year-Old Dancer* is his most famous sculpture. His model was Marie van Goethem, a young Belgian dancer in the Paris Opera Dance School.

©Tate, London/Art Resource, NY

Despite the fact that the little dancer is not dancing, we sense that she is prepared to move almost immediately. The subject matter on one level is the dancer herself, and the content points to her capacity to move, even though she is bronze. Her posture, leg forward, leaning back as if to spring upon the viewer, implies great energy and power. She is small, and her tutu—which differs in every museum displaying the work—clarifies her talent for dance. As we look at her we see her pose as only a dancer would pose. For some viewers the subject matter is not only the fourteen-year-old girl, but dance itself. It is as if Degas had somehow distilled the essence of dance in this one figure.

SCULPTURE AND ARCHITECTURE COMPARED

Architecture is the art of separating inner from outer space so that the inner space can be used for practical purposes. Sculpture does not provide a practically usable inner space. What about the Sphinx and the Pyramid of Cheops (Figure 5-6)? They are the densest and most substantial of all works. They attract us visually and tactilely. But since there is no usable space within the Sphinx, it is sculpture. Within the Pyramid, however, space was provided for the burial of the dead. There is a separation of inner from outer space for the functional use of the inner space. Yet the use of this inner space is so limited that the living often have a difficult time finding it. The inner space is functional only in a restricted sense—is this Pyramid, then, sculpture or architecture? The difficulty of the question points up an important factor to keep in mind. The distinctions between

FIGURE 5-6
The Sphinx and Pyramid of Cheops, Egypt. Fourth dynasty. Circa 2850 BCE. Limestone and masonry. Base of pyramid ca. 13 acres; Sphinx 66 feet high, 172 feet wide.

©Lee A. Jacobus

the arts that we have been and will be making are helpful in order to talk about them intelligibly, but the arts resist neat pigeonholing, and attempts at that are futile.

SENSORY SPACE

The space around a sculpture is sensory rather than empty. Despite its invisibility, sensory space—like the wind—is felt. Sculptures such as Arp's *Growth* (Figure 5-1) are surrounded by radiating vectors, something like the axis lines of painting. But with sculpture, our bodies as well as our eyes are directed. *Growth* is like a magnet drawing us in and around. With relief sculptures, except for very high relief such as the *Mithuna Couple* (Figure 5-4), our bodies tend to get stabilized in one favored position. The framework of front and sides meeting at sharp angles, as in *Giufà, the Moon, the Thieves, and the Guards* (Figure 5-3), limits our movements to 180 degrees at most. Although we are likely to move around within this limited range for a while, our movements gradually slow down, as they do when we finally get settled in a comfortable chair. We are not Cyclops with just one eye, and so we see something of the three-dimensionality of things even when restricted to one position. But even low-relief sculpture encourages some movement of the body, because we sense that different perspectives, however slight, may bring out something we have not directly perceived, especially something more of the three-dimensionality of the materials.

When one of the authors participated with Arp's *Growth*, he had this response:

> I find a warm and friendly presence. I find myself reaching toward the statue rather than keeping my distance.
>
> The Arp seems not only three-dimensional but four-dimensional, because it brings in the element of time so discernibly—a cumulative drama. In addition to making equal demands upon my contemplation, at the same time, each aspect is also incomplete, enticing me on to the next for fulfillment. As I move, volumes and masses change, and on their surfaces points become lines, lines become curves, and curves become shapes. As each new aspect unrolls, there is a shearing of textures, especially at the lateral borders. The marble flows. The leading border uncovers a new aspect, and the textures of the old aspect change. The light flames. The trailing border wipes out the old aspect. The curving surface continuously reveals the emergence of volumes and masses in front, behind, and in depth. What is hidden behind the surfaces is still indirectly perceived, for the textures indicate a mass behind them. As I move, what I have perceived and what I will perceive stand in defined positions with what I am presently perceiving. My moving body links the aspects. A continuous metamorphosis evolves, as I remember the aspects that were and anticipate the aspects to come, the leaping and plunging lights glancing off the surface helping to blend the changing volumes, shapes, and masses. The remembered and anticipatory images resonate in the present perception. My perception of the Arp is alive with motion. The sounds in the museum room are caught, more or less, in the rhythm of that motion. As I return to my starting point, I find it richer, as home seems after a journey.

SCULPTURE AND THE HUMAN BODY

Sculptures generally are more or less a center—the place of most importance that organizes the places around it—of actual three-dimensional space: "more" in the case of sculpture in the round, "less" in the case of low relief. That is why sculpture in the round is more typically sculpture than is the other species. Other things being equal, sculpture in the round, because of its three-dimensional centeredness, brings out the voluminosity and density of things more certainly than does any other kind of sculpture. First, we can see and perhaps touch all sides. But, more important, our sense of density has something to do with our awareness of our bodies as three-dimensional centers thrusting out into our surrounding environment. Philosopher-critic Gaston Bachelard remarks that

> immensity is within ourselves. It is attached to a sort of expansion of being which life curbs and caution arrests, but which starts again when we are alone. As soon as we become motionless, we are elsewhere; we are dreaming in a world that is immense. Indeed, immensity is the movement of a motionless man.[2]

Lachaise's *Floating Figure* (Figure 5-7), with its ballooning buoyancy emerging with lonely but powerful internal animation from a graceful ellipse, expresses not only this feeling but also something of the instinctual longing we have to become one with the world about us. Sculpture in the round, even when it does not

FIGURE 5-7
Gaston Lachaise, *Floating Figure*.
1927. Bronze (cast in 1979–1980).
135 × 233 × 57 cm. National Gallery
of Australia, Canberra. Purchased
1978. This massive sculpture
appears to be "floating" in a
reflective pool. New York's Museum
of Modern Art elevates it on a plinth
in its sculpture garden. The National
Gallery of Australia places its *Floating
Figure* in a reflecting pool.

Courtesy of the National Gallery of
Australia, Canberra and the Lachaise
Foundation

[2]Source: Gaston Bachelard, *The Poetics of Space*. Translation 1964, Orion Press.

portray the human body, often gives us something of an objective image of our internal bodily awareness as related to its surrounding space. Furthermore, when the human body is portrayed in the round, we have the most vivid material image of our internal feelings.

PERCEPTION KEY Exercise in Drawing and Modeling

1. Take a pencil and paper. Close your eyes. Now draw the shape of a human being but leave off the arms.
2. Take some clay or putty elastic enough to mold easily. Close your eyes. Now model your material into the shape of a human being, again leaving off the arms.
3. Analyze your two efforts. Which was easier to do? Which produced the more realistic result? Was your drawing process guided by any factor other than your memory images of the human body? What about your modeling process? Did any significant factors other than your memory images come into play? Was the feel of the clay or putty important in your shaping? Did the awareness of your inner bodily sensations contribute to the shaping? Did you exaggerate any of the functional parts of the body where movement originates, such as the neck muscles, shoulder bones, knees, or ankles? Could these exaggerations, if they occurred, have been a consequence of your inner bodily sensations?

SCULPTURE IN THE ROUND AND THE HUMAN BODY

No object is more important to us than our bodies, which are always with us. Yet when something is continually present to us, we find great difficulty in focusing our attention upon it. Thus, we usually are only vaguely aware of our bodies except when we feel pain or pleasure. Nevertheless, our bodies are part of our most intimate selves—we are our bodies—and, since most of us are narcissists to some degree, most of us have a deep-down driving need to find a satisfactory material counterpoint for the mental images of our bodies. If that is the case, we are likely to be lovers of sculpture in the round. All sculpture always evokes our outward sensations and sometimes our inner sensations. Sculpture in the round often evokes our inward sensations, for such sculpture often is anthropomorphic in some respect. And sculpture in the round that has the human body as its subject matter not only often evokes our inward sensations but also interprets them—as in Michelangelo's *David* (Figure 5-8) and Rodin's *Danaïde* (Figure 5-9).

PERCEPTION KEY *David* and *Danaïde*

1. Compare Michelangelo's *David* with Rodin's *Danaïde*. How does each sculptor establish the gender of his figure? Does Rodin achieve more in terms of gender identity by leaving some of the original marble unfinished?
2. Research the source of each sculptor's narrative: the Bible for David, and the story of the Daughters of Danaos in Greek myth. How well do these works interpret their subject matter?

continued

FIGURE 5-8
Michelangelo Buonarroti, *David.* **1501–1504. Marble, 13 feet high. Accademia, Florence.** The heroic-size *David* stood as Florence's warning to powers that might consider attacking the city-state. It represents Michelangelo's idealization of the human form and remains a Renaissance ideal.

©Lee A. Jacobus

FIGURE 5-9
Auguste Rodin, *Danaïde*. 1885.
Marble, approximately 14 × 28 × 22
inches. Musée Rodin, Paris. *Danaïde* is
from a Greek myth in which the fifty
daughters of Danaos were ordered
to kill their fifty husbands, sons of
Argos, on their wedding night. The
gods punished them by forcing them
to fill bottomless barrels with water.
This Danaïde is shown exhausted
and dispirited by the impossibility of
her task.

©Bridgeman-Giraudon/Art Resource, NY

3. Apart from myth, how quickly, as a viewer, do you react to each sculpture? With which work do you most participate?
4. What is the content of each work? How do you interpret these sculptures once you understand their subject matter?
5. Compare what you feel is the respect Michelangelo and Rodin have for the human figure.

Rodin, one of the greatest sculptors of the human body, wrote that

instead of imagining the different parts of the body as surfaces more or less flat, I represented them as projections of interior volumes. I forced myself to express in each swelling of the torso or of the limbs the efflorescence of a muscle or a bone which lay beneath the skin. And so the truth of my figures, instead of being merely superficial, seems to blossom forth from within to the outside, like life itself.[3]

David and *Danaïde* present ***objective correlatives***—images that are objective in the sense that they are "out there" and yet correlate or are similar to subjective awareness. They clarify inner bodily sensations as well as outward appearance. These are large, highly speculative claims. You may disagree, of course, but we hope they will stimulate your thinking.

When we participate with sculpture such as the *David* and *Danaïde*, we find something of our bodily selves confronting us. If we demanded all of our bodily selves, we would be both disappointed and stupid. Art is always a transformation

---

[3]Source: Auguste Rodin, *Art*, trans. Romilly Fedden (Boston: Small, 1912), p. 65.

of reality, never a duplication. Thus, the absence of the rest of *Danaïde*'s body does not shock us as it would if we were confronting a real woman. Its lack of finish does not ruin our perception of its beauty. The work was only a partial image of a female. But, even so, she is in that partiality exceptionally substantial. The *Danaïde* is substantial because the female shape, texture, grace, sensuality, sexuality, and beauty are interpreted by a form and thus clarified.

The human body is supremely beautiful. To begin with, there is its sensuous charm. There may be other things in the world as sensuously attractive—for example, the full glory of autumn leaves—but the human body also possesses a sexuality that greatly enhances its sensuousness. Moreover, in the human body, mind is incarnate. Feeling, thought, purposefulness—spirit—have taken shape with the *Danaïde*.

EXPERIENCING Sculpture and Physical Size

1. The sculptor Henry Moore claims that "sculpture is more affected by actual size considerations than painting. A painting is isolated by a frame from its surroundings (unless it serves just a decorative purpose) and so retains more easily its own imaginary scale." He makes the further claim that the actual physical size of sculpture has an emotional meaning. "We relate everything to our own size, and our emotional response to size is controlled by the fact that men on the average are between five and six feet high."[4] Now look at *Five Swords*, by Alexander Calder (Figure 5-10), and compare it to *David* and the *Danaïde*. Does the fact that *Five Swords* is much larger than *David*, which in turn is larger than the *Danaïde*, make any significant difference with respect to your tactile sensations?

FIGURE 5-10
Alexander Calder, *Five Swords*. 1976. Sheet metal, bolts, paint, 213 × 264 × 348 inches. Calder's sculpture implies by its form that the swords have been turned into plowshares, which may be seen as a monument to the end of the Vietnam War, one of America's longest wars.

©2017 Calder Foundation, New York/Artists Rights Society (ARS), New York. Photo: ©Art Resource, NY

Size in sculpture can be significant for many reasons. Michelangelo intentionally made *David* large as a political statement in Florence. The great Renaissance sculptor Donatello had created an earlier *David* that was slightly smaller than a life-size boy, partly as a way of emphasizing the fact that the small warrior defeated the large warrior. But Michelangelo's heroic-size figure was a warning to other Italian city-states that Florence was not easy pickings at a time when regional wars were common.

Rodin's *Danaïde* is much smaller than *David*, but its expressiveness, as Rodin suggests, is considerable despite its size. This sculpture, unlike Calder's and Michelangelo's,

[4]Moore, "Notes on Sculpture," p. xxxiv.

continued

is not intended as an outdoor monument. Rather, it is an intimate piece designed to be close to the viewer, even close enough to tempt the viewer to touch and sense its tactile repertoire, from smooth to rough.

Five Swords is a gigantic structure, not in marble, but in steel panels painted a brilliant color. Calder's work needs to have space around it, which is one reason it is located in a huge, parklike setting. We are arrested by the sensa of this piece, and its hugeness when we are near it is an important part of the sensa. Calder's ideas about size are naturally influenced by his own practice as a sculptor of monumental works, some of which dominate huge public spaces in major cities. Unfortunately, photographs in this book can only suggest the differences in size, but if you spend time with sculpture in its own setting, consider how much the size of the work affects your capacity to participate with it.

2. Find and photograph a sculpture whose size seems to contribute importantly to its impact. In your photograph, try to provide a visual clue that would help a viewer see whether the object is huge or tiny.
3. To what extent does your respect for size affect your response to the sculpture?

CONTEMPORARY SCULPTURE

Developments in sculpture are emerging and changing so rapidly that no attempt can be made here even to begin to classify them adequately. But adding to the traditional species (relief sculpture and sculpture in the round), at least five new species have taken hold: space, protest against technology, accommodation with technology, machine, and earth sculpture. In much contemporary sculpture, there is one fairly pervasive characteristic: ***truth to materials***, both in respecting materials and defying them. For some sculptors, for example, one purpose was to reveal the "stoneness" of the stone, or the "woodness" of the wood. But some sculptors, including Michelangelo and Rodin, are committed to defying the limits of, say, marble when depicting the human figure. Some sculptors use nontraditional materials to explore the questions of space, volume, and density.

TRUTH TO MATERIALS

In the flamboyant eighteenth-century *Baroque* and in some of the *Romanticism* of the later nineteenth century, respect for materials tended to be ignored. Karl Knappe referred to a "crisis" in the early twentieth century that "concerns . . . the artistic media":

> An image cannot be created without regard for the laws of nature, and each kind of material has natural laws of its own. Every block of stone, every piece of wood is subject to its own rules. Every medium has, so to speak, its own tempo; the tempo of a pencil or a piece of charcoal is quite different from the tempo of a woodcut. The habit of mind which creates, for instance, a pen drawing cannot simply be applied mechanically to the making of a woodcut; to do this would be to deny the validity of the spiritual as well as the technical tempo.[5]

---

[5]Source: Karl Knappe, quoted in Kurt Herberts, *The Complete Book of Artists—Techniques* (London: Thames and Hudson, 1958), p. 16. Published in the United States by Frederick A. Praeger.

FIGURE 5-11
Henry Moore, *Recumbent Figure.*
1938. Green Hornton stone, 54
inches long. Tate Gallery, London,
Great Britain. *Recumbent Figure* is one
of an enormous number of similar
sculptures by Moore in both stone
and bronze. This stone piece distorts
the figure in ways reminiscent of
Picasso's paintings of the same
period.

Henry Moore, sculptor of *Recumbent Figure* (Figure 5-11), has stated that "every material has its own individual qualities. It is only when the sculptor works direct, when there is an active relationship with his material, that the material can take its part in the shaping of an idea. Stone, for example, is hard and concentrated and should not be falsified to look like soft flesh—it should not be forced beyond its constructive build to a point of weakness. It should keep its hard tense stoniness."[6]

Jeff Koons has made a career by pushing against the idea of truth to materials. His *Balloon Dog (Magenta)* (Figure 5-12) is a whimsical piece and amuses young and old alike. Much of his work seems to be an attempt to call the entire question, What is art? to the forefront. After looking at *Balloon Dog* in Versailles, will you see birthday-party balloon dogs differently?

At the behest of Creative Time Kara E. Walker has confected: A Subtlety, or the Marvelous Sugar Baby, an Homage to the unpaid and overworked Artisans who have refined our Sweet tastes from the cane fields to the Kitchens of the New World on the Occasion of the demolition of the Domino Sugar Refining Plant (Figure 5-13) was constructed in the now-defunct Diamond Sugar Factory in Williamsburg, New York. The setting is ironic, and the depiction of a "black Mammy" as a sphinx is a protest aimed at reminding us that the demand for sugar in the Americas was central to the increased demand for African slaves to work the sugar plantations in the West Indies. The sculpture was site-specific and stayed in place from mid-May to mid-July, slowly decaying.

---

[6]Quoted by Herbert Read, *Henry Moore, Sculptor* (London: A. Zwemmer, 1934), p. 29.

FIGURE 5-12
Jeff Koons, *Balloon Dog (Magenta)*. 1994–2000. Mirror-polished stainless steel with transparent color coating. 121 × 143 × 45 inches. 307.3 × 363.2 × 114.3 cm. *Balloon Dog (Magenta)*, among Koons's most popular works, has been exhibited in the Museum of Modern Art, the Chateau de Versailles, Venice, and elsewhere. Several examples exist in blue, yellow, orange, and magenta. Koons often works against the principles of truth to materials.

©Jeff Koons Installation View: Chateau de Versailles, Jeff Koons Versailles, October 9, 2008 - April 1, 2009, Photo: Laurent Lecat

FIGURE 5-13
Kara Walker, *A Subtlety, or the Marvelous Sugar Baby*, 2014. 35 feet high by 75 feet long.

Photo: Jason Wyche, Artwork ©Kara Walker, courtesy of Sikkema Jenkins & Co., New York

As technology has gained more and more ascendancy, reverence toward natural things has receded. In highly industrialized societies, people tend to revere artificial things, and the pollution of our environment is one result. Another result is the flooding of the commercial market with imitations of primitive sculpture, which are easily identified because of the lack of truth to the materials (test this for yourself). Even contemporary sculptors have lost some of their innocence toward things simply because they live in a technological age. Many sculptors still possess something of the natural way of feeling things, and so they find inspiration in primitive sculpture. Despite its abstract subject matter, Barbara Hepworth's *Pelagos* (Figure 5-14), with its reverence to wood, has a close spiritual affinity to the *Maternity Figure* (Figure 5-25). Truth to materials sculpture is an implicit protest against technological ascendancy.

PERCEPTION KEY Truth to Materials

1. Examine the examples of twentieth-century sculpture in the book. Assuming that these examples are fairly representative, do you find a pervasive tendency to truth to materials? Do you find exceptions, and, if so, how might these be explained?
2. Does *Recumbent Figure* illustrate Moore's point about staying true to materials? If so, point out specifically how this is done.
3. What is the result of the attitude toward truth to materials in the works of Jeff Koons and Kara Walker? Is their work more interesting for defying the traditional views, or does it matter at all? Which of these sculptures most rewards your participation? Which of these sculptures would you most want to own? Is their work more interesting for defying the traditional views, or does it matter at all? Which of these sculptures most rewards your participation? Which of these sculptures would you most want to own?

PROTEST AGAINST TECHNOLOGY

Explicit social protest is part of the subject matter of the works we will discuss by Trova, Segal, and Giacometti, although perhaps only in Trova's *Study: Falling Man (Wheel Man)* (Figure 5-15) is that protest unequivocally directed at technology. Flaccid, faceless, and sexless, this anonymous robot has "grown" spoked wheels instead of arms. Attached below the hips, these mechanisms produce a sense of eerie instability, a feeling that this antiseptically cleansed automaton with the slack, protruding abdomen may tip over from the slightest push. In this inhuman mechanical purity, no free will is left to resist. Human value, as articulated in Aldous Huxley's *Brave New World,* has been reduced to human power, functions performed in the world of goods and services. Since another individual can also perform these functions, the given person has no special worth. His or her value is a unit that can easily be replaced by another.

FIGURE 5-15
Ernest Trova, Study: *Falling Man (Wheel Man)*. **1965. Bronze, 60 × 48 × 20¹³/₁₆ inches.** Trova's sculpture portrays man as part of a machine, implying that in the machine age humans are becoming less and less human. Consider the unidealized human figure in comparison with the Greek ideal.

©Ernest Trova, *Study: Falling Man (Wheel Man)*, 1965. Collection Walker Art Center, Minneapolis, Gift of the T.B. Walker Foundation, 1965.

FIGURE 5-16
Magdalena Abakanowicz, *Bronze Crowd*. 1990–1991. Bronze, 71 × 23 × 15½ inches. Raymond and Patsy Nasher Collection, Nasher Sculpture Center, Dallas, Texas. Magdalena Abakanowicz witnessed the occupation of Poland, her native country, by both the Nazi Germans and the Soviet Russians. *Bronze Crowd* portrays the aloneness that is possible in modern society. Abakanowicz has said, "A crowd is the most cruel because it begins to act like a brainless organism."

Raymond and Patsy Nasher Collection, Nasher Sculpture Center, Dallas, Texas. Art ©Studio Magdalena Abakanowicz

The thirty-six larger-than-life figures in *Bronze Crowd* (Figure 5-16) seem to be the same until one examines them and sees small differences. The absence of their heads is a sign of their having been stripped of dignity and individuality. The space between the figures is sufficient so that a viewer can walk in and around the group and begin to experience what it might be like to be one of them.

In *Bronze Crowd*'s emaciated figures, the huge, solidly implanted feet suggest nostalgia for the earth; the soaring upward of the elongated bodies suggests aspiration for the heavens. The surrounding environment has eaten away at the flesh, leaving lumpy, irregular surfaces with dark hollows. Each figure is without bodily or mental contact with anyone. They stand in an utterly alienated space, but, unlike *Falling Man*, they are headless and unaware. And whereas the habitat of *Falling Man* is the clean, air-conditioned factory or office of *Brave New World*, the figures in *Bronze Crowd* are exposed and organized in soldierly fashion.

Giacometti's people (Figure 5-17), even when in neat galleries, always seem to be in the grubby streets of our decaying cities. The cancer of the city has left only the armatures of bodies stained with pollution and scarred with sickness. There is no center in this city square or any particular exit, nor can we imagine any communication among these citizens. Their very grouping in the square gives them, paradoxically, an even greater feeling of isolation. Each Giacometti figure separates a spot of space from the common place. The disease and utter distress of these vulnerable creatures demand our respectful distance, as if they were lepers to whom help must come, if at all, from some public agency. To blame technology entirely for the dehumanization of society interpreted in these sculptures is an oversimplification, of course. But this kind of work does bring out something of the horror of technology when it is misused.

ACCOMMODATION WITH TECHNOLOGY

Many contemporary sculptors see in technology blessings for humankind. It is true that sculpture can be accomplished with the most primitive tools (that, incidentally, is one of the basic reasons sculpture in primitive cultures usually not only precedes painting but also usually dominates both qualitatively and quantitatively). Nevertheless, sculpture in our day, far more than painting, can take advantage of some of the most sophisticated advances of technology, surpassed in this respect only by architecture. Many sculptors today interpret the positive rather than the negative aspects of technology. This respect for technology is expressed by truth to its materials and the showing forth of its methodology.

Naum Gabo (Figure 5-18), one of the early adopters of current technology, used a number of modern materials, such as cardboard, acrylic plastic, and stainless steel,

FIGURE 5-18
Naum Gabo, *Constructed Head No. 2, 1916 (enlargement 1975)*.
Stainless steel, 70 × 54¼ × 48 inches. Raymond and Patsy
Nasher Collection, Nasher Sculpture Center, Dallas, Texas.

FIGURE 5-19
David Smith, *Cubi X*. 1963. Stainless steel,
10 feet 1⅜ inches × 6 feet 6¾ inches × 2 feet
(308.3 × 199.9 × 61 cm), including steel base
2⅞ × 25 × 23 inches (7.3 × 63.4 × 58.3 cm).
Museum of Modern Art, New York. Robert O.
Lord Fund. *Cubi X* is Smith's cubistic experiment
representing a human figure in planes of
polished steel, akin to the cubistic paintings
of Picasso and others. Smith produced a wide
collection of *Cubi* sculptures.

Art ©The Estate of David Smith/Licensed by VAGA,
New York, NY. Photo: ©The Museum of Modern Art/
Licensed by SCALA/Art Resource, NY

for his constructivist sculptures. He was part of the modernist movement in Russia, and after World War II he moved to the United States, where he used modern engineering techniques for his work.

David Smith's *Cubi X* (Figure 5-19) illustrates truth to technological materials. The stainless steel cylinders of *Cubi X* support a juggling act of hollow rectangular and square cubes that barely touch one another as they cantilever out into space. Delicate buffing modulates the bright planes of steel, giving the illusion of several atmospheric depths and reflecting light like rippling water. Smith writes,

> I like outdoor sculpture and the most practical thing for outdoor sculpture is stainless steel, and I make them and I polish them in such a way that on a dull day, they take on the dull blue, or the color of the sky in late afternoon sun, the glow, golden like the rays, the colors of nature. And in a particular sense, I have used atmosphere in a reflective way on the surfaces. They are colored by the sky and the surroundings, the green or blue of water. Some are down by the water and some are by the mountains. They reflect the colors. They are designed for outdoors.[7]

But Smith's steel is not just a mirror, for in the reflections the fluid surfaces and tensile strength of the steel emerge in a structure that, as Smith puts it, "can face the sun and hold its own."

---

[7]Source: David Smith in Cleve Gray, ed., *David Smith* (New York: Holt, Rinehart and Winston, 1968), p. 123.

MACHINE SCULPTURE

Jean Tinguely is dedicated to humanizing the machine. His *Homage to New York* (Figure 5-20), exhibited at the Museum of Modern Art in 1960, was not only a machine sculpture but a onetime sculpture performance. Tinguely introduced a touch of humor into the world of sculpture as he explored the subject matter of technology in the arts. For those present it was unforgettable. The mechanical parts, collected from junk heaps and dismembered from their original machines, stood out sharply, and yet they were linked by their spatial locations, shapes, and

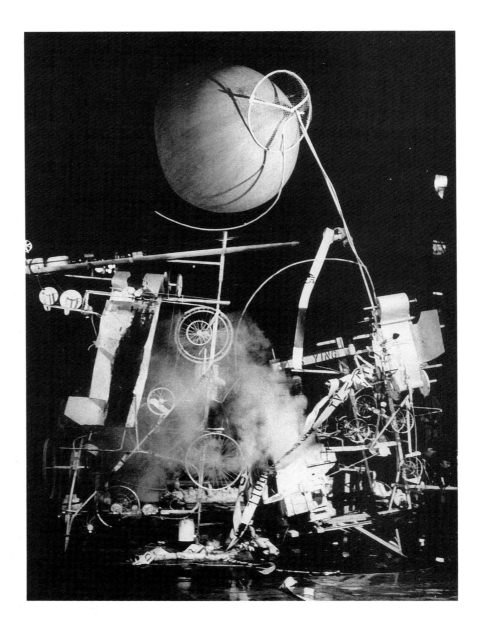

FIGURE 5-20
Jean Tinguely, *Homage to New York*. 1960. Mixed media. Exhibited at the Museum of Modern Art, New York.
Homage to New York was exhibited in the sculpture garden of the Museum of Modern Art in New York, where it operated for some twenty-seven minutes until it destroyed itself. This was a late Dadaist experiment.

textures, and sometimes by nervelike wires. Only the old player piano was intact. As the piano played, it was accompanied by howls and other weird sounds in irregular patterns that seemed to be issuing from the wheels, gears, and rods, as if they were painfully communicating with one another in some form of mechanical speech. Some of the machinery that runs New York City was exposed as vulnerable, pathetic, and comic, but Tinguely humanized this machinery as he exposed it. Even death was suggested, for *Homage to New York* was self-destructing: The piano was electronically wired for burning, and, in turn, the whole structure collapsed.

EARTH SCULPTURE

Another avant-garde sculpture—*earth sculpture*—goes so far as to make the earth itself the medium, the site, and the subject matter. The proper spatial selection becomes absolutely essential, for the earth usually must be taken where it is found. Structures are traced in plains, meadows, sand, snow, and the like, in order to help make us stop and perceive and enjoy the "form site"—the earth transformed to be more meaningful. Usually nature rapidly breaks up the form and returns the site to its less ordered state. Accordingly, many earth sculptors have a special need for the photographer to preserve their art.

Robert Smithson was a pioneer in earthwork sculpture. One of his best-known works is *Spiral Jetty* (Figure 5-21), a 1,500-foot-long coil 15 feet wide that spirals out from a spot on the Great Salt Lake. It is constructed of "mud, precipitated salt crystals, rocks, water," and colorful algae, all of which are now submerged in the lake. At times it reemerges when the water level is low. Because the sculpture is usually hidden, it exists for most viewers only in photographs. This mode of existence offers some interesting problems for those who question the authenticity of such works.

FIGURE 5-21
Robert Smithson, *Spiral Jetty*. 1970. Great Salt Lake, Utah. Mud, salt crystals, rocks, water; length 1,500 feet long and 15 feet wide. Reaching 1,500 feet into the Great Salt Lake is one of the first and most influential of large earth sculptures. Utah officials stopped a recent move to drill for oil nearby.

Collection: DIA Center for the Arts, New York, Photo: Gianfranco Gorgoni, Courtesy of James Cohan Gallery, New York, Art ©Holt-Smithson Foundation/Licensed by VAGA, New York, NY

FOCUS ON **African Sculpture**

Sub-Saharan African sculpture has exerted an important influence on Western art since the late eighteenth century, but it was especially influential on nineteenth- and twentieth-century artists such as Paul Gauguin, Constantine Brancusi, Amedeo Modigliani, Henri Matisse, and especially Pablo Picasso, who developed a large personal collection of African sculpture. Picasso's experiments in Cubism owe their origin to the influence of African sculpture, which had become widely known in Europe in the late nineteenth century.

Because most African sculpture was carved from wood, much of the older artistic heritage has been lost to weathering, repeated use, and even termites. Very little sculpture was made from stone. In certain periods, cast metal sculpture was created for kings in important courts, especially in the Benin culture in Nigeria. Benin cast sculpture, such as *Head of an Oba* (Figure 5-22), was meant to celebrate a ruler. The head was displayed in a temple shrine to connect the next ruler to his predecessor as part of a dynasty, which, in this case, began in the fourteenth century. While some of these cast works are profoundly realistic, in general realism is not the aim of African sculpture. Yet the power of the *Head of an Oba* is undeniable. The face has powerful eyes and lips, and a sense of bulk and density implied in the garment covering the neck as well as the woven hat and what appears to be hair or fiber held with beads. One senses an expression of power, respect, and authority in this work.

The figural distortions common in African sculpture were what most interested Picasso and other Western artists in the early twentieth century. The artists' response to those distortions freed them in important ways, permitting them to emphasize portions of a face or figure to intensify its strength and significance. It also helped Picasso and others create a sense of freedom from being tied to a realistic representation. It gave them a new way to conceive of proportion, shape, and beauty. But the purpose of distortion in African sculpture is less an artistic value than it is an effort to respect the life forces these artists perceived in the enlarged

FIGURE 5-22

Head of an Oba, 16th century, Nigeria, Court of Benin, Edo peoples. Brass. H. 9¼ × W. 8⅝ × D. 9 inches. Metropolitan Museum of Art, New York. The Michael C. Rockefeller Memorial Collection, Bequest of Nelson A. Rockefeller, 1979. Accession Number: 1979.206.86. This work is an example of the Benin lost-wax metal sculpture technique. The original is modeled in bees wax. Casts are formed from clay applied to the original. The casts are dried in the sun. Then the casts are fired in a pit in intense heat that both fires the clay and melts the bees wax. The fired clay casts are then used to form the bronze sculpture.

Source: The Michael C. Rockefeller Memorial Collection, Bequest of Nelson A. Rockefeller, 1979/The Metropolitan Museum of Art

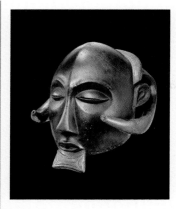

FIGURE 5-23
Luba Helmet Mask. Luba people,
southeastern Congo. Circa 1880.
25½ inches high. Royal Museum for
African Art, Tervuren, Belgium. This is a
strongly modeled mask of what may be
an important person. The ram's horns
and the bird carved on the rear of the
mask may imply supernatural powers.
Many African sculptures refer to
magical powers and the supernatural.

EO.0.0.23470, Collection RMCA Tervuren;
Photo: R. Asselberghs, MRAC Tervuren

FIGURE 5-24
Queen Mother Pendant Mask: Iyoba, 16th century.
Nigeria, Court of Benin. Ivory, iron, copper.
H. 9⅜ × W. 5 × D. 3¼ inches. Metropolitan
Museum of Art, The Michael C. Rockefeller
Memorial Collection, Gift of Nelson A.
Rockefeller, 1972. Accession Number:
1978.412.323. Such portrait masks of women
were rare. This was made for Esigie, the king
of Benin, to honor his mother, Idiaby. It is an
idealized representation, but it was a great
honor. There is only one other like this mask,
in the British Museum.

©Peter Horree/Alamy

eyes, the oversize head, the abdomen, the prominent genitalia, all of which were sources of power for their culture. For a contemporary Western art lover the cultural values are usually unknown, but the effect of the distortions is perceived as being emotionally expressive and visually intensifying.

The *Luba Helmet Mask* (Figure 5-23) is considered one of the most important holdings of the Royal Museum for African Art in Belgium. The modeling and finish of the wood are remarkable, a testament to truth to materials. The powerful nose and deep sculpted eyes dominate, but the bull horns may suggest that the Luba chief, on whom this mask may be based, has supernatural powers. Invisible from the front is a bird carved in the back, also perhaps symbolizing special powers. Originally the lower part of the mask was covered by about ten inches of grass, making it possible to wear the mask in a ceremony. Like the *Head of an Oba* face, this mask exudes extreme dignity, implying that the individual is of high station and great value.

One of the most unusual pieces is *Queen Mother Pendant Mask* (Figure 5-24). It is remarkable first because female masks of royalty are quite rare. It is carved from ivory and then decorated with iron and possibly copper details. It dates to the sixteenth century and was designed as a commemorative mask for the king (Oba) to memorialize his mother, the queen. The use of white ivory connected the image to the ocean because the idea of whiteness implied the purity of the god of the sea, Olokun. Only one other figure of this type is known, a female sculpture in the British Museum.

continued

The *Maternity Figure* (Figure 5-25) celebrates the life force in woman, with a child
held proudly. This work may be viewed from
several positions because it is an example of
sculpture in the round. Its powerful parallel
lines are expressed in stylized breasts, large
arms, and oversized feet, implying stability
and security. Maternity groups are common in African sculpture and some may have
been influenced by Western images of the
Madonna and child, but the African versions
tend to be more dynamic, as in the case of
this sculpture from Congo.

The *Veranda Post: Equestrian Figure and Female Caryatid* (Figure 5-26) is remarkable for
its brilliance in carving and the modeling of the
figures in a highly complex relationship. But it
is even more remarkable for the fact that we
know who the artist was, Olowe of Ise, who may
have carved this functional sculpture in the late
nineteenth or early twentieth century. Like the
female in *Maternity Figure*, the woman below
has an elongated neck, prominent breasts,
careful scarification, and strong angular lines.
She represents ideals of Yoruba female beauty.
Supporting both the horse and its rider, she is
a symbol of power and influence. Other works
by Olowe are often a tribute to the power and
freedom of the women in the community. This
piece was one of several commissioned by a king for a structure in a Yoruba palace
courtyard. Olowe is considered the greatest of Yoruba scultors.

Olowe of Ise was a master carver whose work has been identified because
of his distinctive style. The figures portrayed in the piece represent ideals of
Yoruba dignity, strength, and beauty. The Dallas Museum of Art purchased a
sculpture by Olowe in 2004 for more than $530,000.

FIGURE 5-25
Maternity Figure (Bwanga bwa Cibola)
19th-early 20th century. Democratic
Republic of the Congo, Luluwa peoples.
Wood, metal ring, H. 9¾ × W. 3 ×
D. 2½ inches. (24.8 × 7.6 × 6.4 cm).
Metropolitan Museum of Art, The
Michael C. Rockefeller Memorial
Collection, Bequest of Nelson A.
Rockefeller, Accession number:
1979.206.282. African spiritual
pieces such as this inspired modern
European painters in the early
twentieth century.

©The Metropolitan Museum of Art/Art
Resource, NY

FIGURE 5-26
Olowe of Ise, *The Veranda Post: Equestrian
Figure and Female Caryatid*, Early 20th
century. Wood. 71 ×
11¼ × 11 inches.

Source: Purchase, Lila Acheson Wallace Gift,
1996/The Metropolitan Museum of Art

PERCEPTION KEY African Sculpture

1. Which of the paintings in Chapter 2 seem most influenced by the African sculpture
   discussed here?
2. To what extent do these African sculptures seem to reveal the psychology of the
   figures?
3. Distortion is a powerful device in African sculpture, but it is also powerful in Western art. Comment on the distorted necks of the woman in *Veranda Post*, the mother
   in *Maternity Figure*, and Parmigianino's *The Madonna with the Long Neck* (Figure 4-4).
   How does the use of distortion affect your ability to participate with these works?
4. Examine these five African sculptures for their use of space, simplification of form,
   and sense of dynamics. Which are most stable? Which are most dynamic?
5. How important is the concept of truth to materials for these sculptors?

SCULPTURE IN PUBLIC PLACES

Sculpture has traditionally shared its location with major buildings, sometimes acting as decoration on the building, as in many churches, or acting as a center point of interest, as in the original placement of Michelangelo's *David,* which was positioned carefully in front of the Palazzo Vecchio, the central building of the Florentine government. It stood as a warning not to underestimate the Florentines. Many small towns throughout the world have public sculpture that commemorates wars or other important events.

One of the most popularly successful of contemporary public sculptures has been Maya Ying Lin's *Vietnam Veterans Memorial* (Figure 5-27) in Washington, D.C. Because the Vietnam War was both terribly unpopular and a major defeat, there were fears that any memorial might stir public antagonism. However, the result has been quite the opposite. The piece is a sloping black granite wall, V-shaped, which descends ten feet below grade. On the wall are engraved the names of more than 58,000 dead Americans. Visitors walk along its length, absorbing the seemingly endless list of names. The impact of the memorial grows in part because the list of names grows with each step down the slope. Visitors respond to the memorial by touching the names, sometimes taking rubbings away with them, sometimes simply weeping.

Maya Lin's *Vietnam Veterans Memorial* was a controversial public sculpture when it was first unveiled but has become a most popular attraction both in its place in Washington, D.C., and as a replica tours around the country. Judy Chicago's *The*

FIGURE 5-27
Maya Ying Lin, *Vietnam Veterans Memorial.* 1982. Black granite, V-shaped, 493 feet long, 10 feet high at center. Washington, D.C. Lin designed the memorial when she was an undergraduate. One angle of the wall points to the Washington Monument, the other to the Lincoln Memorial. Its V shape below the ground was intended to suggest a wound in the earth. Incised on it are the names of 58,256 fallen American warriors.

©David Noble

FIGURE 5-28
Judy Chicago, *The Dinner Party*.
1979. Mixed media, each side 48
feet. Elizabeth A. Sackler Center for
Feminist Art, Brooklyn Museum. *The
Dinner Party* consists of thirty-nine
place settings for important women
of myth and history. The work was
produced under the direction of Judy
Chicago by a collective of women
sewing, embroidering, and weaving
to complement the elaborately
designed plates.

Dinner Party (Figure 5-28), in the midst of a powerful wave of feminist activity in the late 1970s, was celebrated by feminists and denounced by opponents of the movement. Although it is not public sculpture in the sense that it is on view outdoors, it once toured the country and attracted huge crowds. It is now in the permanent collection of the Brooklyn Museum of Art. The sculpture includes place settings for thirty-nine mythic and historical women such as Ishtar, Hatshepsut, Sacagawea, Mary Wollstonecraft, Sojourner Truth, Emily Dickinson, and Virginia Woolf. Each place setting has embroidery, napkins, place settings, and a plate with a butterfly design that alludes to female genitalia—one reason for protest against the work. Judy Chicago oversaw the project, but it is the work of many women working in crafts traditionally associated with women, such as sewing and embroidery.

Study (with imagination) Serra's *Sequence* (Figure 5-29), four huge torqued Cor-Ten steel plates installed in the garden of the Museum of Modern Art in summer 2007. We are—as never before—immersed in sculptural space. At both ends we have the chance of entering through one of two openings—one leads into a containment center of settled space; the other pulls us into a seemingly endless curvilinear corridor between two brutal, looming steel walls. Yet strangely, if we wait, we see on the steel intriguing textures and beautiful orange-rust patterns sculpted by time. Still we may feel compressed, confused, perhaps even a touch fearful. To go back is not necessarily an appealing option, for the spaces are narrow, and where are we, anyhow? Normal spatial perception is undermined. The walls appear to close both behind and over us. They seem to sway, and so does the floor. At last we come to the center, overcome with wonder.

FIGURE 5-29
Richard Serra, *Sequence*. 2006. Cor-Ten steel, 12 feet 9 inches × 40 feet 8⅜ inches × 65 feet 2³⁄₁₆ inches. People walk around and in this gigantic work, in which the walls are torqued in such a way as to lean toward the viewer. Critic Ronald Paulson calls Serra the greatest modern sculptor, perhaps the greatest sculptor.

©2017 Richard Serra/Artists Rights Society (ARS), New York. Photo ©Frederick Charles

PERCEPTION KEY Public Sculpture

1. Public sculpture such as that by Maya Lin, Judy Chicago, and Richard Serra usually produces tremendous controversy when it is not representative, such as a conventional statue of a man on a horse, a hero holding a rifle and flag, or a person of local fame. What do you think causes these more abstract works to attract controversy? Do you react negatively or positively to any of these three works?

2. Should artists who plan public sculpture meant to be viewed by a wide-ranging audience aim at pleasing that audience? Should that be their primary mission, or should they simply make the best work they are capable of?

3. Which of the three, *Vietnam Veterans Memorial*, *Sequence*, or *The Dinner Party*, seems least like a work of art to you? Try to convince someone who disagrees with you that it is not a work of art.

4. Choose a public sculpture that is in your community, photograph it, and establish its credentials, as best you can, for making a claim to being an important work of art.

5. If we label Chicago's *The Dinner Party* a feminist work, is it then to be treated as political sculpture? Do you think Lin's *Vietnam Veterans Memorial* is a less political or more political sculpture than Chicago's work? Could Serra's *Sequence* be considered a political work? Would labeling these works as political render them any less important as works of art?

SUMMARY

Sculpture is perceived differently from painting, engaging more acutely our sense of touch and the feeling of our bodies. Whereas painting is more about the visual appearance of things, sculpture is more about things as three-dimensional masses. Whereas painting only represents voluminosity and density, sculpture presents these qualities. Sculpture in the round, especially, brings out the three-dimensionality of objects. No object is more important to us than our bodies, and their "strange thickness" is always with us. When the human body is the subject matter, sculpture more than any other art reveals a material counterpoint for our mental images of our bodies. Traditional sculpture is made by either modeling or carving. Many contemporary sculptures, however, are made by assembling preformed pieces of material. New sculptural techniques and materials have opened developments in avant-garde sculpture that defy classification. Nonetheless, contemporary sculptors, generally, have emphasized truth to materials, respect for the medium that is organized by their forms. Space, protest against technology, accommodation with technology, machine, and earth sculpture are five of the most important new species. Public sculpture is flourishing.

Chapter 6

ARCHITECTURE

We can close the novel, shut off the music, refuse to go to a play or dance, sleep through a movie, shut our eyes to a painting or a sculpture. But we cannot escape from buildings for very long. Fortunately, however, sometimes buildings are works of art—that is, architecture. They draw us to them rather than push us away or make us ignore them. They make our living space more livable. Architecture is the shaping of buildings and space.

Centered Space

Painters do not command real three-dimensional space: They feign it. Sculptors can mold out into space, but generally they do not enfold an enclosed or inner space for our movement. Our passage through the inner spaces of architecture is one of the conditions under which its solids and voids have their effect. In a sense, architecture is a great hollowed-out sculpture that we perceive by moving about both outside and inside. Space is the material of the architect, the primeval cutter,* who carves apart an inner space from an outer space in such a way that both spaces become more fully perceptible and interesting.

Inner and outer space come together on the earth to form a centered and illuminated context or clearing. *Centered space* is the arrangement of things around some paramount thing—the place at which the other things seem to converge. Sometimes

---

*This meaning is suggested by the Greek *architectón*.

FIGURE 6-1
Mortuary Temple of Hatshepsut, Valley of the Kings, Egypt, 15th century BCE. The temple was designed by Senmut, an architect and Hatshepsut's visier and, according to legend, her lover. Hatshepsut (1508–1458 BCE) was the most successful of Egypt's female pharaohs. This is one of the greatest examples of symmetry in early architecture.

©Lee A. Jacobus

this center is a natural site, such as a great mountain, river, canyon, or forest. Sometimes the center is a natural site enhanced by a human-made structure.

Centered space is centripetal, insisting upon drawing us in. There is an in-rush that is difficult to escape, that overwhelms and makes us acquiescent. We perceive space not as a receptacle containing things but rather as a context energized by the positioned interrelationships of things. Centered space has a pulling power that, even in our most harassed moments, we cannot escape feeling. In the Valley of the Kings in Egypt (Figure 6-1), we approach the mortuary temple of the female pharaoh Hatshepsut with a sense of awe. It is, rightly, called the most beautiful of all the temples in the valley, perhaps in all of early Egypt. We find ourselves in the presence of a power beyond our control. We feel the sublimity of space, but, at the same time, the centeredness beckons and welcomes us.

SPACE AND ARCHITECTURE

Architects are the shepherds of space. In turn, the paths around their shelters lead us away from our ordinary preoccupations demanding the use of space. We come to rest. Instead of our using up space, space takes possession of us with a ten-fingered grasp. We have a place to dwell.

Architecture—as opposed to mere engineering—is the creative conservation of space. Architects perceive the centers of space in nature and build to preserve these centers and make them more vital. Architects are confronted by centered spaces that desire to be made, through them, into works. These spaces of nature are not offspring of architects alone but appearances that step up to them, so to speak, and demand protection. If an architect succeeds in carrying through these appeals, the power of the natural space streams forth and the work rises.

The architect typically shelters inner space from outer space in such a way that we can use the inner space for practical purposes at the same time we perceive both spaces and their relationships as more interesting, thus evoking participation. The partitioning of space renders invisible air visible. Inside the building, space is filled with stresses and pressures. Outside the building, space becomes organized and focused. Inner space is anchored to the earth. Outer space converges upon inner space.

Architecture generally creates a strengthened hierarchy in the positioned interrelationships of earth and sky and what is in between. Architecture enhances the centered clearings of nature, accentuating a context in which all our senses can be in harmony with their surroundings. And even when architecture is not present, our memories of architecture, especially of great buildings, teach us how to order the sensations of our natural environment. Aristotle said, "Art completes nature." Every natural environment, unless it has been ruined by humans, lends itself to centering and ordering, even if no architecture is there. The architectural model teaches us how to be more sensitive to the potential centering and ordering of nature. As a result of such intensified sensitivity, we have a context—a special place—within which the sounds, smells, temperatures, breezes, volumes, masses, colors, lines, textures, and constant changes of nature can be ordered into something more than a blooming, buzzing confusion. That special place might be sublimely open, as with the spectacle of an ocean, or cozily closed, as with a bordered brook. In either case, nature is consecrated, and we belong and dwell.

CHARTRES

On a hot summer day many years ago, following the path of Henry Adams, who wrote *Mont-Saint-Michel and Chartres,* one of the authors was attempting to drive from Mont-Saint-Michel to Chartres in time to catch the setting sun through the western rose window of Chartres Cathedral (Figures 6-2 and 6-3). The following is an account of this experience:

> In my rushing anxiety—I had to be in Paris the following day and I had never been to Chartres before—I became oblivious of space except as providing landmarks for my time-clocked progress. Thus I have no significant memories of the towns and countrysides I hurried through. Late that afternoon the two spires of Chartres, like two strangely woven strands of rope let down from the heavens, gradually came into focus. The blue dome of the sky also became visible for the first time, centering as I approached more and more firmly around

FIGURE 6-2
Chartres Cathedral, Chartres. The cathedral, built starting in 1140 and continuing into the fifteenth century, dominates the cityscape. Chartres is considered the greatest of the Gothic cathedrals.

©Alinari Archives/Corbis/Getty Images

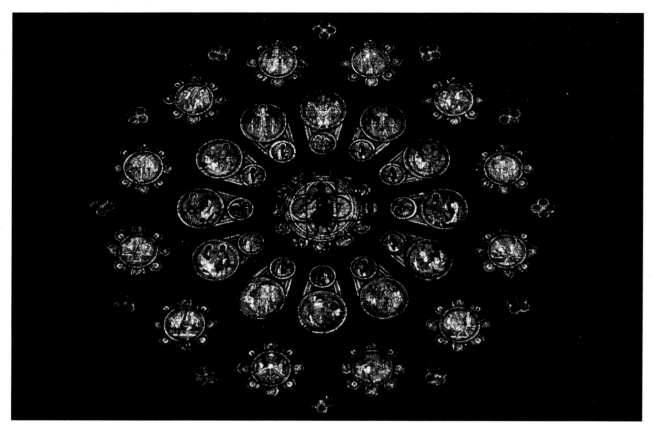

FIGURE 6-3
Chartres Cathedral. The great western rose window. The window casts a powerful light within the cathedral in the later afternoon. Rose windows were designed to cast a "dim, religious light," as the poet John Milton said.

©Lee A. Jacobus

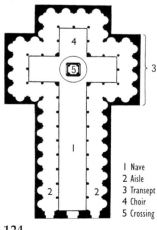

1 Nave
2 Aisle
3 Transept
4 Choir
5 Crossing

the axis of those spires. "In lovely blueness blooms the steeple with metal roof " (Hölderlin). The surrounding fields and then the town, coming out now in all their specificity, grew into tighter unity with the church and sky. I recalled a passage from Aeschylus: "The pure sky desires to penetrate the earth, and the earth is filled with love so that she longs for blissful unity with the sky. The rain falling from the sky impregnates the earth, so that she gives birth to plants and grain for beasts and men." No one rushed in or out or around the church. The space around seemed alive and dense with slow currents all ultimately being pulled to and through the central portal.* Inside, the space, although spacious far beyond the scale of practical human needs, seemed strangely compressed, full of forces thrusting and counterthrusting in dynamic interrelations. Slowly, in the cool silence inlaid with stone,

---

*Chartres, like most Gothic churches, is shaped roughly like a recumbent Latin cross: The front—with its large circular window shaped like a rose and the three vertical windows, or lancets, beneath—faces west. The apse, or eastern end, of the building contains the high altar. The nave is the central and largest aisle leading from the central portal to the high altar. But before the altar is reached, the transept crosses the nave. Both the northern and southern facades of the transept of Chartres contain, like the western facade, glorious rose windows. (Drawing after R. Sturgis)

124

I was drawn down the long nave, following the stately rhythms of the bays and piers. But my eyes also followed the vast vertical stretches far up into the shifting shadows of the vaultings. It was as if I were being borne aloft. Yet I continued down the narrowing tunnel of the nave, but more and more slowly as the pull of the space above held back the pull of the space below. At the crossing of the *transept,* the flaming colors, especially the reds, of the northern and southern roses transfixed my slowing pace, and then I turned back at last to the western rose and the three lancets beneath—a delirium of color, dominantly blue, was pouring through. Earthbound on the crossing, the blaze of the Without was merging with the Within. Radiant space took complete possession of my senses. In the protective grace of this sheltering space, even the outer space which I had dismissed in the traffic of my driving seemed to converge around the center of this crossing. Instead of being alongside things— the church, the town, the fields, the sky, the sun—I was with them, at one with them. This housing of holiness made me feel at home in this strange land.

PERCEPTION KEY Chartres Cathedral

1. Form and function usually work together in classic architecture. What visible exterior architectural details indicate that Chartres Cathedral functions as a church? Are there any visible details that conflict with its function as a church?
2. The two spires of the church were built at different times. Should they have been made symmetrical? What might be some reasons for their not being symmetrical?
3. What seem to be the primary values revealed by the rose window of Chartres?
4. How did the builders satisfy the fourth requirement of architecture: that the building be revelatory? What values does the exterior of the building reveal?
5. What is implied by the fact that the cathedral dwarfs all the buildings near it?

LIVING SPACE

Living space is the feeling of the comfortable positioning of things in the environment, promoting both liberty of movement and paths as directives. Taking possession of space is our first gesture as infants, and sensitivity to the position of other things is a prerequisite of life. Space infiltrates through all our senses, and our sensations of everything influence our perception of space. A breeze broadens the spaciousness of a room that opens on a garden. A sound tells us something about the surfaces and shape of that room. A cozy temperature brings the furniture and walls into intimate relationships. The smell of books gives that space a personality. With living space, since all the senses are involved, the whole body is a center. Furthermore, when we relate to a place of special value, such as the home, a "configurational center" is formed, a place that is a gathering point around which a field of interest is structured.

PERCEPTION KEY Buildings

1. Select a house in your community that strikes you as ugly. Why?
2. Select a house in your community that strikes you as beautiful. Why?
3. Comment on your own home. Is the space warm, inviting, well situated in its site? Is your home architecture or engineering?

continued

4. Comment on an apartment house, a school building, an office building, a gas station, a supermarket—how well do they use space? Is the space inviting?
5. Do you have any buildings that provide a centered space?
6. What are your configurational centers? Which are beautiful? Which are not?

A building that lacks artistic qualities, even if it encloses a convenient void, encourages us to ignore it. Normally we will be blind to such a building and its space as long as it serves its practical purposes. If the roof leaks or a wall breaks down, however, we will only see the building as a damaged instrument. A well-designed building, on the other hand, brings us into living space by centering space. We become aware of the power and embrace of space. Such a building strikes a bargain between what it lets us do and what it makes us do.

FOUR NECESSITIES OF ARCHITECTURE

Architecture is a peculiarly public art because buildings generally have a social function, and many buildings require public funds. More than other artists, architects must consider the public. If they do not, few of their plans are likely to materialize. Thus, architects must be psychologists, sociologists, economists, businesspeople, politicians, and courtiers. They must also be engineers, for they must be able to design structurally stable buildings. And then they need luck.

Architects have to take into account four basic and closely interrelated necessities: technical requirements, function, spatial relationships, and revelatory requirements. To succeed, their structures must adjust to these necessities. As for what time will do to their creations, they can only hope and prepare with foresight. Ultimately every building is susceptible to economic demands and the whims of future taste.

Technical Requirements of Architecture

Of the four necessities, the technical requirements of a building are the most obvious. Buildings must stand and withstand. Architects must know the materials and their potentialities, how to put the materials together, and how the materials will work on a particular site. But they are something more as well—artists. In solving their technical problems, they must also make their forms revelatory. Their buildings must illuminate something significant that we would otherwise fail to perceive.

Consider, for example, the relationship between the engineering requirements and artistic qualities of the Parthenon, 447–432 BCE (Figure 6-4). The engineering was superb, but unfortunately the building was almost destroyed in 1687, when it was being used as an ammunition dump by the Turks and was hit by a shell from a Venetian gun. Basically the technique used was *post-and-lintel* (or post-and-beam) construction. Set on a base, or stylobate, columns (verticals: the posts) support the entablature (horizontals: the lintel), which, in turn, supports the *pediment* (the triangular structure) and roof.

FIGURE 6-4
The Parthenon, Athens. 447–432 BCE. The Parthenon was dedicated to Athena, the patron of Athens. To give its proportions a sense of perfection, a number of imperfections were built into the columns to accommodate the way people must look up to the building.

©Lee A. Jacobus

PERCEPTION KEY The Parthenon and Chartres Cathedral

1. Compare the dominant vertical elements of the Parthenon—the Doric columns and the pediment—with the dominant vertical elements of Chartres Cathedral—the spires, the strong vertical buttresses, and the round window. Each building is dedicated to God or gods. What revelatory function do the strong verticals seem to serve? What might they reveal to those who first saw these buildings?
2. Which building is more dominated by straight lines? What does the emphasis on straight or rounded lines in these buildings imply in terms of revealing religious values?
3. Both buildings are temples. Which seems to you more holy? Which seems to put more trust in God? Compare your views with those of your peers.
4. Examine the elements of the Doric order in Figure 6-5. What values are revealed by the attention to detail in the stylobate, the shaft, and the segments of the capital, the necking, echinus, and abacus? Are these details simply decoration, or are they also functional and revelatory?

Functional Requirements of Architecture

Traditionally architects made their buildings stand in such a way that they revealed their function or use. No one is likely to mistake Chartres Cathedral for an office building. We have seen the conventional structures of too many churches and office buildings to be mistaken about this. Nor are we likely to mistake the Seagram Building (Figure 6-6) for a church. We recognize the functions of these buildings because they are in the conventional shapes that such buildings so often possess.

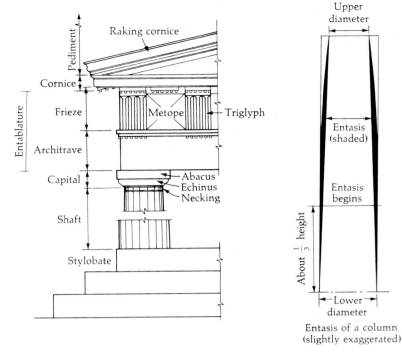

FIGURE 6-5
Elements of the Doric order, the
simplest of the Greek orders and
thus considered most appropriate for
temples.

PERCEPTION KEY Form, Function, Content, and Space

Study Figure 6-2 (Chartres Cathedral) and the Seagram Building Figure 6-6 below.
1. What is the basic function of each of these buildings?
2. How have the respective forms revealed the functions of their buildings? We would argue that both works are architecture because the form of the building is revelatory of the subject matter—of the tension, anguish, striving, and ultimate concern of religious faith—whereas the form of the Seagram Building is revelatory of the stripped-down, uniform efficiency of an American business corporation. Consider every possible relevant argument against this view.

Study one of Frank Lloyd Wright's last and most famous works, the Solomon R. Guggenheim Museum in New York City (Figures 6-7 and 6-8), constructed in 1957–1959 but designed in 1943. Wright wrote,

Here for the first time architecture appears plastic, one floor flowing into another (more like sculpture) instead of the usual superimposition of stratified layers cutting and butting into each other by way of post-and-beam construction. The whole building, cast in concrete, is more like an egg shell—in form a great simplicity—rather than like a crisscross structure. The light concrete flesh is rendered strong enough everywhere to do its work

FIGURE 6-6
Ludwig Mies van der Rohe and Philip Johnson, architects, the Seagram Building, New York City. 1954–1958. An example of the International style popular in midcentury, the building was designed so that the structure of the building would be visible. Without decoration, and with replication of floor upon floor, this building reveals a clear function for "doing business."

©SuperStock

FIGURE 6-7
Frank Lloyd Wright, Solomon R. Guggenheim Museum, New York City. 1957–1959. This was the last great commission for Wright, whose cast concrete design was instantly controversial.

FIGURE 6-8
Solomon R. Guggenheim Museum interior. The floor spirals continuously upward with art hung on the walls. A large transparent skylight is shaped similarly to cathedral rose windows.

by embedded filaments of steel either separate or in mesh. The structural calculations are thus those of cantilever and continuity rather than the post and beam. The net result of such construction is a greater repose, the atmosphere of the quiet unbroken wave: no meeting of the eye with abrupt changes of form.[1]

The term *cantilever* refers to a structural principle in architecture in which one end of a horizontal form is fixed—usually in a wall—while the other end juts out over space. Steel beam construction makes such forms possible; many modern buildings, like the Guggenheim Museum, have forms extending fluidly into space.

PERCEPTION KEY Guggenheim Museum

1. How well does the exterior of the building harmonize with the interior?
2. Does the exterior form reveal the building as an art museum?
3. The museum stands near much larger rectangular buildings. What would be the point of such a sharp contrast with boxlike "post-and-beam" structures? What would such a contrast reveal about the nature of art?
4. The Guggenheim Museum faces Fifth Avenue in New York City. Originally it was to have been located in Central Park. How much difference would that have made to the revelatory qualities of the building?

---

[1]Source: *The Solomon R. Guggenheim Museum*, 1960, The Solomon R. Guggenheim Foundation and Horizon Press, New York, p. 16ff.

Wright solved his technical problems (such as cantilevering) and his functional problems (efficient and commodious exhibition of works of art) with considerable success. Moreover, the building reveals itself as a museum. What else could it be? In the 1950s Wright's design was revolutionary. We think of it now as a museum, but when it was built it contrasted so sharply with the rectangular boxlike structures near it that people were shocked. Indeed, this building stands as a work of art partly because its singular design occupies space as a sculpture would. The Guggenheim Museum in New York began an architectural era in which the relationship of form and function began to be called into question.

Revelatory Requirements of Architecture

The function or use of a building is an essential part of the subject matter of that building, what the architect interprets or gives insight into by means of its form. The function of the Seagram Building is to house offices. The form of that building reveals that function. But does this function exhaust the subject matter of this building? Is only function revealed? Would we, perhaps, be closer to the truth by claiming that involved with this office function are values closely associated with, but nevertheless distinguishable from, this function? That somehow other values, besides functional ones, are interpreted in architecture?

We are claiming that the essential values of contemporary society are a part of all artists' subject matter, part of what they must interpret in their work, and this—because of the public character of architecture—is especially so with architects. Architects (and artists generally) are influenced by the values of their society. In the Middle Ages, religion in the West was supreme and the great buildings of that period were churches and cathedrals. Soon after, the great buildings were palaces and fortresses. Each of these structures reveals the values of the times and the places—in short, of the societies in which they were built. The church, the royal court, and the military protection of the communities were dependent on the services of architects. In the 1950s, when the Seagram Building was constructed, the rise of corporate capitalism was interpreted clearly and efficiently. That is one reason the Guggenheim Museum was so shocking.

Every stone of the Parthenon, in the way it was cut and fitted, reveals something about the values of the Age of Pericles, the fifth century BCE—for example, the emphasis on moderation and harmony, the importance of mathematical measurement and yet its subordination to the eminence of humans and their rationality, as well as the immanence rather than the transcendence of the sacred.

Chartres Cathedral reveals three principal value areas of that medieval region: the special importance of Mary, to whom the cathedral is dedicated; the doctrines of the cathedral school, one of the most important centers of learning in Europe in the twelfth and thirteenth centuries; and the value preferences of the main patrons—the royal family, the lesser nobility, and the local guilds. The windows of the 175 surviving panels and the sculpture, including more than 2,000 carved figures, were a bible in glass and stone for the illiterate, but they were also a visual encyclopedia for the literate. From these structures the iconographer—the decipherer of the meaning of icons or symbols—can trace almost every fundamental value of the society that created Chartres Cathedral: the conception of human history from Adam and Eve to the Last Judgment; church history; ancient lore and contemporary history; the latest scientific knowledge; the curriculum of the cathedral school as divided into the trivium (grammar, logic, and rhetoric) and the quadrivium (arithmetic, geometry, astronomy, and music); the hierarchy of the nobility and the guilds; the code of chivalry and manners; and the hopes and fears of the time.

PERCEPTION KEY **Values and Architecture**

1. Enumerate other values in addition to the functional that may be interpreted by the form of the Seagram Building.
2. Choose another piece of architecture in this chapter and comment on the values reflected in its structure.
3. Is there any building that you know of that does not reflect some values of its place and time?

EARTH-ROOTED ARCHITECTURE

The earth is the securing agency that grounds the place of our existence, our center. In many primitive cultures, it is believed that people are born from the earth. And in many languages, people are the "Earth-born." In countless myths, Mother Earth is the bearer of humans from birth to death. Of all things, the expansive earth, with its mineral resources and vegetative fecundity, most suggests or is symbolic of security. Moreover, since the solidity of the earth encloses its depth in darkness, the earth is also suggestive of mystery and death.

The Earth Mother has a mysterious, nocturnal, even funerary aspect—she is also often a goddess of death. But, as the theologian Mircea Eliade points out, "even in respect of these negative aspects, one thing that must never be lost sight of, is that when the Earth becomes a goddess of Death, it is simply because she is felt to be the universal womb, the inexhaustible source of all creation."[2] Nothing in nature is more suggestive or symbolic of security and mystery than the earth. *Earth-rooted architecture* accentuates this natural symbolism more than any other art.

Site

Architecture that is earth-rooted discloses the earth by drawing our attention to the site of the building, its submission to gravity, its raw materials, and its centrality in outer and inner space. Sites whose surrounding environment can be seen from great distances are especially favorable for helping a building to bring out the earth. The Mortuary Temple of Hatshepsut (Figure 6-1) is profoundly earth-rooted. It appears to be cut out of the stone mountain that cradles it. The site is large and inviting, and the interior is mysterious and extensive. Few buildings in the world are more clearly earth-bound. Even the extraordinary symmetry of its parts, with the repeats of vertical

---

[2]Source: Mircea Eliade, *Myths, Dreams and Mysteries*, trans. Philip Mairet (New York: Harper, 1961), p. 188.

supports and open spaces leading within, reinforces the sense that this building is in place and will never be elsewhere. The deepest section of the temple, the Chapel of Amun, is cut from the rock itself and leads deep into the mountain.

Gravity

The Parthenon (Figure 6-4), because it is on the Acropolis, the highest point in Athens, seems an unlikely candidate for an earth-rooted structure, but as we see it now in ruin we perceive a remarkable tendency for it to appear profoundly weighty. The stones that surround the building give us a clue immediately to the density of its stone columns, and the stones of the support of the original roof imply an inevitable yielding to gravity. The horizontal rectangularity of the entablature follows evenly along the plain of the Acropolis with the steady beat of its supporting columns and quiets their upward thrust. Gravity is accepted and accentuated in this serene stability—the hold of the earth is secure.

James Gibbs's Radcliffe Camera (Figure 6-9) cannot be seen from great distances, although it benefits from a grassy surround that permits us to view it in its entirety.

FIGURE 6-9
James Gibbs, Radcliffe Camera, Oxford University, Oxfordshire, UK. 1737–1748. A library for Oxford University, the building does not have a long vista. It sits amid the many colleges of the university. It was inspired by a sixteenth-century tempietto (little temple) by Donato Bramante. Like the Radcliffe Camera, it was enclosed by other buildings.

©Nikreates/Alamy

It appears to be a temple, but in this case a temple to learning. The classical columns add a sense of weight that roots the building firmly in place. Standing and accounting for its site and its thrust upward, one feels as if it is only the top of a much larger structure that is somehow invisible in the ground below. It is almost impossible to avoid participating with its dramatic form. Our first sense is that the building is the top of a temple and that there is more to come. Yet the dimension—one hundred feet in diameter—impresses us with a sense of both wonder and satisfaction. When we consider its classical columns, its renaissance dome, and the perfection of its circular structure, we begin to understand Gibbs's revelatory purposes. The building reveals the significance of learning, resting on the shoulders of Greece, Rome, and Italian renaissance. It is a symbol of the preservation of civilization through the art of architecture.

The pueblo buildings (Figure 6-10), the Betakin Cliff Dwellings, in the National Navajo Monument are also built out of and into the earth. The habitations are communal, protected by their setting, high into the cliffs. The American Southwest is notable for its adobe structures, adhering tightly to the earth, simple and arrestingly beautiful in their sites. The Pueblo settlements survive even now in partial ruin, striking because of their sense of rootedness in their setting.

Raw Materials

When the medium of architecture is made up totally or in large part of unfinished materials furnished by nature, especially when they are from the site, as in the Betakini Cliff Dwellings, these materials tend to stand forth and help reveal the earthiness of the earth. In this respect, stone, wood, and clay in a raw or

FIGURE 6-10
Betakin Cliff Dwellings. Ancestral (Anasazi) Pueblo buildings. Ruins at the National Navajo Monument in Arizona.

©Witold Skrypczak/Getty Images

FIGURE 6-11
Frank Lloyd Wright, Edgar J.
Kaufmann House, known as
Fallingwater. 1937–1939. Fifty
miles southeast of Pittsburgh, it
was described by *Time* magazine as
Wright's "most beautiful job."

relatively raw state are much more effective than steel, concrete, and glass. If the Parthenon had been made in concrete rather than in native Pentelic marble—the quarries can still be seen in the distance—the building would not grow out of the soil so organically, and some of the feeling of the earth would be dissipated. Also, if the paint that originally covered much of the Parthenon had remained, the effect would be considerably less earthy than at present. Note, however, that the dominant colors were terra-cotta reds, colors of the earth. Wright's Kaufmann house (Figure 6-11) is an excellent example of the combined use of manufactured and raw materials that helps set forth the earth. The concrete and glass bring out by contrast the textures of stone and wood taken from the site, while the lacelike flow of the falling water is made even more graceful by its reflection in the smooth clear flow of concrete and glass. Like a wide-spreading plant, drawing the sunlight and rain to its good earth, this home seems to breathe within its homeland. The Kaufmann house is an excellent example of the combined use of manufactured and raw materials that helps set forth the earth. The concrete and glass bring out by contrast the textures of stone and wood taken from the site, while the lacelike flow of the falling water is made even more graceful by its reflection in the smooth clear flow of concrete and glass. Like a wide-spreading plant, drawing the sunlight and rain to its good earth, this home seems to breathe within its homeland.

PERCEPTION KEY Architecture and Materials

In his *In Praise of Architecture*, the Italian architect Giò Ponti writes, "Beautiful materials do not exist. Only the right material exists. . . . Rough plaster in the right place is the beautiful material for that place. . . . To replace it with a noble material would be vulgar."[3]

1. Do you agree with Ponti?
2. If you agree, refer to examples that corroborate Ponti's point.
3. If you disagree, refer to examples that do not corroborate.

---

[3]Gio Ponte, *In Praise of Architecture*. New York: F.W. Dodge Corporation, 1960.

Centrality

A building that is strongly centered, in both its outer and inner space, helps disclose the earth. Perhaps no building is more centered in its site than the Parthenon, but the weak centering of its inner space slackens somewhat the significance of the earth. Unlike Chartres, there is no strong pull into the Parthenon and, when we get inside, the inner space, as we reconstruct it, is divided in such a way that no certain center can be felt. There is no place to come to an unequivocal standstill as at Chartres. Even Versailles (Figure 6-12), despite its seemingly never-ending partitions of inner space, brings us eventually to somewhat of a center at the bed in Louis XIV's bedroom. Yet this centering is made possible primarily by the view from the room that focuses both the pivotal position of the room in the building and the placement of the room on a straight-line axis to Paris in the far distance. Conversely, the inner space of Chartres, most of which from the crossing can be taken in with a sweep of the eyes, achieves centrality without this kind of dependence upon outside orientation. Buildings such as the Parthenon and Versailles, which divide the inner

FIGURE 6-12
Louis le Vau and Jules Hardouin-Mansart, Palace of Versailles, France. 1661–1687. France was governed from this palace from 1682 until the French Revolution of 1789. Its immensity was designed to house the entire Royal Court in a place several miles from Paris, the official capital of France.

FIGURE 6-13
Giovanni Paolo Panini, Interior of the Pantheon, Rome. Circa 1734. Oil on canvas, 50½ × 39 inches. The Pantheon dates from the second century. It is notable for being one of the only Roman buildings still in use and still intact as it originally was. The interior space is overwhelming in part because it contrasts dramatically with a very plain exterior.

Source: Samuel H. Kress Collection/National Gallery of Art, Washington, D.C.

space with solid partitions, are weaker in inner centrality than buildings without such divisions. The endless boxes within boxes of the Seagram Building (Figure 6-6) negate any possibility of significant inner centering, adding to the unearthiness of this cage of steel and glass.

Buildings in the round, other things being equal, are the most internally centered of all. In the Pantheon (Figure 6-13), almost all the inner space can be seen with a turn of the head, and the grand and clear *symmetry* of the enclosing shell draws

FIGURE 6-14
The Pantheon, Rome, exterior.
117–125 CE. The Greek facade,
eight Egyptian marble Corinthian
pillars, hides the drumlike structure
of the building, which was used as
a Christian church starting in the
seventh century.

©Canali Photobank, Italy

us to the center of the circle, the privileged position, beneath the eye of the dome opening to a bit of the sky. Few buildings root us more firmly in the earth. The massive dome with its stony bluntness seems to be drawn down by the funneled and dimly spreading light falling through the eye. This is a dome of destiny pressing tightly down. We are driven earthward in this crushing ambience. Even on the outside, the Pantheon seems to be forcing down (Figure 6-14). In the circular interior of Wright's Guggenheim Museum (Figure 6-8), not all of the inner space can be seen from the privileged position, but the smoothly curving ramp that comes down like a whirlpool makes us feel the earth beneath as our only support. Whereas in buildings such as Mont-Saint-Michel and Chartres, mass seems to be overcome, the weight lightened, and the downward motion thwarted, in buildings such as the Pantheon and the Guggenheim Museum, mass comes out heavily and down.

SKY-ORIENTED ARCHITECTURE

Architecture that is *sky-oriented* suggests or is symbolic of a world as the generating agency that enables us to project our possibilities and realize some of them. A horizon, always a necessary part of a world, is symbolic of the limitations placed upon our possibilities and realizations. The light and heat of the sun are more symbolic than anything else in nature of generative power. Dante declared, "There is no visible thing in the world more worthy to serve as symbol of God than the Sun; which illuminates with visible life itself first and then all the celestial and mundane bodies." Total darkness, at least until we can envision a world, is terrifying. That is why, as the Preacher of Ecclesiastes proclaims, "The light is sweet, and a pleasant thing it is for the eyes to behold the sun." Architecture organizes a world, usually more tightly than nature, by centering that world on the earth by means of a building. By accentuating the natural symbolism of sunlight, sky, and horizon, sky-oriented architecture opens up a world that is symbolic of our projections into the future.

Such architecture discloses a world by drawing our attention to the sky bounded by a horizon. It accomplishes this by means of making a building appear high and centered within the sky, defying gravity, and tightly integrating the light of outer with inner space. Negatively, architecture that accents a world de-emphasizes the features that accent the earth. Thus, the manufactured materials, such as the steel and glass of the Seagram Building (Figure 6-6), help separate this building from the earth. Positively, architects can accent a world by turning their structures toward the sky in such a way that the horizon of the sky forms a spacious context. Architecture is an art of bounding as well as opening.

PERCEPTION KEY Sky-Oriented Architecture

1. Identify the most sky-oriented building in your local community. Photograph that building from an angle or angles that support your choice.

Stained glass, usually framed within a wall, is activated by penetrating light. Outside, the great western rose window of Chartres (Figure 6-3) is only of sculptural interest. Inside, on a sunny day, the cascade of flashing colors, especially blues, is overwhelming. No photograph can capture the sublimity. There is a "strangeness." Our sight is wired to see light falling on objects rather than shining through them.

2. Try to find in your local community any buildings with powerful stained glass. Do you think stained glass is generally sky-oriented?
3. Do you think stained glass should be classified as an independent art distinct from painting?

Barcelona's Antonio Gaudí created one of the most striking modern buildings in his Sagrada Família (Figures 6-15 to 6-17). Gaudí never lived to see the erection of the four towers that dominate the facade. The interior space is not yet covered with a roof, and this emphasizes the sky-orientation of the building. One's eye is lifted upward by almost every part of the building. Under construction for over a hundred years, it may be at least another hundred years before the church is completed. Work proceeds slowly, guided more or less by Gaudí's general designs. Gaudí developed details and structures based on organic forms of nature through irregular sweeping lines, shapes, and volumes. Geometric designs are subordinated. Textures vary greatly, often with strong contrasts between smooth and rough; and sometimes, especially in the towers, brilliantly colored pieces of glass and ceramics are embedded, sparkling in the sunlight. The effect is both sculptural—dense volumes activating the surrounding space—and organic, as if a forest of plants were stretching into the sky, searching for sunlight. The earth, despite its necessity, is superseded. This is a building for heaven.

FIGURE 6-15
Antonio Gaudí, Sagrada Família
(Church of the Holy Family, interior),
Barcelona. 1883–present. Gaudí
famously relied on organic forms to
create an idiosyncratic style.

©Vanni/Art Resource, NY

FIGURE 6-16
Sagrada Família, interior detail.
Gaudí merged traditional cathedral
details with flowing modern forms.

©Lee A. Jacobus

FIGURE 6-17
Sagrada Família, exterior detail.
Organic forms are clearly visible
on the exterior along with figures
typically found on the exteriors of
Gothic churches.

©Lee A. Jacobus

PERCEPTION KEY Sagrada Família

1. Compare Sagrada Família with Chartres (Figure 6-2). How do their sky-orientations differ? How are they similar? Compare Sagrada Família with any church well known to you. What are the differences?
2. Chartres, Sagrada Família, and Notre Dame-du-Haut (Figure 3-4) are all Catholic churches. Do they each reveal different expressions of religious values?

Axis Mundi

Early civilizations often express a need for a world by centering themselves in relation to the sky by means of an **axis mundi**. Mircea Eliade cites many instances, for example, among the nomadic Australians, whose economy is based on gathering food and hunting small game:

> According to the traditions of an Arunta tribe, the Achipla, in mythical times the divine being Numbakula cosmicized their future territory, created their Ancestor, and established their institutions. From the trunk of a gum tree Numbakula fashioned the sacred pole (*kauwa-auwa*) and, after anointing it with blood, climbed it and disappeared into the sky. This pole (the *axis mundi*) represents a cosmic axis, for it is around the sacred pole that territory becomes habitable, hence is transformed into a world. The sacred pole consequently plays an important role ritually. During their wanderings the Achipla always carry it with them and choose the direction they are to take by the direction toward which it bends. This allows them, while being continually on the move, to be always in "their world" and, at the same time, in communication with the sky into which Numbakula

vanished. For the pole to be broken denotes catastrophe; it is like "the end of the world," reversion to chaos. Spencer and Gillen report that once, when the pole was broken, "the entire clan were in consternation; they wandered about aimlessly for a time, and finally lay down on the ground together and waited for death to overtake them."[4]

Buildings that stretch up far above the land and nearby structures, such as Chartres and Sagrada Família, not only direct our eyes to the sky but also act as a center that orders the sunlight in such a way that a world with a horizon comes into view. The sky both opens up and takes on limits. Such buildings reach up like an *axis mundi,* and the sky reaches down to meet them in mutual embrace. And we are blessed with an orienting center, our motion being given direction and limits.

Defiance of Gravity

The stony logic of the press of the ***flying buttresses*** of Chartres and the arched roof, towers, and spires that carry on their upward thrust seem to overcome the binding of the earth, just as the stone birds on the walls seem about to break their bonds and fly out into the world. The reach up is full of vital force and finally comes to rest comfortably and securely in the bosom of the heavens. Mont-Saint-Michel is even more impressive in this respect, mainly because of the advantages of its site.

Perhaps Brunelleschi's dome of the Cathedral of Florence (Figure 6-18) is the most powerful structure ever built in seeming to defy gravity and achieving height in relation to its site. The eight outside ribs spring up to the cupola with tremendous energy, in part because they repeat the spring of the mountains that encircle

FIGURE 6-18
Filippo Brunelleschi, dome of the Cathedral of Florence. 1420–1436.
One of the great architectural achievements of the Renaissance, the cathedral still dominates the landscape of modern Florence.

©Douglas Pearson/Getty Images

[4]Source: Mircea Eliade, *The Sacred and the Profane*, trans. Willard R. Trask (New York: Harcourt, Brace, 1959), p. 32ff.

Florence. The dome, visible from almost everywhere in and around Florence, appears to be precisely centered in the Arno Valley, precisely as high as it should be in order to organize its sky. The world of Florence begins and ends at the still point of this dome of aspiration.

Integration of Light

When the light of outer space suffuses the light of inner space, especially when the light from the outside seems to dominate or draw the light from the inside, a world is accented. Inside Chartres, the light through the stained glass is so majestic that we cannot fail to imagine the light outside that is generating the transfiguration inside. For a medieval man like Abbot Suger, the effect was mystical, separating the earth from heaven:

> When the house of God, many colored as the radiance of precious jewels, called me from the cares of the world, then holy meditation led my mind to thoughts of piety, exalting my soul from the material to the immaterial, and I seemed to find myself, as it were, in

FIGURE 6-19
Hagia Sophia (Church of the Holy Wisdom of God), Istanbul. 532–537; restored 558, 975. Isadore and Anthemius were nonprofessional architects who used light materials to create a huge well-lighted interior.

©David Pearson/Alamy

some strange part of the universe which was neither wholly of the baseness of the earth, nor wholly of the serenity of heaven, but by the grace of God I seemed lifted in a mystic manner from this lower toward the upper sphere.

For a contemporary person, the stained glass is likely to be felt more as integrating rather than as separating us from a world. Hagia Sophia in Istanbul (Figure 6-19) has no stained glass, and its glass areas are completely dominated by the walls and dome. Yet the subtle placement of the relatively small windows, especially around the perimeter of the dome, seems to draw the light of the inner space up and out. Unlike the Pantheon, the great masses of Hagia Sophia seem to rise. The dome floats gently, despite its diameter of 107 feet, and the great enfolded space beneath is absorbed into the even greater open space outside. We imagine a world.

Sky-oriented architecture reveals the generative activity of a world. The energy of the sun is the ultimate source of all life. The light of the sun enables us to see the physical environment and guides our steps accordingly. "Arise, shine, for thy light is come" (Isaiah 60:1). The sky with its horizon provides a spacious context for our progress. The world of nature vaguely suggests the potentialities of the future. Architecture, however, tightly centers a world on the earth by means of its structures. This unification gives us orientation and security.

EARTH-RESTING ARCHITECTURE

Most architecture accents neither earth nor sky but rests on the earth, using the earth like a platform with the sky as background. *Earth-resting* buildings relate more or less harmoniously to the earth. Mies van der Rohe's residence for Edith Farnsworth (Figure 6-20) in Plano, Illinois, is an example of a very harmonious

FIGURE 6-20
Ludwig Mies van der Rohe,
Farnsworth Residence, Plano, Illinois.
1950. Mies insisted on building with
the interior structure visible from
all angles.

©Jon Miller/Hedrich Blessing, Chicago

relationship. Unlike sky-oriented architecture, the earth-resting type does not strongly organize the sky around itself, as with Chartres (Figure 6-2) or the Cathedral of Florence (Figure 6-18). The sky is involved with earth-resting architecture, of course, but more as backdrop.

With earth-resting architecture—unlike earth-rooted architecture—the earth does not appear as an organic part of the building, as in Wright's Kaufmann house (Figure 6-11). Rather, the earth appears as a stage. Earth-resting buildings, moreover, are usually cubes that avoid cantilevering structures, as in the Kaufmann house, as well as curving lines, as in the Sagrada Família (Figure 6-15). Earth-rooted architecture seems to "hug to" the earth, as with the Pantheon (Figure 6-14), or to grow out of the earth, as with the Kaufmann house. Earth-resting architecture, on the other hand, seems to "sit on" the earth. Thus, because it does not relate to its environment quite as strongly as earth-rooted and sky-oriented architecture, this kind of architecture usually tends to draw to itself more isolated attention with reference to its shape, articulation of the elements of its walls, lighting, and so on.

Earth-resting architecture is usually more appropriate than earth-rooted architecture when the site is severely bounded by other buildings. Perhaps this is a basic deficiency of Wright's Guggenheim Museum (Figure 6-7). In any case, it is obvious that if buildings were constructed close to the Kaufmann house—especially earth-resting or sky-oriented buildings—they would destroy much of the glory of Wright's creation.

EARTH-DOMINATING ARCHITECTURE

Unlike an earth-resting building, an *earth-dominating* building does not sit on but "rules over" the earth. There is a sense of power and aggression. And unlike earth-rooted buildings, such as the Pantheon (Figure 6-14) or the Kaufmann house (Figure 6-11), there is no feeling of an organic relationship between the building and the earth.

Earth-dominating buildings generally are easily identified. Any work of architecture *solicits* attention. But earth-dominating buildings *demand* attention. Usually earth-dominating buildings are large and massive, but those features do not necessarily express earth-dominance. For example, Versailles is huge and heavy, but its vast horizontal spread has, we think, the effect of earth-resting. The earth as a platform holds its own with the palace. You can sense this much better from the ground than from an aerial photograph (Figure 6-12). Study the East Wing of the National Gallery of Art (Figure 6-21). Do you think the building is earth-resting or earth-dominating? As you think about this, compare it to Sagrada Família (Figure 6-15). In Spain, Sagrada Familia is one of the best examples of earth-dominating architecture.

You may find it difficult to locate earth-dominating buildings in your community. Palaces are rare, except in very wealthy communities. Few churches exert anything close to the power of Chartres. Public buildings such as courthouses tend to avoid aggressive appearance. They are expected to be traditional and democratic. And buildings of commerce—from banks to malls—are meant to invite.

FIGURE 6-21
I. M. Pei, East Wing of the National Gallery of Art, Washington, D.C. 1974–1978. The East Wing contains modern and contemporary art. Pei's design features powerful geometric forms.

©Randy Duchaine/Alamy

COMBINATIONS OF TYPES

> **PERCEPTION KEY** The National Gallery and the Long Island Federal Courthouse
>
> 1. Compare I. M. Pei's East Wing addition to the National Gallery with Richard Meier's Courthouse. Which of these better respects the concept of form following function?
> 2. Which of these buildings is more earth-resting? Which is more earth-rooted?
> 3. I. M. Pei relies heavily on the geometric form of the triangle. How do the many triangles visible in I. M. Pei's East Wing (Figure 6-21) and the National Gallery of Art interior (Figure 6-22) express a source of power in the building? In terms of social values, why are these forms revelatory?
> 4. Which geometric forms dominate Meier's Courthouse (Figure 6-23)? In what way are those forms revelatory of the function of the building? In what way are they revelatory of social values?

It seems to us that the Courthouse might best be described as a combination of the earth-resting and the earth-rooted. The earth-resting features, such as the sky as a backdrop and the platform character of the earth, are fairly obvious. The earth-rootedness is also there, however, because of the powerful effect of the huge rotunda that rises at the entrance like a giant tree anchoring the building into the earth. The Courthouse does not just use the earth but seems to belong to it. Some critics have described the rotunda as a huge ugly nose that defaces a handsome face. What do you think? Meier, incidentally, is the architect of the famous Getty Museum in Los Angeles.

FIGURE 6-22
National Gallery of Art interior.
The interior space of the walkway connecting the two wings of the museum is lighted by the triangular skylights visible from the exterior.

©B. O'Kane/Alamy

FIGURE 6-23
Richard Meier, Long Island Federal Courthouse, Central Islip, New York.
2000. A stark white building, it is one of the largest courthouses in the nation. It is designed to accommodate public gatherings as well as numerous individual courts.

©Robert Polidori

Guggenheim Museum Bilbao and The Taj Mahal

Frank Gehry's Guggenheim Museum in Bilbao, Spain, 1991–1997 (Figures 6-24 to 6-26), was the culminating architectural sensation of the twentieth century, surpassing in interest even Wright's Guggenheim of 1959. Gehry, like many contemporary architects, often uses the computer to scan models and flesh out the possibilities

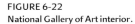

of his designs. The titanium-swathed structure changes drastically and yet harmoniously from every view: For example, from across the Nervion River that cuts through Bilbao the Guggenheim looks something like a whale. The locals say that from the bridge it looks like a colossal artichoke, from the south a bulging, blooming flower. The billowing volumes, mainly cylindrical, spiral upward, as if blown by gently sweeping winds.

Inside, smooth curves dominate perpendiculars and right angles, propelling visitors leisurely from each gallery or room to another with constantly changing perspectives, orderly without conventional order.

FIGURE 6-26
Guggenheim Museum Bilbao, interior. The sculpture is by Richard Serra.

©View Pictures/UIG/Getty Images

PERCEPTION KEY Guggenheim Museum Bilbao

1. Is the Guggenheim earth-rooted, earth-resting, earth-dominating, or sky-oriented? Could it be a combination? It would be helpful if you could examine more photographs (see, for instance, *Frank O. Gehry: The Complete Works*, by Francesco Dal Co and Kurt W. Forster [New York: Monacelli Press, 1998]).
2. Identify a building in your community that is an example of a combination of types. Photograph that building from the angle or angles that support your choice.

EXPERIENCING The Taj Mahal

1. Would you recognize the function of the building if you did not know its name?
2. Which type does this building fulfill, earth-resting, earth-rooted, or sky-oriented?
3. Compare The Taj Mahal with the Temple of Queen Hatshepsut *(Figure 6-1)*. Both are mortuary monuments to women. Which seems more gender-linked? Which is most earth-centered?
4. The Taj Mahal *(Figure 6-27)* has been described as a monument to the love of Shah Jehan for his wife Mumtaz Mahal. What formal qualities suggest that this building is revelatory of Shah Jehan's love? Of what else might the form of The Taj Mahal be considered revelatory?
5. Because the Pyramid of Cheops *(Figure 5-6)*, the Mortuary Temple of Hatshepsut, and The Taj Mahal are all mausoleums, is it possible to think of these buildings as revelatory of memorials to the dead? Which is more instantly recognizable as functioning as a tomb? What might they reveal about attitudes toward death?

continued

The Taj Mahal is one of the most famous buildings in the world. It was built as a monument to Shah Jehan's third wife, Mumtaz Mahal, who died in 1631. When you look at the building, its form is dazzling and compelling, but what is its function? What are the first thoughts that come to mind? For one thing, the minarets at the corner of the site were designed to be used for the call to prayer, so it is reasonable to think of the building as a mosque. There is a separate mosque on the grounds of The Taj Mahal, but The Taj Mahal itself is a mausoleum, a tomb that houses Shah Jehan and his wife Mumtaz Mahal, finished in 1648. The main level holds two sarcophagi (marble burial vaults) that are richly decorated with Arabic religious scripts, but because Islamic law prohibits elaborate decorations on the actual coffins, both Shah Jehan and Mumtaz Mahal are buried in simpler sarcophagi on a lower level, with their faces turned toward Mecca.

Shah Jehan constructed many buildings during his reign over the Mughal Empire in India. The Mughals, descendants of Mongols living in Turkestan, became Muslims in the fifteenth century. Notable for their arts, architecture, and respect for religious freedom, they dominated India in the sixteenth and seventeenth centuries. Their influences were Persian, as illustrated in the "onion" dome of the building, Islamic as illustrated by the copious script acting as decorative features throughout, and Indian as illustrated by the arched doors and windows. The majority population, Hindu citizens, were treated fairly, but the undoing of the great Mughal Empire came with the rise of Shah Jehan's son Aurangzeb, who imposed strict Sharia law on the entire populace and thus doomed the Mughals, whose empire was weakened by revolts and internal decay lasting another century and a half.

FIGURE 6-27
The Taj Mahal, Agra, Uttar Pradesh, India. 1653. Shah Jehan, the Mughal emperor, built The Taj in memory of his wife Mumtaz Mahal, who died in 1631. One of the most visited buildings in the world, it is in some danger because of the subsidence of a nearby river. Its architect, Ustad Ahmad Lahauri, was one of thousands of craftsmen and designers who finished the primary building in a little more than fifteen years.

©Seb c'est bien/Shutterstock RF

High-Rises and Skyscrapers

Some of the most dramatic examples of the combination of types occur when traditional architecture is fused with contemporary architecture, as happens quite often in China and Malaysia. With a population of over 8 million and rapidly growing, closely crowded around a huge and superb port, Kuala Lumpur had Argentine architect Cesar Pelli design the Petronas Towers (Figure 6-28), which was the tallest building in the world in 1996 and is still the tallest twin towers in the world.

From outside, the buildings of Hong Kong as a conglomerate appear overwhelmingly sky-oriented. Most of the skyscrapers appear to penetrate the heavens, aided in their thrust by the uplift of the background mountains. Photographs cannot do justice to this effect. The earthly tops of the Shanghai high-rise type are rare, and the Hong Kong buildings generally are considerably higher than those of Shanghai. "Skyscraper" more than "high-rise" more accurately describes these Hong Kong buildings. Sometimes verticality stretches so powerfully that even the diagonal struts of I. M. Pei's Bank of China Tower (Figure 6-29)—one of the tallest buildings in Hong Kong—may appear to stretch imaginatively beyond the top of the roof into vertical straight lines.

FIGURE 6-28
Petronas Twin Towers, Kuala
Lumpur, Malaysia. Cesar Pelli, 1993–
1996. The tallest twin towers in the
world, these buildings are influenced
by the traditional Buddhist temples
that were common in Southeast
Asia. The influence links temples of
spiritual contemplation with temples
of business.

©lim_atos/123rf.com

From inside the city, the architectural impressions of Hong Kong are generally another story (Figure 6-30). The skyscrapers usually abut, crowd, mirror, and slant into each other, often from odd angles, blocking a full view, closing and overwhelming the spaces between. Unlike New York City, where the grid of broad straight avenues provides breathing room for the skyscraper, the narrow crooked streets that dominate Hong Kong rarely allow for more than truncated views of the buildings. Except on the waterfront, only small patches of the sky are usually visible. The skyscrapers press down. Gravity is overbearing. Sometimes the atmosphere is

FIGURE 6-29
I. M. Pei, Bank of China Tower, Hong Kong. 1982–1990. At seventy-two stories high, this is Hong Kong's tallest building. One of Pei's challenges was to satisfy the needs of feng shui, the proper positioning of the building and its angles.

©QT Luong/terragalleria.com

FIGURE 6-30
Cityscape in Hong Kong. The crowding of buildings is typical in this small city.

©Michel Setboun/The Image Bank/Getty Images

claustrophobic. Inside Hong Kong the skyscrapers are usually more earth-dominating than sky-oriented. In New York City there are a few areas of this kind, but even there, Park Avenue provides an extensive clearing.

PERCEPTION KEY High-Rises in Asia

1. Examine the top structures of the high-rises in Hong Kong. Are these tops horizontally oriented as with the Seagram Building (Figure 6-6), or are they more vertically oriented as with The Taj Mahal?
2. Are these top structures suggestive of structures normally built on and belonging to the earth, such as temples, pagodas, restaurants, and porches?
3. The Chinese usually use the term "high-rise" rather than "skyscraper." Is this significant? If so, in what way?
4. A Chinese architect in Shanghai commented to one of the authors, "In our big cities we build high for practical purposes, just as in the West. But the culture of China is much more traditional than the culture of the West, especially in its arts. With painting, for example, it often takes an expert to identify a twentieth- or twenty-first-century work from earlier centuries. The painter begins by imitating a style and then evolves a style that never loses its roots. Likewise, the Chinese architect tends to be very sensitive to the styles of the past, and that past is more reverent to the earth than to the sky." Is this comment relevant to the toppings of many of the Asian high-rises?

The high-rise in Malmö, Sweden (Figure 6-31)—often described as the "Turning Torso"—by the Spanish architect Santiago Calatrava, provides splendid views for most of the 147 apartments. At the core of the building, stairs and elevators provide internal communication. The service rooms—kitchen, bath, and utilities—are grouped around that core, freeing the living-room spaces for the outside world. The tallest building in Scandinavia, the Turning Torso is bound by struts forming triangles, reducing the use of steel by about 20 percent compared to the conventional box structure such as the Seagram Building.

FIGURE 6-31
Santiago Calatrava, "Turning Torso," high-rise, Malmö, Sweden. 1999–2000. The twisting design derived from one of Calatrava's own sculptures.

©Johan Furusjo/Alamy

PERCEPTION KEY The Turning Torso

1. Is the building sky-oriented?
2. Is it earth-oriented?
3. Is it a combination?

It seems to the authors that the Turning Torso is a combination of sky- and earth-orientation. The horizontal gaps that divide the building disect powerful sweeping vertical edges. The top of the building, unlike the Kuala Lumpur example, has no earthlike structures. Surely this building, especially with its spatial isolation, is sky-oriented. And yet the aptly named Turning Torso seems to be twisting fantastically on the earth as one walks around it. Or from the perspective of our photograph, the building seems to be striding toward the right. Whatever the view, the Turning Torso is horizontally kinetic, totally unlike the static Seagram Building. The Turning Torso is an extraordinary example, we think, of a combination of sky-orientation and earth-domination, unlike the Hong Kong examples, which are sky-oriented and earth-resting.

Study the photograph of Norman Foster's Hearst Tower at Eighth Avenue and Fifty-Seventh Street, New York City (Figure 6-32) . Check the Internet for different

FIGURE 6-32
Norman Foster, Hearst Tower, New York City. 2006. The project was to build on top of a seventy-eight-year-old limestone building whose interior was essentially gutted to accommodate the tower, which rises sharply and suddenly above the conventional lower section.

©Chuck Choi/Arcaid/Getty Images

views. Don't miss this building if you are in New York City, viewing it from different angles. The six lower floors of the original building were gutted except for the four facades. Thus, the tower seems to rise from the top of the facades, which strangely appear to provide a platform.

> ## PERCEPTION KEY Hearst Tower
>
> 1. Does the tower strike you as more or less interesting than the two adjoining skyscrapers? Why?
> 2. Would you describe the building as earth-rooted, earth-dominating, sky-oriented, or some combination? As you think about this, notice how the great triangular panels of glass reflect the sky (at night, of course, there is the reflection of lights).
> 3. Compare the Hearst Tower with the two buildings near it. What is revelatory about the Hearst Tower that is not revelatory about the other buildings?

We suggest that the tower is most accurately described as sky-oriented. The platform's earth-resting effect is overwhelmed by the great soaring beautiful volumes of triangular glass. The tower overwhelms the earth. Its flat topping doesn't penetrate the sky, like the two fellow skyscrapers, but, with its reflecting glass mirrors, it merges with the sky. The tower would seem to be most accurately described as sky-oriented.

FOCUS ON The Alhambra

The Alhambra (Figure 6-33) is one of the world's most dazzling works of architecture. Its beginnings in the Middle Ages were modest, a fortress on a hilly flatland above Granada built by Arab invaders—Moors—who controlled much of Spain. In time, the fortress was added to, and by the fourteenth century the Nasrid dynasty demanded a sumptuous palace and King Yusuf I (1333–1352) began construction. After his death it was continued by his son Muhammad V (1353–1391).

While the needs of a fortress were still evident, including the plain massive exterior walls, the Nasrids wanted the interior to be luxurious, magnificent, and beautiful. The Alhambra is one of the world's most astounding examples of beautifully decorated architecture. The builders created a structure that was different from any that had been built in Islam. But at the same time, they depended on many historical traditions for interior decoration, such as the Seljuk, Mughal, and Fatimid styles. Because Islam forbade the reproduction in art of the human form, we see representations of flowers, plants, vines, and other natural objects in the midst of elaborate designs, including Arabic script.

The aerial view (Figure 6-34) reveals the siting of the Alhambra rising above trees surrounding it. The large square structure was added much later by Charles V, after the Nasrid dynasty collapsed and the Moors were driven from Spain.

The Alhambra was a fortress, a palace, and a residence for supportive staff, and it included a harem and a mosque. The structure of three inner courts was connected to functional complexes, such as a court of justice and a hall of welcoming for ambassadors, the largest interior room. The Court of the Myrtles is a large central space with a pool fed with water through ingenious management of a nearby river. The Court of the Lions (Figure 6-35) is the large reception hall, with doors leading to family tombs, the mosque, and other rooms. The fountain is surrounded by twelve lions, and a different lion spewed water each hour of the day and night.

The delicacy of the slender upright posts supporting Arabic arches is supplemented by the details of the muqarna—layers of stalagtite-like decorative tiles (Figure 6-36). The reflecting light illuminates the spaces above the head of the visitor. One of the authors, standing in the court, felt the sublimity of the colors and the lighting in the open spaces but also evident beneath the overhang leading to the outer rooms. His sense of participation yielded a revelation of the spiritual connection to the beautiful.

One of the unexpected delights of visiting the Alhambra is seeing how the architects took advantage of the very intense spring and summer sunshine in Grenada. The light bathes every surface, and because almost every surface is decorated with tile or with carvings, one

FIGURE 6-33
The Alhambra, Granada, Spain. Circa 1370–1380. "Alhambra" may be translated as red, possibly a reference to the color of the bricks of its outer walls. It sits on high ground above the town.

©Daniel Viñé Garcia/Getty Images RF

FIGURE 6-34
Aerial view of the Alhambra complex. The large square structure was added much later and destroyed part of the original complex. The exterior of the Alhambra is modest and typical of some early fortitifications.

©Manuel Hurtado/Shutterstock RF

continued

FIGURE 6-35
The Court of the Lions, the Alhambra. One of the largest open courts in the Alhambra, the space was for large receptions. The fountain was fed through a hydraulic system, with the lions spewing the fountain's water. Today all twelve lions spew water, but originally each lion took a turn each hour.

©Shaun Egan/Getty Images RF

FIGURE 6-36
Detail of decorations in the columnar supports in the Alhambra. The script is the motto of the Nasrid dynasty: "There is no victor but Allah." The motto of the Nasrid dynasty is repeated hundreds of times carved in stone. But recent examination of decorations in the lower half of the walls has revealed that some of the script is poetry, suggesting that inscriptions high on the ceiling—toward heaven—are drawn from the Qu'ran, while those below are humane.

©Paolo Gallo/Shutterstock RF

sees every design with clarity. The incised carvings on the capitals of each pillar hold a stylized phrase, such as the Nasrid motto, but the carvings yield to the light in surprising ways, changing and enriching the vista through the hours of the day. Today the Alhambra is lighted electrically, but when it was built we must imagine a rich firelight designed to warm the king and his harem. Moreover, the problem of intense summer heat is solved by the open spaces and fenestration (Figure 6-37) angled to the advantage of the prevailing breezes on the high ground.

After many generations of struggle, the Christian Spaniards drove the Moors out of Spain in 1492. Almost immediately, the Alhambra was desecrated and Charles V destroyed part of it to build a large castle with a circular interior space. People destroyed many of the things the Moors left behind, and in time the complex was abandoned to squatters. In the early 1800s English travelers—during the Romantic period—rediscovered the Alhambra and reconstruction and restoration began in earnest. What we see today is the result of more than 200 hundred years of careful uncovering and reclaiming the beauty of the original. Today it is one of the most visited places in Europe.

FIGURE 6-37
The Queen's Window, the Alhambra. One of the most outstanding vistas in the Alhambra, this window is sumptuous in its beauty in part because of the way the Grenadian light seems to wash every surface. The arch high above both openings is constructed of repeated muqarnas layered one receding row upon another. The intensely colored tile decorations on the lower half of the walls are typical of the Islamic effort to use natural forms for enriching the surfaces of almost every room.

©kossarev56/Shutterstock RF

URBAN PLANNING

Nowhere has the use of space become more critical in our time than in the city. In conclusion, therefore, the issues we have been discussing about space and architecture take on special relevance with respect to city planning.

The conglomerate architecture visible in Figure 6-38, surrounding a large church on Park Avenue, New York, makes us aware that the setting of many interesting

FIGURE 6-38
St. Bartholomew's Church on Park Avenue, New York City. 1902. Once a dominant building, it now seems dwarfed by nearby office buildings. Bertram Goodhue was the architect, with the portico done by McKim, Meade, and White.

©Lee A. Jacobus

buildings so completely overwhelms them that we hardly know how to respond. An urban planner might decide to unify styles of buildings or to separate buildings so as to permit us to participate with them more individually. The scene suggests that there has been little or no planning. Of course, some people might argue that such an accidental conglomeration is part of the charm of urban centers. One might feel, for example, that part of the pleasure of looking at a church is responding to its contrast with its surroundings. For some people, a special energy is achieved in such a grouping. A consensus is unlikely. Other people are likely to find the union of old and new styles—without first arranging some kind of happy marriage—a travesty. The dome of a church capped by a skyscraper! The church completely subdued by business! What do you think? These are the kinds of problems, along with political and social complications, that city planners must address.

Consider the view along a canal in Amsterdam (Figure 6-39). The regularity of the buildings implies a form of planning that limits the height and size of each structure. The scale of the city is measured in terms of an individual person—the city is a friendly place, small enough to be comprehended, large enough to provide all the services of a civilized center. In the streets of New York, Shanghai, and Hong Kong, one feels almost swallowed by the looming towers on all sides. In Amsterdam, with its bicycles and picturesque canals, one feels a sense of intimacy and welcoming. Because of the canals, the spaces between rows of buildings are open. Light streams in, even on overcast days.

Figure 6-40 shows the early development of Greenwich Village, New York City. Simplicity, economy, and symmetry determined the shape of buildings that were originally held to four- or five-story walk-ups. The buildings were frequently mixed use, with businesses on the first floor. Obviously the fire escapes, which dominate such buildings, were an afterthought.

FIGURE 6-39
Amsterdam street scene. Some of these buildings date back to the eighteenth century. Five stories seem to be the limit in this neighborhood. These are residential and businesses along the canal.

©Lee A. Jacobus

FIGURE 6-40
A typical facade on an anonymous building in Greenwich Village, New York City. The design is rudimentary and the buildings rarely more than four stories high. This is an earth-centered, humble structure.

©Lee A. Jacobus

PERCEPTION KEY Urban Views

1. Would you prefer to live in a humble building in Greenwich Village or in one of the buildings on a canal in Amsterdam?
2. Suppose St. Bartholomew's Church was no longer being used for religious purposes. As a city planner, would you preserve or destroy it?
3. Do you find the scene around the church visually attractive? Compare this scene with the main avenue of Dubai (Figure 6-41), a city audaciously built on the Persian Gulf in a few recent decades. Dubai's growth was planned and controlled; New York's growth was largely unplanned and little controlled. Would you prefer, other things being more or less equal, to live in a city with architecture like New York or architecture like Dubai?

Suppose spacious parking lots were located around the fringes of the city, rapid public transportation were readily available from those lots into the city, and in the city only public and emergency transportation—most of it underground—were permitted. In place of poisonous fumes, screeching noises, and jammed streets, there could be fresh air, fountains, flowers, sculpture, music, wide-open spaces to walk and talk in and enjoy, benches, and open theaters. Without the danger of being run over, all the diversified characters of a city—theaters, opera, concert halls, museums, shops, offices, restaurants, parks, squares—could take on some spatial unity. Furthermore, we could get to those various places without nervous prostration and the risk of life and limb.

One of the threats to cities around the world is the rising level of the oceans, a result of climate change. The Inuit people living near the North Pole are already

FIGURE 6-41
Main road, Dubai. This nation has been building high-rises and other structures in a pristine environment, making urban planning an absolute necessity.

©Simeone Huber/Getty Images

experiencing the subsidence of their old settlements near the edge of ice that has been secure for ages. People are leaving to move to more southerly areas to avoid calamity. The threats to island nations in the South Pacific have people worried about their future. The disappearance of island nations such as Micronesia—more than 600 islands spanning a million square miles of the Pacific—is already happening. The Seasteading project (Figure 6-42) hopes to provide floating islands for parts of French Polynesia, which is said to be threatened with destruction in less than half a century.

CONCEPTION KEY City Planning

1. Do you think the city ought to be saved? Why not just spread out, without the centralized functions of a city? What advantages does the city alone have? What still gives glamour to such cities as Florence, Venice, Rome, Paris, Vienna, and London?
2. Suppose you are a city planner for New York City, and assume that funds are available to implement your plans. What would you propose? How would you preserve or develop local neighborhoods? Would you start over or build on what exists?
3. Would you allow factories within the city limits? How would you handle transportation to and within the city? For instance, would you allow expressways to slice through the city, as in Detroit and Los Angeles? If you banned private cars from the city, what would you do with the streets? What transportation system would you favor?
4. If floating islands represent a solution to the rising of the oceans, what must they provide in terms of culture to make them livable? Cities are not just a matter of buildings. How can a floating island replicate the culture that it would save?
5. If floating islands are required to save a culture as different and widespread as Micronesia or French Polynesia, who should pay for building the islands? Should the nations who most contributed to the change in climate pay? Should they be responsible for designing and constructing the islands?

#1058

FIGURE 6-42
Seastead floating cities. A non-profit institute is planning floating cities for French Polynesia. The illustration shows a plan for bio-growing bubbles to supply food in the ocean.

Courtesy of the Seasteading Institute

Summary

Architecture is the creative conservation of centralized space—the power of the positioned interrelationships of things. The spatial centers of nature organize things around them, and architecture enhances these centers. Architects carve apart an inner space from an outer space in such a way that both spaces become more fully perceptible, and especially the inner space can be used for practical purposes. A work of architecture is a configurational center, a place of special value, a place to dwell. Architects must account for four basic and closely interrelated necessities: technical requirements, function, spatial relationships, and content. To succeed, their forms must adjust to these necessities. Because of the public character of architecture, moreover, the common or shared values of contemporary society usually are in a direct way a part of architects' subject matter. Architecture can be classified into four main types. Earth-rooted architecture brings out with special force the earth and its symbolisms. Such architecture appears organically related to the site, its materials, and gravity. Sky-oriented architecture brings out with special force the sky and its symbolisms. Such architecture discloses a world by drawing our attention to the sky bounded by a horizon. It accomplishes this positively by means of making a building high and centered within the sky, defying gravity, and tightly integrating the light of outer and inner space. Negatively, this kind of architecture de-emphasizes the features that accent the earth. Earth-resting architecture accents neither earth nor sky but rests on the earth, using the earth as a platform with the sky as backdrop. Earth-dominating architecture rules over the earth. There is a

161

sense of aggression, and such buildings seem to say that humanity is the measure of all things. In recent years, more and more combinations of these four types have been built.

If we have been near the truth, architects are the shepherds of space. And if we are sensitively aware of their buildings and their relationships, we help, in our humble way, to preserve their work. Architects can make space a welcoming place. Such places, like a home, give us a center from which we can orient ourselves to the other places around us. And then in a way we can feel at home anywhere.

©Art Collection 2/Alamy

Chapter 7

LITERATURE

Spoken Language and Literature

The basic medium of literature is spoken language. Eons before anyone thought to write it down, literature was spoken and sung aloud. Homer's great epics, *The Iliad* and *The Odyssey,* may date from 800 BCE or earlier. They were memorized by poets, who sang the epics to the plucking of a harplike instrument while entertaining royalty at feasts. The tradition of memorizing and reciting such immense works survived into the twentieth century.

In the Middle Ages, St. Augustine was surprised to see St. Ambrose reading without making a sound. Before the printing press was invented, monks copied books by hand, and they would speak the words softly to themselves as they wrote. In the fourteenth century, Geoffrey Chaucer wrote down his *Canterbury Tales* for convenience, more than a century before the invention of the printing press. But he read his tales out loud to an audience of courtly listeners who were much more attuned to hearing a good story than to reading it. Today people interested in literature are usually described as readers, which underscores the dependence we have developed on the printed word for our literary experiences. Yet words "sound" even when read silently, and the sound is an essential part of the sense, or meaning, of the words.

Literature—like music, dance, film, and drama—is a serial art. In order to perceive it, we must be aware of what is happening now, remember what happened before, and anticipate what is to come. This is not so obvious with a short lyric poem because we are in the presence of something akin to a painting: It seems to be all there in front of us all at once. But one word follows another: one sentence, one line, or one stanza after another. There is no way to perceive the all-at-onceness of a literary work as we sometimes perceive a painting, although short lyrics come close.

Most lyric poetry was intended to be spoken aloud, and few poems invite recitation more than John Masefield's 1902 poem, "Cargoes." Masefield, the poet laureate of Great Britain for much of his life, had many opportunities to hear English schoolchildren recite this poem for him.

CARGOES

Quinquireme of Nineveh from distant Ophir,
Rowing home to haven in sunny Palestine,
With a cargo of ivory,
And apes and peacocks,
Sandalwood, cedarwood, and sweet white wine.

Stately Spanish galleon coming from the Isthmus,
Dipping through the Tropics by the palm-green shores,
With a cargo of diamonds,
Emeralds, amethysts,
Topazes, and cinnamon, and gold moidores.

Dirty British coaster with a salt-caked smoke stack,
Butting through the Channel in the mad March days,
With a cargo of Tyne coal,
Road-rails, pig-lead,
Firewood, iron-ware, and cheap tin trays.

"Cargoes" is structured into three stanzas representing three historical eras. The first stanza, with its reference to Nineveh, a city in ancient Assyria older than the Bible, points to a marvelous age with incredible wealth and beauty. The Spanish galleon is a reference to the sixteenth century, when gold was brought from the new world to the kings and queens of Spain. The modern age is represented by a "Dirty British coaster" sailing in with a cargo of "pig lead" and "cheap tin trays." Masefield appears to be looking backward to periods of past glory against which the modern age looks tawdry.

The language of the poem is carefully chosen to imply the valuation he gives to each age, just as the brilliance and beauty of the selected cargo ship reveals the quality of that age. A Quinquireme is an ancient galley from more than 2000 years ago. It had three tiers of oars, with five men to each oar. When you say the word "Quinquireme" aloud you may imagine something of richness and beauty, which is what Masefield hopes you will see in your mind's eye. That ship carries cargo that stimulates and satisfies the senses: ivory, touch; peacocks, sight; sandalwood, smell; sweet white wine, taste; and the language, sound.

The Spanish galleon evokes pictures of the grandeur of the high seas in South America. It sails from the "Isthmus," Panama, and its cargo evokes images of wealth and royalty: diamonds, precious stones, and "gold moidores." Just saying the word "moidores" stimulates one to imagine great trunks of spilling magnificent gleaming gold coins.

The "Dirty British coaster," besmirched by its "salt-caked smoke stack" is, by comparison with the first two cargo ships, insignificant and crude. Its cargo may be important to commerce, but it is vulgar. Masefield chooses language carefully. Words like "coal," "Road-rails, pig-lead," and "cheap tin trays" do not come "trippingly off the tongue." Say them aloud and then go back and say the words describing earlier cargo. Masefield makes us feel, through the sound of the words, the distinction among three great historical eras.

> ## PERCEPTION KEY "Cargoes"
>
> 1. Read the poem aloud to someone who has not seen it before. What is his or her reaction to the sounds of the key words? How does he or she evaluate the three cargo ships and their cargoes?
> 2. Which historical era is most successfully represented by Masefield?
> 3. After reading the poem to a friend and asking for an opinion, explain that quin-quiremes were rowed by slaves chained to their seats. Explain that the Spanish galleons were bringing gold stolen from conquered Indians. Then explain to your friend that the British coaster was bringing cheap goods for a democratic society and the seamen were free. How do these details affect your friend's view of the poem? How does it affect your view of the poem?
> 4. Is it appropriate to respond to the poem by introducing information that Masefield may not have intended us to know? What details suggest that Masefield wanted you to ignore the unpleasant aspects of the social conditions of the ancient eras?
> 5. How does additional knowledge of the historical references in the poem condition your understanding of the subject matter of the poem? What is the poem's subject matter?
> 6. What do you think is the content of this poem?

Ezra Pound once said, "Great literature is simply language charged with meaning to the utmost possible degree." The ways in which writers intensify their language and "charge" it with meaning are many. First, they need to attend to the basic elements of literature because, like architecture, a work of literature is, in one sense, a construction of separable elements. The details of a scene, a character or event, or a group of symbols can be conceived of as the bricks in the wall of a literary structure. If one of these details is imperfectly perceived, our understanding of the function of that detail—and, in turn, of the total structure—will be incomplete.

The *theme* (main idea) of a literary work usually involves a structural decision, comparable to an architectural decision about the kind of space being enclosed. Decisions about the sound of the language, the characters, the events, the setting are comparable to the decisions regarding the materials, size, shape, and landscape of architecture. It is helpful to think of literature as works composed of elements that can be discussed individually in order to gain a more thorough perception of them. And it is equally important to realize that the discussion of these individual elements leads to a fuller understanding of the whole structure. Details are organized into parts, and these, in turn, are organized into structure.

Consider Amy Lowell's 1919 poem:

VENUS TRANSIENS*

Tell me,
Was Venus more beautiful
Than you are,

---

*Amy Lowell, "Venus Transiens" from *Poetry: A Magazine of Verse,* ed. Harriet Monroe, April 1915.

When she topped
The crinkled waves,
Drifting shoreward
On her plaited shell?
Was Botticelli's vision
Fairer than mine;
And were the painted rosebuds
He tossed his lady,
Of better worth
Than the words I blow about you
To cover your too great loveliness
As with a gauze
Of misted silver?
For me,
You stand poised
In the blue and buoyant air,
Cinctured by bright winds,
Treading the sunlight
And the waves which precede you
Ripple and stir
The sands at my feet.

Amy Lowell was one of the Imagist School of poets. Imagists relied less on the kind of discourse that John Masefield employed and more on the effort to paint a picture. The references to "crinkled waves," "plaited shell," "painted rosebuds," and "a gauze / Of misted silver" all demand visualization on the part of the reader. The poem begins with three rhetorical questions that the imagery indirectly answers.

The reference in the title is to the *Birth of Venus*, the Renaissance painting of Venus, goddess of love, standing on a seashell on the edge of the ocean, by Sandro Botticelli. Botticelli's Venus is a nude idealizing beauty. Lowell imagines her lover, Amy Dwyer Russell, with whom she lived from 1912 to 1925, as Venus.

The power of imagery in "You stand poised / In the blue and buoyant air, / Cinctured by bright winds / Treading the sunlight" conjures a picture of beauty and desire, emblematic of the goddess of love and the idealization of the living woman to whom the poem is addressed.

Our structural emphasis in the following pages will be on the narrative—both the episodic narrative, in which all or most of the parts are loosely interrelated, and the organic narrative, in which the parts are tightly interrelated. Once we have explored some of the basic structures of literature, we will examine some of the more important details. In everyday language situations, what we say is usually what we mean. But in a work of literature, language is rarely that simple. Language has **denotation**, a literal level where words mean what they obviously say, and **connotation**, a subtler level where words mean more than they obviously say. When we are being denotative, we say the rose is sick and mean nothing more than that. But if we are using language connotatively, we might mean any of several things by such a statement. When the poet William Blake says the rose is sick (see "The Sick Rose" later in this chapter), he is describing a symbolic rose, something very different from a literal rose. Blake may mean that the rose is morally sick, spiritually defective, and that in some ways we are like the rose. The image, metaphor, symbol, irony, and diction (word choices) are the main details of literary language that will be examined. All are found in poetry, fiction, drama, and even the essay.

LITERARY STRUCTURES

The Narrative and the Narrator

The **narrative** is a story told to an audience by a teller controlling the order of events and the emphasis those events receive. Most narratives concentrate upon the events. But some narratives have little action: They reveal depth of character through responses to action. Sometimes the **narrator** is a character in the fiction; sometimes the narrator pretends an awareness of an audience other than the reader. However, the author controls the narrator; and the narrator controls the reader. Participate with the following narrative poem by Alfred, Lord Tennyson.

ULYSSES

It little profits that an idle king,
By this still hearth, among these barren crags,
Match'd with an aged wife, I mete and dole
Unequal laws unto a savage race,
That hoard, and sleep, and feed, and know not me.
I cannot rest from travel; I will drink
Life to the lees. All times I have enjoy'd
Greatly, have suffer'd greatly, both with those
That loved me, and alone; on shore, and when
Thro' scudding drifts the rainy Hyades
Vext the dim sea. I am become a name;
For always roaming with a hungry heart
Much have I seen and known,– cities of men
And manners, climates, councils, governments,
Myself not least, but honor'd of them all,–
And drunk delight of battle with my peers,
Far on the ringing plains of windy Troy.
I am a part of all that I have met;
Yet all experience is an arch wherethro'
Gleams that untravell'd world whose margin fades
For ever and for ever when I move.
How dull it is to pause, to make an end,
To rust unburnish'd, not to shine in use!
As tho' to breathe were life! Life piled on life
Were all too little, and of one to me
Little remains; but every hour is saved
From that eternal silence, something more,
A bringer of new things; and vile it were
For some three suns to store and hoard myself,
And this gray spirit yearning in desire
To follow knowledge like a sinking star,
Beyond the utmost bound of human thought.

This is my son, mine own Telemachus,
to whom I leave the sceptre and the isle,–

Well-loved of me, discerning to fulfill
This labor, by slow prudence to make mild
A rugged people, and thro' soft degrees
Subdue them to the useful and the good.
Most blameless is he, centred in the sphere
Of common duties, decent not to fail
In offices of tenderness, and pay
Meet adoration to my household gods,
When I am gone. He works his work, I mine.

There lies the port; the vessel puffs her sail;
There gloom the dark, broad seas. My mariners,
Souls that have toil'd, and wrought, and thought with me,--
That ever with a frolic welcome took
The thunder and the sunshine, and opposed
Free hearts, free foreheads,-- you and I are old;
Old age hath yet his honor and his toil.
Death closes all; but something ere the end,
Some work of noble note, may yet be done,
Not unbecoming men that strove with Gods.
The lights begin to twinkle from the rocks;
The long day wanes; the slow moon climbs; the deep
Moans round with many voices. Come, my friends.
'T is not too late to seek a newer world.
Push off, and sitting well in order smite
The sounding furrows; for my purpose holds
To sail beyond the sunset, and the baths
Of all the western stars, until I die.
It may be that the gulfs will wash us down;
It may be we shall touch the Happy Isles,
And see the great Achilles, whom we knew.
Tho' much is taken, much abides; and tho'
We are not now that strength which in old days
Moved earth and heaven, that which we are, we are,--
One equal temper of heroic hearts,
Made weak by time and fate, but strong in will
To strive, to seek, to find, and not to yield.

PERCEPTION KEY "Ulysses"

1. Who narrates this poem?
2. What do the events of the poem reveal about the narrator?
3. To whom is the narrator telling this story? Why?
4. Did the narrator have an exciting life? Is having an exciting life important for a full understanding of the poem?
5. What is the narrator telling us?
6. Where is the narrator while telling this story?

The narrator of "Ulysses" is Ulysses, the hero of Homer's *Odyssey*. Ulysses is the Roman name for the Greek hero Odysseus. In Homer, Ulysses spends ten years at the battle of Troy and another ten years coming home to Ithaca to his wife, Penelope. At the time of Tennyson's poem, the great hero is an old man, but he is tired of staying at home and anxious to test his mettle—to see if he can live a life of adventure. For Ulysses the question is whether he can find a way to make life worth living. Do you admire Ulysses for demanding that he go off again on an adventure, or do you think he should stay at home with his wife, who waited twenty years for him? How do you think Tennyson would have answered that question?

The Episodic Narrative

An *episodic narrative* describes one of the oldest kinds of literature, embodied by *epics* such as Homer's *Odyssey*. We are aware of the overall structure of the story centering on the adventures of Odysseus, but each adventure is almost a complete entity in itself. We develop a clear sense of the character of Odysseus as we follow him in his adventures, but this does not always happen in episodic literature. The adventures sometimes are not only completely disconnected from one another, but the thread that is intended to connect everything—the personality of the *protagonist* (the main character)—also may not be strong enough to keep things together. Sometimes the character may even seem to be a different person from one episode to the next. This is often the case in oral literature, compositions by people who told or sang traditional stories rather than by people who wrote their narratives. In oral literature, the tellers or singers may have gathered adventures from many sources and joined them in one long narrative. The likelihood of disconnectedness in such a situation is quite high. But disconnectedness is sometimes desirable. It may offer compression, speed of pacing, and variety of action that sustains attention. Some of the most famous episodic narratives are novels: Fielding's *Tom Jones,* Defoe's *Moll Flanders,* and Saul Bellow's *The Adventures of Augie March.* The following excerpt is an episode from Miguel de Cervantes's *Don Quixote.*

CHAPTER VIII. OF THE GOOD FORTUNE WHICH THE VALIANT DON QUIXOTE HAD IN THE TERRIBLE AND UNDREAMT-OF ADVENTURE OF THE WINDMILLS, WITH OTHER OCCURRENCES WORTHY TO BE FITLY RECORDED

At this point they came in sight of thirty or forty windmills that there are on plain, and as soon as Don Quixote saw them he said to his squire, "Fortune is arranging matters for us better than we could have shaped our desires ourselves, for look there, friend Sancho Panza, where thirty or more monstrous giants present themselves, all of whom I mean to engage in battle and slay, and with whose spoils we shall begin to make our fortunes; for this is righteous warfare, and it is God's good service to sweep so evil a breed from off the face of the earth."

"What giants?" said Sancho Panza.

"Those thou seest there," answered his master, "with the long arms, and some have them nearly two leagues long."

"Look, your worship," said Sancho; "what we see there are not giants but windmills, and what seem to be their arms are the sails that turned by the wind make the millstone go."

"It is easy to see," replied Don Quixote, "that thou art not used to this business of adventures; those are giants; and if thou art afraid, away with thee out of this and betake thyself to prayer while I engage them in fierce and unequal combat."

So saying, he gave the spur to his steed Rocinante, heedless of the cries his squire Sancho sent after him, warning him that most certainly they were windmills and not giants he was going to attack. He, however, was so positive they were giants that he neither heard the cries of Sancho, nor perceived, near as he was, what they were, but made at them shouting, "Fly not, cowards and vile beings, for a single knight attacks you."

A slight breeze at this moment sprang up, and the great sails began to move, seeing which Don Quixote exclaimed, "Though ye flourish more arms than the giant Briareus, ye have to reckon with me."

So saying, and commending himself with all his heart to his lady Dulcinea, imploring her to support him in such a peril, with lance in rest and covered by his buckler, he charged at Rocinante's fullest gallop and fell upon the first mill that stood in front of him; but as he drove his lance-point into the sail the wind whirled it round with such force that it shivered the lance to pieces, sweeping with it horse and rider, who went rolling over on the plain, in a sorry condition.

Sancho hastened to his assistance as fast as his ass could go, and when he came up found him unable to move, with such a shock had Rocinante fallen with him. "God bless me!" said Sancho, "did I not tell your worship to mind what you were about, for they were only windmills? and no one could have made any mistake about it but one who had something of the same kind in his head."

"Hush, friend Sancho," replied Don Quixote, "the fortunes of war more than any other are liable to frequent fluctuations; and moreover I think, and it is the truth, that that same sage Friston who carried off my study and books, has turned these giants into mills in order to rob me of the glory of vanquishing them, such is the enmity he bears me; but in the end his wicked arts will avail but little against my good sword."

"God order it as he may," said Sancho Panza, and helping him to rise got him up again on Rocinante, whose shoulder was half out; and then, discussing the late adventure, they followed the road to Puerto Lapice, for there, said Don Quixote, they could not fail to find adventures in abundance and variety, as it was a great thoroughfare.

For all that, he was much grieved at the loss of his lance, and saying so to his squire, he added, "I remember having read how a Spanish knight, Diego Perez de Vargas by name, having broken his sword in battle, tore from an oak a ponderous bough or branch, and with it did such things that day, and pounded so many Moors, that he got the surname of Machuca, and he and his descendants from that day forth were called Vargas y Machuca. I mention this because from the first oak I see I mean to rend such another branch, large and stout like that, with which I am determined and resolved to do such deeds that thou mayest deem thyself very fortunate in being found worthy to come and see them, and be an eyewitness of things that will with difficulty be believed."

"Be that as God will," said Sancho, "I believe it all as your worship says it; but straighten yourself a little, for you seem all on one side, may be from the shaking of the fall."

"That is the truth," said Don Quixote, "and if I make no complaint of the pain it is because knights-errant are not permitted to complain of any wound, even though their bowels be coming out through it."

"If so," said Sancho, "I have nothing to say; but God knows I would rather your worship complained when anything ailed you. For my part, I confess I must complain however small the ache may be; unless this rule about not complaining extends to the squires of knights-errant also."

Don Quixote could not help laughing at his squire's simplicity, and he assured him he might complain whenever and however he chose, just as he liked, for, so far, he had never read of anything to the contrary in the order of knighthood.

—tr. John Ormsby

> **PERCEPTION KEY** Episodic Narrative: *Don Quixote*
>
> 1. For which character is this action an adventure?
> 2. What tells you that there will be more adventures?
> 3. How well do we know the personality of Quixote? Of Sancho Panza?
> 4. What is the subject matter of the narrative? What is its content?
> 5. Determine how much Cervantes is emphasizing the action at the expense of developing the characters. Is action or psychology more important?

Miguel de Cervantes Saavedra called this episode, the seventh in the first book of *The Ingenious Gentleman Don Quixote de la Mancha,* "The Terrifying Adventure of the Windmills." It is one of more than a hundred episodes in the book, and it is the most memorable and most famous. The excerpt here is only a small part of that episode, but it gives a clear indication of the nature of the entire book. Quixote has driven himself a bit crazy through his reading of the adventures of the old-style knights and has imagined himself to be one. Therefore, if he is a knight he must have adventures, so he goes out to seek his fortune and runs into what he thinks are giants with long arms. Killing them will make him a hero, and he imagines that they guard a fortune that will pay the way for the rest of their adventures.

Don Quixote rides the aging Rocinante and dreams of his heroine, the "lady Dulcinea," a local girl who hardly knows he is alive. Quixote's squire, Sancho Panza, is a simple man riding an ass. As the episodes go on he longs more and more for home but cannot persuade his aging and frail companion to stop looking for more adventures.

Since Cervantes wrote this book in the seventeenth century (contemporary with Shakespeare), literature has been drenched with adventurers and their sidekicks. Hundreds of novels, films, television shows, and radio plays have featured the pattern of the heroic avenger righting wrongs with the aid of a devoted assistant. Sherlock Holmes and Dr. Watson, the Lone Ranger and Tonto, Batman and Robin are only a few of the incredible number spawned by the genius of Cervantes. The episodic narrative works best when the character of the protagonist is clearly portrayed and consistent throughout. Don Quixote is such a character, so clearly portrayed he has become a part of folklore.

The Organic Narrative

The term *organic* implies a close relationship of all the details in a narrative. Unlike episodic narratives, the **organic narrative** unifies both the events of the narrative and the nature of the character or characters in it. Everything relates to the center of the narrative in a meaningful way so that there is a consistency to the story that is not broken into separable narratives. An organic narrative can be a narrative poem or a prose narrative of any length, so long as the material in the narrative coheres and produces a sense of unity.

The following short story, Maxim Gorky's "Her Lover," is first-person narration, in which the narrative is limited to what the unnamed narrator has been told by a friend, who, essentially, is also an unnamed narrator. The student tells us the story he heard about Teresa, an unfortunate woman living alone and friendless in the same kind of simplicity as the narrator. In the course of the story the narrator reveals that his sense of class superiority is slowly challenged when he understands the complete dimension of the circumstances of Teresa's life and her need for love. As you read, consider how the characters relate to one another and how Gorky uses the details of the narrative to build sympathy for Teresa's situation.

HER LOVER

An acquaintance of mine once told me the following story.

When I was a student at Moscow I happened to live alongside one of those ladies whose repute is questionable. She was a Pole, and they called her Teresa. She was a tallish, powerfully-built brunette, with black, bushy eyebrows and a large coarse face as if carved out by a hatchet—the bestial gleam of her dark eyes, her thick bass voice, her cabman-like gait and her immense muscular vigour, worthy of a fishwife, inspired me with horror. I lived on the top flight and her garret was opposite to mine. I never left my door open when I knew her to be at home. But this, after all, was a very rare occurrence. Sometimes I chanced to meet her on the staircase or in the yard, and she would smile upon me with a smile which seemed to me to be sly and cynical. Occasionally, I saw her drunk, with bleary eyes, tousled hair, and a particularly hideous grin. On such occasions she would speak to me.

"How d'ye do, Mr. Student!" and her stupid laugh would still further intensify my loathing of her. I should have liked to have changed my quarters in order to have avoided such encounters and greetings; but my little chamber was a nice one, and there was such a wide view from the window, and it was always so quiet in the street below—so I endured.

And one morning I was sprawling on my couch, trying to find some sort of excuse for not attending my class, when the door opened, and the bass voice of Teresa the loathsome resounded from my threshold:

"Good health to you, Mr. Student!"

"What do you want?" I said. I saw that her face was confused and supplicatory . . . It was a very unusual sort of face for her.

"Sir! I want to beg a favour of you. Will you grant it me?"

I lay there silent, and thought to myself:

"Gracious! . . . Courage, my boy!"

"I want to send a letter home, that's what it is," she said; her voice was beseeching, soft, timid.

"Deuce take you!" I thought; but up I jumped, sat down at my table, took a sheet of paper, and said:

"Come here, sit down, and dictate!"

She came, sat down very gingerly on a chair, and looked at me with a guilty look.

"Well, to whom do you want to write?"

"To Boleslav Kashput, at the town of Svieptziana, on the Warsaw Road . . ."

"Well, fire away!"

"My dear Boles . . . my darling . . . my faithful lover. May the Mother of God protect thee! Thou heart of gold, why hast thou not written for such a long time to thy sorrowing little dove, Teresa?"

I very nearly burst out laughing. "A sorrowing little dove!" more than five feet high, with fists a stone and more in weight, and as black a face as if the little dove had lived all its life in a chimney, and had never once washed itself! Restraining myself somehow, I asked:

"Who is this Bolest?"

"Boles, Mr. Student," she said, as if offended with me for blundering over the name, "he is Boles—my young man."

"Young man!"

"Why are you so surprised, sir? Cannot I, a girl, have a young man?"

She? A girl? Well! "Oh, why not?" I said. "All things are possible. And has he been your young man long?"

"Six years."

"Oh, ho!" I thought. "Well, let us write your letter . . ."

And I tell you plainly that I would willingly have changed places with this Boles if his fair correspondent had been not Teresa but something less than she.

"I thank you most heartily, sir, for your kind services," said Teresa to me, with a curtsey. "Perhaps *I* can show *you* some service, eh?"

"No, I most humbly thank you all the same."

"Perhaps, sir, your shirts or your trousers may want a little mending?" I felt that this mastodon in petticoats had made me grow quite red with shame, and I told her pretty sharply that I had no need whatever of her services.

She departed.

A week or two passed away. It was evening. I was sitting at my window whistling and thinking of some expedient for enabling me to get away from myself. I was bored; the weather was dirty. I didn't want to go out, and out of sheer ennui I began a course of self-analysis and reflection. This also was dull enough work, but I didn't care about doing anything else. Then the door opened. Heaven be praised! Some one came in.

"Oh, Mr. Student, you have no pressing business, I hope?"

It was Teresa. Humph!

"No. What is it?"

"I was going to ask you, sir, to write me another letter."

"Very well! To Boles, eh?"

"No, this time it is from him."

"Wha-at?"

"Stupid that I am! It is not for me, Mr. Student, I beg your pardon. It is for a friend of mine, that is to say, not a friend but an acquaintance—a man acquaintance. He has a sweetheart just like me here, Teresa. That's how it is. Will you, sir, write a letter to this Teresa?"

I looked at her—her face was troubled, her fingers were trembling. I was a bit fogged at first—and then I guessed how it was.

"Look here, my lady," I said, "there are no Boleses or Teresas at all, and you've been telling me a pack of lies. Don't you come sneaking about me any longer. I have no wish whatever to cultivate your acquaintance. Do you understand?"

And suddenly she grew strangely terrified and distraught; she began to shift from foot to foot without moving from the place, and spluttered comically, as if she wanted to say something and couldn't. I waited to see what would come of all this, and I saw and felt that, apparently, I had made a great mistake in suspecting her of wishing to draw me from the path of righteousness. It was evidently something very different.

"Mr. Student!" she began, and suddenly, waving her hand, she turned abruptly towards the door and went out. I remained with a very unpleasant feeling in my mind. I listened. Her door was flung violently to—plainly the poor wench was very angry . . . I thought it over, and resolved to go to her, and, inviting her to come in here, write everything she wanted.

I entered her apartment. I looked round. She was sitting at the table, leaning on her elbows, with her head in her hands.

"Listen to me," I said.

Now, whenever I come to this point in my story, I always feel horribly awkward and idiotic. Well, well!

"Listen to me," I said.

She leaped from her seat, came towards me with flashing eyes, and laying her hands on my shoulders, began to whisper, or rather to hum in her peculiar bass voice:

"Look you, now! It's like this. There's no Boles at all, and there's no Teresa either. But what's that to you? Is it a hard thing for you to draw your pen over paper? Eh? Ah, and *you*, too! Still such a little fair-haired boy! There's nobody at all, neither Boles, nor Teresa, only me. There you have it, and much good may it do you!"

"Pardon me!" said I, altogether flabbergasted by such a reception, "what is it all about? There's no Boles, you say?"

"No. So it is."

"And no Teresa either?"

"And no Teresa. I'm Teresa."

I didn't understand it at all. I fixed my eyes upon her, and tried to make out which of us was taking leave of his or her senses. But she went again to the table, searched about for something, came back to me, and said in an offended tone:

"If it was so hard for you to write to Boles, look, there's your letter, take it! Others will write for me."

I looked. In her hand was my letter to Boles. Phew!

"Listen, Teresa! What is the meaning of all this? Why must you get others to write for you when I have already written it, and you haven't sent it?"

"Sent it where?"

"Why, to this—Boles."

"There's no such person."

I absolutely did not understand it. There was nothing for me but to spit and go. Then she explained.

"What is it?" she said, still offended. "There's no such person, I tell you," and she extended her arms as if she herself did not understand why there should be no such person. "But I wanted him to be . . . Am I then not a human creature like the rest of them? Yes, yes, I know, I know, of course . . . Yet no harm was done to any one by my writing to him that I can see . . ."

"Pardon me—to whom?"

"To Boles, of course."

"But he doesn't exist."

"Alas! alas! But what if he doesn't? He doesn't exist, but he *might!* I write to him, and it looks as if he did exist. And Teresa—that's me, and he replies to me, and then I write to him again . . ."

I understood at last. And I felt so sick, so miserable, so ashamed, somehow. Alongside of me, not three yards away, lived a human creature who had nobody in the world to treat her kindly, affectionately, and this human being had invented a friend for herself!

"Look, now! you wrote me a letter to Boles, and I gave it to some one else to read it to me; and when they read it to me I listened and fancied that Boles was there. And I asked you to write me a letter from Boles to Teresa—that is to me. When they write such a letter for me, and read it to me, I feel quite sure that Boles is there. And life grows easier for me in consequence."

"Deuce take you for a blockhead!" said I to myself when I heard this.

And from thenceforth, regularly, twice a week, I wrote a letter to Boles, and an answer from Boles to Teresa. I wrote those answers well . . . She, of course, listened to them, and wept like anything, roared, I should say, with her bass voice. And in return for my thus moving her to tears by real letters from the imaginary Boles, she began to mend the holes I had in my socks, shirts, and other articles of clothing. Subsequently, about three months after this history began, they put her in prison for something or other. No doubt by this time she is dead.

My acquaintance shook the ash from his cigarette, looked pensively up at the sky, and thus concluded:

Well, well, the more a human creature has tasted of bitter things the more it hungers after the sweet things of life. And we, wrapped round in the rags of our virtues, and regarding others through the mist of our self-sufficiency, and persuaded of our universal impeccability, do not understand this.

And the whole thing turns out pretty stupidly—and very cruelly. The fallen classes, we say. And who are the fallen classes, I should like to know? They are, first of all, people with the same bones, flesh, and blood and nerves as ourselves. We have been told this day after day for ages. And we actually listen—and the devil only knows how hideous the whole thing is. Or are we completely depraved by the loud sermonising of humanism? In reality, we also are fallen folks, and, so far as I can see, very deeply fallen into the abyss of self-sufficiency and the conviction of our own superiority. But enough of this. It is all as old as the hills—so old that it is a shame to speak of it. Very old indeed—yes, that's what it is!

—Anonymous translator

PERCEPTION KEY Narrator in "Her Lover"

1. Who narrates the story?
2. What is the attitude of the student narrator? Why does he hold the social views that he begins the story with?
3. How does the narrator present Teresa to us? What does he expect our view of Teresa will be?
4. How many levels of narrative are in this story?
5. Gorky reveals a change in the narrator's views about Teresa and humanity. When does that change begin to take place?
6. To what extent do you as a reader find yourself accepting the student's point of view in the beginning of the story? What change does this story effect in you?
7. Do you believe that the story itself comes from "an acquaintance," or is it the primary narrator's story?

The first-level narrator is first person, but we do not know who he is. The second-level narrator is known only as "Mr. Student," which tells us that he has had little interaction with Teresa but that Teresa knows he can write, which she cannot. The social status of the two characters in the story is established in the first few words. The young student regards the older woman with some contempt. The student says she is a "powerfully-built brunette, with black, bushy eyebrows and a large coarse face as if carved out by a hatchet—the bestial gleam of her dark eyes, her thick bass voice, her cabman-like gait and her immense muscular vigour, worthy of a fishwife." She "inspired me with horror." The narrator expects his listener to picture Teresa and agree with his view of her.

Gorky's use of two levels of narration has the effect of separating the observer of the original narrative from the narrator who has heard the story and passes it on to us. Therefore, there is a narrative distance on the part of the unnamed man who tells us the story—and that permits him to set the story up in a way that helps us understand better the change that happens to the characters. The unnamed narrator does not judge the story that Mr. Student tells about his response to Teresa's requests.

We learn very quickly that while Mr. Student thinks of himself as superior to Teresa, she sees them as both on the same social level. She does not judge him the way he judges her. She also does not see herself as he sees herself as "a little dove." When he reacts in astonishment at her writing a love letter, she says, "Cannot I, a girl, have a young man?" The narrator then learns that Boles has been her "young man" for six years. It is at this point that the narrator begins to alter his thinking about her.

Gorky uses many narrative techniques, such as irony, comparison and contrast, and the revelation of the psychological interior of his character. We are given insight into Mr. Student's thoughts, into his psychology, which is marked by a sense of superiority because of his education and Teresa's lack of education. Mr. Student also judges Teresa on her appearance and only begins to change his feelings about her after listening to her expressing her need for love. The letters she writes to Boles never arrive. The letters she writes as Boles to herself provide her with a sense of happiness. The very act of writing has made her happy. The act of writing the letters changed Mr. Student, who said, "I understood at last. And I felt so sick, so miserable, so ashamed, somehow. Alongside of me, not three yards away, lived a human creature who had nobody in the world to treat her kindly, affectionately, and this human being had invented a friend for herself!"

The story ends with the narrator reflecting not on Teresa and her "lover" but on himself and people like him (and us): "We also are fallen folks, and, so far as I can see, very deeply fallen into the abyss of self-sufficiency and the conviction of our own superiority."

The Quest Narrative

The *quest narrative* is simple enough on the surface: A protagonist sets out in search of something valuable that must be found at all cost. Such, in simple terms, is the plot of almost every adventure yarn and adventure film ever written. However, where most such yarns and films content themselves with erecting impossible obstacles that the heroes overcome with courage, imagination, and skill, the quest narrative has other virtues. Herman Melville's *Moby-Dick,* the story of Ahab's determination to find and kill the white whale that took his leg, is also a quest narrative. It achieves unity by focusing on the quest and its object. But at the same time, it explores in great depth the psychology of all those who take part in the adventure. Ahab becomes a monomaniac, a man who obsessively concentrates on one thing. The narrator, Ishmael, is like an Old Testament prophet in that he has lived the experience, has looked into the face of evil, and has come back to tell the story to anyone who will listen, hoping to impart wisdom and sensibility to those who were not there. The novel is centered on the question of good and evil. When the novel begins, those values seem fairly clear and well defined. But as the novel progresses, the question becomes murkier and murkier because the actions of the novel begin a reversal of values that is often a hallmark of the quest narrative.

Because most humans feel uncertain about their own nature—where they have come from, who they are, where they are going—it is natural that writers from all cultures should invent fictions that string adventures and character development on the thread of the quest for self-understanding. This quest attracts our imaginations and sustains our attention. Then the author can broaden and deepen the meaning of the quest until it engages our concepts of ourselves. As a result, the reader usually identifies with the protagonist.

The quest structure in Ralph Ellison's *Invisible Man* is so deeply rooted in the novel that the protagonist has no name. We know a great deal about him because he narrates the story and tells us about himself. He is black, Southern, and, as a young college student, ambitious. His earliest heroes are George Washington Carver and Booker T. Washington. He craves the dignity and the opportunity he associates with their lives. But things go wrong. He is dismissed unjustly from his college in the South and must leave home to seek his fortune. He imagines himself destined for better things and eagerly pursues his fate, finding a place to live and work up North, beginning to find his identity as a black man. He discovers the sophisticated urban society of New York City, the political incongruities of communism, the complexities of black nationalism, and the subtleties of his relationship with white people, to whom he is an invisible man. Yet he does not hate the whites, and in his own image of himself he remains an invisible man. The novel ends with the protagonist in an underground place he has found and that he has lighted, by tapping the lines of the electric company, with almost 1400 electric lightbulbs. Despite this colossal illumination, he still cannot think of himself as visible. He ends his quest without discovering who he is beyond this fundamental fact: He is invisible. Black or white, we can identify in many ways with this quest, for Ellison is showing us that invisibility is in all of us.

PERCEPTION KEY **The Quest Narrative**

Read a quest narrative. Some suggestions: Ralph Ellison, *Invisible Man*; Mark Twain, *The Adventures of Huckleberry Finn*; Herman Melville, *Moby-Dick*; J. D. Salinger, *The Catcher in the Rye*; Graham Greene, *The Third Man*; Franz Kafka, *The Castle*; Albert Camus, *The Stranger*; and Toni Morrison, *Beloved*. How does the quest help the protagonist get to know himself or herself better? Does the quest help you understand yourself better? Is the quest novel you have read basically episodic or organic in structure?

The quest narrative is central to American culture. Mark Twain's *Huckleberry Finn* is one of the most important examples in American literature. But, whereas *Invisible Man* is an organic quest narrative, because the details of the novel are closely interwoven, *Huckleberry Finn* is an episodic quest narrative. Huck's travels along the great Mississippi River qualify as episodic in the same sense that *Don Quixote,* to which this novel is closely related, is episodic. Huck is questing for freedom for Jim, but also for freedom from his own father. Like Don Quixote, Huck comes back from his quest richer in the knowledge of who he is. One might say Don Quixote's quest is for the truth about who he is and was, since he is an old man when he begins. But Huck is an adolescent, and so his quest is for knowledge of who he is and can be.

The Lyric

The *lyric*, usually a poem, primarily reveals a limited but deep feeling about some thing or event. The lyric is often associated with the feelings of the poet, although it is not uncommon for poets to create narrators distinct from themselves and to explore hypothetical feelings, as in Tennyson's "Ulysses."

If we participate, we find ourselves caught up in the emotional situation of the lyric. It is usually revealed to us through a recounting of the circumstances the poet reflects on. T. S. Eliot speaks of an *objective correlative*: an object that correlates with the poet's feeling and helps express that feeling. Eliot has said that poets must find the image, situation, object, event, or person that "shall be the formula for that *particular* emotion" so that readers can comprehend it. This may be too narrow a view of the poet's creative process, because poets can understand and interpret emotions without necessarily undergoing them. Otherwise, it would seem that Shakespeare, for example, and even Eliot would have blown up like overcompressed boilers if they had had to experience directly all the feelings they interpreted in their poems. But, in any case, it seems clear that the lyric has feeling—emotion, passion, or mood—as basic in its subject matter.

The word "lyric" implies a personal statement by an involved writer who feels deeply. In a limited sense, lyrics are poems to be sung to music. Most lyrics before the seventeenth century were set to music—in fact, most medieval and Renaissance lyrics were written to be sung with musical accompaniment. And the writers who composed the words were usually the composers of the music—at least until the seventeenth century, when specialization began to separate those functions.

John Keats (1795–1821), an English poet of the Romantic period, died of tuberculosis. The following *sonnet* is grounded in his awareness of early death:

When I have fears that I may cease to be
Before my pen has glean'd my teeming brain,
Before high-piled books, in charact'ry,
Hold like rich garners the full-ripen'd grain;
When I behold, upon the night's starr'd face,
Huge cloudy symbols of a high romance,
And think that I may never live to trace
Their shadows, with the magic hand of chance;
And when I feel, fair creature of an hour!
That I shall never look upon thee more,
Never have relish in the faery power
Of unreflecting love! then on the shore
Of the wide world I stand alone, and think
Till love and fame to nothingness do sink.

> **PERCEPTION KEY** "When I Have Fears . . ."
>
> 1. This poem has no setting (environmental context), yet it establishes an atmosphere of uncertainty and, possibly, of terror. How does Keats create this atmosphere?
> 2. The poet is dying and knows he is dying—why does he then labor so over the rhyme and meter of this poem? What does the poem do for the dying narrator?
> 3. What do the rhyming words do to help clarify the content of the poem?

Keats interprets a terrible personal feeling. He realizes he may die before he can write his best poems. The epitaph Keats chose for his headstone just before he died, "Here lies one whose name was writ in water," is one of the most sorrowful lines of all poetry. He was wrong in believing that his poems would not be read by posterity. Moreover, his work is so brilliant that we cannot help wondering what else he might have done. Had Chaucer, Shakespeare, Milton, Proust, or Joyce died at twenty-six, we might not know their names, for their important work was yet to come.

It is not difficult for us to imagine how Keats must have felt. The lyric mode usually relies not on narrative but on our ability to respond to the circumstances described. In this poem, Keats has important resources. One is the fact that since we all will die, we can sympathize with the thought of death cutting a life's work short. The tone Keats establishes in the poem—one of direct speech, honestly said, not overdone or melodramatic—helps him communicate his feelings. It gives the poem an immediacy: one human being telling another something straight from the heart. Keats modulates the tone slightly, slowing things down enough at the end of the poem for us to sense and share the despairing contemplative mood "to nothingness do sink."

A different approach is apparent in John Donne's "Death Be Not Proud," a seventeenth-century poem by one of England's greatest churchmen. By personifying Death, Donne is able to comment on its power and the company it keeps. This is an example of a witty poem—wit being the imaginative power that finds the comparisons here: of death and sleep, death as a slave to fate, death as yielding to resurrection.

> Death be not proud, though some have called thee
> Mighty and dreadfull, for, thou art not soe,
> For, those, whom thou think'st, thou dost overthrow,
> Die not, poore death, nor yet canst thou kill mee.
> From rest and sleepe, which but thy pictures bee,
> Much pleasure, then from thee, much more must flow,
> And soonest our best men with thee doe goe,
> Rest of their bones, and soules deliverie.
> Thou art slave to Fate, Chance, kings, and desperate men,
> And dost with poyson, warre, and sicknesse dwell,
> And poppie, or charmes can make us sleepe as well,
> And better then thy stroake; why swell'st thou then?
> One short sleepe past, wee wake eternally,
> And death shall be no more; death, thou shalt die.

PERCEPTION KEY "Death Be Not Proud"

1. Read the poem aloud to a friend. Where do your emphases fall? Underline the emphatic words or syllables before you do the actual reading.
2. By comparison, read aloud any of the other lyrics in this section. How does the line structure of that poem control the way you read the lines? Where do the emphases fall? Try to characterize the differences between the line structures of the two poems.

Numerous lyric poems have inspired paintings and pieces of music. John Waterhouse's 1893 painting *La Belle Dame Sans Merci* (Figure 7-1) is an interpretation of the famous poem by John Keats. It is more than an illustration. Waterhouse imagines the knight yielding to an irresistible, childlike maiden. In keeping with the prescriptions of the Pre-Raphaelite Brotherhood, Waterhouse chooses a medieval setting and a romantic narrative.

FIGURE 7-1
John Waterhouse, *La Belle Dame Sans Merci*. 1893. Oil on Canvas. 43½ x 32 inches. Hessisches Landesmuseum, Darmstadt, Germany.

©Art Collection 2/Alamy

LA BELLE DAME SANS MERCI

Ah, what can ail thee, knight at arms,
Alone and palely loitering?
The sedge is withered from the lake,
        And no birds sing.

Ah, what can ail thee, knight at arms,
So haggard and so woe-begone?
The squirrel's granary is full,
        And the harvest's done.

I see a lily on thy brow,
With anguish moist and fever dew;
And on thy cheeks a fading rose
        Fast withereth too.

I met a lady in the meads
Full beautiful, a fairy's child;
Her hair was long, her foot was light,
        And her eyes were wild.

I made a garland for her head
And bracelets too, and fragrant zone;
She looked at me as she did love,
        And made sweet moan.

I set her on my pacing steed,
And nothing else saw all day long,
For sidelong would she bend, and sing
        A fairy's song.

She found me roots of relish sweet,
And honey wild, and manna dew;
And sure in language strange she said,
        I love thee true.

She took me to her elfin grot,
And there she gazed and sighed full sore,
And there I shut her wild wild eyes—
        With kisses four.

And there she lulled me asleep,
And there I dreamed, ah woe betide,
The latest dream I ever dreamed
        On the cold hill side.

I saw pale kings, and princes too,
Pale warriors, death-pale were they all;
They cried—"La belle Dame sans merci
        Hath thee in thrall!"

I saw their starved lips in the gloam
With horrid warning gaped wide,
And I awoke, and found me here
        On the cold hill's side.

And this is why I sojourn here,
Alone and palely loitering,
Though the sedge is withered from the lake,
And no birds sing.

1. "La Belle Dame Sans Merci" (the beautiful lady without pity) is a ballad. Ballads are often sung. What qualities would make this poem easy to sing?
2. Where and when does this poem seem to be set?
3. What does John Waterhouse's painting tell us about how he has interpreted the poem?
4. How important is visual imagery in this poem?
5. Comment on the power of repetition—of sounds, words, and stanzas. How does repetition create what some critics have called the "hypnotic power of this poem"?

The setting dominates the poem. The vegetation is "withered," "the harvest's done," and therefore it is cold and wintry. The first three stanzas are spoken by a narrator to the knight, who is "haggard and woe-begone." The narrator asks, "What can ail thee?" which tells us that the knight is not just sad but possibly ill. Keats wrote this poem sick with tuberculosis and knew he had very little time to live. He loved Fanny Brawne but could not marry her because of his illness. The imagery in the poem is solemn and threatening even to a knight. The fairy woman conquers him easily because he has no defenses. Is she a symbol of death? If so, why is she so appealing, so beautiful, so irresistible?

The knight, discovered by the narrator, is in shock. He has had an experience with "the other world" of fairy, a world that suggests the Middle Ages, when this poem seems to take place. In the early nineteenth century, the age of Romanticism, the idea of knights and otherworldly spirits was attractive to artists and poets alike. Images like the "lily on thy brow," a symbol of funerals and death, were common. The romantic notion of "making love with death" was also common in 1819 when this poem was written because people often died young.

The "lady in the meads" is a *femme fatalle*, dangerous and desirable. The knight cannot resist her and makes love with her. Medieval lore always warned against connubial affection with a woman of the spirit world. Usually it resulted in death. But in this poem the knight survives to tell his story because, ironically, the fairy takes pity on him after showing him in a dream "pale kings, and princes too, Pale warriors, death pale were they all." His vision was of the underworld, and the knight's own countenance is a mirror of that world in the second line of the poem when he is "alone and palely loitering." "Loitering" is a strange word to describe a knight, who is usually on a quest.

John Waterhouse's Pre-Raphaelite painting interprets the poem but includes tiny flowers and a lush spring landscape. The fairy is a lovely young woman luring the knight, in full armor, by winding her "long" hair around his neck. He is clearly as captured in the painting as in the poem.

Emily Dickinson lived in her family house for most of her life, never married, and kept most of her personal romantic interests to herself, so that biographers can only speculate on the kind of delight and joy that she seems to be describing in "I Taste a Liquor Never Brewed," which was originally published in *Poems* (1890), edited by Thomas Wentworth Higginson and Mabel Loomis Todd. Her method is to be indirect and not to specify the issues at the heart of her lyric. She uses metaphors, such as "Inebriate of air am I," which is both specific and yet completely abstract and untranslatable. We have no idea what precise intoxication she is talking about—perhaps the joy of finding love, or perhaps the mere joy of loving life itself. She talks about the headiness of inebriation without having resorted to any liquor known to man. She shares the same kind of intoxication that is experienced by the "drunken bee" and the butterfly among flowers. Even when they cease at the end of summer, she will continue to experience delight. She will continue to feel the delight of life until the angels ("seraphs") and the saints come to see her at the end of life.

XX.

I taste a liquor never brewed,
From tankards scooped in pearl;
Not all the vats upon the Rhine
Yield such an alcohol!

Inebriate of air am I,
And debauchee of dew,
Reeling, through endless summer days,
From inns of molten blue.

When landlords turn the drunken bee
Out of the foxglove's door,
When butterflies renounce their drams,
I shall but drink the more!

Till seraphs swing their snowy hats,
And saints to windows run,
To see the little tippler
Leaning against the sun!

PERCEPTION KEY "I Taste a Liquor Never Brewed"

1. Read the poem aloud. To what extent do the open vowels and the rich rhymes give a "musical" quality to your reading?
2. Listen to someone else read the poem and ask the same question: How musical is this poem?
3. Set the poem to music. If you are a musician, sing the poem aloud and decide what kind of emotional quality the poem has when set to music.
4. The imagery and language seem designed to describe an emotional state in the poet's or the reader's experience. Describe as best you can the emotional content of the poem.
5. Is this poem describing a positive experience or a negative experience? Does the indirectness of the imagery enhance the effect of the poem or limit it?
6. What do you think Emily Dickinson means by "inns of molten blue" and "debauchee of dew"? Who is the "little tippler" at the end of the poem?
7. How would you describe Emily Dickinson's relationship with nature?

LITERARY DETAILS

So far we have been analyzing literature with reference to structure, the overall order. But within every structure are details that need close examination in order to properly perceive the structure.

Language is used in literature in ways that differ from everyday uses. This is not to say that literature is artificial and unrelated to the language we speak but, rather, that we sometimes do not see the fullest implications of our speech and rarely take full advantage of the opportunities language affords us. Literature uses language to reveal meanings that are usually absent from daily speech.

Our examination of detail will include image, metaphor, symbol, irony, and diction. They are central to literature of all *genres*.

Image

An image in language asks us to imagine or "picture" what is referred to or being described. An image appeals essentially to our sense of sight, but sound, taste, odor, and touch are sometimes involved. One of the most striking resources of language is its capacity to help us reconstruct in our imaginations the "reality" of perceptions. This resource sometimes is as important in prose as in poetry. Consider, for example, the following passage from Joseph Conrad's *Youth:*

> The boats, fast astern, lay in a deep shadow, and all around I could see the circle of the sea lighted by the fire. A gigantic flame arose forward straight and clear. It flares fierce, with noises like the whirr of wings, with rumbles as of thunder. There were cracks, detonations, and from the cone of flame the sparks flew upwards, as man is born to trouble, to leaky ships, and to ships that burn.

PERCEPTION KEY Conrad's *Youth* and Imagery

1. What does Conrad ask us to see in this passage?
2. What does he ask us to hear?
3. What do his images make us feel?
4. Comment on the imageless second half of the last sentence.

In *Youth,* this scene is fleeting, only an instant in the total structure of the book. But the entire book is composed of such details, helping to engage the reader's participation.

Because of its tendency toward the succinct, poetry usually contains stronger images than prose, and poetry usually appeals more to our senses (Conrad's prose being an obvious exception). Listen to the following poem by T. S. Eliot:

I

PRELUDES

The winter evening settles down
With smell of steaks in passageways.
Six o'clock.
The burnt-out ends of smoky days.
And now a gusty shower wraps
The grimy scraps
Of withered leaves about your feet
And newspapers from vacant lots;

The showers beat
On broken blinds and chimney-pots,
And at the corner of the street
A lonely cab-horse steams and stamps.

And then the lighting of the lamps.

Source: T.S. Eliot, "Preludes," *Poems*, New York: Alfred A. Knopf, 1920. Alfred A. Knopf, a division of Random House, Inc.

PERCEPTION KEY "Preludes"

1. What happens in the poem? What does the title mean?
2. What senses are imaginatively stimulated?
3. Does the poem appeal to and evoke one particular sense more than the others? If so, which one and why?
4. Where is the poet? Is he talking to you?

In the early years of the twentieth century the imagist school of poetry developed, with the intention of writing poems that avoided argument and tried to say everything only in images. Ezra Pound's poem is one of the best examples of that approach.

IN A STATION OF THE METRO

The apparition of these faces in the crowd;
Petals on a wet, black bough.

The Metro is the subway system in Paris, which Pound used in 1916 when he wrote this poem. The poem is in two parts. Ask yourself how they relate to each other, and at the same time ask yourself which line has the image. How complete is this poem?

Metaphor

Metaphor helps writers intensify language. Metaphor is a comparison designed to heighten our perception of the things compared. For example, in the following poem, Shakespeare compares his age to the autumn of the year and himself to a glowing fire that consumes its vitality. The structure of this sonnet is marked by developing one metaphor in each of three quatrains (a group of four rhyming lines) and a couplet that offers a summation of the entire poem.

SONNET 73

That time of year thou mayst in me behold
When yellow leaves, or none, or few, do hang
Upon those boughs which shake against the cold,
Bare ruined choirs, where late the sweet birds sang.
In me thou see'st the twilight of such day

As after sunset fadeth in the west,
Which by and by black night doth take away,
Death's second self, that seals up all in rest.
In me thou see'st the glowing of such fire
That on the ashes of his youth doth lie,
As the death-bed whereon it must expire,
Consumed with that which it was nourished by.
    This thou perceiv'st, which makes thy love more strong,
    To love that well which thou must leave ere long.

> ### PERCEPTION KEY Shakespeare's 73rd Sonnet
>
> 1. The first metaphor compares the narrator's age with autumn. How are "yellow leaves, or none" appropriate for comparison with someone's age? What is implied by the comparison? The "bare ruined choirs" are the high place in the church—what place, physically, would they compare with in a person's body?
> 2. The second metaphor is the "sunset" fading "in the west." What is this compared with in someone's life? Why is the imagery of the second quatrain so effective?
> 3. The third metaphor is the "glowing" fire. What is the point of this metaphor? What is meant by the fire's consuming "that which it was nourished by"? What is being consumed here?
> 4. Why does the conclusion of the poem, which contains no metaphors, follow logically from the metaphors developed in the first three quatrains?

The standard definition of the metaphor is that it is a comparison made without any explicit words to tell us a comparison is being made. The *simile* is the kind of comparison that has explicit words: "like," "as," "than," "as if," and a few others. We have no trouble recognizing the simile, and we may get so used to reading similes in literature that we recognize them without any special degree of awareness.

The Chinese poet Wang Chang-Ling (698–756), a major T'ang dynasty poet, shows the power of the metaphor in a poetic tradition very different from that of the West.

SO-FEI GATHERING FLOWERS

In a dress of gauzy fabric
    Of the 'Lien' leaf's emerald hue
So-fei glides amongst the lilies
    Sprinkled with the morning dew.

Rose-hued are the lotus-blossoms,
    Rose-hued, too, the maiden's cheeks;
Is it So-fei's form I follow,
    Or the flowers she seeks?

Now I hear a song arising
    From the lotus bowers,
Which distinguishes the maiden
    From her sister flowers.

    —tr. Charles Budd

Wang Chang-Ling metaphorizes a beautiful young woman, So-fei, as a flower in her garden. She wears "gauzy fabric" and does not walk but "glides" among the lilies. Just as the lotus blossoms are rose hued, So-fei is "rose hued." The poet is so taken by the vision of So-fei that when he hears her singing he thinks this is the only way in which he can distinguish her "from her sister flowers." Instead of striking bluntly and immediately, the metaphoric language of Chang's poem resounds with such nuance that we are aware of its cumulative impact only after reading and rereading.

Metaphor pervades poetry, but we do not always realize how extensive the device is in other kinds of literature. Prose fiction, drama, essays, and almost every other form of writing use metaphors. Poetry in general, however, tends to have a higher metaphoric density than other forms of writing, partly because poetry is somewhat distilled and condensed to begin with.

Since literature depends so heavily on metaphor, it is essential that we reflect on its use. One kind of metaphor tends to evoke an image and involves us mainly on a perceptual level—because we perceive in our imaginations something of what we would perceive were we there. To see So-fei as sister to the flowers in her garden we need the description of the blossoms. This kind we shall call a *perceptual metaphor*. Another kind of metaphor tends to evoke ideas, gives us information that is mainly conceptual. This kind of metaphor we shall call a *conceptual metaphor*. The implications of seeing So-fei not only as a woman, but as a flower demands an act of cognition. Once we begin to make the comparison, many ideas may be introduced. For example, as the flower blooms for only a short time, are we to think that the poet is fearful that So-fei's beauty may fade quickly? One must be careful with metaphors.

Symbol

The *symbol* is a further use of metaphor. Being a metaphor, it is a comparison between two things, but unlike most perceptual and conceptual metaphors, only one of the things compared is clearly stated. The symbol is clearly stated, but what it is compared with (sometimes a very broad range of meanings) is only hinted at.

Perhaps the most important thing to remember about the symbol is that it implies rather than explicitly states meaning. We sense that we are dealing with a symbol in those linguistic situations in which we believe there is more being said than meets the eye. Most writers are quite open about their symbols, as William Blake was in his poetry. He saw God's handiwork everywhere, but he also saw forces of destruction everywhere. Thus, his poetry discovers symbols in almost every situation and/or thing, not just in those situations and things that are usually accepted as meaningful. The following poem is an example of Blake's technique. At first the poem may seem needlessly confusing, because we do not know how to interpret the symbols. But a second reading begins to clarify their meaning.

THE SICK ROSE

O rose, thou art sick!
  The invisible worm,
That flies in the night,
  In the howling storm,

Has found out thy bed
Of crimson joy;
And his dark secret love
Does thy life destroy.

Source: William Blake, "The Sick Rose," *Songs of Experience*, 1794.

PERCEPTION KEY **"The Sick Rose"**

1. The rose and the worm stand as opposites in this poem, symbolically antagonistic. In discussion with other readers, explore possible meanings for the rose and the worm.
2. The bed of crimson joy and the dark secret love are also symbols. What are their meanings? Consider them closely in relation to the rose and the worm.
3. What is not a symbol in this poem?

Blake used such symbols because he saw a richness of implication in them that linked him to God. He thus shared in a minor way the creative act with God and helped others understand the world in terms of symbolic meaningfulness. For most other writers, the symbol is used more modestly to expand meaning, encompassing deep ranges of suggestion. The symbol has been compared with a stone dropped into the still waters of a lake: The stone itself is very small, but the effects radiate from its center to the edges of the lake. The symbol is dropped into our imaginations, and it, too, radiates with meaning. But the marvelous thing about the symbol is that it tends to be permanently expansive: Who knows where the meaningfulness of Blake's rose ends?

Blake does not tell us that his rose and worm are symbolic, but we readily realize that the poem says very little worth listening to if we do not begin to go beyond its literal meaning. The fact that worms kill roses is more important to gardeners than it is to readers of poetry. But that there is a secret evil that travels mysteriously to kill beautiful things is not as important to gardeners as to readers of poetry.

Prose fiction has made extensive use of the symbol. In Melville's *Moby-Dick,* the white whale is a symbol, but so, too, is Ahab. The quest for Moby-Dick is itself a symbolic quest. The albatross in Samuel Coleridge's "The Ancient Mariner" is a symbol, and so is the Ancient Mariner's stopping one of the wedding guests to make him hear the entire narrative. In these cases, the symbols operate both structurally, in the entire narrative, and in the details.

In those instances in which there is no evident context to guide us, we should interpret symbols with extreme care and tentativeness. Symbolic objects usually have a well-understood range of meaning that authors such as Blake depend on. For instance, the rose is often thought of in connection with beauty, romance, and love. The worm is often thought of in connection with death, the grave, and—if we include the serpent in the Garden of Eden (Blake had read Milton's *Paradise Lost*)— the worm also suggests evil, sin, and perversion. Most of us know these things. Thus, the act of interpreting the symbol is usually an act of bringing this knowledge to the forefront of our minds so that we can use it in our interpretations.

Irony implies contradiction of some kind. It may be a contradiction of expectation or a contradiction of intention. For example, much sarcasm is ironic. Apparent compliments are occasionally digs intended to be wickedly amusing. In literature, irony can be one of the most potent of devices. For example, in Sophocles's play *Oedipus Rex*, the prophecy is that Oedipus will kill his father and marry his mother. What Oedipus does not know is that he has been adopted and taken to another country, so when he learns his fate he determines to leave home in order not to harm his parents. Ironically, he heads to Thebes and unknowingly challenges his true father, a king, at a crossroads and kills him. He then answers the riddle of the Sphinx, lifting the curse from the land—apparently a good outcome—but is then wed to the wife of the man he has killed. That woman is his mother. These events are part of a pattern of tragic irony, and in narrative literature this is a powerful device.

Edwin Arlington Robinson's poem "Richard Cory" is marked by regular meter, simple rhyme, and a basic pattern of four four-line stanzas. There is very little if any imagery in the poem, very little metaphor, and possibly no symbol, unless Richard Cory is the symbol. What gives the poem its force is the use of irony.

RICHARD CORY

Whenever Richard Cory went down town,
We people on the pavement looked at him:
He was a gentleman from sole to crown,
Clean favored, and imperially slim.

And he was always quietly arrayed,
And he was always human when he talked;
But still he fluttered pulses when he said,
"Good-morning," and he glittered when he walked.

And he was rich—yes, richer than a king—
And admirably schooled in every grace:
In fine, we thought that he was everything
To make us wish that we were in his place.

So on we worked, and waited for the light,
And went without the meat, and cursed the bread;
And Richard Cory, one calm summer night,
Went home and put a bullet through his head.

Source: Edwing Arlington Robinson, "Richard Cory," *The Children of the Night*, 1897.

The irony lies in the contrast between the wealthy, accomplished, polished Richard Cory, and the struggling efforts of his admirers to keep up with him. Ultimately the most powerful irony is that the man everyone idolized did not love himself enough to live. For an admired person to have everything and then "put a bullet through his head" simply does not seem reasonable. And yet, that is what happened.

Diction

Diction refers to the choice of words. But because the entire act of writing involves the choice of words, the term "diction" is usually reserved for literary acts (speech as well as the written word) that use words chosen especially carefully for their impact. The diction of a work of literature will sometimes make that work seem inevitable, as if there were no other way of saying the same thing, as in Hamlet's "To be or not to be." Try saying that in other words.

In Robert Herrick's poem, we see an interesting example of the poet calculating the effect of specific words in their context. Most of the words in "Upon Julia's Clothes" are single-syllable words, such as "then." But the few polysyllables—"vibration" with three syllables and the most unusual four-syllable word "liquefaction"—lend an air of intensity and special meaning to themselves by means of their syllabic contrast. There may also be an unusual sense in which those words act out or imitate what they describe.

UPON JULIA'S CLOTHES

Whenas in silks my Julia goes,
Then, then, methinks, how sweetly flows
That liquefaction of her clothes.

Next, when I cast mine eyes, and see
That brave vibration, each way free,
O, how that glittering taketh me!

Source: Herrick, Robert, "Upon Julia's Clothes," *Works of Robert Herrick, Alfred Pollard*, ed. London: Lawrence & Bullen 1891, pg.77.

PERCEPTION KEY "Upon Julia's Clothes"

1. The implications of the polysyllabic words in this poem may be quite different for different people. Read the poem aloud with a few people. Ask for suggestions about what the polysyllables do for the reader. Does their complexity enhance what is said about Julia? Their sounds? Their rhythms?
2. Read the poem to some listeners who are not likely to know it beforehand. Do they notice such words as "liquefaction" and "vibration"? When they talk about the poem, do they observe the use of these words? Compare their observations with those of students who have read the poem in this book.
3. Examine other poems in this chapter for the unexpected, unusual, or striking diction. Is Pound's use of "apparition" a good example of diction?

We have been giving examples of detailed diction. Structural diction produces a sense of linguistic inevitability throughout the work. The careful use of structural diction can sometimes conceal a writer's immediate intention, making it important for us to be explicitly aware of the diction until it has made its point. Jonathan Swift's essay *A Modest Proposal* is a classic example. Swift most decorously suggests that the solution to the poverty-stricken Irish farmer's desperation is the sale of his infant children—for the purpose of serving them up as plump, tender roasts for Christmas dinners in England. The diction is so subtly ironic that it is with some difficulty that many readers finally realize Swift is writing *satire*. By the time we reach the following passage, we should surely understand the irony:

I have been assured by a very knowing American of my acquaintance in London, that a young healthy child well nursed is at a year old a most delicious, nourishing, and wholesome food, whether stewed, roasted, baked, or boiled; and I make no doubt that it will equally serve in a fricasee or a ragout.

Many kinds of diction are available to the writer, from the casual and conversational to the archaic and the formal. Every literary writer is sensitive, consciously or unconsciously, to the issues of diction, and every piece of writing solves the problem in its own way. When the choice of words seems so exact and right that the slightest tampering diminishes the value of the work, then we have literature of high rank. Then, to paraphrase Robert Frost, "Like a piece of ice on a hot stove the poem rides on its own melting." No writer can tell you exactly how he or she achieves "inevitability," but much of it depends upon sound and rhythm as it relates to sense.

FOCUS ON   Po Chü'i, Poet of the T'ang Dynasty

Perhaps the most revered of Chinese poets, Po Chü'i (also known as Bai Juyi) (772–846) lived during the T'ang dynasty (618–907), a period in which poetry and the arts flourished and Imperial China recovered from a serious rebellion. Po left as many as 3,500 poems, written while he was also an important governor of several provinces. His life was guided by Confucian ideals, a commitment to social service and moral actions. Simplicity, despite his connection with royal courts, was a guide for Po. He enjoyed a busy life in the city of Chang'an, an important center of government. His poetry aimed at communicating with ordinary people as well as the elite. He is said to have shown his poetry to a peasant woman and revising any lines that were not clear to her.

In China he is well known for satirical poetry designed to stimulate improvement of society, but he is much admired for his shorter poems that seem often to be observations on the moments of everyday life that prompt a meditative response. Like many Chinese poets of the period, Po describes nature and the landscape, often dramatic, that he sees in travel or in his own garden. He has been described as the most influential poet of the time, even though the T'ang dynasty produced a number of the greatest poets in Chinese history. Because these poems are in translation, the question of diction—word choice—is not relevant to our discussion, but these poems often use metaphor, imagery, and symbol.

"An Early Rising" describes his travel to a meeting with the emperor, conducted usually at 6:30 am, and requiring a very early start with many problems along the journey. He envies Ch'en Chü-shih, the hermit who can stay in bed all morning. Ironically, Po lived at the end of his life in an abandoned monastery and referred to himself as a hermit.

AN EARLY RISING (Addressed to Ch'en, the Hermit)

At Ch'ang-an—a full foot of snow;
A rising at dawn—to bestow congratulations on the Emperor.
Just as I was nearing the Gate of the Silver Terrace,
After I had left the suburb of Hsin-ch'ang
On the high causeway my horse's foot slipped;
In the middle of the journey my lantern suddenly went out.
Ten leagues riding, always facing to the North;

continued

The cold wind almost blew off my ears.
I waited for the bell outside the Five Gates;
I waited for the summons within the Triple Hall.
My hair and beard were frozen and covered with icicles;
My coat and robe—chilly like water.
Suddenly I thought of Hsien-yu Valley
And secretly envied Ch'en Chü-shih,
In warm bed-socks dozing beneath the rugs
And not getting up till the sun has mounted the sky.

—tr. Arthur Waley

Like many people close to power, Po was not always praised, and sometimes he was envied. He fell from grace at one point in his life and was condemned for writing some poems that displeased his enemies. In the following poem he explains that writing poems can be dangerous.

MADLY SINGING IN THE MOUNTAINS

There is no one among men that has not a special failing:
And my failing consists in writing verses.
I have broken away from the thousand ties of life:
But this infirmity still remains behind.
Each time that I look at a fine landscape:
Each time that I meet a loved friend,
I raise my voice and recite a stanza of poetry
And am glad as though a God had crossed my path.
Ever since the day I was banished to Hsün-yang
Half my time I have lived among the hills.
And often, when I have finished a new poem,
Alone I climb the road to the Eastern Rock.
I lean my body on the banks of white stone:
I pull down with my hands a green cassia branch.
My mad singing startles the valleys and hills:
The apes and birds all come to peep.
Fearing to become a laughing-stock to the world,
I choose a place that is unfrequented by men.

—tr. Arthur Waley

Po, Like many great writers who suffered exile, wrote about the pain of his banishment from the wonderful dynamic city of Chang'an.

EXILE

Across great plains of yellow sand,
        Where the whistling winds are blown,
Over the cloud-topped mountain peaks,
        They wend their way alone.

Few are the pilgrims that attain
        Mount Omi's heights afar;
And the bright gleam of their standard grows
        Faint as the last pale star.

Dark the Sezchuan waters loom,
    Dark the Sezchuan hills,
And day and night the Emperor's life
    An endless sorrow fills.

The brightness of the foreign moon
    Saddens his lonely heart;
And a sound of a bell in the evening rain
    Doth rend his soul apart.

        —tr. L. Cranmer-Byng

Po meditated on the beauty of Lake Shang but saw, too, the significance of this beauty to the meaning of his own life and its perishability.

LAKE SHANG

Oh! she is like a picture in the spring,
This lake of Shang, with the wild hills gathering
Into a winding garden at the base
Of stormless waters; pines, deep blue, enlace
The lessening slopes, and broken moonlight
    gleams
Across the waves like pearls we thread in
    dreams.
Like a woof of jasper strands the corn unfolds,
Field upon field beyond the quiet wolds;
The late-blown rush flaunts in the dusk serene
Her netted sash and slender skirt of green.
Sadly I turn my prow toward the shore,
The dream behind me and the world before.
O Lake of Shang, his feet may wander far
Whose soul you hold mirrored as a star.

        —tr. L. Cranmer-Byng

In "The Ancient Wind," a meditation on aging and death, Po compares himself to a single pine tree left alone in the landscape. All his senses are involved in this poem and the images are direct, simple, and powerful in the manner that later poets emulate even today.

THE ANCIENT WIND

The peach blooms open on the eastern wall —
I breathe their fragrance, laughing in the glow
Of golden noontide. Suddenly there comes
The revelation of the ancient wind,
Flooding my soul with glory; till I feel
One with the brightness of the first far dawn,
One with the many-colored spring; and all
The secrets of the scented hearts of flowers
Are whispered through me; till I cry aloud.
Alas! how grey and scentless is the bloom
Of mortal life! This — this alone I fear,

continued

That from yon twinkling mirror of delight
The unreal flowers may fade; that with the breath
Of the fiery flying Dragon they will fall
Petal by petal, slowly, yet too soon,
Into the world's green sepulchre. Alas!
My little friends, my lovers, we must part,
And, like some uncompanioned pine that stands,
Last of the legions on the southern slopes,
I too shall stand alone, and hungry winds
Shall gnaw the lute-strings of my desolate heart.

—tr. L. Cranmer-Byng

PERCEPTION KEY Po Chü'i, Poet of the T'ang Dynasty

1. Give some thought to examining the imagery in these poems. What does the poet see? What does he hear? What does he feel? What does he smell?
2. Does "the world's green sepulchre" in "The Ancient Wind" act as a metaphor or a symbol, or both?
3. Are these poems simple enough for most people? What makes them valuable as poems? Choose any poem and comment on its subject matter and its content.
4. Po talks often about the weather. Are his examples metaphors, imagery, or none of those?
5. There may be no images, metaphors, or symbols in "Madly Singing in the Mountains." If that is true, what gives it the status of poetry and art? What is the subject matter, and what is the content?
6. Listen to someone read one of these poems aloud—perhaps even try to sing the poem. In what ways does listening to the poem alter your sense of its significance?

SUMMARY

Our emphasis throughout this chapter has been on literature as the wedding of sound and sense. Literature is not passive; it does not sit on the page. It is engaged actively in the lives of those who give it a chance. A reading aloud of some of the literary samples in this chapter—especially the lyric—illustrates the point.

We have been especially interested in two aspects of literature: its structure and its details. Any artifact is composed of an overall organization that gathers details into some kind of unity. It is the same in literature, and before we can understand how writers reveal the visions they have of their subject matters, we need to be aware of how details are combined into structures. The use of image, metaphor, symbol, and diction, as well as other details, determines in an essential sense the content of a work of literature.

Structural strategies, such as the choice between a narrative or a lyric, will determine to a large extent how details are used. There are many kinds of structures besides the narrative and the lyric, although these two offer convenient polarities that help indicate the nature of literary structure. It would be useful for any student of literature to discover how many kinds of narrative structures—in addition to the already discussed episodic, organic, and quest structures—can be used. And it also would be useful to determine how the different structural strategies tend toward the selection of different subject matters. We have made some suggestions as starters: pointing out the capacity of the narrative for reaching into a vast range of experience, especially for revealing psychological truths, and the capacity of the lyric for revealing feeling.

©Joan Marcus

Chapter 8

THEATER

We sit in the darkened theater with many strangers. We sense an air of anticipation, an awareness of excitement. People cough, rustle about, then suddenly become still. Slowly the lights on the stage begin to come up, and we see actors moving before us, apparently unaware of our presence. They are in rooms or spaces similar to those that we may be in ourselves at the end of the evening. Eventually they begin speaking to one another much the way we might ourselves, sometimes saying things so intimate that we are uneasy. They move about the stage, conducting their lives in total disregard for us, only hinting occasionally that we might be there in the same space with them.

At first we feel that despite our being in the same building with the actors, we are in a different world. Then slowly the distance between us and the actors begins to diminish until, in a good play, our participation erases the distance. We thrill with the actors, but we also suffer with them. We witness the illusion of an action that has an emotional impact for us and changes the way we think about our own lives. Great plays such as *Hamlet, Othello, The Misanthrope, Death of a Salesman, A Streetcar Named Desire,* and *Long Day's Journey into Night* can have the power to transform our awareness of ourselves and our circumstances. It is a mystery common to much art: that the illusion of reality can affect the reality of our own lives.

Drama is a collaborative art that represents events and situations, either realistic and/or symbolic, that we witness happening through the actions of actors in a play on a stage in front of a live audience. According to the greatest dramatic critic, Aristotle (384–322 BCE), the *elements of drama* are as follows:

Plot: a series of events leading to disaster for the main characters who undergo reversals in fortune and understanding but usually ending with a form of enlightenment—sometimes of the characters, sometimes of the audience, and sometimes of both

Character: the presentation of a person or persons whose actions and the reason for them are more or less revealed to the audience

Diction: the language of the drama, which should be appropriate to the action

Thought: the ideas that underlie the plot of the drama, expressed in terms of dialogue and soliloquy

Spectacle: the places of the action, the costumes, set designs, and visual elements in the play

Music: in Greek drama, the dialogue was sometimes sung or chanted by a chorus, and often this music was of considerable emotional importance; in modern drama, music is rarely used in serious plays, but it is of first importance in the musical theater

Aristotle conceived his theories in the great age of Greek *tragedy*, and therefore much of what he has to say applies to tragedies by such dramatists as Aeschylus (ca. 525–456 BCE), especially his trilogy, *Agamemnon, The Libation Bearers,* and *The Eumenides.* Sophocles (ca. 496–406 BCE) wrote *Oedipus Rex, Antigone,* and *Oedipus at Colonus;* and Euripides (ca. 485–406 BCE), the last of the greatest Greek tragedians, wrote *Andromache, Medea,* and *The Trojan Women.* All of these plays are still performed around the world, along with comedies by Aristophanes (ca. 448–385 BCE), the greatest Greek writer of comedies. His plays include *Lysistrata, The Birds, The Wasps,* and *The Frogs.* These plays often have a satirical and political purpose and set a standard for much drama to come.

Plot involves rising action, climax, falling action, *denouement*. For Aristotle, the tragic hero quests for truth. The moment of truth—the climax—is called *recognition*. When the fortune of the protagonist turns from good to bad, the *reversal* follows. The strongest effect of tragedy occurs when recognition and reversal happen at the same time, as in Sophocles's *Oedipus Rex* (Figure 8-1).

The protagonist, or leading character, in the most powerful tragedies fails not only because of fate, which is a powerful force in Greek thought, but also because of a *flaw in character (hamartia)*, a disregard of human limitations. The protagonist in the best tragedies ironically brings his misfortune upon himself. In *Oedipus Rex,* for example, the impetuous behavior of Oedipus works well for him until he decides to leave "home." Then his rash actions bring on disaster. Sophocles shows us that something of what happens to Oedipus could happen to us. We pity Oedipus and fear for him. Tragedy, Aristotle tells us, arouses pity and fear and by doing so produces in us a *catharsis*, a purging of those feelings, wiping out some of the horror.

FIGURE 8-1
Oedipus Rex. In the Tyrone Guthrie Theatre production, 1973, the shepherd tells Oedipus the truth about his birth and how he was prophesied to kill his father and marry his mother.

Courtesy Guthrie Theater.
Photo: Michael Paul

The drama helps us understand the complexities of human nature and the power of our inescapable destinies.

Dialogue and Soliloquy

The primary dramatic interchanges are achieved by dialogue, the exchange of conversation among the characters. In older plays, the individual speech of a character might be relatively long, and then it is answered by another character in the same way. In more-modern plays, the dialogue is often extremely short. Sometimes a few minutes of dialogue will contain a succession of speeches only five or six words in length. The following is an example of a brief dialogue between Algernon and his manservant, Lane, from Oscar Wilde's *The Importance of Being Earnest.*

> Algernon: A glass of sherry, Lane.
>
> Lane: Yes, sir.
>
> Algernon: Tomorrow, Lane, I'm going Bunburying.
>
> Lane: Yes, sir.
>
> Algernon: I shall probably not be back till Monday. You can put up my dress clothes, my smoking jacket, and all the Bunbury suits—

Lane: Yes, sir. *(Handing sherry.)*

Algernon: I hope tomorrow will be a fine day, Lane.

Lane: It never is, sir.

Algernon: Lane, you're a perfect pessimist.

Lane: I do my best to give satisfaction, sir.

In this passage, Algernon plans to visit an imaginary friend, Bunbury, an invention designed to help him avoid dinners and meetings that he cannot stand. The dialogue throughout the play is quick and witty, and the play is generally regarded as one of the most amusing comedies. As in most plays, the dialogue moves the action forward by telling us about the importance of the situations in which the actors speak. This example is interesting because, while brisk, its last line introduces an amusing irony, revealing the ironic soul of the entire play.

The *soliloquy*, on the other hand, is designed to give us insight into the character who speaks the lines. In the best of soliloquies we are given to understand that characters are speaking to themselves, not to the audience—the term "aside" is used to describe such speeches. Because the character is alone we can trust to the sincerity of the speech and the truths that it reveals. Hamlet's soliloquies in Shakespeare's play are among the most famous in literature. Here, Hamlet speaks at a moment in the play when the tension is greatest:

Hamlet: To be, or not to be, that is the question:

    Whether 'tis nobler in the mind to suffer

    The slings and arrows of outrageous fortune,

    Or to take arms against a sea of troubles,

    And by opposing end them. To die, to sleep—

    No more—and by a sleep to say we end

    The heart-ache and the thousand natural shocks

    That flesh is heir to. [3.1.57–64]

There is nothing superficial about this speech, nor the many lines that come after it. Hamlet considers suicide and, once having renounced it, considers what he must do. The many soliloquies in *Hamlet* offer us insight into Hamlet's character, showing us an interiority, or psychological existence, that is rich and deep. In the Greek tragedies, some of the function of the modern soliloquy was taken by the Chorus, a group of citizens who commented in philosophic fashion on the action of the drama.

PERCEPTION KEY Soliloquy

A soliloquy occurs when a character alone onstage reveals his or her thoughts. Study the use of the soliloquy in Shakespeare's *Hamlet* (3.3.73–96, 4.4.32–66) and in Tennessee Williams's *The Glass Menagerie* (Tom's opening speech, Tom's long speech in scene 5, and his opening speech in scene 6). What do these soliloquies accomplish? Is their purpose different in these two plays? Are soliloquies helpful in all drama? What are their strengths and weaknesses?

ARCHETYPAL PATTERNS

Theater originated from ancient rituals that had their roots in religious patterns such as death and rebirth. One such pattern is the ritual of sacrifice—which implies that the individual must be sacrificed for the commonweal of society. Such a pattern is *archetypal*—a basic psychological pattern that people apparently react to on a more or less subconscious level. These patterns, **archetypes**, are deep in the *myths* that have permeated history. We feel their importance even if we do not recognize them consciously.

Archetypal drama aims at symbolic or mythic interpretations of experience. For instance, one's search for personal identity, for self-evaluation, a pattern repeated in all ages, serves as a primary archetypal structure for drama. This archetype is the driving force in Sophocles's *Oedipus Rex,* Shakespeare's *Hamlet,* August Wilson's *The Piano Lesson,* Arthur Miller's *Death of a Salesman,* and many more plays—notably, but by no means exclusively, in tragedies. (As we shall see, **comedy** also often uses this archetype.) This archetype is powerful because, while content to watch other people discover their identities, we may find that we are not the people we want others to think we are.

The power of the archetype derives, in part, from our recognition of a pattern that has been repeated by the human race throughout history. The psychologist Carl Jung, whose work spurred critical awareness of archetypal patterns in all the arts, believed that the greatest power of the archetype lies in its capacity to reveal through art the "imprinting" of human experience. Maud Bodkin, a critic who developed Jung's views, explains the archetype this way:

> The special emotional significance going beyond any definite meaning conveyed attributes to the stirring in the reader's mind, within or beneath his conscious response, of unconscious forces which he terms "primordial images" or archetypes. These archetypes he describes as "psychic residua of numberless experiences of the same type," experiences which have happened not to the individual but to his ancestors, and of which the results are inherited in the structure of the brain.[1]

The quest narrative (see Chapter 7) is an example of an archetypal structure, one that recurs in drama frequently. For instance, Hamlet is seeking the truth about his father's death (Aristotle's recognition), but in doing so, he is also trying to discover his own identity as it relates to his mother. Sophocles's *Oedipus* is the story of a man who kills his father, marries his mother, and suffers a plague on his lands. He discovers the truth (recognition again), and doom follows (Aristotle's reversal). He blinds himself and is ostracized. Freud thought the play so archetypal that he saw in it a profound human psychological pattern, which he called the "Oedipus complex": the desire of a child to get rid of the same-sex parent and to have a sexual union with the parent of the opposite sex. Not all archetypal patterns are so shocking, but most reveal an aspect of basic human desires. Drama—because of its immediacy and compression of presentation—is, perhaps, the most powerful means of expression for such archetypes.

Some of the more important archetypes include those of an older man, usually a king in ancient times, who is betrayed by a younger man, his trusted lieutenant, with regard to a woman. This is the theme of Lady Gregory's *Grania.* The loss of innocence, a variation on the Garden of Eden theme, is another

---

[1]Maud Bodkin, *Archetypal Patterns in Poetry* (New York: Oxford University Press, 1934), p. 1.

favorite, as in August Strindberg's *Miss Julie* and Henrik Ibsen's *Ghosts* and *The Wild Duck*. Tom Stoppard's *Arcadia* combines two archetypes: loss of innocence and the quest for knowledge. However, no archetype seems to rival the quest for self-identity. That quest is so common that it is even parodied, as in Wilde's *The Importance of Being Earnest*.

The four seasons set temporal dimensions for the development of archetypes because the seasons are intertwined with patterns of growth and decay. The origins of drama, which are obscure beyond recall, may have been linked with rituals associated with the planting of seed, the reaping of crops, and the entire complex issue of fertility and death. In *Anatomy of Criticism*, Northrop Frye associates comedy with spring, romance with summer, tragedy with autumn, irony and satire with winter. His associations suggest that some archetypal drama may be rooted in connections between human destiny and the rhythms of nature. Such origins may account for part of the power that archetypal drama has for our imaginations, for the influences that derive from such origins are pervasive in all of us. These influences may also help explain why tragedy usually involves the death of a hero—although, sometimes, as in the case of Oedipus, death is withheld—and why comedy frequently ends with one or more marriages, as in Shakespeare's *As You Like It, Much Ado about Nothing,* and *A Midsummer Night's Dream,* with their suggestions of fertility.

CONCEPTION KEY Archetypes

1. Whether or not you do additional reading, consider the recurrent patterns you have observed in dramas—include television dramas or television adaptations of drama. Can you find any of the patterns we have described? Do you see other patterns showing up? Do the patterns you have observed seem basic to human experience? For example, do you associate gaiety with spring, love with summer, death with fall, and bitterness with winter? What season seems most appropriate for marriage?

GENRES OF DRAMA: TRAGEDY

Carefully structured plots are basic for Aristotle, especially for tragedies. The action must be probable or plausible, but not necessarily historically accurate. Although noble protagonists are essential for great tragedies, Aristotle allows for tragedies with ordinary protagonists. In these, plot is much more the center of interest than character. Then we have what may be called action dramas, never, according to Aristotle, as powerful as character dramas, other things being equal. Action dramas prevail on the popular stage and television. But when we turn to the great tragedies that most define the genre, we think immediately of great characters: Oedipus, Agamemnon, Prometheus, Hamlet, Macbeth, King Lear.

Modern drama tends to avoid traditional tragic structures because modern concepts of morality, sin, guilt, fate, and death have been greatly altered. Modern psychology explains character in ways the ancients either would not have understood or would have disputed. Critics have said that there is no modern tragedy because there can be no character noble enough to engage our heartfelt sympathy. Moreover, the acceptance of chance as a force equal to fate in our lives has also reduced the power of tragedy in modern times. Greek myth—used by modern playwrights like Eugene O'Neill—has a diminished vitality in modern tragedy. It may be that the return of a strong integrating myth—a world vision that sees the actions of humanity as tied into a large scheme of cosmic or sacred events—is a prerequisite for producing a drama that we can recognize as truly tragic, at least in the traditional sense. This may be an overstatement. What do you think?

The Tragic Stage

Our vision of tragedy focuses on two great ages—ancient Greece and Renaissance England. These two historical periods share certain basic ideas: for instance, that there is a "divine providence that shapes our ends," as Hamlet says, and that fate is immutable, as the Greek tragedies tell us. Both periods were marked by considerable prosperity and public power, and both ages were deeply aware that sudden reversals in prosperity could change everything. In addition, both ages had somewhat similar ideas about the way a stage should be constructed. The relatively temperate climate of Greece permitted an open amphitheater, with seating on three sides of the stage. The Greek architects often had the seats carved out of hillside rock, and their attention to acoustics was so remarkable that even today in some of the surviving Greek theaters, as at Epidaurus, a whisper on the stage can be heard in the farthest rows. The Elizabethan stages were roofed wooden structures jutting into open space enclosed by stalls in which the well-to-do sat (the not-so-well-to-do stood around the stage), providing for sight lines from three sides. Each kind of theater was similar to a modified theater-in-the-round, such as is used occasionally today. A glance at Figures 8-2 through 8-4 shows that the Greek and Elizabethan theaters were very different from the standard theater of our time—the *proscenium* theater.

The proscenium acts as a transparent "frame" separating the action taking place on the stage from the audience. The Greek and Elizabethan stages are not so explicitly framed, thus involving the audience more directly spatially and, in turn, perhaps, emotionally. In the Greek theater, the action took place in a circle called the "orchestra." The absence of a separate stage put the actors on the same level as those seated at the lowest level of the audience.

Stage Scenery and Costumes

Modern theater depends on the scenery and costumes for much of its effect on the audience. Aristotle considered these ingredients as part of the spectacle, what we see when we are in the theater. Greek drama used a basic set, as seen in Figure 8-5, with an open space, the orchestra, and a building, the skene, against which the actors played.

FIGURE 8-2
Theater at Epidaurus, Greece. Circa 350 BCE. The theater, which has a capacity of more than 10,000 patrons, was used for early Greek tragedy and is still used for performances.

©Tuul/Robert Harding World Imagery

FIGURE 8-3
Modern rendering of DeWitt's 1596 drawing of the interior of an Elizabethan theater in London. This is typical of those in which Shakespeare's plays were performed.

©Lee A. Jacobus

FIGURE 8-4
The auditorium and proscenium of the Royal Opera House, Covent Garden, London. The proscenium arch is typical of theaters from the eighteenth century to the present. It has been compared with the fourth wall of the drama within.

©Topham/The Image Works

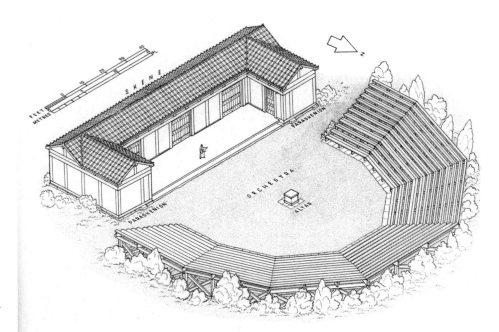

FIGURE 8-5
Eretria, Greece. Early Greek theater.
The orchestra was the area for the chorus to act in, and for the primary actors. The paraskenion was used for entrances and exits, and the skene was a backdrop for the actors.

Greek actors wore simple clothing and distinguished their parts by the use of elaborate masks, some of which included a megaphone to help project the voices. The paraskenion provided entrances and exits, and the skene usually represented a home or palace against which the action was set. The presence of the altar indicates the religious nature of the festival of Dionysus, during which plays were presented. Because the Greeks held their festivals in the daytime, no special lighting was necessary. Shakespearean and Elizabethan plays were staged in the afternoon and used little stage scenery. The words of the play established the place and time of the action.

Elaborate lighting and painted flats to establish the locale of the action became the norm in the late seventeenth century and after. Candlelight was used ingeniously in the late seventeenth century, but by the eighteenth century oil lamps replaced lights in the theater and onstage.

The Drury Lane Theatre in London was the most popular theater of its time. As seen in Figure 8-6, it made extensive use of artificial lighting, while the stage was decorated with detailed painted sets simulating the environment in which the actors moved. Such efforts at realistic staging had become the norm with impressive speed, and even today we expect the stage to produce a sense of realism.

In Shakespeare's time, some of the most impressive and imaginative costumes were not on the public stage, but in the special entertainments at the courts of Queen Elizabeth and King James, as shown in Figure 8-7. They were called masques, entertainments with mythic narratives, elaborate music and costumes, and much dancing. Masques were very expensive to produce and were usually performed only once for special celebrations.

FIGURE 8-6
Theatre Royal, Drury Lane, 1812.
London's Drury Lane was the
most popular theater of its time.
Its lighting system was advanced,
and the scenery was painted and
constructed to produce an illusion
of reality.

FIGURE 8-7
**Spirit Torchbearer, costume design
by Inigo Jones, 1613.** Inigo Jones was
an architect and stage designer for
entertainments at court. His fanciful
Spirit was intended for a royal
masque written by Thomas Campion
to honor the marriage of King James
I's daughter, Elizabeth.

©Devonshire Collection, Chatsworth/
Reproduced by permission of Chatsworth
Settlement Trustees/Bridgeman Images

For a contemporary audience, *Romeo and Juliet* is easier to participate with than most Greek tragedies because, among other reasons, its tragic hero and heroine, although aristocratic, are not a king and a queen. Their youth and innocence add to their remarkable appeal. The play presents the archetypal story of lovers whose fate—mainly because of the hatred their families bear each other—is sealed from the first. The archetype of lovers who are not permitted to love enacts a basic struggle among forces that lie so deep in our psyches that we need a drama such as this to help reveal them. It is the struggle between light and dark, between the world in which we live on the surface of the earth with its light and openness and the world of darkness, the underworld of the Greeks and the Romans, and the hell of the Christians. Young lovers represent life, the promise of fertility, and the continuity of the human race. Few subject matters could be more potentially tragic than that of young lovers whose promise is plucked by death.

The play begins with some ominous observations by Montague, Romeo's father. He points out that Romeo, through love of a girl named Rosaline (who does not appear in the play), comes home late in the morning and locks "fair daylight out," making for himself an "artificial night." Montague tells us that Romeo stays up all night, comes home, pulls down the shades, and converts day into night. These observations seem innocent enough unless one is already familiar with the plot; then it seems a clear and tragic irony: that Romeo, by making his day a night, is already foreshadowing his fate. After Juliet has been introduced, her nurse wafts her off-stage with an odd bit of advice aimed at persuading her of the wisdom of marrying Count Paris, the man her mother has chosen. "Go, girl, seek happy nights to happy days." At first glance, the advice seems innocent. But with knowledge of the entire play, it is prophetic, for it echoes the day/night imagery Montague has applied to Romeo. Shakespeare's details invariably tie in closely with the structure. Everything becomes relevant.

When Romeo first speaks with Juliet, not only is it night but they are in Capulet's orchard: symbolically a place of fruitfulness and fulfillment. Romeo sees her and imagines her, not as chaste Diana of the moon, but as his own luminary sun: "But soft! What light through yonder window breaks? / It is the East, and Juliet is the sun!" He sees her as his "bright angel." When she, unaware he is listening below, asks, "O Romeo, Romeo! Wherefore art thou Romeo? / Deny thy father and refuse thy name," she is touching on profound concerns. She is, without fully realizing it, asking the impossible: that he not be himself. The denial of identity often brings great pain, as witness Oedipus, who at first refused to believe he was his father's child. When Juliet asks innocently, "What's in a name? That which we call a rose / By any other name would smell as sweet," she is asking that he ignore his heritage. The mythic implications of this are serious and, in this play, fatal. Denying one's identity is rather like Romeo's later attempt to deny day its sovereignty.

When they finally speak, Juliet explains ironically that she has "night's cloak to hide me" and that the "mask of night is upon my face." We know, as she speaks, that eternal night will be on that face, and all too soon. Their marriage, which occurs offstage as act 2 ends, is also performed at night in Friar Lawrence's cell, with his hoping that the heavens will smile upon "this holy act." But he is none too sure. And before act 3 is well under way, the reversals begin. Mercutio, Romeo's friend, is slain because of Romeo's intervention. Then Romeo slays Tybalt, Juliet's cousin, and finds himself doomed to exile from both Verona and Juliet. Grieving for the dead Tybalt and the banished Romeo, Juliet misleads her father into thinking the only cure for her condition is a quick marriage to Paris, and Romeo comes to spend their one night of love together before he leaves Verona. Naturally they want the night to last and last—again an irony we are prepared for—and when daylight springs, Romeo and Juliet have a playful argument over whether it is the nightingale or the lark that sings. Juliet wants Romeo to stay, so she defends the nightingale; he knows he must go, so he points to the lark and the coming light. Then both, finally, admit the truth. His line is "More light and light—more dark and dark our woes."

Another strange archetypal pattern, part of the complexity of the subject matter, has begun here: the union of sex and death as if they were aspects of the same thing. In Shakespeare's time, death was a metaphor for making love, and often when a singer of a love song protested that he was dying, he expected everyone to understand that he was talking about the sexual act. In *Romeo and Juliet,* sex and death go together, both literally and symbolically. The first most profound sense of this appears in Juliet's pretending death in order to avoid marrying Paris. She takes a potion from Friar Lawrence—who is himself afraid of a second marriage because of possible bigamy charges—and she appears, despite all efforts of investigation, quite dead.

When Romeo hears that Juliet has been placed in the Capulet tomb, he determines to join her in death as he was only briefly able to do in life. The message Friar Lawrence had sent by way of another friar explaining the counterfeit death did not get through to Romeo. And it did not get through because genuine death, in the form of plague, had closed the roads to Friar John. When Romeo descends underground into the tomb, he unwillingly fights Paris. After killing Paris, Romeo sees the immobile Juliet. He fills his cup (a female symbol) with poison and drinks. When Juliet awakes from her potion and sees both Paris and Romeo dead, she can get no satisfactory answer for these happenings from Friar Lawrence. His fear is so great that he runs off as the authorities bear down on the tomb. This leaves Juliet to give Romeo one last kiss on his still warm lips, then plunge his dagger (a male symbol) into her heart and die (Figure 8-8).

Earlier, when Capulet thought his daughter was dead, he exclaimed to Paris, "O son, the night before thy wedding day / Hath Death lain with thy wife. There she lies, / Flower as she was, deflowered by him. / Death is my son-in-law, Death is my heir." At the end of the play, both Juliet and his real son-in-law, Romeo, are indeed married in death. The linkage of death and sex is ironically enacted in their final moments, which include the awful misunderstandings that the audience beholds in sorrow, that make Romeo and Juliet take their own lives for love of each other. And among the last lines is one that helps clarify one of the main themes: "A glooming peace this morning with it brings. / The sun for sorrow will not show his head." Theatergoers have mourned these deaths for generations, and the promise that these two families will now finally try to get along together in a peaceful manner does not seem strong enough to brighten the ending of the play.

FIGURE 8-8
Romeo and Juliet in the tomb.
Worcester Foothills Theater
production, 2003, directed by Edward
Isser. Juliet awakes to find Romeo's
body after he has drunk poison. She
will seize his dagger and follow him
to the grave.

©ArenaPal/Topham/The Image Works

PERCEPTION KEY Tragedy

1. While participating with *Romeo and Juliet*, did you experience pity and fear for the protagonists? Catharsis (the purging of those emotions)?
2. Our discussion of the play did not treat the question of the tragic flaw (hamartia): the weakness of character that brings disaster to the main characters. One of Romeo's flaws may be rashness—the rashness that led him to kill Tybalt and thus be banished. But he may have other flaws as well. What might they be? What are Juliet's tragic flaws, if any?
3. You may not have been able to see *Romeo and Juliet,* but perhaps other tragedies are available. Try to see any of the tragedies by Aeschylus, Sophocles, or Shakespeare; Ibsen's *Ghosts;* John Millington Synge's *Riders to the Sea;* Eugene O'Neill's *Long Day's Journey into Night;* Tennessee Williams's *The Glass Menagerie;* or Arthur Miller's *Death of a Salesman.* Analyze the issues of tragedy we have raised. For example, decide whether the play is archetypal. Are there tragic flaws? Are there reversals and recognitions of the sort Aristotle analyzed? Did the recognition and reversal occur simultaneously? Are the characters important enough—if not noble enough—to excite your compassion for their sorrow and suffering?
4. If you were to write a tragedy, what modern figure could be a proper tragic protagonist? What archetypal antagonist would be appropriate for your tragedy? What tragic flaw or flaws would such a modern antagonist exhibit?

Ancient Western comedies were performed at a time associated with wine making, thus linking the genre with the wine god Bacchus and his relative Comus—from whom the word "comedy" comes. Comedy, like tragedy, achieved institutional status in ancient Greece. Some of the earliest comedies, along with satyr plays, were frankly phallic in nature, and many of the plays of Aristophanes, the master of **Old Comedy**, were raucous and coarse. Plutarch was offended by plays such as *The Clouds, The Frogs, The Wasps,* and especially *Lysistrata,* the world's best-known phallic play, concerning a situation in which the women of a community withhold sex until the men agree not to wage any more war. At one point in the play, the humor centers on the men walking around with enormous erections under their togas. Obviously Old Comedy is old in name only, since it is still present in the routines of nightclub comedians and the bawdy entertainment halls of the world.

In contrast, the **New Comedy** of Menander, with titles such as *The Flatterer, The Lady from Andros, The Suspicious Man,* and *The Grouch,* his only surviving complete play, concentrated on common situations in the everyday life of the Athenian. It also avoided the brutal attacks on individuals, such as Socrates, which characterize much Old Comedy. Historians credit Menander with developing the comedy of manners, the kind of drama that satirizes the manners of a society as the basic part of its subject matter.

Old Comedy is associated with our modern farce, burlesque, and the broad humor and make-believe violence of slapstick. New Comedy tends to be suave and subtle. Concentrating on manners, New Comedy developed *type characters*, for they helped focus upon the foibles of social behavior. Type characters, such as the gruff and difficult man who turns out to have a heart of gold, the good cop, the bad cop, the ingenue, the finicky person, or the sloppy person—all these work well in comedies. Such characters can become *stereotypes*—with predictable behavior patterns—although the best dramatists usually make them complex enough so that they are not completely predictable.

The comic vision celebrates life and fecundity. Typically in comedy, all ends well; conflicts are resolved; and, as often in Shakespeare's comedies, the play concludes with feasting, revelry, and a satisfying distribution of brides to the appropriate suitors. We are encouraged to imagine that they will live happily ever after.

PERCEPTION KEY Type Characters

1. In *The Odd Couple*, Felix Unger, a finicky opera-loving neatnik, lives with Oscar Madison, a slob whose life revolves around sports. What is inherently funny about linking different type characters like them?

2. Type characters exist in all drama. What types are Romeo, Juliet, the Nurse, and Friar Lawrence? How close do they stay to their types?

3. To what extent is Hamlet a type character? Is it possible that the character of Hamlet actually created the dark-hued melancholiac as a type that did not exist before Shakespeare created him?

4. What type characters do you remember from your experiences with drama? What are the strengths of such characters? What are their limitations?

Comedy, like tragedy, may use archetypal patterns. A blocking character, personified by a parent or controlling older person, is often pitted against the younger characters who wish to be married. The "parent" can be any older person who blocks the younger people, usually by virtue of controlling their inheritance or their wealth. The blocking character, for social or mercenary reasons, schemes to stop the young people from getting together.

Naturally, the blocking character fails. But the younger characters do not merely win their own struggle. They usually go on to demonstrate the superiority of their views over those of the blocking character. For example, they may demonstrate that true love is a better reason for marrying than is merging two neighboring estates. One common pattern is for two lovers to decide to marry regardless of their social classes. The male, for instance, may be a soldier or a student but not belong to the upper class to which the female belongs. But often at the last minute, through means such as a birthmark (as in *The Marriage of Figaro*) or the admission of another character who knew all along, the lower-class character will be shown to be a member of the upper class in disguise. Often the character himself will not know the truth until the last minute in the drama. This is a variant of Aristotle's recognition in tragedy, although it does not have the unhappy consequences. In all of this, New Comedy is usually in tacit agreement with the ostensible standards of the society it entertains. It only stretches the social standards and is thus evolutionary rather than revolutionary.

Blocking characters may be misers, for example, whose entire lives are devoted to mercenary goals, although they may not be able to enjoy the money they heap up; or malcontents, forever looking on the dark side of humanity; or hypochondriacs, whose every move is dictated by their imaginary illnesses. Such characters are so rigid that their behavior is a form of vice. The effort of the younger characters is often to reform the older characters, educating them away from their entrenched and narrow values toward accepting the idealism and hopefulness of the young people who, after all, are in line to inherit the world that the older people are reluctant to turn over. Few generations give way without a struggle, and this archetypal struggle on the comic stage may serve to give hope to the young when they most need it, as well as possibly to help educate the old so as to make the real struggle less terrible.

PERCEPTION KEY Old and New Comedy

Studying comedy in the abstract is difficult. It is best for you to test what has been discussed above by comparing our descriptions and interpretations with your own observations. If you have a chance to see some live comedy onstage, use that experience, but if that is impossible, watch some television comedy.

1. Is there criticism of society? If so, is it savage or gentle?
2. Are there blocking characters? If so, do they function somewhat in the ways described above? Are there any new twists?
3. See or read at least two comedies. How many type or stereotype characters can you identify? Is there an example of the braggart tough guy? The big lover? The poor but honest fellow? The dumb cop? The absentminded professor? Do types or stereotypes dominate? Which do you find more humorous? Why?

On the walls beside many stages, especially the ancient, we find two masks: the tragic mask with a downturned mouth and the comic mask with an upturned mouth. If there were a third mask, it would probably have an expression of bewilderment, as if someone had just asked an unanswerable question. Mixing the genres of tragedy and comedy in a drama may give such a feeling. Modern audiences are often left with many unanswered questions when they leave the theater. They are not always given resolutions that wrap things up neatly. Instead, **tragicomedy** tends, more than either tragedy or comedy, to reveal the **ambiguities** of the world. It does not usually end with the finality of death or the promise of a new beginning. It usually ends somewhere in between.

The reason tragicomedy has taken some time to become established as a genre may have had something to do with the fact that Aristotle did not provide an analysis—an extraordinary example of a philosopher having great influence on the arts. Thus, for a long time, tragicomedy was thought of as a mixing of two pure genres and consequently inferior in kind. The mixing of tragedy and comedy is surely justified, if for no other reason than the mixture works so well, as proved by most of the marvelous plays of Chekhov. This mixed genre is a way of making drama truer to life. As playwright Sean O'Casey commented to a college student, "As for the blending 'Comedy with Tragedy,' it's no new practice—hundreds have done it, including Shakespeare. . . . And, indeed, Life is always doing it, doing it, doing it. Even when one lies dead, laughter is often heard in the next room. There's no tragedy that isn't tinged with humour, no comedy that hasn't its share of tragedy—if one has eyes to see, ears to hear." Much of our best modern drama is mixed in genre so that, as O'Casey points out, it is rare to find a comedy that has no sadness to it or a tragedy that is unrelieved by laughter.

A PLAY FOR STUDY: *RIDERS TO THE SEA*

Riders to the Sea (1904, see Figure 8-9) was John Millington Synge's first success with the famed Abbey Theatre in Dublin. It follows some of the Aristotelian demands for tragedy. It is enacted in one day in the time it takes to play. The primary character, Maurya, while not royalty, is ennobled and heroic because of her stoicism. Moreover, the power of fate, a Greek force, seems to be at work in this modern age, despite the allusions to Christianity in the form of the young priest who carelessly assures Maurya that God will not let her be left without any men to look after her. Maurya—whose name is close to the Greek moira, fate—is a powerful figure whose final speeches are among the most lyrical and moving in all of Irish drama. The setting is on one of the the remote Aran islands, off the west coast of Ireland in the Atlantic. The passage from the island to the coast is treacherous, which is why so many of the men have died trying to make a living on the water. Even today the islanders use the old-fashioned boats to make the trip, sometimes towing animals in the water behind them. While it seems that the play carries the weight of doom throughout, the point Synge makes is that life in the remote spaces of Ireland demands resourcefulness and a transcendent grace in the women who survive.

FIGURE 8-9
The Druid Synge Production of *Riders to the Sea*, 2005, Galway, Ireland.

Image by Keith Pattison, courtesy of Druid

RIDERS TO THE SEA

John Millington Synge

Persons in the Play
MAURYA (*an old woman*)

BARTLEY (*her son*)

CATHLEEN (*her daughter*)

NORA (*a younger daughter*)

MEN *and* WOMEN

SCENE: An Island off the West of Ireland.

(*Cottage kitchen, with nets, oil-skins, spinning wheel, some new boards standing by the wall, etc.*

Cathleen, a girl of about twenty, finishes kneading cake, and puts it down in the pot-oven by the fire; then wipes her hands, and begins to spin at the wheel. NORA, a young girl, puts her head in at the door.)

NORA (In a low voice.): Where is she?

CATHLEEN: She's lying down, God help her, and may be sleeping, if she's able.

(*Nora comes in softly, and takes a bundle from under her shawl.*)

CATHLEEN (*Spinning the wheel rapidly.*): What is it you have?

NORA: The young priest is after bringing them. It's a shirt and a plain stocking were got off a drowned man in Donegal.

(*Cathleen stops her wheel with a sudden movement, and leans out to listen.*)

NORA: We're to find out if it's Michael's they are, some time herself will be down looking by the sea.

CATHLEEN: How would they be Michael's, Nora. How would he go the length of that way to the far north?

NORA: The young priest says he's known the like of it. "If it's Michael's they are," says he, "you can tell herself he's got a clean burial by the grace of God, and if they're not his, let no one say a word about them, for she'll be getting her death," says he, "with crying and lamenting."

(The door which Nora half closed is blown open by a gust of wind.)

CATHLEEN (*Looking out anxiously.*): Did you ask him would he stop Bartley going this day with the horses to the Galway fair?

NORA: "I won't stop him," says he, "but let you not be afraid. Herself does be saying prayers half through the night, and the Almighty God won't leave her destitute," says he, "with no son living."

CATHLEEN: Is the sea bad by the white rocks, Nora?

NORA: Middling bad, God help us. There's a great roaring in the west, and it's worse it'll be getting when the tide's turned to the wind. (*She goes over to the table with the bundle.*) Shall I open it now?

CATHLEEN: Maybe she'd wake up on us, and come in before we'd done. (*Coming to the table.*) It's a long time we'll be, and the two of us crying.

NORA (*Goes to the inner door and listens.*): She's moving about on the bed. She'll be coming in a minute.

CATHLEEN: Give me the ladder, and I'll put them up in the turf-loft, the way she won't know of them at all, and maybe when the tide turns she'll be going down to see would he be floating from the east.

(They put the ladder against the gable of the chimney; Cathleen goes up a few steps and hides the bundle in the turf-loft. Maurya comes from the inner room.)

MAURYA (*Looking up at Cathleen and speaking querulously.*): Isn't it turf enough you have for this day and evening?

CATHLEEN: There's a cake baking at the fire for a short space. (*Throwing down the turf*) and Bartley will want it when the tide turns if he goes to Connemara.

(NORA picks up the turf and puts it round the pot-oven.)

MAURYA (*Sitting down on a stool at the fire.*): He won't go this day with the wind rising from the south and west. He won't go this day, for the young priest will stop him surely.

NORA: He'll not stop him, mother, and I heard Eamon Simon and Stephen Pheety and Colum Shawn saying he would go.

MAURYA: Where is he itself?

NORA: He went down to see would there be another boat sailing in the week, and I'm thinking it won't be long till he's here now, for the tide's turning at the green head, and the hooker tacking from the east.

CATHLEEN: I hear some one passing the big stones.

NORA (*Looking out.*): He's coming now, and he's in a hurry.

BARTLEY (*Comes in and looks round the room. Speaking sadly and quietly.*): Where is the bit of new Rope, Cathleen, was bought in Connemara?

CATHLEEN (*Coming down.*): Give it to him, Nora; it's on a nail by the white boards. I hung it up this morning, for the pig with the black feet was eating it.

NORA (*Giving him a rope.*): Is that it, Bartley?

MAURYA: You'd do right to leave that rope, Bartley, hanging by the boards (*Bartley Takes the rope*). It will be wanting in this place, I'm telling you, if Michael is washed up to-morrow morning, or the next morning, or any morning in the week, for it's a deep grave we'll make him by the grace of God.

BARTLEY (*Beginning to work with the rope.*): I've no halter the way I can ride down on the mare, and I must go now quickly. This is the one boat going for two weeks or beyond it, and the fair will be a good fair for horses I heard them saying below.

MAURYA: It's a hard thing they'll be saying below if the body is washed up and there's no man in it to make the coffin, and I after giving a big price for the finest white boards you'd find in Connemara.

(She looks round at the boards.)

BARTLEY: How would it be washed up, and we after looking each day for nine days, and a strong wind blowing a while back from the west and south?

MAURYA: If it wasn't found itself, that wind is raising the sea, and there was a star up against the moon, and it rising in the night. If it was a hundred horses, or a thousand horses you had itself, what is the price of a thousand horses against a son where there is one son only?

BARTLEY (*Working at the halter, to Cathleen.*): Let you go down each day, and see the sheep aren't jumping in on the rye, and if the jobber comes you can sell the pig with the black feet if there is a good price going.

MAURYA: How would the like of her get a good price for a pig?

BARTLEY (*To Cathleen*): If the west wind holds with the last bit of the moon let you and NORA get up weed enough for another cock for the kelp. It's hard set we'll be from this day with no one in it but one man to work.

MAURYA: It's hard set we'll be surely the day you're drownd'd with the rest. What way will I live and the girls with me, and I an old woman looking for the grave?

(BARTLEY *lays down the halter, takes off his old coat, and puts on a newer one of the same flannel.*)

BARTLEY (*To Nora.*): Is she coming to the pier?

NORA (*Looking out.*): She's passing the green head and letting fall her sails.

BARTLEY (*Getting his purse and tobacco.*): I'll have half an hour to go down, and you'll see me coming again in two days, or in three days, or maybe in four days if the wind is bad.

MAURYA (*Turning round to the fire, and putting her shawl over her head.*): Isn't it a hard and cruel man won't hear a word from an old woman, and she holding him from the sea?

CATHLEEN: It's the life of a young man to be going on the sea, and who would listen to an old woman with one thing and she saying it over?

BARTLEY: (*Taking the halter.*) I must go now quickly. I'll ride down on the red mare, and the gray pony'll run behind me . . . The blessing of God on you. (*He goes out.*)

MAURYA (*Crying out as he is in the door.*): He's gone now, God spare us, and we'll not see him again. He's gone now, and when the black night is falling I'll have no son left me in the world.

CATHLEEN: Why wouldn't you give him your blessing and he looking round in the door? Isn't it sorrow enough is on every one in this house without your sending him out with an unlucky word behind him, and a hard word in his ear?

(MAURYA *takes up the tongs and begins raking the fire aimlessly without looking round.*)

NORA (*Turning towards her.*): You're taking away the turf from the cake.

CATHLEEN (*Crying out.*): The Son of God forgive us, Nora, we're after forgetting his bit of bread. (*She comes over to the fire.*)

214

NORA: And it's destroyed he'll be going till dark night, and he after eating nothing since the sun went up.

CATHLEEN (*Turning the cake out of the oven.*): It's destroyed he'll be, surely. There's no sense left on any person in a house where an old woman will be talking for ever.

(*Maurya sways herself on her stool.*)

CATHLEEN (*Cutting off some of the bread and rolling it in a cloth; to Maurya.*): Let you go down now to the spring well and give him this and he passing. You'll see him then and the dark word will be broken, and you can say "God speed you," the way he'll be easy in his mind.

MAURYA (*Taking the bread.*): Will I be in it as soon as himself?

CATHLEEN: If you go now quickly.

MAURYA (*Standing up unsteadily.*): It's hard set I am to walk.

CATHLEEN (*Looking at her anxiously.*): Give her the stick, Nora, or maybe she'll slip on the big stones.

NORA: What stick?

CATHLEEN: The stick Michael brought from Connemara.

MAURYA (*Taking a stick Nora gives her.*): In the big world the old people do be leaving things after them for their sons and children, but in this place it is the young men do be leaving things behind for them that do be old.

(*She goes out slowly. Nora goes over to the ladder.*)

CATHLEEN: Wait, Nora, maybe she'd turn back quickly. She's that sorry, God help her, you wouldn't know the thing she'd do.

NORA: Is she gone round by the bush?

CATHLEEN (*Looking out.*): She's gone now. Throw it down quickly, for the Lord knows when she'll be out of it again.

NORA (*Getting the bundle from the loft.*): The young priest said he'd be passing to-morrow, and we might go down and speak to him below if it's Michael's they are surely.

CATHLEEN (*Taking the bundle.*): Did he say what way they were found?

NORA (*Coming down.*): "There were two men," says he, "and they rowing round with poteen before the cocks crowed, and the oar of one of them caught the body, and they passing the black cliffs of the north."

CATHLEEN (*Trying to open the bundle.*): Give me a knife, Nora, the string's perished with the salt water, and there's a black knot on it you wouldn't loosen in a week.

NORA (*Giving her a knife.*): I've heard tell it was a long way to Donegal.

CATHLEEN (*Cutting the string.*): It is surely. There was a man in here a while ago—the man sold us that knife—and he said if you set off walking from the rocks beyond, it would be seven days you'd be in Donegal.

NORA: And what time would a man take, and he floating?

(*Cathleen opens the bundle and takes out a bit of a stocking. They look at them eagerly.*)

CATHLEEN (*In a low voice.*): The Lord spare us, Nora! Isn't it a queer hard thing to say if it's his they are surely?

NORA: I'll get his shirt off the hook the way we can put the one flannel on the other (*she looks through some clothes hanging in the corner.*) It's not with them, Cathleen, and where will it be?

CATHLEEN: I'm thinking Bartley put it on him in the morning, for his own shirt was heavy with the salt in it (*pointing to the corner*). There's a bit of a sleeve was of the same stuff. Give me that and it will do.

(*Nora brings it to her and they compare the flannel.*)

CATHLEEN: It's the same stuff, Nora but if it is itself aren't there great rolls of it in the shops of Galway, and isn't it many another man may have a shirt of it as well as Michael himself?

NORA (*Who has taken up the stocking and counted the stitches, crying out.*): It's Michael, Cathleen, it's Michael; God spare his soul, and what will herself say when she hears this story, and Bartley on the sea?

CATHLEEN (*Taking the stocking.*): It's a plain stocking.

NORA: It's the second one of the third pair I knitted, and I put up three score stitches, and I dropped four of them.

CATHLEEN (*Counts the stitches.*): It's that number is in it (*crying out.*) Ah, Nora, isn't it a bitter thing to think of him

floating that way to the far north, and no one to keen him but the black hags that do be flying on the sea?

NORA (*Swinging herself round, and throwing out her arms on the clothes.*): And isn't it a pitiful thing when there is nothing left of a man who was a great rower and fisher, but a bit of an old shirt and a plain stocking?

CATHLEEN (*After an instant.*): Tell me is herself coming, Nora? I hear a little sound on the path.

NORA (*Looking out.*): She is, Cathleen. She's coming up to the door.

CATHLEEN: Put these things away before she'll come in. Maybe it's easier she'll be after giving her blessing to Bartley, and we won't let on we've heard anything the time he's on the sea.

NORA (*Helping Cathleen to close the bundle.*): We'll put them here in the corner.

(*They put them into a hole in the chimney corner. Cathleen goes back to the spinning-wheel.*)

NORA: Will she see it was crying I was?

CATHLEEN: Keep your back to the door the way the light'll not be on you. (*Nora sits down at the chimney corner, with her back to the door. Maurya comes in very slowly, without looking at the girls, and goes over to her stool at the other side of the fire. The cloth with the bread is still in her hand. The girls look at each other, and NORA: points to the bundle of bread.*)

CATHLEEN (*After spinning for a moment.*): You didn't give him his bit of bread?

(*Maurya begins to keen softly, without turning round.*)

CATHLEEN: Did you see him riding down? (*Maurya goes on keening.*)

CATHLEEN (*A little impatiently.*): God forgive you; isn't it a better thing to raise your voice and tell what you seen, than to be making lamentation for a thing that's done? Did you see Bartley, I'm saying to you?

MAURYA (*With a weak voice.*): My heart's broken from this day.

CATHLEEN (*As before.*): Did you see Bartley?

MAURYA: I seen the fearfulest thing.

CATHLEEN (*Leaves her wheel and looks out.*): God forgive you; he's riding the mare now over the green head, and the gray pony behind him.

MAURYA (*Starts, so that her shawl falls back from her head and shows her white tossed hair. With a frightened voice.*): The gray pony behind him.

CATHLEEN: (*Coming to the fire.*) What is it ails you, at all?

MAURYA (*Speaking very slowly.*): I've seen the fearfulest thing any person has seen, since the day Bride Dara seen the dead man with the child in his arms.

CATHLEEN: and NORA: Uah.

(*They crouch down in front of the old woman at the fire.*)

NORA: Tell us what it is you seen.

MAURYA: I went down to the spring well, and I stood there saying a prayer to myself. Then Bartley came along, and he riding on the red mare with the gray pony behind him (*she puts up her hands, as if to hide something from her eyes.*) The Son of God spare us, Nora!

CATHLEEN: What is it you seen.

MAURYA: I seen Michael himself.

CATHLEEN (*Speaking softly.*): You did not, mother; it wasn't Michael you seen, for his body is after being found in the far north, and he's got a clean burial by the grace of God.

MAURYA (*A little defiantly.*): I'm after seeing him this day, and he riding and galloping. Bartley came first on the red mare; and I tried to say "God speed you," but something choked the words in my throat. He went by quickly; and "the blessing of God on you," says he, and I could say nothing. I looked up then, and I crying, at the gray pony, and there was Michael upon it—with fine clothes on him, and new shoes on his feet.

CATHLEEN (*Begins to keen.*): It's destroyed we are from this day. It's destroyed, surely.

NORA: Didn't the young priest say the Almighty God wouldn't leave her destitute with no son living?

MAURYA (*In a low voice, but clearly.*): It's little the like of him knows of the sea. . . . Bartley will be lost now, and let you call in Eamon and make me a good coffin out of the white

boards, for I won't live after them. I've had a husband, and a husband's father, and six sons in this house—six fine men, though it was a hard birth I had with every one of them and they coming to the world— and some of them were found and some of them were not found, but they're gone now the lot of them . . . There were Stephen, and Shawn, were lost in the great wind, and found after in the Bay of Gregory of the Golden Mouth, and carried up the two of them on the one plank, and in by that door.

(*She pauses for a moment, the girls start as if they heard something through the door that is half open behind them.*)

NORA (*In a whisper.*): Did you hear that, Cathleen? Did you hear a noise in the north-east?

CATHLEEN (*In a whisper.*): There's some one after crying out by the seashore.

MAURYA (*Continues without hearing anything.*): There was Sheamus and his father, and his own father again, were lost in a dark night, and not a stick or sign was seen of them when the sun went up. There was Patch after was drowned out of a curagh that turned over. I was sitting here with Bartley, and he a baby, lying on my two knees, and I seen two women, and three women, and four women coming in, and they crossing themselves, and not saying a word. I looked out then, and there were men coming after them, and they holding a thing in the half of a red sail, and water dripping out of it—it was a dry day, Nora—and leaving a track to the door.

(*She pauses again with her hand stretched out towards the door. It opens softly and old women begin to come in, crossing themselves on the threshold, and kneeling down in front of the stage with red petticoats over their heads.*)

MAURYA (*Half in a dream, to Cathleen.*): Is it Patch, or Michael, or what is it at all?

CATHLEEN: Michael is after being found in the far north, and when he is found there how could he be here in this place?

MAURYA: There does be a power of young men floating round in the sea, and what way would they know if it was Michael they had, or another man like him, for when a man is nine days in the sea, and the wind blowing, it's hard set his own mother would be to say what man was it.

CATHLEEN: It's Michael, God spare him, for they're after sending us a bit of his clothes from the far north.

(She reaches out and hands MAURYA the clothes that belonged to Michael. Maurya stands up slowly, and takes them into her hands. NORA looks out.)

NORA: They're carrying a thing among them and there's water dripping out of it and leaving a track by the big stones.

CATHLEEN *(In a whisper to the women who have come in.)*: Is it Bartley it is?

ONE OF THE WOMEN: It is surely, God rest his soul.

(Two younger women come in and pull out the table. Then men carry in the body of Bartley, laid on a plank, with a bit of a sail over it, and lay it on the table.)

CATHLEEN *(To the women, as they are doing so.)*: What way was he drowned?

ONE OF THE WOMEN: The gray pony knocked him into the sea, and he was washed out where there is a great surf on the white rocks.

(Maurya has gone over and knelt down at the head of the table. The women are keening softly and swaying themselves with a slow movement. Cathleen and Nora kneel at the other end of the table. The men kneel near the door.)

MAURYA *(Raising her head and speaking as if she did not see the people around her.)*: They're all gone now, and there isn't anything more the sea can do to me. . . . I'll have no call now to be up crying and praying when the wind breaks from the south, and you can hear the surf is in the east, and the surf is in the west, making a great stir with the two noises, and they hitting one on the other. I'll have no call now to be going down and getting Holy Water in the dark nights after Samhain, and I won't care what way the sea is when the other women will be keening. *(To Nora)*. Give me the Holy Water, Nora, there's a small sup still on the dresser. *(Nora gives it to her.)*

MAURYA *(Drops Michael's clothes across Bartley's feet, and sprinkles the Holy Water over him.)*: It isn't that I haven't prayed for you, Bartley, to the Almighty God. It isn't that I haven't said prayers in the dark night till you wouldn't know what I'd be saying; but it's a great rest I'll have now, and it's time surely. It's a great rest I'll have now, and great sleeping in the long nights after Samhain, if it's only a bit of wet flour we do have to eat, and maybe a fish that would be stinking.

(She kneels down again, crossing herself, and saying prayers under her breath.)

CATHLEEN *(To an old man.)*: Maybe yourself and Eamon would make a coffin when the sun rises. We have fine white boards herself bought, God help her, thinking Michael would be found, and I have a new cake you can eat while you'll be working.

THE OLD MAN *(Looking at the boards.)*: Are there nails with them?

CATHLEEN: There are not, Colum; we didn't think of the nails.

ANOTHER MAN: It's a great wonder she wouldn't think of the nails, and all the coffins she's seen made already.

CATHLEEN: It's getting old she is, and broken.

(Maurya stands up again very slowly and spreads out the pieces of Michael's clothes beside the body, sprinkling them with the last of the Holy Water.)

NORA *(In a whisper to Cathleen)*: She's quiet now and easy; but the day Michael was drowned you could hear her crying out from this to the spring well. It's fonder she was of Michael, and would any one have thought that?

CATHLEEN *(Slowly and clearly.)*: An old woman will be soon tired with anything she will do, and isn't it nine days herself is after crying and keening, and making great sorrow in the house?

MAURYA *(Puts the empty cup mouth downwards on the table, and lays her hands together on Bartley's feet.)*: They're all together this time, and the end is come. May the Almighty God have mercy on Bartley's soul, and on Michael's soul, and on the souls of Sheamus and Patch, and Stephen and Shawn *(bending her head))*; and may He have mercy on my soul, Nora, and on the soul of every one is left living in the world.

(She pauses, and the keen rises a little more loudly from the women, then sinks away.)

MAURYA *(Continuing)*: Michael has a clean burial in the far north, by the grace of the Almighty God. Bartley will have a fine coffin out of the white boards, and a deep grave surely. What more can we want than that? No man at all can be living for ever, and we must be satisfied.

(She kneels down again and the curtain falls slowly.)

▶ EXPERIENCING *Riders to the Sea*

1. Plot: What happens in this drama? Who changes in what way?
2. Ideas: What ideas are important in this drama? Could this be said to be a drama of ideas rather than a drama of action?

The plot of *Riders to the Sea* is virtually a straight line in that the question at the beginning of the play, whether Michael has been found dead, is answered step by step through the inquiry of the bundle the young priest brings. The shirt and stocking are ordinary enough, but through the analysis of the stitching Michael's death is confirmed quickly. Then the question is whether Bartley will risk his life now that he is the only man left in the family. Of course, we feel his sense of need to prove himself and he becomes the archetype of the reckless youth seeking his identity on the sea. The plot has a sense of inevitability about it, but that does not make it any less painful to watch because the result of the action of the drama is the abandonment of the women who must live on.

If this is a drama of ideas, it is about the idea of fate at work in the modern world. Here fate takes the form of the wild environment. The Aran islands are harsh and the poverty of the people who live on them is cruel. To raise a family and to live even for a short time in this part of Ireland has always been known to be daunting, challenging even the most dutiful of people. In some ways, too, the play is about the relationships of men and women. Maurya reels off a litany of the men who have perished, leaving their women behind them. Synge lived on one of the Aran islands for a time and knew the characters that he portrayed. He knew the recklessness of the men and the stoic patience and hopefulness of the women. *Riders to the Sea* is his hymn to a people for whom he had great admiration.

3. Character: Are there type characters in this play? Are the men types? Are the women type characters?
4. Setting: Where is the action set? Why is the setting of critical importance to the ideas in the drama?
5. Genre: What qualifies this play as a tragedy? Is it, for you, a satisfying drama? Does Maurya qualify as a tragic heroine?

FOCUS ON **Musical Theater: *Hamilton***

Most of the plays discussed so far do not emphasize music, but in *The Poetics,* Aristotle includes it as an essential part of the dramatic experience: "a very real factor in the pleasure of the drama." The great Greek tragedies were chanted to musical instruments, and the music had a significant effect on the audiences. Most of the great Elizabethan plays included music, some of which came at important moments in the action. Shakespeare's plays especially are noted for numerous beautiful and moving songs.

In modern times, the Broadway musical theater represents one of the most important contributions made by the United States to the stage. The musical plays that have developed since the early part of the twentieth century have been produced around the globe, and today they are being written and performed in many nations abroad. The Broadway musical is now an international drama that is in most cases more popular than standard drama. In the twenty-first century, musical plays attract much greater audiences over longer runs than virtually any straight drama. *The Fantasticks,* for example—a simple love story featuring a blocking character and two young lovers—ran for forty-two years with a piano accompaniment and essentially one hit song, "Try to Remember That Night in September."

Unlike most famous musicals, the Pulitzer Prize musical *Hamilton* (Figures 8-10, 8-11, and 8-12) did not derive its narrative from a novel or play, but from a biography by a historian. Lin-Manuel Miranda, who had written an earlier successful hip-hop musical, *In the Heights,* set in the Latino neighborhood of Washington Heights, New York, read the biography of Hamilton and realized he shared many of his qualities, especially that of having been an outsider.

Alexander Hamilton, apart from being on the ten-dollar bill in honor of his having established sound banking procedures after the American Revolution, took an important part in the Revolution itself. He hoped to lead a military contingent in the 1770s, but George Washington needed him in his camp with him as his aide. He performed great service to Washington and was rewarded with important responsibilities in the new government, including helping to shape the relationship between the federal and state responsibilities.

Alexander Hamilton's life was filled with adventure and achievement, so it provided a thrilling basis for the musical. He was born out of wedlock, with a father who disappeared and a mother who died when he was a teenager. He was orphaned in the British West Indies and found his way to New York, where he became part of the movement for independence. After the war he was named Secretary of the Treasury and took part in politics. He opposed Aaron Burr, also a brilliant young man, when Burr ran against Jefferson for the presidency. Their competition annoyed Burr because Hamilton succeeded where he failed. Ultimately, they took part in a duel across the river in New Jersey. Hamilton fired in the air, but Burr shot and killed him.

Miranda took the material of Hamilton's extraordinarily adventurous and responsible life and dramatized it in a way that was specifically novel, using a mixed cast of actors singing and dancing in a hip-hop style that was thought by some to be inappropriate for the musical theater. However, *Hamilton* became an instant hit, selling out all the seats in the Public Theater and then doing the same on Broadway. It became a must-see for all theater goers in its first year on the stage. Miranda performed some of the songs at the White House in a special appearance.

FIGURE 8-10
Hamilton, **the Pulitzer Prize–winning hip-hop musical.** Originating in the Public Theater in New York, it moved to Broadway in 2015. Lin-Manuel Miranda, center, plays the title role in the hip-hop-influenced musical *Hamilton,* at the Public Theater.

©Sara Krulwick/The New York Times/Redux

FIGURE 8-11
Phillipa Soo, left, as Eliza Schuyler and Lin-Manuel Miranda as Alexander Hamilton in *Hamilton.* **May 10, 2016.** Alexander Hamilton, an illegitimate orphan from the West Indies, marries a member of one of America's great families. He will eventually become embroiled in a great scandal and lose his family.

©Joan Marcus

What made *Hamilton* different was the use of hip-hop lyrics, which depend on music, rapping dialogue, and intense and surprising rhymes. A typical passage is this, from the song "My Shot": "If we win our independence / Is that a guarantee of freedom for our descendants? / Or will the blood we shed begin an endless / Cycle of vengeance and death with no defendants?" Miranda saw that rap was the voice of his generation and the people he hoped to reach in his drama. The surprise was that he reached not only those people but also audiences that never credited hip-hop and rap as serious art. Miranda, though he came late to the art, is known as one of the best freestyle rappers.

Of course, musical theater has been successful for years. *Cats,* based on T. S. Eliot's *Old Possum's Book of Practical Cats,* stayed on Broadway for almost 7,500 performances, longer than Michael Bennett's *A Chorus Line,* which lasted for 6,137 performances. Other contemporary long-running musicals are *The Phantom of the Opera* (8,700 on Broadway, 9,500 in London), *Beauty and the Beast, Chicago,* and *The Lion King.* A number of musical plays in addition to *Hamilton* have won the Pulitzer Prize for Drama: *Of Thee I Sing* (1932); *South Pacific* (1950); *A Chorus Line* (1976); *Sunday in the Park with George* (1985); and *Rent* (1996).

FIGURE 8-12

Lin-Manuel Miranda, center, and the company of *Hamilton*. This Pulitzer Prize–winning musical play starred Lin-Manuel Miranda, who wrote the music and lyrics and directed the production. He devised this drama after reading Ron Chernow's historical biography, *Alexander Hamilton*.

©Joan Marcus

Most musicals include extensive choreography, often by celebrated modern dancers, such as Agnes de Mille in *Oklahoma!,* Jerome Robbins in *The King and I,* Gower Champion in *42nd Street,* and Bob Fosse in *Chicago, Dancin',* and *All That Jazz.*

The musical theater can be especially rich in spectacle, with massed dance scenes and popular songs that have a life outside the drama, as in the case of musicals by Cole Porter, Jerome Kern, and Richard Rodgers. But some musicals also treat serious subjects, as in Jerome Kern's and Oscar Hammerstein's *Show Boat,* which comes closer to being a drama than a musical in part because of its treatment of slavery in the South. It was adapted from Edna Ferber's novel, and partly through the powerful song "Ol' Man River," it has become one of the most moving of musicals. One interesting aspect of Broadway musicals is that they have often been successfully transformed into excellent films, bringing them to audiences around the world.

PERCEPTION KEY Musical Theater: *Hamilton*

1. If possible, see *Hamilton* on stage or snippits online in video clips. Comment on the dynamics of the presentation and the language. Comment, too, on the question of the ideas in the drama.
2. The American revolution is part of the subject matter of *Hamilton,* but Miranda uses the musical to praise immigrants and to argue for justice today. How effective is his use of ideas in the service of justice?

3. Has Lin-Manuel Miranda discovered a new archetype in the portrayal of the home-less orphan immigrant who comes to a new country and makes good? Or is this just the archetype of the American Dream?

4. If you have the chance to see either a live or filmed version of one of the musicals mentioned above, explain what you feel has been added to the drama by the use of music and song.

5. If possible, compare *Hamilton* with its source, Ron Chernow's biography, *Alexander Hamilton*.

6. Given that people generally do not communicate with one another in song, how can we consider musicals as being realistic and true to life? If not, why are musicals so powerful and popular among audiences? Isn't realism a chief desirable quality in drama? Does the hip-hop style make the songs more or less realistic?

7. Try reading the book and lyrics of *Hamilton*. How effective do you think this work would be on the stage if there were no music with it? What is missing besides the music?

8. Musical comedy dominates the popular stage. There is no obvious musical tragedy (*Oedipus Rex* or *Hamlet*, for example). However, given that Alexander Hamilton is killed at the end of *Hamilton*, does that make it a musical tragedy?

EXPERIMENTAL DRAMA

We have seen exceptional experimentation in modern drama in the Western world. Samuel Beckett wrote plays with no words at all, as with *Acts without Words*. One of his plays, *Not I,* has an oversized mouth talking with a darkened, hooded fig-ure, thus reducing character to a minimum. In *Waiting for Godot,* plot is greatly reduced in importance. In *Endgame* (Figure 8-13), two of the characters are immo-bilized in garbage cans. Beckett's experiments have demonstrated that even when

FIGURE 8-13
Samuel Beckett's *Endgame*. Elaine Stritch, Nell, and Alvin Epstin, Nagg, in the Brooklyn Academy of Music's Spring 2008 production. First produced in 1957, *Endgame* continues to be performed worldwide. Nell and Nagg are parents of Hamm, played by John Turturro. Ostensibly, the play suggests the end of the world, with characters who are unable to move or change.

©Richard Termine

the traditional elements of drama are de-emphasized or removed, it is still possible for drama to evoke intense participative experiences. Beckett has been the master of doing away with everything inessential.

Another important thrust of experimental drama has been to assault the audience. Antonin Artaud's "Theater of Cruelty" has regarded audiences as comfortable, pampered groups of privileged people. Peter Weiss's play—*The Persecution and Assassination of Marat as Performed by the Inmates of the Asylum at Charenton under the Direction of the Marquis de Sade* (or *Marat/Sade*)—obviously was influenced by Artaud's radical antiestablishment thinking. Through a depiction of insane inmates contemplating the audience at a very close range, it sought to break down the traditional security associated with the proscenium theater. *Marat/Sade* ideally was performed in a theater-in-the-round with the audience sitting on all sides of the actors and without the traditional fanfare of lights dimming for the beginning and lighting up for the ending. The audience is deliberately made to feel uneasy throughout the play. The depiction of intense cruelty within the drama is there because, according to Weiss, cruelty underlies all human events, and the play attempts a revelation of that all-pervasive cruelty. The audience's own discomfort is a natural function of this revelation.

Richard Schechner's *Dionysus in '69* also did away with spatial separation. The space of the theater was the stage space, with a design by Jerry Rojo that made players and audience indistinguishable. The play demanded that everyone become part of the action; in some performances—and in the filmed performance—most of the players and audience ended the drama with a modern-day orgiastic rite. Such experimentation, indeed, seems extreme. But it is analogous to other dramatic events in other cultures, such as formal religious and celebratory rites.

PERCEPTION KEY Experimental Drama

Should you have the chance to experience a drama produced by any of the directors or groups mentioned above, try to distinguish its features from those of the more traditional forms of drama. What observations can you add to those made above? Consider the kinds of satisfaction you can get as a participant. Is experimental drama as satisfying as traditional drama? What are the differences? To what extent are the differences to be found in the details? The structure? Are experimental dramas likely to be episodic or organic? Why?

SUMMARY

The subject matter of drama is the human condition as represented by action. By emphasizing plot and character as the most important elements of drama, Aristotle helps us understand the priorities of all drama, especially with reference to its formal elements and their structuring. Aristotle's theory of tragedy focuses on the fatal flaw of the protagonist. Tragedy and comedy both have archetypal patterns that help define them as genres. Some of the archetypes are related to the natural rhythms of the seasons and focus, in the case of tragedy, on the endings of things, such as death (winter) and, in the case of comedy, on the beginnings of things, such as romance (spring). The subject matter of tragedy is the tragic—sorrow and suffering. The subject matter of comedy is the comic—oddball behavior and joy.

Comedy has several distinct genres. Old Comedy revels in broad humor. New Comedy satirizes the manners of a society; its commentary often depends on type and stereotype characters. Tragicomedy combines both genres to create a third genre. The ambiguity implied by tragedy joined with comedy makes this a particularly flexible genre, suited to a modern world that lives in intense uncertainty. Musical drama sometimes veers toward social commentary, or even social satire. The success of musical drama in modern times suggests that Aristotle was correct in assuming the importance of music in drama on an almost equal footing with its other elements. The experiments in modern drama have broken away from traditional drama, creating fascinating insights into our time. The human condition shifts from period to period in the history of drama, but somehow the constancy of human concerns makes all great dramatists our contemporaries.

©Brand X Pictures/PunchStock RF

Chapter 9

MUSIC

Music is one of the most powerful of the arts partly because sounds—more than any other sensory stimulus—create in us involuntary reactions, pleasant or unpleasant. Live concerts, whether of the Chicago Symphony Orchestra, Wynton Marsalis at Lincoln Center, or Bruce Springsteen and the E Street Band on tour, usually produce delight in their audiences. Yet, in all cases, the people rarely analyze the music. It may seem difficult to connect analysis with the experience of listening to music, but everyone benefits from an understanding of some of the fundamentals of music.

Hearing and Listening

Music can be experienced in two basic ways: "hearing" or "listening." *Hearers* do not attempt to perceive accurately either the structure or the details of the form. They hear a familiar melody such as the Beatles' "Strawberry Fields," which may trigger associations with John Lennon, early rock and roll, and perhaps even the garden in Central Park dedicated to his memory. But aside from the melody, little else—such as the details of chord progression, movement toward or away from tonic and dominant—is heard sensitively. The case is much the same with classical music. Most hearers prefer richly melodic music, such as Tchaikovsky's Fifth Symphony, whose second movement especially contains lush melodies that can trigger romantic associations. But when one asks hearers if the melody was repeated exactly or varied, or whether the melody was moved from one instrumental family to another, they cannot say. They are concentrating on the associations evoked by the music rather than on the details and structure of the music.

A hearer of hard rock is likely to attend as much to the performer as to the sonic effects. Powerful repetitive rhythms and blasting sounds trigger visceral responses so strong that dancing or motion—often wild—becomes imperative. Another kind of hearer is "suffused" or "permeated" by music, bathing in sensuous sounds, as many people will do with their earphones tuned to soft rock, new age, or easy-listening sounds. In this nonanalytic but attractive state of mind, the music spreads through the body rhythmically, soothingly. It feels great, and that is enough.

The *listeners*, conversely, concentrate their attention upon the form, details as well as structure. They could answer questions about the structure of Tchaikovsky's Fifth Symphony. And a listener, unlike a hearer, would be aware of the details and structure of works such as the Rolling Stones' "Sympathy for the Devil." Listeners focus on the form that informs, that creates content. Listeners do not just listen: They listen for something—the content.

PERCEPTION KEY Hearing and Listening

1. Play one of your favorite pieces of music. Describe its overall organization or structure. Is there a clear melody? Is there more than one melody? If so, are they similar to one another or do they contrast with one another? Is the melody repeated? Is it varied or the same? Do different instruments play it? If there are lyrics, are they repeated?
2. Describe details such as what kind of rhythm is used. Is it varied? If so, how? Is there harmony? What kind of instruments are played? How do these details fit into the structure?
3. Play the first movement of Beethoven's Third Symphony (the *Eroica*). Answer the same questions for this piece as were asked in questions 1 and 2. Later, we will analyze this movement. You may wish to compare your responses now with those you have after studying the work.

THE ELEMENTS OF MUSIC

Before trying to describe the subject matter of music, we will introduce some of the important terms and concepts essential to a clear discussion of music. We begin with some definitions and then analyze the basic musical elements of tone, consonance, dissonance, rhythm, tempo, melody, counterpoint, harmony, dynamics, and contrast. A common language about music is prerequisite to any intelligible analysis.

Tone

A sound with one definite frequency or a sound dominated by one definite frequency is a *tone*. Most music is composed of a succession of tones. We hear musical patterns because of our ability to hear and remember tones as they are played in succession. Every musical instrument will produce overtones, called harmonic partials, that, while sometimes faint, help us identify one instrument from another. Each of the notes on the piano is a tone whose sound vibrates at a specific number of cycles per second (hertz, or Hz). The note A below middle C vibrates at 220 Hz; middle C vibrates at 262.63 Hz; and the G above vibrates at 392. But each note will also produce overtones that are fainter than the primary tone. For instance, the note A below middle C produces these tones:

A: 220 Hz + 440 Hz + 660 Hz + 880 Hz and possibly 1,100 Hz

Each of the overtones will grow fainter than the primary tone, and the exact loudness and quality of the overtones will define for our ears whether we hear a saxophone or a trumpet or a piano. All the blending of instruments will contribute to the color (metaphorically) of the sounds we hear. Thus, the tonal color of a jazz group will differ from a heavy metal band, which will differ from a traditional rock-and-roll group, which in turn will differ greatly from a major orchestra. Each group may play the same sequence of tones, but we will hear the tones differently because of the arrangement of instruments and their tonal qualities.

Consonance

When two or more tones are sounded simultaneously and the result is easeful and pleasing to the ear, the resultant sound is said to be consonant. The phenomenon of *consonance* may be qualified by several things. For example, what sounds dissonant or produces tension often becomes more consonant after repeated hearings. Thus, the sounds of the music of a different culture may seem dissonant at first but consonant after some familiarity develops. Also, there is the influence of context: A combination of notes or chords may seem dissonant in isolation or within one set of surrounding notes while consonant within another set. In the C major scale, the strongest consonances will be the eighth (C + C′) and the fifth (C + G), with the third (C + E), the fourth (C + F), and the sixth (C + A) being only slightly less consonant. Use Figure 9-1 if helpful, and sound the preceding chords on a piano.

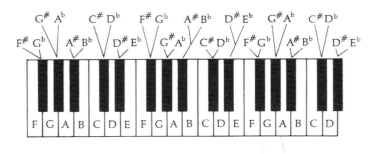

FIGURE 9-1
Notes of the piano keyboard.

Dissonance

Just as some tones sounding together tend to be stable and pleasant, other tones sounding together tend to be unstable and unpleasant. This unpleasantness is a result of wave interference and a phenomenon called "beating," which accounts for the instability we perceive in *dissonance*. The most powerful dissonance is achieved when notes close to one another in pitch are sounded simultaneously. The second (C + D) and the seventh (B + C) are both strongly dissonant. Dissonance is important in building musical tension, since the desire to resolve dissonance with consonance is strong in almost everyone. There is a story that Mozart's wife would retaliate against her husband during or after some quarrel by striking a dissonant chord on the piano. Wolfgang would be forced to come from wherever he was and play a resounding consonant chord to relieve the unbearable tension.

Rhythm

Rhythm refers to the temporal relationships of sounds. Our perception of rhythm is controlled by the accent or stress on given notes and their duration. In the waltz, the accent is heavy on the first note (of three) in each musical measure. In most jazz music, the stress falls on the second and fourth notes (of four) in each measure. Marching music, which usually has six notes in each measure, emphasizes the first and fourth notes.

Tempo

Tempo is the speed at which a composition is played. We perceive tempo in terms of beats, just as we perceive the tempo of our heartbeat as seventy-two pulses per minute, approximately. Many tempos have descriptive names indicating the general time value. *Presto* means "very fast"; *allegro* means "fast"; *andante* means "at a walking pace"; *moderato* means at a "moderate pace"; *lento* and *largo* mean "slow." Sometimes metronome markings are given in a score, but musicians rarely agree on any exact time figure. Tension, anticipation, and one's sense of musical security are strongly affected by tempo.

Melodic Material: Melody, Theme, and Motive

Melody is usually defined as a group of notes played one after another, having a perceivable shape or having a perceivable beginning, middle, and end. Usually a melody is easily recognizable when replayed. Vague as this definition is, we rarely find ourselves in doubt about what is or is not a melody. We not only recognize melodies easily but also can say a great deal about them. Some melodies are brief, others extensive; some slow, others fast; some playful, others somber. A *melodic line* is a vague melody, without a clear beginning, middle, and end. A *theme* is a melody that undergoes significant modifications in later passages. Thus, in the first movement of Beethoven's *Eroica* symphony, the melodic material is more accurately described as themes than melodies. On the other hand, the melodic material of "Swing Low, Sweet Chariot" (Figure 9-4) is clear and singable. A *motive* is the briefest intelligible and self-contained fragment or unit of a theme—for example, the famous first four notes of Beethoven's Symphony no. 5.

Counterpoint

In the Middle Ages, the monks composing and performing church music began to realize that powerful musical effects could be obtained by staggering the melodic lines. This is called *counterpoint*—playing one or more themes or melodies or motives against each other, as in folk songs such as "Row, Row, Row Your Boat." Counterpoint implies an independence of simultaneous melodic lines, each of which can, at times, be most clearly audible. Their opposition creates tension by virtue of their competition for our attention.

Harmony

Harmony is the sounding of tones simultaneously. It is the vertical dimension, as with a chord (Figure 9-2), as opposed to the horizontal dimension, of a melody. The harmony that most of us hear is basically chordal. A *chord* is a group of notes sounded together that has a specific relationship to a given key: The chord C-E-G, for example, is a major triad in the *key* of C major. At the end of a composition in the key of C, the major triad will emphasize the sense of finality—more than any other technique we know.

G or treble clef

F or bass clef

FIGURE 9-2
Harmony—the vertical element.

Chords are particularly useful for establishing *cadences*: progressions to resting points that release tensions. Cadences move from relatively unstable chords to stable ones. You can test this on a piano by first playing the notes C-F-A together, then playing C-E-G (consult Figure 9-1 for the position of these notes on the keyboard). The result will be obvious. The first chord establishes tension and uncertainty, making the chord unstable, while the second chord resolves the tension and uncertainty, bringing the sequence to a stable conclusion. You probably will recognize this progression as one you have heard in many compositions—for example, the "Amen" that closes most hymns. The progression exists in every key with the same sense of moving to stability.

Harmony is based on apparently universal psychological responses. All humans seem to perceive the stability of consonance and the instability of dissonance. The effects may be different due to cultural conditioning, but they are predictable within a limited range. In the 1940s one anthropologist, when told about a Samoan ritual in which he was assured he could hear original Samoan music—as it had existed from early times—hauled his tape recorder to the site of the ceremonies, waited until dawn, and when he heard the first stirrings turned on his machine and captured the entire group of Samoans singing "You are my sunshine, my only sunshine." The anthropologist was disappointed, but his experience underscores the universality of music.

Dynamics

One of the most easily perceived elements of music is *dynamics*: loudness and softness. Composers explore dynamics—as they explore keys, tone colors, melodies, rhythms, and harmonies—to achieve variety, to establish a pattern against which they can play, to build tension and release it, and to provide the surprise that can delight an audience. Two terms, *piano* ("soft") and *forte* ("loud"), with variations such as *pianissimo* ("very soft") and *fortissimo* ("very loud"), are used by composers to identify the desired dynamics at a given moment in the composition. A gradual buildup in loudness is called a *crescendo*, whereas a gradual reduction is called a *decrescendo*. Most compositions will have some of each, as well as passages that sustain a dynamic level.

Contrast

One thing that helps us value dynamics in a given composition is the composer's use of contrast. But contrast is of value in other ways. When more than one instrument is involved, the composer can contrast *timbres*. The brasses, for example, may be used to offer tonal contrast to a passage that may have been played by the strings. The percussion section, in turn, can contrast with both those sections, with high-pitched bells and low-pitched kettledrums covering a wide range of pitch and timbre. The woodwinds create very distinctive tone colors, and the composer writing for a large orchestra can use all of the families of instruments in ways designed to exploit the differences in the sounds of these instruments even when playing the same notes.

Composers may approach rhythm and tempo with the same attention to contrast. Most symphonies begin with a fast movement (usually labeled *allegro*) in the major key, followed by a slow movement (usually labeled *andante*) in a related or contrasting key, then a third movement with bright speed (usually labeled *presto*), and a final movement that resolves to some extent all that has gone before—again at a fast tempo (*molto allegro*), although sometimes with some contrasting slow sections within it, as in Beethoven's *Eroica*.

THE SUBJECT MATTER OF MUSIC

In music, as in other arts, content is achieved by the form's transformation of subject matter. The question of music's subject matter is dealt with in many ways by critics. Our approach is to identify two kinds of subject matter: feelings (emotions, passions, and moods) and sound.

Music cannot easily imitate nature, unless it does so the way bird songs and clocks sometimes appear in Haydn's symphonies or as Beethoven does in his *Pastoral* Symphony when he suggests a thunderstorm through his music. Other musicians sometimes use sirens or other recognizable sounds as part of their composition.

Program music attempts to provide a musical "interpretation" of a literary text, as in Tchaikovsky's *Overture: Romeo and Juliet,* in which the opening clarinet and oboe passages seem dark and forbidding, as if foreshadowing the tragedy to come. *La Mer,* by Claude Debussy, is an interpretation of the sea. His subtitles for sections of his work are "From Dawn to Noon at Sea," "Gambols of the Waves," and "Dialogue between the Wind and the Sea." For many listeners, the swelling of the music implies the swelling of the sea, just as the music's peacefulness suggests the pacific nature of the ocean.

However, our view is that while a listener who knows the program of *La Mer* may experience thoughts about the sea, listeners who do not know the program will still respond powerfully to the music on another level. It is not the sea, after all, that is represented in the music, but the feelings Debussy evoked by his experience of the sea as mediated by his composition. Thus, the swelling moments of the composition, along with the more lyrical and quiet moments, are perceived by the listener in terms of sound, but sound that evokes an emotional response that pleases both those who know the program and those who do not. This then means there is no strict relationship between the structures of our feelings and the structures of music, but there is clearly a general and worthwhile relationship that pleases us.

Feelings

Feelings are composed of sensations, emotions, passions, and moods. Any stimulus from any art produces a sensation. **Emotions** are strong sensations felt as related to a specific stimulus. **Passions** are emotions elevated to great intensity. **Moods** sometimes arise from no apparent stimulus, as when we feel melancholy for no apparent reason. In our experience, all these feelings mix together and can be evoked by music. No art reaches into our life of feeling more deeply than music.

In some important ways, music is congruent with our feelings and is thus capable of clarifying and revealing them to us. Nervous-sounding music can make us feel nervous, while calm, languorous music can relax us. A slow passage in a minor key, such as a funeral march, will produce a response quite different from that of a spritely dance. These extremes are obvious, of course, but they only indicate the profound richness of the emotional resources of music in the hands of a great composer.

Things get most interesting when music begins to clarify and produce emotional states that are not nameable. We name only a small number of the emotions we feel: joy, sorrow, guilt, horror, alarm, fear, calm, and many more. But those that can be named are only a scant few of those we feel. Music has an uncanny ability to give us insight into the vast world of emotions we cannot name.

The philosopher Susanne Langer has said that music has the capacity to educate our emotional life. She can say this because she believes, as we do, that music has feeling as part of its subject matter. She maintains that

> the tonal structures we call "music" bear a close logical similarity to the forms of human feelings—forms of growth and attenuation, flowing and stowing, conflict and resolution, speed, arrest, terrific excitement, calm, or subtle activation and dreamy lapses—not joy and sorrow perhaps, but the poignancy of either and both—the greatness and brevity and eternal passing of everything vitally felt. Such is the pattern, or logical form, of sentience, and the pattern of music is that same form worked out in pure, measured sound and silence. Music is a tonal analogue of emotive life.[1]

---

[1]Susanne Langer, *Feeling and Form* (New York: Scribner's, 1953), p. 27.

Roger Scruton, a contemporary philosopher who has considered this problem extensively, says this about emotion in music:

> The use of the term "expression" to describe the content of music reflects a widespread view that music has meaning because it connects in some way with our states of mind.[2]

These examples of the close similarity between the structures of music and feelings are fairly convincing because they are extreme. Most listeners agree that some music has become associated with gloomy moods, while other music has become associated with exhilaration. Much of this process of association undoubtedly is the result of cultural conventions that we unconsciously accept. But presumably there is something in the music that is the basis for these associations, and Langer has made a convincing case that the basis is in the similarity of musical and emotional structures.

Music creates structures that are something like what we feel during nonmusical experiences. We perceive outside something of what we usually perceive inside. When we listen to the anguish of the funeral march in the second movement of Beethoven's *Eroica*, we perceive the structures of anguish but not what evoked the anguish. Beethoven interprets and, in turn, clarifies those structures, gives us insight into them. Understanding tragic music brings satisfaction, analogous to the satisfaction that comes from understanding tragic drama. But there is a fundamental difference: Tragic drama is about what causes painful feelings; tragic music is about the structure of painful feelings. The subject matter of tragic drama is the outside world; the subject matter of tragic music is the inside world.

EXPERIENCING Chopin's Prelude 7 in A Major

Frederic Chopin (1810–1839) is frequently described as having created the most beautiful solo piano music. He was born in Poland and often used folk melodies and forms, such as mazurkas and polonaises. He lived a short but privileged life, and while spending his last years of life in Paris he was heralded as a genius by Robert Schumann, then one of Europe's most famous pianists. Chopin met Aurore Dudevant, known in literary society as George Sand, a scandalous feminist who wore men's clothes, smoked cigars, and took lovers as she liked. Chopin was living with her in Majorca in 1838 when he composed his Preludes, a cycle of twenty-four short pieces, one in each of the major and minor keys.

We do not know if he intended these pieces to be played as a sequence or if they were to be played independently, like musical jewels. Like most important Romantic music, they are often charged with strong feeling. The first prelude is melodic, but agitated. The second has a melancholic feeling, the third is light-hearted, and later pieces are stormy, explosive, calm, and expressive. We can see in each of the preludes a different "feeling," which we may or may not describe as emotional, or as inviting an emotional response. Each is also carefully crafted and would satisfy the musical demands of any formalist critic or technician.

Prelude 7 (Figure 9-3) is the shortest of the preludes, but it is also one of the most feelingful. Further, it is approachable by an intermediate player. It is in the key of A major, whose scale has the C, F, and G sharped. The harmonies in the bass clef are

continued

---

[2]Roger Scruton, *The Aesthetics of Music* (Oxford: Oxford University Press, 1996), p. 346.

mostly simple reinforcements of the main A major chords of the first and second bars. The harmonies become complex in bars 12 and 13, then become simple, aiming at the final resolution of an A major chord: A + E in the bass and A + C# + A in the treble.

The time signature is that of a waltz, with the first beat stressed, followed by two unstressed notes. The first three bars have two themes, the first an introduction, the second a rising passage to high A, indicating a tension needing release. The following three bars are lower in the scale and offer some release. But the twelfth and thirteenth bars add unexpected B# and D# rising to A# and C#—totally unexpected—the highest notes in the composition. They create novel chords, bright and challenging, and reward us by a "soft landing" at the end in the major chord of A, releasing the tension and informing us emotionally in complex meditative ways.

PRELUDE
Op. 28, No. 7

Frederic Chopin

FIGURE 9-3
Complete sheet music for Prelude 7 in A major, Chopin's shortest prelude.

Prelude 7 is to be played very slowly. You can hear several recordings online (search Chopin Prelude 7). Follow the score as you listen. Each player takes a different approach, and each player finds a different expressiveness in the composition.

1. After hearing the piece, do you think it has an emotional content? If so, how would you describe it?
2. How do different pianists interpret the content of Prelude 7?
3. If you can play this piece, describe the awareness of your own feelings. Is there a clear emotional content, or is the piece unemotional?
4. Is the piece memorable?

PERCEPTION KEY Feelings and Music

1. Listen to a piece of instrumental music by Claude Debussy, such as *La Mer, Claire de Lune, Golliwogg's Cake Walk*, or a piece from *Children's Corner*. Determine what, if any, feelings the music excites in you. Compare your observations with those of other listeners. Is there a consensus among your peers, or is there a wide variation in emotional response?
2. Listen to a piece such as Duke Ellington's *Diminuendo in Blue and Crescendo in Blue*, with Paul Gonsalves on saxophone (YouTube). What range of feelings and emotions seem to be excited in the audience? In you?
3. Listen to a piece of church music, such as Sergey Rachmaninov's *Vespers*. Describe your emotional reaction to the music. Is there such a thing as religious music? If so, what are its identifying qualities?

Music may not only evoke feelings in the listener but also reveal the structures of those feelings. Presumably, then, the form of *An Alpine Symphony* by Richard Strauss not only evokes feelings analogous to the feelings a day climbing in the Alps would arouse in us but also interprets those feelings and gives us insight into them. The Formalists of music, such as Eduard Hanslick and Edmund Gurney,[3] deny any connection of music with nonmusical situations. For them, the apprehension of the tonal structures of music is made possible by a unique musical faculty that produces a unique and wondrous effect, and they refuse to call that effect anything that suggests alliance with everyday feelings. They consider the grasp of the form of music so intrinsically valuable that any attempt to relate music to anything else is spurious.

As Igor Stravinsky, one of the greatest composers of the twentieth century, insisted, "Music is by its very nature essentially powerless to express anything at all."[4] In other words, the Formalists deny that music has a subject matter, and, in turn, this means that music has no content, that the form of music has no revelatory meaning. We think that the theory of the Formalists is plainly inadequate, but it is an important warning against thinking of music as a springboard for hearing, for nonmusical associations and sentimentalism. Moreover, much work remains—building on the work of philosophers of art such as Langer and Scruton—to make clearer the mechanism of how the form of music evokes feeling and yet at the same time interprets or gives us insight into those feelings.

Much simpler—and more generally accepted than either the Formalist theory of Hanslick and Gurney or our own theory—is the Expressionist theory: Music evokes feelings. Composers express or communicate their feelings through their music to their audiences. We should experience, more or less, the same feelings as the composer. But Mozart was distraught both psychologically and physically when he composed the *Jupiter* Symphony, one of his last and greatest works, and melancholy was the pervading feeling of his life shortly before his untimely death. Yet where is the melancholy in that symphony? Certainly there is melancholy in his *Requiem,* also one of his last works. But do we simply undergo melancholy in listening to the *Requiem*? Is it alone evoked in us and nothing more? Is there not a transformation of melancholy? Does not the structure of the music—"out there"—allow us to perceive the structure of melancholy and thus understand it better? If so, then the undoubted fact that the *Requiem* gives extraordinary satisfaction to most listeners is given at least partial explication by our theory that music reveals as well as evokes emotion.

SOUND

Apart from feelings, sound might also be thought of as one of the subject matters of music, because in some music it may be that the form gives us insight into sounds. This is somewhat similar to the claim that colors may be the subject matter of some abstract painting. The tone C in a musical composition, for example, has its analogue in natural sounds, as in a bird song, somewhat the way the red in an abstract

---

[3]Eduard Hanslick, *The Beautiful in Music,* trans. Gustav Cohen (London: Novello, 1891), and Edmund Gurney, *The Power of Sound* (London: Smith, Elder, 1880).
[4]*Igor Stravinsky, an Autobiography* (New York: Simon and Schuster, 1936), p. 83.

painting has its analogue in natural colors. However, the similarity of a tone in music to a tone in the nonmusical world is rarely perceived in music that emphasizes tonal relationships. In such music, the individual tone usually is so caught up in its relationships with other tones that any connection with sounds outside the music seems irrelevant. It would be rare, indeed, for someone to hear the tone C in a Mozart sonata and associate it with the tone C of some bird song.

Tonal relationships in most music are very different in their context from the tones of the nonmusical world. Conversely, music that does not emphasize tonal relationships—such as many of the works of John Cage—can perhaps give us insight into sounds that are noises rather than tones. Since we are surrounded by noises of all kinds—humming machines, talking people, screeching cars, and banging garbage cans, to name a few—we usually turn them off in our conscious minds so as not to be distracted from more important matters. This is such an effective turnoff that we may be surprised and sometimes delighted when a composer introduces such noises into a musical composition. Then, for once, we listen to rather than away from them, and then we may discover these noises to be intrinsically interesting, at least briefly.

PERCEPTION KEY The Content of Music

1. Select two brief instrumental compositions you enjoy. Choose one that you believe has recognizable emotions as its primary musical content. Choose another that you believe has sounds rather than tones as its primary musical content. Listen to both with a group of people to see if they agree with you. What is the result of your experiment?
2. Choose one piece of popular music that evokes strong emotion in you. Listen to it with people older or younger than you and determine whether they have similar emotional reactions.
3. What piece of music convinces you that the content of music is related to the expression of feeling? What piece of music convinces you otherwise?
4. Find a piece of music that you and a friend disagree about in terms of its apparent emotional content. If you think it expresses one kind of emotion, passion, or mood, and your friend thinks it expresses a totally different kind of emotion, passion, or mood, would that then call into question the theory that the content of music is connected to feelings?
5. To what extent do you think the emotional content of a piece of popular music may result in great differences of opinion among listeners of different generations? Do you and your parents listen to the same music? Do your parents listen to the same kind of music their parents listened to?

TONAL CENTER

A composition written mainly in one scale is said to be in the key that bears the name of the tonic, or tonal center, of that scale. A piece in the key of F major uses the scale of F major, although in longer, more complex works, such as symphonies, the piece may use other, related keys in order to achieve variety. The tonal center of a composition in the key of F major is the tone F. We can usually expect such a composition to begin on F, to end on it, and to return to it frequently to establish stability. Each return to F builds a sense of security in the listener, while each movement

Swing Low, Sweet Chariot

FIGURE 9-4
"Swing Low, Sweet Chariot." The
song is a Negro spiritual written
by Wallace Willis some time before
the emancipation of the slaves
in America (1862). Willis was a
freedman, a Choctaw, whose music
was recorded by the Jubilee Singers,
students at Fisk University, in 1909.
Both Anton Dvořák and Eric Clapton
are credited with incorporating the
melody in their music.

away usually builds a sense of insecurity or tension. The listener perceives the tonic as the basic tone because it establishes itself as the anchor, the point of reference for all the other tones.

After beginning with A in the familiar melody of "Swing Low, Sweet Chariot" (Figure 9-4), the melody immediately moves to F as a weighty rest point. The melody rises no higher than D and falls no lower than C. (For convenience, the notes are labeled above the notation in the figure.) Most listeners will sense a feeling of completeness in this brief composition as it comes to its end. But the movement in the first four bars, from A downward to C, then upward to C, passing through the tonal center F, does not suggest such completeness; rather, it prepares us to expect something more. If you sing or whistle the tune, you will see that the long tone, C, in bar 4 sets up an anticipation that the next four bars attempt to satisfy. In bars 5 through 8, the movement downward from D to C, then upward to A, and finally to the rest point at F suggests a temporary rest point. When the A sounds in bar 8, however, we are ready to move on again with a pattern that is similar to the opening passage: a movement from A to C and then downward through the tonal center, as in the opening four bars. Bar 13 is structurally repetitious of bar 5, moving from D downward, establishing firmly the tonal center F in the last note of bar 13 and the first four tones of bar 14. Again, the melody continues downward to C, but when it returns in measures 15 and 16 to the tonal center F, we have a sense of almost total stability. It is as if the melody has taken us on a metaphoric journey: showing us at the beginning where "home" is, the limits of our movement away from home, and then the pleasure and security of returning to home.

The tonal center F is home, and when the lyrics actually join the word "home" in bar 4 with the tone C, we are a bit unsettled. This is a moment of instability. We do not become settled until bar 8, and then again in bar 16, where the word "home" falls on the tonal center F, which we have already understood—simply by listening—as the real home of the composition. This composition is very simple, but also subtle, using the resources of tonality to excite our anticipations for instability and stability.

PERCEPTION KEY "Swing Low, Sweet Chariot"

1. What is the proportion of tonic notes (F) to the rest of the notes in the composition? Can you make any judgments about the capacity of the piece to produce and release tension in the listener on the basis of the recurrence of F?
2. Are there any places in the composition where you expect F to be the next note but it is not? If F is always supplied when it is expected, what does that signify for the level of tension the piece creates?
3. On the one hand, the ending of this piece produces a strong degree of finality. On the other hand, in the middle section the sense of finality is not nearly as strong. Is this difference between the middle section and the ending effective? Explain.
4. Does this music evoke feeling in you? If so, what kind of feeling? Does the music interpret this feeling, help you understand it? If so, how does the music do this?
5. Would a piece that always produced what is expected be interesting? Or would it be a musical cliché? What is a musical cliché?

MUSICAL STRUCTURES

The most familiar musical structures are based on repetition—especially repetition of melody, harmony, rhythm, and dynamics. Even the refusal to repeat any of these may be effective mainly because the listener usually anticipates repetition. Repetition in music is particularly important because of the serial nature of the medium. The ear cannot retain sound patterns for very long, and thus it needs repetition to help it hear the musical relationships.

Theme and Variations

A theme with variations on that theme constitutes a favorite structure for composers, especially since the seventeenth century. We are usually presented with a clear statement of the theme that is to be varied. The theme is sometimes repeated so that we have a full understanding, and then modifications of the theme follow. "A" being the original theme, the structure unfolds as A^1-A^2-A^3-A^4-A^5 . . . and so on to the end of the variations. Some marvelous examples of structures built on this principle are Bach's *Art of Fugue*, Beethoven's *Diabelli Variations*, Brahms's *Variations on a Theme by Joseph Haydn*, and Elgar's *Enigma Variations*.

Rondo

The first section or refrain of a ***rondo*** will include a melody and perhaps a development of that melody. Then, after a contrasting section or episode with a different melody, the refrain is repeated. Occasionally early episodes are also repeated, but usually not so often as the refrain. The structure of the rondo is sometimes in the pattern A-B-A-C-A—either B or D—and so on, ending with the refrain A. The rondo may be slow, as in Mozart's *Hafner Serenade,* or it may be played with blazing speed, as in Weber's *Rondo Brillante.*

Fugue

The *fugue*, a specialized structure of counterpoint, was developed in the seventeenth and eighteenth centuries and is closely connected with Bach and his *Art of Fugue*. Most fugues feature a melody—called the "statement"—which is set forth clearly at the beginning of the composition, usually with the first note the tonic of its key. Thus, if the fugue is in C major, the first note of the statement is likely to be C. Then that same melody more or less—called the "answer"—appears again, usually beginning with the dominant note (the fifth note) of that same key. The melodic lines of the statements and answers rise to command our attention and then submerge into the background as episodes of somewhat contrasting material intervene. Study the diagram in Figure 9-5 as a suggestion of how the statement, answer, and episode at the beginning of a fugue might interact. As the diagram indicates, the melodic lines often overlap, as in the popular song "Row, Row, Row Your Boat."

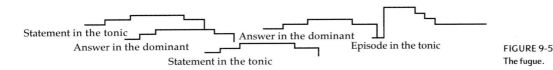

Statement in the tonic   Answer in the dominant   Episode in the tonic

Answer in the dominant

Statement in the tonic

FIGURE 9-5
The fugue.

Sonata Form

The eighteenth century brought the **sonata form** to full development, and many contemporary composers still find it very useful. Its overall structure basically is A-B-A, with these letters representing the main parts of the composition and not just melodies. The first A is the exposition, with a statement of the main theme in the tonic key of the composition and usually a secondary theme or themes in the dominant key (the key of G, for example, if the tonic key is C). A theme is a melody that is not merely repeated, as it usually is in the rondo, but is instead developed in an important way. In the A section, the themes are usually restated but not developed very far. This full development of the themes occurs in the B, or development, section, with the themes normally played in closely related keys. The development section explores contrasting dynamics, timbres, tempos, rhythms, and harmonic possibilities inherent in the material of the exposition. In the third section, or recapitulation, the basic material of the first section, or exposition, is more or less repeated, usually in the tonic key. After the contrasts of the development section, this repetition in the home key has the quality of return and closure.

The sonata form is ideal for revealing the resources of melodic material. For instance, when contrasted with a very different second theme, the principal theme of the exposition may take on a surprisingly new quality, as in the opening movement of Beethoven's *Eroica.*

The symphony is usually a four-movement structure, often employing the sonata form for its opening and closing movements. The middle movement or movements normally are contrasted with the first and last movements in dynamics, tempos, timbres, harmonies, and melodies. The listener's ability to perceive how the sonata form functions within most symphonies is essential if the total structure of the symphony is to be comprehended.

PERCEPTION KEY Sonata Form

1. Listen to and then examine closely the first movement of a symphony by Haydn or Mozart. That movement, with few exceptions, will be a sonata form. If a score is available, it can be helpful. (You do not have to be a musician to read a score.) Identify the exposition section—which will come first—and the beginning of the development section. Then identify the end of the development and the beginning of the recapitulation section. At these points, you should perceive some change in dynamics, tempo, and movements from home key or tonic to contrasting keys and back to the tonic. You need not know the names of those keys in order to be aware of the changes.
2. Once you have developed the capacity to identify these sections, describe the characteristics that make each of them different. Note the different characteristics of melody, harmony, timbre, dynamics, rhythm, tempo, and contrapuntal usages.
3. Listen to Haydn's Symphony no. 104, the *London*. It is available on YouTube played by the Bavarian Radio Symphony Orchestra. Listen closely for the A-B-A patterns within the first movement. Identify the repeated melodic material and consider the ways in which the orchestra varies the melodies as the piece progresses. How does watching the orchestra play help you identify theme and variation?

Symphony

The symphony marks one of the highest developments in the history of Western instrumental music (Figure 9-6). The symphony is so flexible a structure that it has flourished in every musical era since the Baroque period in the early eighteenth century. The word "symphony" implies a "sounding together." From its beginnings, through its full and marvelous development in the works of Haydn, Mozart, Beethoven, and Brahms, the symphony was particularly noted for its development of harmonic structures. Harmony is the sounding together of tones that have an established relationship to one another. Because of its complexity, harmony is a subject most composers must study in great depth during their apprentice years.

Triadic harmony (the sounding of three tones of a specific chord, such as the basic chord of the key C major, C-E-G, or the basic chord of the key F major, F-A-C) is common to most symphonies, especially before the twentieth century. Even in classical symphonies, however, such as Mozart's, the satisfaction that the listener has in triadic harmony is often withheld in order to develop musical ideas that will resolve their tensions only in a full, resounding chordal sequence of triads.

The symphony usually depends on thematic development. All the structures that we have discussed—theme and variations, rondo, fugue, and sonata form—develop melodic material, and some or all of them are often included in the symphony.

FIGURE 9-6
The BBC Symphony Orchestra.

©ArenaPal/Clive Barda/Topham/The
Image Works

In general, as the symphony evolved into its conventional structure in the time of Haydn and Mozart, the four movements were ordered as follows: first movement, sonata form; second movement, A-B-A or rondo; third movement, minuet; fourth movement, sonata form or rondo. There were exceptions to this order even in Haydn's and Mozart's symphonies, and in the Romantic and following periods the exceptions increased as the concern for conventions decreased.

The relationships between the movements of a symphony are flexible. On the one hand, the same melodic or key or harmonic or rhythmic approach may not prevail in all the movements. The sequence of movements may then seem arbitrary. On the other hand, some symphonies develop similar material through all movements, and then the sequence may seem less, if at all, arbitrary. This commonality of material is relatively unusual because its use for three or four movements can rapidly exhaust all but the most sustaining and profound material.

A comparison of the tempo markings of several symphonies by important composers usually shows several similarities: fast opening and closing movements with at least one slower middle movement. An alteration of tempo can express a profound change in the feeling of a movement. Our ears depend on the predictable alteration of tempo for finding our way through the whole symphony. In such large

FIGURE 9-7

The first theme of movement 1 of Haydn's Symphony no. 104. The first theme of the symphony is played by the strings alone after a brief introduction by the entire orchestra. The top line is played by the first violins, the second line by the second violins, the third line by the violas, and the bottom line by the cellos. The Bavarian Radio Symphony Orchestra performs this symphony on YouTube.

structures, we need all the signposts we can get, since it is easy to lose one's way through a piece that may last an hour or more. The following tempo markings in Figures 9-7 and 9-8 are translated loosely:

Haydn, Symphony no. 104 in A Major, the *London*
1. *Adagio, allegro* (slowly, fast)
2. *Andante* (moderately slow)
3. *Menuetto* and *trio*: allegro (slow dance, fast)
4. *Finale*: *Spiritoso* (ending, lively)

Mozart, Symphony no. 41 in C Major, the *Jupiter*
1. *Allegro vivace* (fast and lively)
2. *Andante cantabile* (slow and songlike)
3. *Allegretto* (dancelike)
4. *Allegro molto* (very fast)

The tempo markings, such as *andante* and *allegro,* in these and other symphonies, including those of modern composers, such as Charles Ives and Igor Stravinsky, suggest that each movement is designed with other movements in mind. That is, each movement offers a contrast to those that come before or after it. Composers of symphonies have many means besides tempo by which to achieve contrast, especially rhythm. The first movement is often written in 4/4 time, which means that there are four quarter notes in each measure, with the first especially and the third usually getting accents. The rhythms of the second movement are so varied that no general pattern is discernible. The third movement, especially in the early period of the symphony (Haydn and Mozart), usually is a dancelike minuet—3/4 time, three quarter notes to a measure, with the first note receiving the accent. Occasionally in the second and third movements, march time is used, either 6/8 time or 2/4 time. In 6/8 time, there are six eighth notes to a measure, with the first and fourth receiving the accent. In 2/4 time, the first of the two quarter notes receives the accent.

FIGURE 9-8

Opening bars of Mozart's Symphony no. 41 in C Major, the *Jupiter*. The opening bars are dynamic, with the entire orchestra, loud in bars 1, 5, and 9 contrasting soft, simple passages in bars 2, 3, and 4, and bars 6, 7, and 8. You can watch Nikolaus Harnoncourt conduct the Chamber Orchestra of Europe on YouTube using an orchestra similar to Mozart's.

Sometimes this produces the "oom-pah" sound we associate with marching bands. The fourth movement, usually a sonata form or a rondo, normally returns to 4/4 time.

Contrast is also achieved by varying the dynamics, with opposing loud and soft passages likely to be found in any movement. We might expect the middle movements, which are normally shorter than the first and last, to use less dynamic shifting. We usually expect the last movement to build to a climax that is smashing and loud. Variations in the length of movements add to contrast. And since the symphony is usually played by a large orchestra, the composer has a variety of instrumental families to depend on for adding contrast of tone colors. A theme, for instance, can be introduced by the violins, passed on to the woodwinds, then passed on to the horns, only to return to the violins. Secondary themes can be introduced by flutes or piccolos so as to contrast with the primary themes developed by other families of instruments. A secondary theme is often very different in length, pitch, and rhythmic character from a primary theme, thus achieving further contrast. Sometimes a theme or a developmental passage is played by a single instrument in a solo passage and then with all the instruments in that family playing together. Once the theme has been introduced by a single instrument or a small group, it may be played by the entire orchestra. These contrasts should hold our attention—for otherwise we miss much of what is going on—helping us to grasp the melodic material by showing us how it sounds in different timbres and ranges of pitch (higher in the flutes, lower in the cellos). The exceptional possibilities for achieving contrast in the symphony account, in part, for its sustaining success over the centuries.

We readily perceive contrasts in tempo, time signature, dynamics, and instrumentation, even if we are not trained and do not have access to the score of the composition. But there are subtler means of achieving contrast. For one thing, even within a specific movement, a composer will probably use a number of different keys. Usually they are closely related keys, such as C major followed by G major, or F major followed by C major. The dominant tone is the fifth tone, and one of the most convenient ways of moving from key to key is to follow the cycle of fifths, confident that each new key will clearly relate to the key that precedes it. Distant keys, A major to, say, D minor, can produce a sense of incoherence or uncertainty. Such motions between keys often are used to achieve this effect.

The average listener cannot always tell just by listening that a passage is in a new key, although practiced musicians can tell immediately. The exploration of keys and their relationships is one of the more interesting aspects of the development portions of most symphonies. The very concept of development, which means the exploration of a given material, is sometimes best realized by playing the same or similar material in different keys, finding new relationships among them. Our awareness of an especially moving passage is often due to the subtle manipulation of keys that analysis with a score might help us better understand. For the moment, however, let us concentrate on what the average listener can detect in the symphony.

PERCEPTION KEY The Symphony

Listen to Haydn's Symphony no. 104, the *London*, or to Mozart's Symphony no. 41, the *Jupiter*. Haydn and Mozart established the form. Both symphonies can be heard on YouTube. Respond to each movement by keeping notes with the following questions in mind.

1. Is the tempo fast, medium, or slow? Is it the same throughout? How much contrast is there in tempo within the movement? Between movements?
2. Can you hear the differences in time signatures—such as the difference between waltz time and marching time?
3. How much difference in dynamics is there in a given movement? From one movement to the next? Are some movements more uniform in loudness than others?
4. Identify melodic material as treated by single instruments, groups of instruments, or the entire orchestra.

5. Are you aware of the melodic material establishing a tonal center, moving away from it, then returning? (Perhaps only practiced listeners will be able to answer this in the affirmative.)
6. As a movement is coming to an end, is your expectation of the finale carefully prepared for by the composer? Is the finale sensed as surprising or inevitable?

FOCUS ON Beethoven's Symphony in Eb Major, No. 3, *Eroica*

Beethoven's "heroic" symphony is universally acclaimed by musicians and critics as a symphonic masterpiece. It has some of the most daring innovations for its time, and it succeeds in powerfully unifying its movements by developing similar material throughout, especially the melodic and the rhythmic. The symphony, finished in 1804, was intended to celebrate the greatness of Napoleon, whom Beethoven regarded as a champion of democracy and the common man. But when Napoleon declared himself emperor in May 1804, Beethoven, his faith in Napoleon betrayed, was close to destroying the manuscript. However, the surviving manuscript indicates that he simply tore off the dedication page and substituted the general title *Eroica*.

The four movements of the symphony follow the tempo markings we would expect of a classical symphony, but there are a number of important ways in which the *Eroica* is unique in the history of musical structures. The first movement, marked *allegro con brio* (fast, breezy), is a sonata form with the main theme of the exposition based on a triadic chord in the key of Eb major that resoundingly opens the movement. The development section introduces a number of related keys, and the recapitulation ultimately returns to the home key of Eb major. There is a **coda** (a section added to the end of the recapitulation) so extended that it is a second development section as well as a conclusion. After avoidance of the home key in the development, the Eb major finally dominates in the recapitulation and the coda. The movement is at least twice as long as the usual first movements of earlier symphonies, and no composer before had used the coda in such a developmental way. Previously the coda was quite short and repetitive. The size of the movement, along with the tight fusion of themes and their harmonic development into such a large structure, was very influential on later composers. The feelings that are evoked and revealed are profound and enigmatic.

The slow second movement is dominated by a funeral march in 2/4 time, with a very plaintive melody and a painfully slow tempo (in some performances), and an extremely tragic mood prevails. In contrast with the dramatic and vivid first movement, the second movement is sobering, diminishing the reaches of power explored in such depth in the first movement. The second movement uses a fugue in one of its later sections, even though the tempo of the passage is so slow as to seem to "stretch time." Despite its exceptional slowness, the fugue, with its competing voices and constant, roiling motion, seems appropriate for suggesting heroic, warlike feelings. The structure is a rondo: A-B-A'-C-A''-B'-D-A-''', A being the theme of the funeral march, the following A's being variations. The other material, including the fugue in C, offers some contrast, but because of its close similarity to the march theme, it offers no resolution.

The relief comes in the third movement, marked **scherzo**, which is both lively (*scherzo* means "joke") and dancelike. The movement is derivative from the first movement, closely linking the two in an unprecedented way. The time signature is the same

continued

as a minuet, 3/4, and the melodic material is built on the same triadic chord as in the first movement. And there is the same rapid distribution from one group of instruments to another. However, the third movement is much briefer than the first, while only a little briefer than the last.

The finale is marked *allegro molto* (very fast). A theme and variation movement, it is a catchall. It includes two short fugues, a dance using a melody similar to the main theme of the first movement, which is not introduced until after a rather decorative opening, and a brief march. Fast and slow passages are contrasted in such a fashion as to give us a sense of a recapitulation of the entire symphony. The movement brings us triumphantly to a conclusion that is profoundly stable. At this point, we can most fully appreciate the powerful potentialities of the apparently simple chord-based theme of the first movement. Every tonal pattern that follows is ultimately derivative, whether by approximation or by contrast, and at the end of the symphony the last triumphal chords are characterized by total inevitability and closure. The feelings evoked and revealed defy description, although there surely is a progression from yearning to sorrow to joy to triumph.

The following analysis will be of limited value without your listening carefully to the symphony more than once. If possible, use a score, even if you have no musical training. Ear and eye can coordinate with practice.

Listening Key: The Symphony

Beethoven, Symphony No. 3, OPUS 55, *Eroica*
Performed by George Szell and the Cleveland Orchestra.

Listen to the symphony using the timings of this recording. Before reading the following discussion, listen to the symphony. Then, study the analysis and listen again, this time participatively. Your enjoyment will likely be much greater.

Movement I: *Allegro Con Brio*. **Fast, Breezy.**
Sonata form, 3/4 time, E♭ major: Timing: 14:46; Track 1.

The first two chords are powerful, staccato, isolated, and compressed (Figure 9-9). They are one of the basic chords of the home key of E♭ major: G-E♭-B♭-G. Then at the third measure (Figure 9-10), the main theme, generated from the opening chord of the symphony, is introduced. Because it is stated in the cellos, it is low in pitch and somewhat portentous, although not threatening. Its statement is not quite complete, for it unexpectedly ends on a C♯ (♯ is the sign for sharp). The horns and clarinets take the theme at bar 15 (0:19), only to surrender it at bar 20 (0:23) to a group of ascending tones closely related to the main theme.

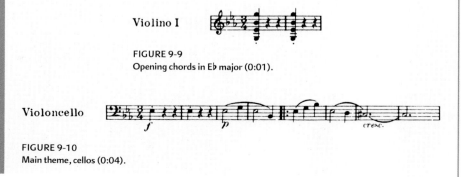

FIGURE 9-9
Opening chords in E♭ major (0:01).

FIGURE 9-10
Main theme, cellos (0:04).

The second theme is in profound contrast to the first. It is a very brief and incomplete pattern (and thus could also be described as a motive) of three descending tones moved from one instrument to another in the woodwinds, beginning with the oboes at bar 45 (Figure 9-11). This theme is unstable, like a gesture that needs something to complete its meaning. And the following motive of dotted eighth notes at bars 60 through 64 played by flutes and bassoons (Figure 9-12) is also unstable.

FIGURE 9-11
Second theme, oboes at bar 45 (0:54).

FIGURE 9-12
Flutes and bassoons at bars 60 through 64 (1:14).

This is followed by a rugged rhythmic passage, primarily audible in the violins, preparing us for a further incomplete thematic statement at bar 83, a very tentative, delicate interlude. The violin passage that preceded it (Figure 9-13) functions here and elsewhere as a link in the movement between differing material. Getting this passage firmly in your memory will help you follow the score, for it returns dependably.

FIGURE 9-13
Violin passage preceding bar 83 (1:19).

Many passages have unsettling fragments, such as the dark, brooding quality of the cello and contrabass motive shown in Figure 9-14, which sounds as a kind of warning, as if it were preparing us for something like the funeral march of the second movement. It repeats much later in variation at bar 498, acting again as an unsettling passage. Many other passages also appear to be developing into a finished statement, only to trail off. Some commentators have described these passages as digressions, but this is misleading, because they direct us to what is coming.

FIGURE 9-14
Cello and contrabass motive (1:57).

The exposition starts to end at bar 148 (3:03), with a long passage in B♭, the measures from 148 to 152 hinting at the opening theme, but they actually prepare us for a dying-down action that joins with the development. In George Szell's rendition, as in most recordings, the repeat sign at 156 is ignored. Instead, the second ending

continued

(bars 152 to 159) is played, and this passage tends to stretch and slow down, only to pick up when the second theme is played again in descending patterns from the flutes through all the woodwinds (3:16).

The development section is colossal, from bars 156 to 394, beginning at 3:18. The main theme recurs first at 178 (3:48) in shifting keys in the cellos, then is played again in B♭ from 186 to 194 (3:55), very slow and drawn out. Contrasting passages mix in so strongly that we must be especially alert or we will fail to hear the main theme. The momentum speeds up around bar 200 (4:16), where the main theme is again played in an extended form in the cellos and the contrabasses. The fragmented motives contribute to a sense of incompleteness, and we do not have the fullness of the main theme to hold on to. The fragmentary character of the second theme is also emphasized, especially between bars 220 and 230 (4:39). When we reach the crashing discords at bar 275 (5:44), the following quieting down is a welcome relief. The subsequent passage is very peaceful and almost without direction until we hear again the main theme in B♭ at bar 300 (6:21), then again at 312 (6:37) in the cellos and contrabasses. The music builds in loudness and then quiets down, and then the main theme is stated clearly in the bassoons, preparing for an extended passage that includes the main theme in the woodwinds building to a mild climax in the strings at bar 369 (Figure 9-15).

FIGURE 9-15
Strings at bar 369 (7:53).

The remainder of this passage is marvelously mysterious, with the strings maintaining a steady tremolo and the dynamics brought down almost to a whisper. The horn enters in bar 394 (8:24), playing the main theme in virtually a solo passage. Bars 394 and 395 are two of the most significant measures of the movement because of the way in which they boldly announce the beginning of the recapitulation. The horns pick up the main theme again at bar 408 (8:32), loud and clear, and begin the restatement of the exposition section. The recapitulation begins at bar 394 (8:24) and extends to bar 575 (12:05). It includes a brief development passage, treating the main theme in several unusual ways, such as the tremolo statement in the violins at bars 559 to 565 (Figure 9-16).

FIGURE 9-16
Violins at bars 559 to 565 (11:50).

The long, slow, quiet passages after bar 575 (12:05) prepare us for the incredible rush of power that is the coda—the "tail," or final section, of the movement. The triumphal quality of the coda—which includes extended development, especially of the main theme—is most perceptible, perhaps, in the juxtaposition of a delightful running violin passage from bar 631 to bar 639 (13:31), with the main theme and a minimal variation played in the horns. It is as if Beethoven is telling us that he has perceived the musical problems that existed with his material, mastered them, and now is celebrating with a bit of simple, passionate, and joyous music.

PERCEPTION KEY Movement I of the *Eroica*

1. Describe the main theme and the second theme. What are their principal qualities of length, "tunefulness," range of pitch, rhythm, and completeness? Could either be accurately described as a melody? Which is easier to whistle or hum? Why could the second theme be plausibly described as a motive? Do the two themes contrast with each other in such a way that the musical quality of each is enhanced? If so, how?

2. What are the effects of hearing the main theme played in different keys, as in bars 3 to 7 (0:04), bars 184 to 194 (3:55), and bars 198 to 206 (4:16)? All these passages present the theme in the cellos and contrabasses. What are the effects of the appearance of the theme in other instrumental families, such as the bassoons at bar 338 (7:12) in the development section and the horns at bar 408 (8:32) in the recapitulation section? Does the second theme appear in a new family of instruments in the development section?

3. How clearly perceptible do you find the exposition, development, recapitulation, and coda sections? Describe, at least roughly, the feeling qualities of each of these sections.

4. Many symphonies lack a coda. Do you think Beethoven was right in adding a coda, especially such a long and involved one? If so, what does it add?

5. If possible, record the movement, but begin with the development section; then follow with the recapitulation, exposition, and coda sections. Does listening to this "reorganization" help clarify the function of each section? Does it offer a better understanding of the movement as it was originally structured? Does this "reorganization" produce significantly different feeling qualities in each section?

Before going on to the next Perception Key, give your ear a rest for a brief time. Then come back to the symphony and listen to it all the way through. Sit back and enjoy it. Then consider the following questions.

PERCEPTION KEY The *Eroica*

1. In what ways are the four movements tied together? Does a sense of relatedness develop for you?

2. Is the symphony properly named? If so, what qualities do you perceive in it that seem "heroic"?

3. Comment on the use of dynamics throughout the whole work. Comment on variations in rhythms.

4. Is there a consistency in the thematic material used throughout the symphony? Are there any inconsistencies?

5. Do you find that fatigue affects your responses to the second movement or any other portion of the symphony? The act of creative listening can be very tiring. Could Beethoven have taken that into consideration?

6. Are you aware of a variety of feeling qualities in the music? Does there seem to be an overall plan to the changes in these qualities as the symphony unfolds?

7. What kind of feelings (emotion, passion, or mood) did the *Eroica* arouse in you? Did you make discoveries of your inner life of feeling because of your responses to the *Eroica*?

BLUES AND JAZZ: POPULAR AMERICAN MUSIC

So far, our emphasis is on classical music because its resources are virtually inexhaustible and its development, over many centuries and continuing today, has reached a pitch of refinement that matches that of painting, architecture, and literature. But other kinds of music in addition to opera, symphonies, and chamber music affect modern listeners. The blues, which developed in the African American communities in the southern United States, has given rise to a wide number of styles—among them jazz, which has become an international phenomenon, with players all over the world.

The term "blues" was used early to describe a form of music developed in the black communities in the South, and it seems to describe a range of feelings, although the blues was never a music implying depression or despair. Rather, it implied a soulful feeling as expressed in the blue notes of the scale and in the lyrics of the songs. The music that later developed from the blues is characterized by the enthusiasm of its audiences and the intense emotional involvement that it demands, especially in the great auditoriums and outdoor venues that mark the most memorable concerts seen by thousands of fans.

The blues evolved into a novel musical form by relying on a slightly different scale with blue notes: C E♭ F F♯ G B♭ C. Compare that with the standard C major scale: C D E F G A B C. The standard C scale has no sharps or flats, so the blues scale has a totally different feel. If you can play these scales, you will hear how different they are. The structure of the blues is twelve measures with a constant pattern of chord progressions, which is then repeated for another twelve measures. Out of this original pattern, jazz developed in the early years of the twentieth century.

Jazz began in New Orleans with the almost mythic figures of Buddy Bolden, the great trumpet player in Lincoln Park in the first years of 1900, and Jelly Roll Morton, who claimed to have single-handedly invented jazz. King Oliver's band in New Orleans was enormously influential, and when New Orleans was "cleaned up" by the U.S. Navy in 1917—drugs and prostitution were forced out of town—jazz moved up the Mississippi River to Chicago, where Louis Armstrong's powerful trumpet dominated jazz for more than a dozen years (Figure 9-17). The large, primarily white society bands, such as Paul Whiteman's Orchestra, introduced jazz to large radio audiences by employing great jazz stars such as Bix Beiderbecke, Jimmy and Tommy Dorsey, Hoagy Carmichael, and Jack Teagarden. Fortunately, all these orchestras recorded widely in the 1920s, and their music can be heard online at any of a number of sources.

The hot jazz of the time is marked by an extensive use of the blues scale, a powerful rhythm emphasizing the second and fourth beats of each measure, and a delight in counterpoint ensemble playing and dynamic solos that show off the talent of virtuoso players. The rhythm section was usually drums, piano, and guitar or bass. The horns, trumpet, clarinet, and trombone played most of the melodic material, supplying complex harmonic support while individuals were soloing. Some of their best recorded tunes were "Willie the Weeper," "Wild Man Blues," "Twelfth Street Rag," and "Chicago Breakdown." They were an energetic and exciting band playing the best jazz of the period.

Larger orchestras, such as the swing bands of Benny Goodman, Count Basie, Jimmy Lunceford, and Duke Ellington, had to rely less on improvisation and

FIGURE 9-17
**Louis Armstrong and the Hot Seven,
the dynamic mid-1920s band that
made some legendary recordings in
1927.** Armstrong is in the middle,
playing trumpet. His wife, Lil Hardin,
is at the piano. Johnny St. Cyr
played banjo, Johnny Dodds clarinet,
Baby Dodds drums, John Thomas
trombone, and Pete Briggs tuba.
The group can be heard at www
.redhotjazz.com.

©JP Jazz Archive/Redferns/Getty Images

counterpoint and more on ensemble playing. Their music was smoother, more har-
monically secure, and less exciting except when a soloist stood for his improvised
twelve or twenty-four measures. But even in the big bands, the emphasis on the
weak beats (the second and fourth of each measure) and the use of syncopation and
the anticipation of the beats helped keep a sense of power and movement in the
music, even though it may have been played more or less the same way in concert
after concert. Big band music was originally designed for dancing, and the best of
the jazz groups kept to that concept.

Miles Davis (Figure 9-18) has been compared with Picasso because of his various
stylistic periods, from the early bop of the late 1940s to the cool jazz of the 1950s
and 1960s and then the rock-fusion jazz of the *Bitches Brew* album in 1970, which
introduced electronic instruments. Charlie Parker, John Coltrane, Herbie Hancock,
Ron Carter, Bill Evans, Lee Konitz, Chick Corea, and many more giants of jazz were
among the members of Davis's groups, including the late sextet. *Sketches of Spain,*
1960, arranged by his friend Gil Evans, is an example of Davis's use of folk melodies
to produce a classical jazz album.

Contemporary jazz musicians, such as Wynton Marsalis (Figure 9-19), Diana
Krall, Cyrus Chesnut, Esperanza Spalding, the late Geri Allen, Keith Jarrett, Joshua
Redman, Christian McBride, Wayne Shorter, and Chuchu Valdés, are all in the
tradition of the great improvisational players of the twentieth century. The essence
of jazz is improvisation and, to an extent, competition. The early jazz bands often
competed with one another in "cutting contests" to see which band was better.
Players of the same instruments, such as the saxophone, have sometimes performed
onstage in intense competition to help raise the excitement level of the music.

FIGURE 9-18
Miles Davis.

©David Warner Ellis/Redferns/Getty Images

FIGURE 9-19
Wynton Marsalis opens Jazz Appreciation Month by performing and lecturing at the Kimmel Center for the Performing Arts. The Grammy Award winner performed with members of the Jazz at Lincoln Center Orchestra.

©Ricky Fitchett/Zuma Press, Inc./Alamy

ROCK AND ROLL AND RAP

Rock and roll has its roots in R&B—rhythm and blues—popular in the 1940s in the United States primarily among black radio audiences. Joe Turner, an early R&B man, composed "Shake, Rattle, and Roll," but it did not become a hit until Bill Haley recorded it in 1955. Louis Jordan's Tympany Five, Bo Diddley, and Muddy Waters were some of the major predecessors of rock and roll, and Ike Turner may have had the first true rock-and-roll record in 1951. However, the wide acceptance of rock and roll began only after white groups and singers began to adopt the black style. Elvis Presley was the first rock-and-roll star, with hit records beginning in the mid-1950s. Bill Haley's Comets, originally a country-western band, adopted the new style in "Rock around the Clock," the first rock tune to be used in the popular 1955 film *Blackboard Jungle,* in which rioting students destroy a high school teacher's collection of jazz records—obviously symbolic of a period of musical revolution.

Rock music and jazz are essentially countercultural art forms with codes for sexual behavior, and they usually went unobserved by general audiences. Rock groups were aided by the invention of the electric guitar in 1931. Les Paul popularized the Gibson solid-body electric guitar, and by the 1960s almost all rock-and-roll music was amplified, which made possible the great concerts of Led Zeppelin, the Who, Cream, Steve Miller Band, the Beatles, the Grateful Dead, and the Rolling Stones, all of whom began to tour internationally. The Beatles, a small group, were especially political during the 1960s and 1970s when they condemned the Vietnam War and popularized Indian mysticism. Some of these groups still appear, and all can be heard on the Internet and seen on YouTube and other sharing sites.

One of the most enduring of the classic age of rock groups is the Rolling Stones, whose tune "(I Can't Get No) Satisfaction," 1965, is still a hit when performed by Mick Jagger and Keith Richards (Figure 9-20). Their band began in 1962, endures today, and is widely available on Internet sharing sites. The Rolling Stones presented concerts marked by wild gyrations of Mick Jagger, while the cool and cerebral Keith Richards stayed behind, playing complex riffs inspiring the band. Both Jagger and Richards wrote most of their hits, and, unlike jazz groups, the Rolling Stones helped establish the pattern of great rock bands writing their own material rather than "covering" other people's music.

Styles in popular music evolve almost seamlessly from earlier styles and become apparent as a distinct form of music only when a major figure has a hit that catches the attention of a wide audience. Hip-hop and rap music have their roots in gospel, shout, and blues, just as do jazz and rock and roll. The use of amplified instruments, simple chord patterns—often the use of no more than three chords—and a heavy back beat (great stress on beats two and four) throughout a composition mark most of rock and later music. The lyrics are often personal, political, and usually countercultural—aimed at a youthful audience that sees itself as naturally rebellious.

Rap stars like Tupac Shakur recorded hundreds of tracks about life on the streets and the violence in the neighborhood. Tupac was killed in Las Vegas after an incident with gangs. Notorious B.I.G. was famous at the same time and feuded with Tupac. Later rap figures tend to develop the narratives beyond the neighborhood, like Eminem, Jay Z, Sean Combs, Drake, and Future. However, the music is still

FIGURE 9-20

Mick Jagger and Keith Richards of the Rolling Stones, in concert.
Mick Jagger and Keith Richards joined Ian Stewart and the original leader Brian Jones in 1962 with the Rolling Stones, adding the drummer Charlie Watts and bassist Bill Wyman. This band was part of the "British Invasion" that solidified the international credentials of rock and roll.

©Robert Galbraith/Reuters/Alamy

subversive and often a form of protest. Rap has been called misogynistic and sometimes racist, but it is an evolving form. The driving rhythm of rap remains, but as in the Pulitzer Prize–winning *Hamilton*, the resources of rap may be much less limited than its critics have thought.

Today, popular music includes most styles derived from blues, and most of it is strictly commercial, designed to make money. But some of it derives from a serious artistic purpose that has little to do with making money. Serious lovers of popular music usually look for evidence of sincerity in the music they prefer. It is not always easy to detect. But all that aside, the elements of popular music are those of all music: tone, rhythm, tempo, consonance, dissonance, melody, counterpoint, harmony, dynamics, and contrast.

> ## PERCEPTION KEY Popular Music
>
> 1. Choose a number of popular pieces, and identify their style (blues, jazz, punk, rock, rap, country, etc.). Decide whether this music seems to clarify a feeling state or states for you.
> 2. Select a piece of popular music that does not satisfy you. Listen to it several times and then explain what qualities the music has that you feel are insufficient for you to consider it a successful composition.
> 3. Listen to a composition by the Rolling Stones or another rock group that interests you. Comment on the band's respective use of rhythm, consonance and dissonance, melody, and harmony.
> 4. Select a popular composition and comment on its use of rhythm and tempo. Can you see connections with the use of rhythm and tempo in classical music?

5. Which of the elements of music is most imaginatively used in the popular composition that you currently listen to most?
6. Listen to George Gershwin's *Rhapsody in Blue*. It was written for piano and jazz band. Is Gershwin's composition classical in style, or is it jazz? What qualifies it as belonging to or not belonging to popular music?
7. Do you find structures in popular music like those of classical music—for example, theme and variations, rondos, fugues, sonatas, and so on? Which structure, if any, seems to dominate?
8. How closely related are popular music styles to those of classical music? How does understanding classical music help in appreciating popular music?

SUMMARY

We began this chapter by suggesting that feelings and sounds are the primary subject matters of music. This implies that the content of music is a revelation of feelings and sounds—that music gives us a more sensitive understanding of them. However, as we indicated in our opening statements, there is considerable disagreement about the subject matter of music, and so there is disagreement about the content of music. If music does reveal feelings and sounds, the way it does so is still one of the most baffling problems in the philosophy of art.

Given the basic theory of art as revelation, as we have been presupposing in this book, a couple of examples of how that theory might be applied to music are relevant. In the first place, some music apparently clarifies sounds as noises and tones. Music gives us insight into the resources of tonality in much the way painting gives us insight into the resources of color and visual sensa.

There seems to be evidence that music gives us insight into our feelings; for example, the last movement of Mozart's *Jupiter* symphony may excite a feeling of joy. The second movement—the funeral march—of Beethoven's *Eroica* symphony may evoke a feeling of sadness. In fact, "joy" and "sadness" are general terms that only very crudely describe our feelings. We experience all kinds of different joys and different sadnesses, and the names language gives to these are often imprecise.

Music, with its capacity to evoke feelings, and with a complexity of detail and structure that in many ways is greater than that of language, may be able to reveal or interpret feeling with much more precision than language. Perhaps the form of the last movement of the *Jupiter* symphony—with its clear-cut rising melodies, bright harmonies and timbres, brisk strings, and rapid rhythms—is somehow analogous to the form of a certain kind of joy. Perhaps the last movement of the *Eroica* is somehow analogous to a different kind of joy. And if so, then perhaps we find revealed in those musical forms clarifications or insights about joy. Such explanations are highly speculative. However, they not only are theoretically interesting but also may intensify one's interest in music. There is mystery about music, unique among the arts; that is part of its fascination. In addition to classical music, modern popular styles such as blues, jazz, rock and roll, and rap all have capacity to evoke intense participation resulting from the use of standard musical elements such as rhythm, tone color, melody, and harmony. They produce feeling states that can be complex and subtle in proportion to the seriousness and commitment of the artists and composers.

©Robbie Jack/Corbis/Getty Images

Chapter 10

DANCE

Dance—moving bodies shaping space—shares common ground with kinetic sculpture. In abstract dance, the center of interest is upon visual patterns, and thus there is common ground with abstract painting. Dance, however, usually includes a narrative, performed on a stage with scenic effects, and thus has common ground with drama. Dance is rhythmic, unfolding in time, and thus has common ground with music. Most dance is accompanied by music, and dance is often incorporated in opera. According to the psychologist Havelock Ellis: "Dancing is the loftiest, the most moving, the most beautiful of the arts, because it is no mere translation or abstraction from life; it is life itself."[1]

Subject Matter of Dance

At its most basic level, the subject matter of dance is abstract motion of bodies, but a much more pervasive subject matter of the dance is feeling. Our ability to identify with other human bodies is so strong that the perception of feelings exhibited by the dancer often evokes feelings in ourselves. The choreographer, creator of the dance, interprets those feelings. And if we participate, we may understand those feelings and ourselves with greater insight. In Trisha Brown's dance *Present Tense* (2003) (Figure 10-1), the very joy of movement is clearly expressed by the intensity of the dancers. The music was by John Cage and the set by Elizabeth Murray. Brown was notable for combining her choreography with music and set design by noted modern artists. Brown's interpretation of the joy of movement is infectious, demanding a kinesthetic response from the audience.

---

[1]Havelock Ellis, *The Dance of Life* (Boston: Houghton Mifflin, 1923).

FIGURE 10-1
Trisha Brown's company in *Present Tense*, **at the Brooklyn Academy of Music, 2016.** Trisha Brown's *Set and Reset, Foray Forêt, Present Tense*, and others have been the most admired of the postmodern dances, incorporating music from Laurie Anderson and set designs from Robert Rauschenberg.

©Andrea Mohin/The New York Times/Redux

States of mind are a further dimension that may be the subject matter of dance. Feelings, such as pleasure and pain, are relatively transient, but a state of mind is a disposition or habit that is not easily superseded. For example, jealousy usually involves a feeling so strong that it is best described as a passion. Yet jealousy is more than just a passion, for it is an orientation of mind that is relatively enduring. Thus, José Limón's *The Moor's Pavane* explores the jealousy of Shakespeare's *Othello*. In Limón's version, Iago and Othello dance around Desdemona and seem to be directly vying for her affections. *The Moor's Pavane* represents an interpretation of the states of mind Shakespeare dramatized, although it can stand independently of the play and make its own contribution to our understanding of jealousy.

Since states of mind are felt as enduring, the serial structure of the dance is an appropriate vehicle for interpreting that endurance. The same can be said of music, of course, and its serial structure, along with its rhythmic nature, is the fundamental reason for the wedding of music with dance. Even silence in some dances seems to suggest music, since the dancer exhibits visual rhythms, something like the rhythms of music. But the showing of states of mind is achieved only partly through the elements dance shares with music. More basic is the body language of the dancing bodies. Perhaps nothing—not even spoken language—exhibits states of mind more clearly or strongly.

1. The claim that dance can interpret the inner life of feeling with exceptional power implies, perhaps, that no other art surpasses dance in this respect. Why would such a claim be made?

The fact that dance is usually considered the first art in the cultivation of culture among all civilizations may have something to do with the possibility that dance expresses and refines the emotional life of the dancer. Religious circle dances seem to be common in all civilizations, just as spontaneous movement on the part of individuals in a social setting will, almost contagiously, attract participants who would otherwise just stand around. When one person starts dancing, usually a great many will follow suit.

FIGURE 10-2
Pavithra Reddy and Bijayini Satpathy in the Nrityagram Dance ensemble's production *Sriyah* at the King's Theatre as part of the Edinburgh International Festival.

©Robbie Jack-Corbis/Getty Images

Dances of celebration are associated with weddings around the world, often with precise movements and precise sections that seem to have an ancient pretext associated with fertility and the joy of love. Likewise, some dance simply celebrates the joy of life, as in the Nrityagram performance (Figure 10-2), which reveals an elevation of spirit that interprets an inner life of sheer delight. See Nrityagram on YouTube.

Social dances not only interpret the inner life of feeling, but at times they can both produce an inner life of feeling in us and control that feeling. In ballroom dancing, for example, the prescribed movements are designed to channel our sense of our body's motion and thus to help constrain our feelings while we dance. Alternatively, rock and hip-hop dancing involve a high degree of improvisation and some of the movements will depend on the feeling-state of the dancer at the moment of the dance.

Other arts may equal dance in this respect, but most of us have had experiences in which we find ourselves dancing expressively with friends or even alone as a way of both producing and sustaining a feeling-state that we find desirable and occasionally overwhelming.

2. Compare dance and music in terms of their power to reveal the inner life of feeling.
3. Represent one of the following states of mind by bodily motion: love, jealousy, self-confidence, pride. Have others in your group do the same. Do you find such representations difficult to perceive when others do them?
4. Try to move in such a way as to represent no state of mind at all. Is it possible? Discuss this with your group.
5. Representing or portraying a state of mind allows one to recognize that state. Interpreting a state of mind gives one insight into that state. In any of the experiments above, did you find any examples that went beyond representation and interpretation? If so, what made this possible? What does artistic form have to do with this?

FORM

The subject matter of dance can be moving visual patterns, feelings, states of mind, narrative, or various combinations. The form of the dance—its details and structure—gives us insight into the subject matter. But in dance, the form is not as clearly perceptible as it usually is in painting, sculpture, and architecture. The visual arts normally "sit still" long enough for us to reexamine everything. But dance moves on relentlessly, like literature in recitation, drama, and music, preventing us from reexamining its details and organization. We can only hope to hold in memory a detail for comparison with an ensuing detail, and those details as they help create the structure.

Therefore, one prerequisite for thorough enjoyment of the dance is the development of a memory for dance movements. The dance will usually help us in this task by the use of repetitive movements and variations on them. It can do for us what we cannot do for ourselves: present once again details for our renewed consideration. Often the dance builds tension by withholding movements we want to have repeated. Sometimes it creates unusual tension by refusing to repeat any movement at all. Repetition or the lack of it—as in music or any serial art—becomes one of the most important structural features of the dance.

The dance, furthermore, achieves a number of kinds of balance. In terms of the entire stage, usually dancers in a company balance themselves across the space allotted to them, moving forward, backward, left, and right as well as in circles. Centrality of focus is important in most dances and helps us unify the shapes of the overall dance. The most important dancers are usually at the center of the stage, holding our attention while subordinate groups of dancers balance them on the sides of the stage. Balance is also a structural consideration for both individual dancers (Figure 10-5) and groups (Figure 10-3).

FIGURE 10-3
Eleonora Abbagnato of the Paris Opera Ballet performing in *Le Sacre du Printemps* by Pina Bausch. Interpreting the ritual Rite of Spring, Igor Stravinsky's dynamic symphonic piece almost caused riots in 1913. Bausch interprets the erotic joy implied in the music and in the rituals celebrated in ancient Greece.

©Julien Benhamou

The positions of the ballet dancer also imply basic movements for the dancer, movements that can be maneuvered, interwoven, set in counterpoint, and modified as the dance progresses. As we experience the dance, we can develop an eye for the ways in which these movements combine to create the dance. Modern dance develops a different movement vocabulary of dance, as one can see from the illustrations in Figures 10-1 and 10-7 to 10-16.

DANCE AND RITUAL

Since the only requirement for dance is a body in motion, dance probably precedes all other arts. In this sense, dance comes first. And when it comes first, it is usually connected to a ritual that demands careful execution of movements in precise ways to achieve a precise goal. The dances of most cultures were originally connected with either religious or practical hunting or agricultural acts, all often involving magic.

Some dance has sexual origins and often is a ritual of courtship. Since this phenomenon has a correlative in nature—the courtship dances of birds and many other animals—many cultures occasionally imitated animal dances. Certain movements in Mandan Indian dances, for instance, can be traced to the leaps and falls of western jays and mockingbirds that, in finding a place to rest, will stop, leap into the air while spreading their wings for balance, then fall suddenly, only to rise into the air again.

Dance of all kinds draws much of its inspiration from the movements and shapes of nature: the motion of a stalk of wheat in a gentle breeze, the scurrying of a rabbit, the curling of a contented cat, the soaring of a bird, the falling of leaves, the sway of waves. These kinds of events have supplied dancers with ideas and examples for their own movement. A favorite movement pattern for the dance is that of the spiral nautilus:

The circle is another of the most pervasive shapes of nature. The movements of planets and stars suggest circular motion, and, more mundanely, so do the rings working out from a stone dropped in water. In a magical-religious way, circular dances sometimes have been thought to bring the dancers—and therefore humans in general—into a significant harmony with divine forces in the universe. The planets and stars are heavenly objects in circular motion, so it was reasonable for early dancers to feel that they could align themselves with these divine forces by means of dance.

Ritual Dance

Tourists can see rain dances in the American Southwest even today. The floor pattern of the dance is not circular but a modified spiral. The dancers, properly costumed, form a line and are led by a priest, who at specific moments spreads cornmeal on the ground, symbolizing his wish for the fertility of the ground. The ritual character of the dance is clearly observable in the pattern of motion, with dancers beginning by moving toward the north, then turning west, south, east, north, west, south, and ending toward the east. The gestures of the dancers, like the gestures in most rituals, have definite meanings and functions. For example, the dancers' loud screams are designed to awaken the gods and arrest their attention, the drumbeat suggests thunder, and the dancers' rattles suggest the sound of rain.

PERCEPTION KEY **Dance and Contemporary Rituals**

1. Contemporary rituals, especially weddings and state funerals, involve motion that can be considered dance motion. What other contemporary rituals involve dance motion? Do we need to know the meanings of the ritual gestures in order to appreciate the motion of the ritual?
2. How much common ground do we share with early dancers in trying to give meaning to our gestures, either in a generally accepted dance situation or out of it?
3. Are there dances that can be considered as serving functions similar to those of the dances we have described? Consider, for instance, the dancing at rock concerts. Is the dancing at Rave clubs ritual dance? Are there other instances?

Social Dance

Social dance is not dominated by religious or practical purposes. It is a form of recreation and social enjoyment. Country dance—for example, the eighteenth-century English Playford dances—is a species of folk dance that has traces of ancient origins, because country people tended to perform dances in specific relationship to special periods in the agricultural year, such as planting and harvesting. These were periods of celebration, when people in villages and farms came together to share good fellowship and thanksgiving.

Folk dances are the dances of the people—whether ethnic or regional in origin—and they are often carefully preserved, sometimes with contests designed to keep the dances alive. The dancers often wear the peasant costumes of the region they represent. Virtually every nation has its folk dance tradition.

The Court Dance

The court dances of the Middle Ages and Renaissance developed into more stylized and less openly energetic modes than the folk dance, for the court dance was performed by a different sort of person and served a different purpose. Participating in court dances signified high social status. Some of the older dances were the volta, a favorite at Queen Elizabeth's court in the sixteenth century, with the male dancer hoisting the female dancer in the air from time to time; the pavane, a stately dance popular in the seventeenth century; the minuet, popular in the eighteenth century, performed by groups of four dancers at a time; and the eighteenth-century German allemande—a dance performed by couples who held both hands, turning about one another without letting go. These dances and many others were favorites at courts primarily because they were enjoyable—not because they performed a religious or practical function. Because the dances were also pleasurable to look at, it very quickly became commonplace at court to have a group of onlookers as large as or larger than the group of dancers. Soon professional dancers appeared at more-significant court functions, such as the Elizabethan and Jacobean masques, which were mixed-media entertainments in which the audience usually took some part—particularly in the dance sequences.

PERCEPTION KEY Social Dance

1. How would you evaluate rock dancing? Why does rock dancing demand loud music? Does the performing and watching of spontaneous and powerful muscular motions account for some of the popularity of rock dancing? If so, why? Explain what the viewer and the dancer, respectively, might derive from the experience of rock dancing. Substitute hip-hop for rock and answer the same questions.
2. Try to see an authentic folk dance. Describe the basic differences between folk dance and rock dance. Is the basic subject matter of the folk dance visual patterns, or feelings, or states of mind, or narrative? Or some combination of these? If so, what is the mix? Answer the same questions for rock dances and hip-hop.
3. Break and rock dancing for the young, square and ballroom dancing for the old— why the divided generational appeal? Country dance seems to appeal to both young and old.

BALLET

The origins of ballet usually are traced to the early seventeenth century, when dancers performed interludes between scenes of an opera. Eventually the interludes grew more important, until finally ballets were performed independently.

A considerable repertory of ballets has been built up in the last three centuries. Some of the ballets many of us are likely to see are Lully's *Giselle*; *Les Sylphides*, with music by Chopin; Tchaikovsky's *Nutcracker*, *Swan Lake*, and *Sleeping Beauty*; *Coppélia*, with music by Delibes; and *The Rite of Spring*, with music by Stravinsky. All these ballets—like most ballets—have a *pretext*, a narrative line or story around which the ballet is built (Figure 10-4). In this sense, the ballet has as its subject matter a story that is interpreted by means of stylized movements such as the *arabesque*, the bourrée, and the relevé, to name a few. Our understanding of the story is basically conditioned by our perception of the movements that present the story to us. It is astounding how, without having to be obvious and without having to resort very often to everyday gestures, ballet dancers can present a story to us in an intelligible fashion. Yet it is not the story or the movement that constitutes the ballet: It is the meld of story and movement.

FIGURE 10-4
A scene from George Balanchine's *Nutcracker*, with music by Pyotr Ilych Tchaikovsky, based on E. T. A. Hoffmann's *The Nutcracker and the Mouse King*. Here, Clara has freed the Prince and journeyed with him to the world of the fairies as the Snowflakes gather in a blizzard in the last scene of act 1 by the New York City Ballet.

©Paul Kolnik

PERCEPTION KEY Narrative and Bodily Movement

1. Without training, we cannot perform ballet movements, but all of us can perform some dance movements. By way of experiment and to increase our understanding of the meld of narrative and movement, try representing a narrative by bodily motion to a group of onlookers. Choose a narrative poem from our chapter on literature, or choose a scene from a play that may be familiar to you and your audience. Let your audience know the pretext you are using, since this is the normal method of most ballets. Avoid movements that rely exclusively on facial expressions or simple mime to communicate story elements. After your presentation, discuss with your audience their views about your success or failure in presenting the narrative. Discuss, too, your problems as a dancer, what you felt you wanted your movement to reveal about the narrative. Have others perform the experiment, and discuss the same points.

2. Even the most rudimentary movement attempting to reveal a narrative will bring in interpretations that go beyond the narrative alone. As a viewer, discuss what you believe the other dancers added to the narrative.

Swan Lake

One of the most popular ballets of all time is Tchaikovsky's *Swan Lake (Le Lac des Cygnes),* composed from 1871 to 1877 and first performed in 1894 (act 2) and 1895 (complete). The choreographers were Leon Ivanov and Marius Petipa. Tchaikovsky originally composed the music for a ballet to be performed for children, but its fascination has not been restricted to young audiences. With Margot Fonteyn and Rudolf Nureyev, the reigning dancers in this ballet in modern times, *Swan Lake* has been a resounding favorite on television and film, not to mention repeated sellout performances in dance theaters the world over.

Act 1 opens with the principal male dancer, the young Prince Siegfried, attending a village celebration. His mother, the Queen, finding Siegfried sporting with the peasants, decides that it is time for him to marry someone of his own station and settle into the nobility. After she leaves, a **pas de trois**—a dance with three dancers, in this instance Siegfried and two maids—is interrupted by the Prince's slightly drunk tutor, who tries to take part in some of the dancing but is not quite able. When a flight of swans is seen overhead, the Prince resolves to go hunting.

The opening scene of act 2 is on a moonlit lake, with the arch magician Rothbart tending his swans. The swans, led by Odette, are maidens he has enchanted. They can return to human form only at night. Odette's movements are imitated by the entire group of swans, movements that are clearly influenced by the motions of the swan's long neck and by the movements we associate with birds—for example, an undulating motion executed by the dancers' arms and a fluttering executed by the legs. Siegfried comes upon the swans and restrains his hunters from shooting at them. He falls in love with Odette, now in her human form, all of whose motions are characterized by the softness and grace of a swan (Figure 10-5). Siegfried learns that Odette is enchanted and that she cannot come to the ball at which the Queen has planned to arrange his marriage. Siegfried also learns that if he vows his love to her and keeps his vow, he can free her from the enchantment. She warns him that Rothbart will do everything to trick him into breaking the vow, but Siegfried is determined to be steadfast. As dawn arrives, the lovers part and Rothbart retrieves his swans.

Act 3 commences with the ball the Queen has arranged for presenting to Siegfried a group of princesses from whom he may choose. Each princess, introduced in lavish native costume with a retinue of dancers and retainers, dances the folk dance of her country, such as the allemande, the czardas, the tarantella. But suddenly Rothbart enters in disguise with his own daughter, Odile, who looks exactly like Odette. Today most performances require that Odette and Odile be the same dancer, although the parts were originally written for two dancers. Siegfried and Odile dance the famous Black Swan **pas de deux**, a dance notable for its virtuosity. It features almost superhuman leaps on the part of Siegfried, and it involves thirty-two rapidly executed whipping turns (fouettés) on the part of Odile. Her movement is considerably different in character from that of Odette. Odile is more angular, is less delicate, and in her black costume seems much less the picture of innocence Odette had seemed in her soft white costume. Siegfried's movements suggest great joy at being with Odette, for he does not realize that this is really Odile, the magician's daughter.

FIGURE 10-5
Matthew Golding as Siegfried and
Natalia Ossipova as Odette in act 2
of *Swan Lake* with the corps de ballet
of the Royal Ballet at Covent Garden,
London.

©A Pennefather/Royal Opera House/
ArenaPAL/The Image Works

When the time comes for Siegfried to choose among the princesses for his wife, he rejects them all and presents Odile to the Queen as his choice. Once Siegfried has committed himself to her, Rothbart exults and takes Odile from him and makes her vanish. Siegfried, who has broken his vow to Odette, realizes he has been duped and ends the act by rushing out to find the real Odette.

Like a number of other sections of the ballet, act 4 has a variety of versions that interpret what is essentially similar action (Figure 10-6). Siegfried, in finding Odette by the lake at night, sacrifices himself for her and breaks the spell. They are joined in death and are beyond the power of the magician. Some versions of the ballet aim for a happy ending and suggest that though Siegfried sacrifices himself for Odette, he does not die. In this happy-ending version, Odette, upon realizing that Siegfried had been tricked, forgives him. Rothbart raises a terrible storm in order to drown all the swans, but Siegfried carries Odette to a hilltop, where he is willing to die with her if necessary. This act of love and sacrifice breaks the spell, and the two of them are together as dawn breaks.

Another version concentrates on spiritual victory and reward after death in a better life than that which was left behind. Odette and the swans dance slowly and sorrowfully together, with Odette rising in a stately fashion in their midst. When Siegfried comes, he begs her to forgive him, but nothing can break the magician's spell. Odette and he dance, they embrace, and she bids him farewell and casts herself mournfully into the lake, where she perishes. Siegfried, unable to live without her, follows her into the lake. Then, once the lake vanishes, Odette and Siegfried are revealed in the distance, moving away together as evidence that the spell was broken in death.

The story of *Swan Lake* has archetypal overtones much in keeping with the Romantic age in which it was conceived. John Keats, who wrote "La Belle Dame

FIGURE 10-6
The Royal Ballet rehearses their
production of *Swan Lake*. Here,
Rothbart's enchanted swans dance
together in a classic pose.

©Reuters/Alamy

Sans Merci" fifty years before this ballet was created, was fascinated by the ancient stories of men who fell in love with supernatural spirits, which is what the swan-Odette is, once she has been transformed by magic. Likewise, the later Romantics were fascinated by the possibilities of magic and its implications for dealing with the forces of good and evil. This interest in magic and the supernatural is coupled with the Wagnerian interest in heroism and the implications of the sacrifice of the hero for the thing he loves. But Tchaikovsky—like Wagner, whose hero in the *Ring of the Niebelungs* is also a Siegfried, whose end with Brünnhilde is similar to the ending in *Swan Lake*—concentrates on the human valor of the Prince and its implication for transforming evil into good.

PERCEPTION KEY *Swan Lake*

1. If you can see a production or video of *Swan Lake*, focus on a specific act and comment in a discussion with others on the suitability of the bodily movements for the narrative subject matter of that act. Are feelings or states of mind interpreted as well as the narrative? If so, when and how?
2. What characteristic bodily motions seem to repeat themselves in the dances performed by Siegfried and Odette?
3. If someone who has had training in ballet is available, you might try to get him or her to present a small portion of the ballet for your observation and discussion. What would be the most important kinds of questions to ask such a person?

MODERN DANCE

The origins of *modern dance* are usually traced to the American dancers Isadora Duncan and Ruth St. Denis. They rebelled against the stylization of ballet, with ballerinas dancing on their toes and executing the same basic movements in every performance. Duncan insisted on natural movement, often dancing in bare feet with gossamer drapery that revealed her body and legs in motion (Figure 10-7). She felt that the emphasis ballet places on the movement of the arms and legs was restrictive. Her insistence on placing the center of motion just below the breastbone was based on her feeling that the torso had been neglected in the development of ballet. She believed, too, that the early Greek dancers, whom she wished to emulate, had placed their center of energy at the solar plexus. Her intention was to return to natural movement in dance, and this was one effective method of doing so.

FIGURE 10-7
Isadora Duncan at the Parthenon,
photographed by Edward Steichen.

The developers of modern dance who followed Duncan (she died in 1927) built on her legacy. In her insistence on freedom with respect to clothes and conventions, she infused energy into the dance that no one had ever seen before. Although she was a native Californian, her successes and triumphs were primarily in foreign lands, particularly in France and Russia. Her performances differed greatly from the ballet. Instead of developing a dance built on a pretext of the sort that underlies *Swan Lake,* Duncan took more-abstract subject matters—especially moods and states of mind—and expressed her understanding of them.

Duncan's dances were lyrical, personal, and occasionally extemporaneous. Since, she insisted, there were no angular shapes in nature, she would permit herself to use none. Her movements rarely came to a complete rest. An interesting example of her dance, one in which she does come to a full rest, is recounted by a friend. It was performed in a salon for close friends, and its subject matter seems to be human emergence on the planet:

> Isadora was completely covered by a long loose robe with high draped neck and long loose sleeves in a deep muted red. She crouched on the floor with her face resting on the carpet. In slow motion with ineffable effort she managed to get up on her knees. Gradually with titanic struggles she rose to her feet. She raised her arms toward heaven in a gesture of praise and exultation. The mortal had emerged from primeval ooze to achieve Man, upright, liberated, and triumphant.[2]

Martha Graham, Erick Hawkins, José Limón, Doris Humphrey, and other innovators who followed Duncan developed modern dance in a variety of directions. Graham created some dances on themes of Greek tragedies, such as *Medea.* In addition to his *Moor's Pavane,* Limón is well known for his interpretation of Eugene O'Neill's play *The Emperor Jones,* in which a slave escapes to an island only to become a despised and hunted tyrant. Humphrey, who was a little older than Graham and Limón, was closer to the original Duncan tradition in such dances as *Water Study, Life of the Bee,* and *New Dance,* a 1930s piece that was very successfully revived in 1972.

PERCEPTION KEY Pretext and Movement

1. Devise a series of movements that will take about one minute to complete and that you are fairly sure do not tell a story. Then perform these movements for a group and question them on the apparent pretext of your movement. Do not tell them in advance that your dance has no story. As a result of this experiment, ask yourself and the group whether it is possible to create a sequence of movements that will not suggest a story line to some viewers. What would this mean for dances that try to avoid pretexts? Can there really be abstract dance?
2. Without explaining that you are not dancing, represent a familiar human situation to a group by using movements that you believe are not dance movements. Is the group able to understand what you represented? Do they think you were using dance movements? Do you believe it possible to have movements that cannot be included in a dance? Are there, in other words, nondance movements?

---

[2]From *Christian Science Monitor,* December 4, 1970, © 1970 Christian Science Monitor. All rights reserved. Used by Permission and protected by the Copyright Laws of the United States. The printing, copying, redistribution, or retransmission of this Content without express written permission is prohibited.

Alvin Ailey's Revelations

One of the classics of modern dance is Alvin Ailey's *Revelations* (Figure 10-8), based largely on African American spirituals and experience. It was first performed in January 1960, and hardly a year has gone by since without its having been performed to highly enthusiastic crowds. Ailey refined *Revelations* somewhat over the years, but its impact has brought audiences to their feet for standing ovations at almost every performance. After Ailey's untimely death at the age of fifty-eight, the company was directed by Judith Jamison, one of the great dancers in Ailey's company.

Some of the success of *Revelations* stems from Ailey's choice of the deeply felt music of the spirituals to which the dancers' movements are closely attuned. But, then, this is also one of the most noted qualities of a ballet like *Swan Lake,* which has one of the richest orchestral scores in the history of ballet. Music, unless it is program music, is not, strictly speaking, a pretext for a dance, but there is a perceptible connection between, say, the rhythmic characteristics of a given music and a dance composed in such a way as to take advantage of those characteristics. Thus, in *Revelations* the energetic movements of the dancers often appear as visual, bodily transformations of the rhythmically charged music.

Try to see *Revelations.* Several sites online present segments of the dance, but none show it in its entirety. We will point out details and structures, an awareness of which may prove helpful for refining your experience not only of this dance but of modern dance in general. Beyond the general pretext of *Revelations*—that of African American experience as related by spirituals—each of its separate sections has its own pretext. But none of them is as tightly or specifically narrative as is usually the case in ballet. In *Revelations,* generalized situations act as pretexts.

The first section of the dance is called "Pilgrim of Sorrow," with three parts: "I Been Buked," danced by the entire company (about twenty dancers, male and female);

FIGURE 10-8
The Alvin Ailey Dance Company in *Revelations,* **a suite of dances to gospel music.**

©Zuma Press, Inc./Alamy

"Didn't My Lord Deliver Daniel," danced by only a few dancers; and "Fix Me Jesus," danced by one couple. The general pretext is the suffering of African Americans, who are, like the Israelites of the Old Testament, taking refuge in their faith in the Lord. The most dramatic moments in this section are in "Didn't My Lord Deliver Daniel," a statement of overwhelming faith characterized by close ensemble work. The in-line dancers parallel the rhythms of the last word of the hymn: "Dan´-i-el´," accenting the first and last syllables with powerful rhythmic movements.

The second section, titled "Take Me to the Water," is divided into "Processional," danced by eight dancers; "Wading in the Water," danced by six dancers; and "I Want to Be Ready," danced by a single male dancer. The whole idea of "Take Me to the Water" suggests baptism, a ritual that affirms faith in God—the source of energy of the spirituals. "Wading in the Water" is particularly exciting, with dancers holding a stage-long bolt of light-colored fabric to represent the water. The dancers shimmer the fabric to the rhythm of the music, and one dancer after another crosses over the fabric, symbolizing at least two things: the waters of baptism and the Mosaic waters of freedom. It is this episode that originally featured the charismatic Judith Jamison in a long white gown and holding a huge parasol as she danced.

The third section is called "Move, Members, Move," with the subsections titled "Sinner Man," "The Day Is Past and Gone," "You May Run Home," and the finale "Rocka My Soul in the Bosom of Abraham." In this last episode, a sense of triumph over suffering is projected, suggesting the redemption of a people by using the same kind of Old Testament imagery and musical material that opened the dance. The entire section takes as its theme the lives of people after they have been received into the faith, with the possibilities of straying into sin. It ends with a powerful rocking spiritual that emphasizes forgiveness and the reception of the people (the "members") into the bosom of Abraham, according to the prediction of the Bible. This ending features a large amount of ensemble work and is danced by the entire company, with rows of male dancers sliding forward on their outspread knees and then rising all in one sliding gesture, raising their hands high. "Rocka My Soul in the Bosom of Abraham" is powerfully sung again and again until the effect is almost hypnotic.

The subject matter of *Revelations* is in part that of feelings and states of mind. But it is also more obviously that of the struggle of a people as told—on one level—by their music. The dance has the advantage of a powerfully engaging subject matter even before we witness the interpretation of that subject matter. And the way in which the movements of the dance are closely attuned to the rhythms of the music tends to evoke intense participation, since the visual qualities of the dance are powerfully reinforced by the aural qualities of the music.

PERCEPTION KEY *Revelations*

1. A profitable way of understanding the resources of *Revelations* is to take a well-known African American spiritual such as "Swing Low, Sweet Chariot" (see Figure 9-4) and supply the movements that it suggests to you. Once you have done so, ask yourself how difficult it was. Is it natural to move to such music?
2. Instead of spirituals, try the same experiment with popular music such as rock and rap. What characteristics does such music have that stimulate motion?
3. Is there anything archetypal in the subject matter of *Revelations*?

Martha Graham

Quite different from the Ailey approach is the "Graham technique," taught in Graham's own school in New York as well as in colleges and universities across the country. Like Ailey, Graham was a *virtuoso* dancer and organized her own company. After Isadora Duncan, no one has been more influential in modern dance. Graham's technique is reminiscent of ballet in its rigor and discipline. Dancers learn specific kinds of movements and exercises designed to be used as both preparation for and part of the dance. Graham's contraction, for example, is one of the most common movements one is likely to see: It is the sudden pulling in of the diaphragm with the resultant relaxation of the rest of the body. This builds on Duncan's emphasis on the solar plexus and adds to that emphasis the systolic and diastolic rhythms of heartbeat and pulse. The movement is very effective visually as well as being particularly flexible in depicting feelings and states of mind. It is a movement unknown in ballet, from which Graham always wished to remain distinct.

Graham's dances at times have been very literal, with narrative pretexts quite similar to those found in ballet. *Night Journey,* for instance, is an interpretation of *Oedipus Rex* by Sophocles. The lines of emotional force linking Jocasta and her son-husband, Oedipus, are strongly accentuated by the movements of the dance as well as by certain props onstage, such as ribbons that link the two at times. In Graham's interpretation, Jocasta becomes much more important than she is in the original drama. This is partly because Graham saw the female figures in Greek drama—such as *Phaedra* (Figure 10-9)—as much more fully dimensional than we have normally understood them. By means of dancing their roles, she was able to reveal the complexities of their characters. In dances such as her *El Penitente,* Graham experimented with states of mind as the subject matter. Thus, the featured

FIGURE 10-9
Martha Graham in *Phaedra***, based on the Greek myth concerning the love of Phaedra for Hippolytus, the son of her husband, Theseus.** Graham performed numerous dances based on Greek myths because she felt energized by their passion.

©Jack Mitchell/Getty Images

FIGURE 10-10
The Batsheva Dance Company.

©robbie jack/Corbis/Getty Images

male dancer in loose white trousers and tunic, moving in slow circles about the stage with a large wooden cross, is a powerful interpretation of penitence.

Batsheva Dance Company

The Batsheva Dance Company (Figures 10-10 and 10-11), founded by Martha Graham and Baroness Batsheva Rothschild in Tel Aviv in 1964, derived from Graham's performing and teaching in Israel. By the mid-1970s both Graham and Rothschild had withdrawn to let the company find its own way. Eventually its current director, Ohad Naharin, who had begun with Graham's company in New York, took over and reshaped Batsheva Dance Company into an internationally respected troupe. Batsheva has appeared frequently in the United States and throughout Europe. It is respected for its imaginative dances and the risk taking that has been its trademark.

FIGURE 10-11
Batsheva Dance Company, *Decadance.*
2017.

Photo: Maxim Waratt. Courtesy of Batsheva
Dance Company

Naharin, because of a personal injury that threatened his spine, developed Gaga movement, a special way to train and special movements that permitted him to recover and dance again. The Gaga training has been widely used and is now taught worldwide. Just as Graham developed her style based on the contraction of the body, Naharin developed his by imagining the spinal column to slither like a snake. Dancers are sometimes asked to dance like spaghetti in boiling water.

In the 2017 dance *Decadance*, Naharin sums up the past twenty-five years of the company by presenting excerpts from its repertory. In one dance set to Passover music, the dancers, in a circle, systematically take off their jackets, then their shirts, all the while tossing each in the air to resemble the flight of birds. Some conservatives in Israel protested, but the dance has been popular wherever it has played.

Pilobolus and Momix Dance Companies

The innovative modern dance companies Pilobolus and Momix perform around the world and throughout the United States. They originated in 1970 at Dartmouth College with four male dancers and choreographers Alison Chase and Martha Clarke. Their specialty involves placing moving bodies in acrobatic positions. Moses Pendleton, principal dancer in Pilobolus and director of the dance company Momix, choreographed *F.L.O.W. (For Love of Women)* and had it performed by Diana Vishneva, one of Russia's finest Mariinsky ballerinas (Figure 10-12). Vishneva performs on a highly reflective floor, producing a complex visual dynamic that complements other parts of the dance. Such intense moments characterize much of the style that Pendleton has developed with Momix and echoes some of the acrobatics of the Pilobolus company. *Suspended*, with dancers Renée Jaworski and Jennifer Macavinta (Figure 10-13), shows the Pilobolus company's commitment to the principle that choreography is an art dependent on the body, not just on music, pretext, or lighting.

FIGURE 10-12
Diana Vishneva, from Russia's Mariinsky Ballet, dancing in Moses Pendleton's *F.L.O.W. (For the Love of Women)* at the New York City Center in 2008. Pendleton's emphasis on the body is intensified here by the reflective floor and the acrobatic position.

©Richard Termine/The New York Times/Redux

FIGURE 10-13
Renée Jaworski and Jennifer Macavinta in the Pilobolus Dance Company's *Suspended*, emphasizing the body in space. The Pilobolus company is known for its highly experimental and daring dances, sometimes involving nudity.

©John Kane

FIGURE 10-14

Amber Star Merkens and Domingo Estrada Jr. with fellow members of the Mark Morris Dance Group performing in *Dido and Aeneas* as part of Lincoln Center's Mostly Mozart Festival at the Rose Theater. Set to the music for Henry Purcell's opera, *Dido and Aeneas*, this is considered Morris's finest dance.

©Andrea Mohin/The New York Times/Redux

Mark Morris Dance Group

The Mark Morris Dance Group was created—"reluctantly," he has said—in 1980 because he found he could not do the dances he wanted with other existing companies. Morris and his company were a sensation from the first, performing in New York from 1981 to 1988.

Morris's first major dance was a theatrical piece with an intricate interpretation of Handel's music set to John Milton's lyric poems: *L'Allegro, il Penseroso, ed il Moderato*. The title refers to three moods: happiness, melancholy, and restfulness. David Dougill commented on the "absolute rightness to moods and themes" with Milton's poems and Handel's music. Morris's *Dido and Aeneas* (Figure 10-14) was first performed in 1989 but continues to be produced because of its importance and its impact. Based on Virgil's *Aeneid*, it focuses on the tragic love affair of a king and queen in ancient Rome. Morris continues to be one of the most forceful figures in modern dance throughout the world.

FOCUS ON **Theater Dance**

Dance has taken a primary role in many live theater productions throughout the world. In most cases, dance supports a narrative and shares the stage with spoken actors or, as in the case of opera and in musicals, with singers and music. In the 1920s the rage was for revues that showcased dance teams or dance productions, as in the London revue *Blackbirds*, which introduced "The Black Bottom" dance. Lavish revues in the early 1930s, such as the Ziegfeld Follies, staged lush dance productions, while other revues like *The Great Waltz* featured dance in the service of the biography of Johann Strauss. The dancing was lavish, not original, but the show was enormously successful.

The great dance piece for the postwar era was Jerome Robbins's staging of Leonard Bernstein's *West Side Story* in 1957 (Figure 10-15). The play was innovative on many levels, but with the genius of Robbins, who was at home with ballet as well as modern dance, it was a major moment in the history of dance on stage. A loose adaptation of *Romeo and Juliet*, the play pitted the migrants from Puerto Rico, who by 1957 had peopled New York's West Side from 58th to 85th Street, against the earlier immigrants, mostly poor Irish, Italians, African Americans, and Jews. The play not only told a love story but, at the same time, introduced a sociological theme. The dances were central to the story and remain the most memorable images from that first production, the following film production, and the countless revivals of the drama.

In 2000 Susan Stroman introduced another major dance piece at Lincoln Center, in the very same neighborhood portrayed by *West Side Story*. In the 1960s Lincoln

FIGURE 10-15

A scene from the new Broadway revival of *West Side Story*. 2009. *West Side Story*, 1957. Book by Arthur Laurents, music by Leonard Bernstein, lyrics by Stephen Sondheim, choreography by Jerome Robbins.

©Sara Krulwick/The New York Times/Redux

Center replaced the tenement areas that had housed earlier Puerto Rican migrants. *Contact* (Figure 10-16) was an almost-pure dance theater piece. It had no continuous narrative but instead focused on the idea of swing dance. It was inspired by Stroman's experience in a late-night New York club, seeing a woman in a yellow dress in a group of people dancing to swing music. The dancing in *Contact* was set to three rudimentary "stories" centering on love relationships, but there was no dialogue to carry the narrative along.

The first segment, "Swinging," featured an eighteenth-century girl on a real swing being pushed by two men. The sexual emblem of that era was a swing, and the opening scene reproduced in tableau the famous French painting by Jean-Honoré Fragonard that was understood to symbolize infidelity. The second segment, "Did You Move?," was set in a restaurant with an abusive husband and an unhappy wife who lives out her sexual fantasies by dancing with a busboy, the headwaiter, and some diners. The third segment, "Contact," featured the girl in the yellow dress choosing from among a number of men as dancing partners. One of them is a successful advertising man who has come to an after-hours pool hall nightclub with suicide on his mind. The girl in the yellow dress enchants him, but as he reaches out for her, she disappears, then reappears, keeping him suspended and constantly searching.

Most of the music in *Contact* was taped contemporary songs, but the last section of the piece featured the great Benny Goodman version of "Sing, Sing, Sing" from his Carnegie Hall concert in 1938. The reviews of *Contact* emphasized the sexiness of the entire production. When it came time for Broadway to give out the Tony Awards in 2000, it was decided that *Contact* was unique, partly because it did not use original or live music, and was given a special Tony as a theatrical dance production, rather than as a standard musical.

FIGURE 10-16

Debra Yates in Susan Stroman's *Contact*. 2000. Susan Stroman conceived this theatrical dance event after seeing swing dancers in a New York club. The show won several awards.

©Paul Kolnik

POPULAR DANCE

Popular styles in dance change rapidly from generation to generation. Early in the twentieth century, the Charleston was the exciting dance for young people; then in the 1930s and 1940s, it was swing dancing and jitterbugging. In the 1960s, rock dancing took over, then disco; and then in the 1980s break dancing led into the 1990s hip-hop (Figure 10-17). Recently a resurgence in ballroom dancing has spawned not only competitions at a professional level but also widespread competitions in urban middle schools across the United States.

Street dancing can still be seen on the streets of many cities where young dancers put out the hat for tips. But it is also becoming a mainline form of dance seen on the stage and television. It is marked by sheer energy and virtuoso moves suggesting the one-time competitiveness of jazz music.

In films, great dancers like Fred Astaire and Ginger Rogers as well as Donald O'Connor, Gene Kelly, Cyd Charisse, and many more, captivated wide audiences. The Nicholas Brothers (Figure 10-18) were among the most dazzling tap dancers on film. *Stormy Weather* (1943) was their favorite film, but one of their best dances was in *Orchestra Wives* (1942). Some of Fred Astaire's great films are *Flying Down to Rio* (1933), *Swing Time* (1936), *Shall We Dance?* (1937), and *Daddy Long Legs* (1955). Gene Kelly and Cyd Charisse are famous for *Singin' in the Rain* (1952), one of the best-loved of all dance films.

Fortunately, dance films are almost universally available on DVD and video, and as a result it is still possible for us to see the great work of our best dancers, whatever their style.

FIGURE 10-17
Hip-hop dancing.

©Chau Doan/LightRocket/Getty Images

FIGURE 10-18
The Nicholas Brothers, Harold and Fayard, were showstopping dancers in films such as this, *Sun Valley Serenade*, 1941, during a time when great dance was the staple of movies throughout the world.

SUMMARY

Through the medium of the moving human body, the form of dance can reveal visual patterns or feelings or states of mind or narrative or, more probably, some combination. The first step in learning to participate with the dance is to learn the nature of its movements. The second is to be aware of its different kinds of subject matter. The content of dance gives us insights into our inner lives, especially states of mind, that supplement the insights of music. Dance has the capacity to transform a pretext, whether it be a story, a state of mind, or a feeling. Our attention should be drawn into participation with this transformation. The insight we get from the dance experience depends on our awareness of this transformation.

Note: Many of the dance companies and their dances can be seen in full or in part in online video-sharing services such as YouTube, Hulu, Veoh, Metacafe, Google Videos, and others.

©Nan Goldin

Chapter 11

PHOTOGRAPHY

PHOTOGRAPHY AND PAINTING

The first demonstration of photography took place in Paris in 1839, when Louis J. M. Daguerre (1787–1851) astonished a group of French artists and scientists with the first Daguerreotypes. The process was almost instantaneous, producing a finely detailed monochrome image on a silver-coated copper plate. At that demonstration, the noted French painter Paul Delaroche declared, "From today painting is dead." An examination of his famous painting *Execution of Lady Jane Grey* (Figure 11-1) reveals the source of his anxiety. Delaroche's reputation was built on doing what the photograph does best—reproducing exact detail and exact perspective. However, the camera could not yet reproduce the large size or the colors that make Delaroche's painting powerful.

> ### PERCEPTION KEY Execution of Lady Jane Grey
>
> 1. What aspects of Delaroche's style of painting would have made him think of photography as a threat? In what ways is this painting similar to a photograph?
> 2. Why is it surprising to learn that this painting was exhibited five years before Delaroche saw a photograph—actually before the invention of photography?
> 3. Examine Delaroche's painting for attention to detail. This is a gigantic work, much larger than any photograph could be at mid-nineteenth century. Every figure is reproduced with the same sharpness, from foreground to background. To what extent is that approach to sharpness of focus like or unlike what might have been achieved by a photograph of this scene?
> 4. How does color focus our attention in Delaroche's painting?

FIGURE 11-1
Paul Delaroche, *Execution of Lady Jane Grey*. 1843. Oil on canvas, 97 × 117 inches. National Gallery, London, Great Britain. Delaroche witnessed the first demonstration of photography in 1839 and declared, "From today painting is dead." His enormous painting had great size and brilliant color, two ways, for the time being, in which photography could be superseded.

©HIP/Art Resource, NY

Some early critics of photography complained that the camera does not offer the control over the subject matter that painting does. But the camera does offer the capacity to crop and select the area of the final print, the capacity to alter the aperture of the lens and thus control the focus in selective areas, as well as the capacity to reveal movement in blurred scenes, all of which only suggest the ability of the instrument to transform visual experience into art.

Many early photographs exhibit the capacity of the camera to capture and control details in a manner that informs the viewer about the subject matter. For example, in his portrait of Isambard Kingdom Brunel (1857), a great builder of steamships (Figure 11-2), Robert Howlett exposed the negative for a shorter time and widened the aperture of his lens (letting in more light), thus controlling the depth of field (how much is in focus). Brunel's figure is in focus, but surrounding objects are in soft focus, rendering them less significant. The pile of anchor chains in the background is

FIGURE 11-2
Robert Howlett, *Isambard Kingdom Brunel*. 1857. This portrait of a great English engineer reveals its subject without flattery, without a sense of romance, and absolutely without a moment of sentimentality. Yet the photograph is a monument to power and industry.

©Heritage Image Partnership Ltd/Alamy

massive, but the soft focus makes them subservient to Brunel. The huge chains make this image haunting, but if they were in sharp focus, they would have distracted from Brunel. In *Execution of Lady Jane Grey,* almost everything is in sharp focus, while the white of Jane's dress and the red of the executioner's leggings focus our attention.

Brunel's posture is typical of photographs of the mid-nineteenth century. We have many examples of men lounging with hands in pockets and cigar in mouth, but few paintings portray men this way. Few photographs of any age show us a face quite like Brunel's. It is relaxed, as much as Brunel could relax, but it is also impatient, "bearing with" the photographer. And the eyes are sharp, businessman's eyes. The details of the rumpled clothing and jewelry do not compete with the sharply rendered face and the expression of control and power. Howlett has done, by simple devices such as varying the focus, what many portrait painters do by much more complex means—reveal something of the character of the model.

Julia Margaret Cameron's portrait of Sir John Herschel (1867) (Figure 11-3) and Étienne Carjat's portrait of the French poet Charles Baudelaire (1870) (Figure 11-4) use a plain studio background. But their approaches are also different from each other. Cameron, who reported being interested in the way her lens could soften detail, isolates Herschel's face and hair. She drapes his shoulders with a black velvet shawl so that his clothing will not tell us anything about him or distract us from his face. Cameron catches the stubble on his chin and permits his hair to "burn out," so we perceive it as a luminous halo. The huge eyes, soft and bulbous with their deep curves of surrounding flesh, and the downward curve of the mouth are depicted

fully in the harsh lighting. While we do not know what he was thinking, the form of this photograph reveals him as a thinker of deep ruminations. He was the chemist who first learned how to permanently fix a silver halide photograph in 1839.

The portrait of Baudelaire, on the other hand, includes simple, severe clothing, except for the poet's foulard, tied in a dashing bow. Baudelaire's intensity creates the illusion that he is looking at us. Carjat's lens was set for a depth of field of only a few inches. Thus, Baudelaire's face is in focus, but not his shoulders. What Carjat could not control, except by waiting for the right moment to uncover the lens (at this time, there was no shutter because there was no "fast" film), was the exact expression he could catch.

One irony of the Carjat portrait is that Baudelaire, in 1859, had condemned the influence of photography on art, declaring it "art's most mortal enemy." He thought that photography was adequate for preserving visual records of perishing things but that it could not reach into "anything whose value depends solely upon the addition of something of a man's soul." Baudelaire was a champion of imagination and an opponent of realistic art: "Each day art further diminishes its self-respect by bowing down before external reality; each day the painter becomes more and more given to painting not what he dreams but what he sees."[1]

An impressive example of the capacity of the photographic representation is Timothy O'Sullivan's masterpiece, *Canyon de Chelley, Arizona,* made in 1873 (Figure 11-5). Many photographers have gone back to this scene, but none has treated it quite the way O'Sullivan did. O'Sullivan chose a moment of intense side-lighting, which falls on the rock wall but not on the nearest group of buildings. One question you might ask about this photograph is whether it reveals the "stoniness" of this rock wall in a manner similar to the way Cézanne's *Mont Sainte-Victoire* (see Figure 2-4) reveals the "mountainness" of the mountain.

---

[1]Charles Baudelaire, *The Mirror of Art* (London: Phaidon, 1955), p. 230.

FIGURE 11-5
Timothy O'Sullivan, *Canyon de Chelley, Arizona.* 1873. The American West lured photographers with unwieldy equipment to remote locations such as this. Other photographers have visited the site, but none has outdone O'Sullivan, who permitted the rock to speak for itself.

Source: The J. Paul Getty Museum

EXPERIENCING Photography and Art

1. Do you agree with Baudelaire that photography is "art's most mortal enemy"? What reasons might Baudelaire have had for expressing such a view?

For some time, photography was not considered an art. Indeed, some people today do not see it as an art because they assume the photograph is an exact replica of what is in front of the camera lens. On the other hand, realism in art had been an ideal since the earliest times, and sculptures such as *David* (see Figure 5-8) aimed at an exact replica of a human body, however idealized. Modern artists such as Andy Warhol blur the line of art by creating exact replicas of objects such as Campbell's soup cans, so the question of replication is not the final question in art. Baudelaire saw that painters could be out of work—especially portrait painters—if photography were widespread. Yet, his own photographic portrait is of powerful artistic interest today.

For Baudelaire, photographs were usually Daguerreotypes, which means they were one of a kind. The "print" on silvered copper was the photograph. There was no negative and no way of altering the tones in the print. Shortly after, when the Daguerreotype process was superseded by inventions such as the glass plate negative, it became possible to subtly alter details within the photograph much as a painter might alter the highlights in a landscape or improve the facial details in a portrait. This is a matter of craft, but it became clear that in careful selection of what is in the photographic print, along with the attention to manipulating the print, in the fashion of Ansel Adams's great photographs of Yosemite, the best photographers became artists. Were Baudelaire alive to see how photography has evolved, he may well have changed his opinion. The work of Julia Margaret Cameron, Timothy O'Sullivan, Eugène Atget, Alfred Stieglitz, Edward Steichen, and Edward Weston changed the world's view of whether or not photography is an art.

2. Baudelaire's writings suggest that he believed art depended on imagination and that realistic art was the opponent of imagination. How valid do you feel this view is? Is it not possible for imagination to have a role in making a photograph?
3. Read a poem from Baudelaire's most celebrated volume, *The Flowers of Evil*. You might choose "Twilight: Evening" from a group he called "Parisian Scenes." In what ways is his poem unlike a photograph?
4. Considering his attitude toward photography, why would he have sat for a portrait such as Carjat's? Would you classify this portrait as a work of art? What does the photograph reveal?

The most detailed portions of the photograph are the striations of the rock face, whose tactile qualities are emphasized by the strong sidelighting. The stone buildings in the distance have smoother textures, particularly as they show up against the blackness of the cave. That the buildings are only twelve to fifteen feet high is indicated by comparison with the height of the barely visible men standing in the ruins. Thus, nature dwarfs the work of humans. By framing the canyon wall, and by waiting for the right light, O'Sullivan has done more than create an ordinary "record" photograph. He has concentrated on the subject matter of the puniness and softness of humans, in contrast with the grandness and hardness of the canyon. The content centers on the extraordinary sense of stoniness—symbolic of permanence—as opposed to the transience of humanity, made possible by the capacity of the camera to transform realistic detail.

PHOTOGRAPHY AND PAINTING: THE PICTORIALISTS

Pictorialists are photographers who use the achievements of painting, particularly realistic painting, in their effort to realize the potential of photography as art. The early pictorialists tried to avoid the head-on directness of Howlett and Carjat, just as they tried to avoid the amateur's mistakes in composition, such as inclusion of distracting details and imbalance. The pictorialists controlled details by subordinating them to structure. They produced compositions that usually relied on the same underlying structures found in most nineteenth-century paintings until the dominance of the Impressionists in the 1880s. Normally, the most important part of the subject matter was centered in the frame. Pictorial lighting, also borrowed from painting, often was sharp and clearly directed, as in Alfred Stieglitz's *Paula* (Figure 11-6).

The pictorialist photograph was usually soft in focus, centrally weighted, and carefully balanced symmetrically. By relying on the formalist characteristics of

FIGURE 11-6
Alfred Stieglitz, *Sunrays, Paula*. 1889.
Stieglitz photographed Paula in such
a way as to suggest the composition
of a painting, framing her in darkness
while bathing her in window light.

Source: Library of Congress, Prints and
Photographs Division [LC-DIG-ds-00183]

early- and mid-nineteenth-century paintings, pictorialist photographers often evoked emotions that bordered on the sentimental. Indeed, one of the complaints modern commentators have about the development of pictorialism is that it was emotionally shallow.

Rarely criticized for sentimentalism, Alfred Stieglitz was, in his early work, a master of the pictorial style. His *Paula,* done in 1889, places his subject at the center in the act of writing. The top and bottom of the scene are printed in deep black. The light, streaking through the venetian blind and creating lovely strip patterns, centers on Paula. Her profile is strong against the dark background partly because Stieglitz removed, during the printing process, one of the strips that would have fallen on her lower face. The strong vertical lines of the window frames reinforce the verticality of the candle and echo the back of the chair.

A specifically photographic touch is present in the illustrations on the wall: photographs arranged symmetrically in a triangle (use a magnifying glass). Two prints of the same lake-skyscape are on each side of a woman in a white dress and hat. The same photograph of this woman is on the writing table in an oval frame. Is it Paula? The light in the room echoes the light in the oval portrait. The three hearts in the arrangement of photographs are balanced; one heart touches the portrait of a young man. We wonder if Paula is writing to him. The cage on the wall has dominant vertical lines, crossing the light lines cast by the venetian blind. Stieglitz may be suggesting that Paula, despite the open window, may be in a cage of her own. Stieglitz has kept most of the photograph in sharp focus because most of the details have something to tell us. If this were a painting of the early nineteenth century—for example, one by Delaroche—we would expect much the same style. We see Paula in a dramatic moment, with dramatic light, and with an implied narrative suggested by the artifacts surrounding her. It is up to the viewer to decide what, if anything, the drama implies.

> **PERCEPTION KEY** Pictorialism and Sentimentality
>
> 1. Pictorialists are often condemned for their sentimentality. What is sentimentality? Is it a positive or negative quality in a photograph?
> 2. Is *Paula* sentimental? What is its subject matter and what is its content?
> 3. To what extent is sentimentality present in the work of Cameron or Carjat? Which photographs in this chapter could be considered sentimental?

Both paintings and photographs, of course, can be sentimental in subject matter. The severest critics of such works complain about their *sentimentality*: the falsifying of feelings by demanding responses that are superficial or easy to come by. Sentimentality is usually an oversimplification of complex emotional issues. It also tends to be mawkish and self-indulgent. The case of photography is special because we are accustomed to the harshness of the camera. Thus, when the pictorialist finds tenderness, romance, and beauty in everyday occurrences, we become suspicious. We may be more tolerant of painting doing those things, but in fact we should be wary of any such emotional "coloration" in any medium if it is not restricted to the subject matter.

The pictorialist approach, when not guilty of sentimentalism, has great strengths. The use of lighting that selectively emphasizes the most important features of the subject matter often helps in creating meaning. Borrowing from the formal structures of painting also may help clarify subject matter. Structural harmony of the kind we generally look for in representational painting is possible in photography. Although it is not limited to the pictorialist approach, it is clearly fundamental to that approach.

STRAIGHT PHOTOGRAPHY

In his later work, beginning around 1905, Alfred Stieglitz pioneered the movement of *straight photography*, a reaction against pictorialism. The *f/64 Group*, working in the 1930s, and a second school, the *Documentarists*, continue the tradition. Straight photographers took the position that, as Aaron Siskind said in the 1950s, "Pictorialism is a kind of dead end making everything look beautiful." The straight photographer wanted things to look essentially as they do, even if they are ugly.

Straight photography aimed toward excellence in photographic techniques, independent of painting. Susan Sontag summarizes: "For a brief time—say, from Stieglitz through the reign of Weston—it appeared that a solid point of view had been erected with which to evaluate photographs: impeccable lighting, skill of composition, clarity of subject, precision of focus, perfection of print quality."[2] Some of these qualities are shared by pictorialists, but new principles of composition—not

---

[2] Susan Sontag, *On Photography* (New York: Farrar, Straus, and Giroux, 1977), p. 136.

derived from painting—and new attitudes toward subject matter helped straight photography reveal the world straight, as it really is.

The f/64 Group

The name of the group derives from the small aperture, f/64, which ensures that the foreground, middle ground, and background will all be in sharp focus. The group declared its principles through manifestos and shows by Edward Weston, Ansel Adams, Imogen Cunningham, and others. It continued the reaction against pictorialism, adding the kind of nonsentimental subject matter that interested the later Stieglitz. Edward Weston, whose early work was in the soft-focus school, developed a special interest in formal organizations. He is famous for his nudes and his portraits of vegetables, such as artichokes, eggplants, and green peppers. His nudes rarely show the face, not because of modesty but because the question of the identity of the model can distract us from contemplating the formal relationships of the human body.

Weston's *Nude* (Figure 11-7) shows many characteristics of work by the f/64 Group. The figure is isolated and presented for its own sake, the sand being equivalent to a photographer's backdrop. The figure is presented not as a portrait of a given woman but rather as a formal study. Weston wanted us to see the relationship between legs and torso, to respond to the rhythms of line in the extended body, and to appreciate the counterpoint of the round, dark head against the long, light linearity of the body. Weston enjoys some notoriety for his studies of peppers, because his approach to vegetables was similar to his approach to nudes. We are to appreciate the sensual curve, the counterpoints of line, the reflectivity of skin, the harmonious proportions of parts.

FIGURE 11-7
Edward Weston, *Nude.* **1936.**
Weston's approach to photography was to make everything as sharp as possible and to make the finest print possible. He was aware he was making photographs as works of art.

FIGURE 11-8
Ansel Adams. Church, Taos Pueblo, 1941.

Source: National Archives Catalog

Weston demanded objectivity in his photographs. "I do not wish to impose my personality upon nature (any of life's manifestations), but without prejudice or falsification to become identified with nature, to know things in their very essence, so that what I record is not an interpretation—my ideas of what nature should be—but a revelation."[3] One of Weston's ideals was to capitalize on the capacity of the camera to be objective and impersonal, an ideal that the pictorialists usually rejected.

The work of Ansel Adams establishes another ideal of the f/64 Group: the fine print. Even some of the best early photographers were relatively casual in the act of printing their negatives. Adams spent a great deal of energy and skill in producing the finest print the negative would permit, sometimes spending days to print one photograph. He developed a special system (the Zone System) to measure tonalities in specific regions of the negative so as to control the final print, keeping careful records so that he could duplicate the print at a later time. In even the best of reproductions, it is difficult to point to the qualities of tonal gradation that constitute the fine print. Only the original can yield the beauties that gradations of silver or platinum can produce. His photograph of the church at the Taos Pueblo (Figure 11-8) reveals the character of the southwest adobe architecture while at the same time making us feel the gritty texture of the surfaces of the walls. He has found a moment when the desert light has illuminated the interior and vertical spaces while bathing the walls in a relieving shade. Like Timothy O'Sullivan before him, Adams has made every effort to give us a convincing sense of place, and to some extent a sense of time as well.

---

[3]*The Daybooks of Edward Weston*, ed. Nancy Newhall, 2 vols. (New York: Aperture, 1966), vol. 2, p. 241.

THE DOCUMENTARISTS

Time is critical to the Documentarist, who portrays a world that is disappearing so quickly we cannot see it go. Henri Cartier-Bresson used the phrase "the decisive moment" to define that crucial interaction of shapes and spaces, formed by people and things, that tells him when to snap his shutter. Not all his photographs are decisive; they do not all catch the action at its most intense point. But those that do are pure Cartier-Bresson.

Many Documentarists agree with Stieglitz's description of the effect of shapes on his own feelings. Few contemporary Documentarists, however, who are often journalists like Cartier-Bresson, can compose the way Stieglitz could. But the best develop an instinct—usually nurtured by years of visual education—for the powerful statement, as one can see in Eddie Adams's *Execution in Saigon* (Figure 2-2).

Eugène Atget spent much of his time photographing in Paris in the early morning, when no one would bother him. He must have been in love with Paris and its surroundings because he photographed for many years, starting in the late 1800s and continuing to his death in 1927. Generally there are no people in his views of Paris, although he did an early series on some street traders, such as organ grinders, peddlers, and even prostitutes. His photographs of important Parisian monuments, such as his view of the Petit Trianon (Figure 11-9), are distinctive for their subtle drama. Most commercial photographs of this building ignore the dramatic reflection in the pond, and none of them permit the intense saturation of dark tones in the surrounding trees and in the water reflection. The more one ponders this photograph, the more

FIGURE 11-9
Eugène Atget, *Trianon, Paris.* **1923–1924.** Atget was rediscovered in the 1960s when it became clear he was not just making record photographs but finding ways of intensifying the visual elements to make a statement about how we see.

©The Museum of Modern Art/Scala/Art Resource, NY

FIGURE 11-10
Paul Strand, *Wall Street, New York*,
1916. Paul Strand photographed
New York in the early part of
the century, but moved on to
photograph churches in Mexico,
where he moved during the
Depression. He photographed in
small villages in Maine and in Italy.
Later, he also made films. *Wall Street,
New York* was published in Camera
Work, no. 48, October 1916, plate I.

Source: Library of Congress, Prints and
Photographs Division [LC-USZ62-97529]

one feels a sense of dramatic uncertainty and perhaps even urgency. The many ways in which Atget balances and contrasts the visual elements at the same time make the experience of the image intense. Atget's work did not refer to painting: It created its own photographic reference. We see a photograph, not just a thing photographed.

Paul Strand (Figure 11-10) takes a somewhat different approach from Atget, although he worked in the same tradition at approximately the same time. He used a view camera on a tripod and roamed the streets of New York early in the morning, just as Atget did. But unlike Atget, Strand photographed people as well as buildings, and the content of his photographs was, while artful, less abstract. Yet, like Atget, he looked for strong formal ingredients, as in his remarkable 1915 portrait of workers walking uphill on Wall Street during an economic boom. The building, the Morgan Trust, with its huge dark recessed panels, dwarfs the men and women marching past toward work. The Morgan Trust was a symbol of solidity and reliability, and while Strand could hardly have expected the outcome years later in 1929, all that solidity crumbled in the nation's most devastating Great Depression. The country, whose economy depended on Wall Street, was thrown into unemployment and general poverty for more than ten years. Strand's photograph contrasts the tiny upright people with the sharp diagonal of their shadows on the sidewalk, matched by the diagonal light molding of the building. Above them the powerful upright stone verticals and black panels seem, in retrospect, almost sinister. Strand began documenting people going to work in the financial district, but history now sees him as having documented their progress toward unemployment as a result of the excesses of Wall Street financiers.

Unlike Atget and Paul Strand, who used large cameras, Cartier-Bresson used the 35-mm Leica and specialized in photographing people. He preset his camera in order to work fast and instinctively. His *Behind the Gare St. Lazare* (Figure 11-11) is a perfect example of his aim to capture an image at the "decisive moment." The figure leaping from the wooden ladder has not quite touched the water, while his reflection awaits him. The entire image is a tissue of reflection, with the spikes of the fence reflecting the angles of the fallen ladder. The circles in the foreground are repeated in the wheelbarrow's reflection and the white circles in the poster. Moreover, the figure in the white poster appears to be a dancer leaping in imitation of the man to the right. The focus of the entire image is somewhat soft because Cartier-Bresson preset his camera so that he could take the shot instantly without adjusting the aperture. The formal relationship of elements in a photograph such as this can produce various kinds of significance or apparent lack of significance. The best Documentarists

FIGURE 11-12
Dorothea Lange, *Migrant Mother.*
1936. This is one of the most
poignant records of the Great
Depression in which millions moved
across the nation looking for work.
Lange did a number of photographs
of this family in a very short time.

Source: Library of Congress, Prints and
Photographs Division [LC-USZ62-95653]

search for the strongest coherency of elements while also searching for the decisive
moment. That moment is the split-second peak of intensity, and it is defined especially with reference to light, spatial relationships, and expression.

Dorothea Lange and Walker Evans were Documentarists who took part in a federal
program to give work to photographers during the Depression of the 1930s. Both created careful formal organizations. Lange (Figure 11-12) stresses centrality and balance
by placing the children's heads next to the mother's face, which is all the more compelling because the children's faces do not compete for our attention. The mother's
arm leads upward to her face, emphasizing the other triangularities of the photograph.
Within ten minutes, Lange took four other photographs of this woman and her children, but none could achieve the power of this photograph. Lange caught the exact
moment when the children's faces turned and the mother's anxiety came forth with
utter clarity, although the lens mercifully softens its focus on her face, while leaving

her shabby clothes in sharp focus. This softness helps humanize our relationship with the woman. Lange gives us an unforgettable image that brutally and yet sympathetically imparts a deeper understanding of what the Depression was for many.

Berenice Abbott, aiming at a career in sculpture and art, left Ohio State after two semesters and went to Paris. She became an assistant to the photographer Man Ray and began using a camera, thus finding her calling. She became noted in Paris for her photographs of distinguished artists and writers, such as James Joyce. Man Ray introduced her to the work of Eugene Atget, whom she photographed, and when he died she gathered as many of his negatives as she could and returned to the United States to publish a book of his work. Her experience in New York in the 1930s led her to produce her own photographs, studies of New York City that have become legendary. Like other good photographers in the Great Depression, she was supported by a federal grant.

The subjects of *Blossom Restaurant*, one of her most powerful photographs (Figure 11-13), are the Blossom Restaurant and Jimmy's Barber Shop, which were both in the basement of the Boston Hotel at 103–105 Bowery. The Bowery in lower Manhattan was then a refuge for the down and out. The Boston Hotel, a flophouse, rented rooms for 30 cents a night. Meals at the restaurant were 15 cents or 30 cents. The image is alive with strong contrast and a brilliant sense of busyness, indicating what Abbott interpreted as the extraordinary vigor of the city despite the pain of the Depression.

Walker Evans's photograph (Figure 11-14) shows us a view of Bethlehem, Pennsylvania, and the off-center white cross reminds us of what has become of the message of Christ. The vertical lines are accentuated in the cemetery stones and repeated in

FIGURE 11-13
Berenice Abbott, *Blossom Restaurant.*
October 24, 1935.

©The Museum of the City of New York/Art Resource, NY

the telephone lines, the porch posts, and finally the steel-mill smokestacks. The aspi-
rations of the dominating verticals, however, are dampened by the strong horizontals,
which, because of the low angle of the shot, tend to merge from the cross to the roofs.
Evans equalizes focus, which helps compress the space so that we see the cemetery on
top of the living space, which is immediately adjacent to the steel mills where some of
the people who live in the tenements work and where some of those now in the cemetery died. This compression of space suggests the closeness of life, work, and death.
We see a special kind of sadness in this steel town—and others like it—that we may
never have seen before. Evans caught the right moment for the light, which intensifies
the white cross, and he aligned the verticals and horizontals for their best effect.

PERCEPTION KEY The Documentary Photographers

1. Are any of these documentary photographs sentimental?
2. Some critics assert that these photographers have made interesting social doc-
   uments, but not works of art. What arguments might support their views? What
   arguments might contest their views?
3. Contemporary photographers and critics often highly value the work of Atget because it is "liberated" from the influence of painting. What does it mean to say that
   his work is more photographic than it is painterly?
4. What is the subject matter of each photograph? What is the content of each photograph? Is the "**RAILOWSKY**" poster in Figure 11-11 a pun?

FIGURE 11-15
Bruce Davidson, *Opening at the Metropolitan Museum of Art*. 1969. Gelatin-silver print. Metropolitan Museum of Art. Gift of the Hundredth Anniversary Committee, 1974. Bruce Davidson has caught a moment of what seems to be fun at the museum. Is the hand in the upper frame wittily waving goodbye to the woman who steps toward the photographer? Do the visitors to the museum seem interested in the art? Is this photograph ironic?

THE MODERN EYE

Photography has gone in so many directions that classifications tend to be misleading. The snapshot style, however, has become somewhat identifiable, a kind of rebellion against the earlier movements, especially the pictorial. Janet Malcolm claims, "Photography went modernist not, as has been supposed, when it began to imitate modern abstract art but when it began to study snapshots."[4] No school of photography established a snapshot canon. It seems to be a product of amateurs, a kind of folk photography. The snapshot appears primitive, spontaneous, and accidental. But the snapshot may not be unplanned and accidental, as is evidenced, for instance, in the powerful work of Bruce Davidson and Nan Goldin.

Bruce Davidson respected the work of Walker Evans and Henri Cartier-Bresson enough to concentrate on what he thought photography did best: describe the human scene faithfully. Like Cartier-Bresson, Davidson took advantage of a small camera—in the case of *Opening at the Metropolitan Museum of Art* (Figure 11-15), to produce a square image. Davidson has a long history of association with the Metropolitan Museum of Art, and particularly of photographing visitors and curators. *Opening at the Metropolitan Museum of Art* is a fine example of the snapshot aesthetic: The photograph appears to be totally unplanned and apparently unrefined. As in so many snapshots, the head of the primary figure—the woman in white—is cut off. A hand that seems random and incoherent appears above the shiny steel construction. The construction itself is unidentified and it is impossible to know whether it is a work of art or part of the air conditioning. The very fact that the viewer may be confounded by what is shown seems to be part of the point of the photograph. Yet, when we examine the photograph carefully, studying the forms and the figures, some of whom hold cocktails, we begin to see how Davidson wanted us to respond to the image. For one thing, he has chosen a powerful contrast between the striking steel construction and the people who are nearby. The woman in white seems amused at the fact that she needs to duck to get past it, while the men who stay behind are totally unidentifiable and in the dark. All we really see of them is their

[4]Janet Malcolm, *Diana and Nikon: Essays on the Aesthetics of Photography* (Boston: David Godine, 1980), p. 113.

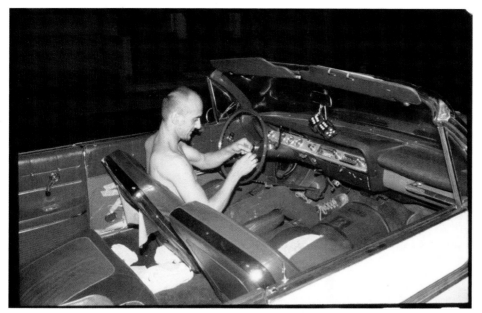

FIGURE 11-16
Nan Goldin, *Bruce in His Red Car.*
1981. Goldin adopted the snapshot
style early on. She constantly
photographed those around her,
often marginalized people and
junkies. She regarded them as her
family.

©Nan Goldin

hands. The frame is broken into segments, each of which seems a photographic statement in itself. Together they have the snapshot virtue of apparent incoherence while the reality is that the action is totally coherent. What Davidson achieves here is what all good photographers want to achieve: We are forced to look at the photograph as an object in itself, and not just as the record of an event. This photograph is made revelatory by virtue of its formal qualities.

At age eleven Nan Goldin suffered the trauma of her older sister's suicide, eventually turning to drugs and leaving home. But a teacher gave her a way of getting herself together with the gift of a camera, which she responded to immediately. Influenced by films of Andy Warhol and Federico Fellini, in Boston she lived among a group of drag queens and photographed them out of respect for their way of life. "My desire was to show them as a third gender, as another sexual option, a gender option. And to show them with a lot of respect and love, to kind of glorify them because I really admire people who can recreate themselves and manifest their fantasies publicly. I think it's brave."[5] Many of her photographs of the LGBT community are in her best-known book, *The Ballad of Sexual Dependency.* Unfortunately, she lost many of her early subjects to overdose. Some of her later work has been in fashion photography and in studying family life. Her snapshot style seems effortless, but she makes her images intense and direct, if not simple and casual.

Nan Goldin's *Bruce in His Red Car* (Figure 11-16) shows a man in his blazing red car, fumbling with the key to the steering wheel lock. It is not clear whether he is worried about having his car stolen or if he is stealing it. The prominent dice hanging from the rearview mirror "spell" boxcars, an ironic comment. Is this a sociological statement or a simple record of an event? How is one to interpret the photographer's comment on Bruce and his car?

[5]Stephen Westfall, "Interview with Nan Goldin," BOMB Magazine 37, Fall 1991.

FIGURE 11-17
Carrie Mae Weems, *Untitled (Man smoking)*. 1990. Gelatin silver print, 27¼ × 27¼ inches. Museum of Modern Art.

©Carrie Mae Weems. Courtesy of the artist and Jack Shainman Gallery, New York

Untitled (Man smoking) (Figure 11-17) is the second image (of twenty) in Carrie Mae Weems's famous project, *The Kitchen Table* (1990). Like her contemporary, Cindy Sherman, this project positions the photographer as the protagonist in a series of images that contains an implied narrative, a portrait of the artist discovering who she is in relation to her man, her child, her friends, and herself. Each image is a self-portrait taken from the same angle, including the kitchen table on and around which much of the life of a woman is lived.

The situation in *Untitled (Man smoking)* is filled with anticipation. The look on the woman's eyes, implying concern, becomes the visual center of the image. The room is filled with sexual tension and a search for emotional understanding between the man and woman. The images in the book are accompanied by fourteen text panels. The panel nearest to *Untitled (Man smoking)* includes the line "Together they were falling for that ole black magic." The visual details, playing cards—the man's hand shows two hearts—the snacks, the whisky, and the almost empty glasses, imply that they have been playing a game. But the expression in the eyes of the woman suggests that she wonders if the game is over. The parallel angles of the arms, hands both covering their mouths, as well as the repetition of curves in the bowl, glasses, and chairs intensify the visual field and create a powerful sense of unity.

The poster of Malcolm X on the wall implies that the man and woman are socially conscious of the movement toward black power. The entire Kitchen Table project has become a significant statement in contemporary feminism while at the same time becoming a landmark in photographic art.

Like Nan Goldin, Tina Barney photographs people she knows, people she is related to, and people who are similar to her in their social milieu. Whereas Goldin photographs those in the LGBT community, Barney photographs the wealthy and the entitled both locally in Long Island and New York and in her overseas communities in Europe.

Because she prints her photographs in large size, four feet by five feet, she employs a view camera with an 8 × 10 inch negative. This means she uses a tripod and often "stages" the set and suggests how her subject should pose. The result is sometimes static, but at the same time her process gives her exceptional detail and full control over lighting and produces rich color. The Art Institute of Chicago has said, "Barney was thus one of the first photographers to present color work on a grand scale that rivaled most twentieth-century paintings." Many modern photographers have moved to producing very large photographs to satisfy the needs of museums as well as collectors.

Barney's extensive body of work indicates that she is essentially a portraitist who welcomes unplanned events, such as people deciding to be part of a photograph at the last minute. She says she takes "a lot of pictures and when I am shooting, I almost go into a trance. It happens so fast that not until afterwards can I see whether all of the elements coalesce. It's like magic."

The Europeans: The Hands (Figure 11-18) may or may not be social commentary. Its title, however, seems to help us begin a search for visual similarities and differences. For one thing, the huge painting behind the man and boy features a hand grasping the breast of what may be a potential lover (or rape victim). The right hand on the Oceanic wood sculpture to the left seems to be over its heart, while the left hand is missing altogether. The sex of the sculpture may seem ambiguous, while the gender of the other figures is explicit. The crossed arms of the man and boy imply a sense of security, perhaps withholdingness. The facial expressions of the man and boy may be interpreted in any of a number of ways.

Unlike a photograph taken in the snapshot style, this photograph is intentional. The richness of the environment, the steel and glass table, the chairs, the circular light overhead—as well as the figures—are placed to have an effect.

FIGURE 11-18
The Europeans: The Hands. 2002.
Chromogenic print, 48 × 60 inches.
Tina Barney, like many contemporary photographers, began with what she knew. She said, "I don't feel it's social commentary because I am not judging them; it's all instinct. For me, it's a great visual feast."

Courtesy Paul Kasmin Gallery

Traditional photography is very much about cameras, lenses, and shutter speeds, all of which control what the photographer is likely to capture. Ansel Adams was important for his contributions about how to produce a fine-art print, establishing a system that aimed to get the best image out of a negative. Today most fine-art photography is the result of digital cameras and digital, chromogenic prints. Because digital images can be altered almost infinitely, fine-art photographers have largely abandoned the principles of printing only what the camera sees. In some cases a single image can be the product of dozens of photographs, all layered together to produce an image that might be impossible in real life. Even in the cases in which we see a single image, the photographer can easily alter the contrast and colors of the original so as to produce an artistically effective print. The result of all this is to free photographers from the limitations of the equipment while permitting them to make prints large enough to compete directly with paintings, as in the case of Figure 11-19, Cindy Sherman's eight-foot-high portrait.

Cindy Sherman is one of the few American photographers to have had a one-woman show at the prestigious Whitney Museum in New York City. Her work has annoyed, confounded, and alarmed many people both ignorant and well informed about photography as an art. Some of Sherman's work is condemned because it seems designed to horrify the audience with images of garbage, offal, vomit, and body parts. For many years she photographed herself in various costumes, with makeup and guises that showed her almost limitless capacity to interpret her personality. Those color photographs often had a snapshot quality and probably were most interesting when seen as a group rather than individually.

Untitled #466 is one of a series of imagined wealthy and privileged modern women. Sherman poses herself as if she were in a painting. The background, the Cloisters in New York City, was photographed separately and the two images were layered together. The contrast between the religious echoes of the Cloisters and the sumptuous secular blue caftan, richly decorated, with Sherman's dangling gold earrings and gold rings is designed to inform us about the significance of the image. Because this is such a large photograph, eight feet high, we can see every detail. The reveal of the cheap plastic sandal and the low-quality stocking implies that the surface is not entirely to be trusted. Sherman has subtly transformed the apparent subject matter and has produced a form-content that, like much contemporary photography, is the result of very careful staging.

One of China's emerging photographers, Wang Qingsong (Figure 11-20), uses all the resources of digital manipulation and collage to make statements that are often subversive and ironic.

Can I Cooperate with You? is a testament to foreign influences in modern China. We see the two most familiar

FIGURE 11-19
Cindy Sherman, *Untitled #466.* **2008.** Cindy Sherman uses herself to create her images. She chooses interesting locations and changes her makeup to alter her appearance and create a mystery about her.

Courtesy of the artist and Metro Pictures

FIGURE 11-20
Wang Qingsong, *Can I Cooperate with You?* **2000.** Wang Qingsong has been influenced by standard commercial advertising and propaganda, but he turns it on its ear by adding subversive touches.

Courtesy of Wang Qingsong

American emblems of McDonald's and Coca-Cola, but we also see a European in a rickshaw pedaled by a Chinese man. Two figures are half-size, observing the action, and the swarm of people around the rickshaw seem involved in acclimating themselves to change. The figure on the left holds a tiny Chinese flag as if trying to preserve traditional Chinese values. The style, with the seamless backdrop, is obviously a comment on popular advertising. He has said, "The countless contradictions I see around me and the ever-present crisis of modernization are what determine my photographic work."

Color is also part of the subject matter, as it is in Bill Gekas's *Plums* (Figure 11-21), and can be appreciated somewhat the way one appreciates the color of a painting.

Bill Gekas, a photographer from Melbourne, Australia, is a businessman who sometimes accepted commissions for photographic portraits. When he began photographing his five-year-old daughter in poses and in settings that emulated the Flemish and Dutch masters of the seventeenth century, he drew attention from around the world. By drawing on the visual techniques of the old masters, he was able to expand the role of modern photography.

Gregory Crewdson sets up his photographic subject matter in a manner reminiscent of preparation for a feature film. At times, he needs cranes, lights, and as many as thirty assistants to get the effect he wants. He spends months on a single image. The photograph in Figure 11-22 alludes to the drowning of Ophelia in *Hamlet*. Crewdson's Ophelia has left her slippers on the stairs and has apparently entered the water on purpose, as did Shakespeare's Ophelia. To get this effect, Crewdson appears to have flooded an ordinary living room, positioned the artificial lights, and captured the sunlight all at the same time. Ophelia's eyes are open, her expression calm, and the colors of the scene are carefully balanced. The level of drama in the photograph is intense, yet the reclined, passive figure of Ophelia lends an almost peaceful quality to the image.

FIGURE 11-21
Bill Gekas, *Plums*. 2012. Digital print. Gekas produces a setting with careful control of the colors and lighting and emulates the old master paintings that inspire him.

©Bill Gekas

FIGURE 11-22
Gregory Crewdson, *Untitled*. 2001. Like many contemporary art photographers, Crewdson sometimes spends days or weeks assembling the material for his work. His use of multiple light sources helps give his work an unsettling quality.

Courtesy of the artist and Gagosian Gallery

PERCEPTION KEY The Modern Eye

1. Compare the photographic values of Bruce Davidson's *Opening at the Metropolitan Museum of Art* with those of Carrie Weems's *Untitled (Man smoking)*. In which are the gradations of tone from light to dark more carefully modulated? In which is the selectivity of the framing more consciously and apparently artistic? In which is the subject matter more obviously transformed by the photographic image? In which is the form more fully revealed?

2. Examine the photographs by Paul Strand, Henri Cartier-Bresson, and Bruce Davidson. What are the characteristics of the best snapshot photographs? What have these three images got in common? What are their differences? How do we react to them in comparison with the carefully staged work of portraitist Tina Barney? Which do you prefer?

3. Which digital photograph more transforms its subject matter by the use of color? What is the ultimate effect of that transformation on the viewer?

4. Cindy Sherman and Gregory Crewdson both build sets to make their photographs. Given that the sets are artificial, and to an extent their subject matter is artificial, can their work be said to be truly representational? What distinguishes their work from that of a Documentarist like Ansel Adams or Berenice Abbott?

5. Photocopy any of the color photographs to produce a black-and-white image. What has been lost in the reproduction? Why is color important to those photographs?

6. Look at some of your own photographs. What school of photography do you belong in? Which photographer is closest to your style?

SUMMARY

The capacity of photography to record reality faithfully is both a virtue and a fault. It makes many viewers of photographs concerned only with what is presented (the subject matter) and leaves them unaware of the way the subject matter has been represented (the form). Because of its fidelity of presentation, photography seems to some to have no transformation of subject matter. This did not bother early photographers, who were delighted at the ease with which they could present their subject matter. The pictorialists, on the other hand, relied on nineteenth-century representational painting to guide them in their approach to form. Their carefully composed images are still valued by many photographers. But the reaction of the straight photographers, who wished to shake off any dependence on painting and disdained sentimental subject matter, began a revolution that emphasized the special qualities of the medium: especially the tonal range of the silver or platinum print (and now color print), the impersonality of the sharply defined object (and consequent lack of sentimentality), spatial compression, and selective framing. The revolution has not stopped there but has pushed on into unexpected areas, such as the exploration of the snapshot and the rejection of the technical standards of the straight photographers. Many contemporary photographers are searching for new ways of photographic seeing based on the capacity of digital cameras and computers to transform and manipulate images. They are more intent on altering rather than recording reality. This is a very interesting prospect.

Source: Warner Brothers

Chapter 12

CINEMA

The history of cinema is, to an extent, dominated by technology. The earliest feature films were black and white, usually projected at twenty-four frames per second, and silent. In the first few years of the twentieth century, they were often projected outdoors in town squares or indoors in social clubs and general-purpose public buildings, but soon special theaters appeared with incredible speed around the world. In 1926 sound permitted both music and dialogue to accompany the visual images. Some films were in color in the 1920s and 1930s, but color films did not become standard until the 1940s and 1950s. Improvements in sound and image size, as well as experiments in 3-D films, followed and continue today. The most dramatic recent change is the abandonment of celluloid film in favor of digital production and digital projection. Since 2013 the industry has been almost entirely digital, so the term "film," while out of date, is still useful for us in discussing theatrical features.

THE SUBJECT MATTER OF FILM

Except in its most reductionist form, the subject matter of most great films is difficult to isolate and restate in words. You could say that death is the subject matter of Bergman's *The Seventh Seal* (Figure 12-1). But you would also need to observe that the knight's sacrifice to save the lives of others—which he accomplishes by playing chess with Death—is also part of the subject matter of the film. As David Cook explains in *A History of Narrative Film,* there is a complexity of subject matter in film that is rivaled only by literature.

FIGURE 12-1
Ingmar Bergman's *The Seventh Seal*
(1957). The knight plays chess with
Death in order to save the lives of
the traveling citizens in the distance.
The close shot balances the knight
and Death in sharp focus, while
the citizens are in soft focus. In
chess, a knight sacrifice is often a
ploy designed to achieve a stronger
position, as in this film.

©AF archive/Alamy

It may be that the very popularity of film and the ease with which we can access it lead us to ignore the form and the insights form offers into subject matter. For example, is it really possible to catch the subtleties of form of a great film in one viewing? Yet how many of us see a great film more than once? Audiences generally enjoy, but rarely analyze, films. Some of the analysis that follows may help your enjoyment as well as your analyses.

Except perhaps for opera, film more than any of the other arts involves collaborative effort. Most films are written by a scriptwriter, then planned by a director, who may make many changes. However, even if the director is also the scriptwriter, the film needs a producer, camera operators, an editor, designers, researchers, costumers, actors, and actresses. Auteur criticism regards the director as equivalent to the *auteur*, or author, of the film. For most moviegoers, the most important persons involved with the film will almost surely be not the director but the stars who appear in the film. George Clooney, Angelina Jolie, Julia Roberts, Meryl Streep, and Denzel Washington are more famous than such directors of stature as Ingmar Bergman, Federico Fellini, Lina Wertmuller, Akira Kurosawa, Jane Campion, or Alfred Hitchcock.

DIRECTING AND EDITING

The two dominant figures in early films were directors who did their own *editing*: D. W. Griffith and Sergei Eisenstein, unquestionably the great early geniuses of filmmaking. They managed to gain control over the production of their works so that they could craft their films into a distinctive art. Some of their films are still considered among the finest ever made. *The Birth of a Nation* (1916) and *Intolerance* (1918) by Griffith, and *Battleship Potemkin* (1925) and *Ivan the Terrible* (1941–1946) by Eisenstein, are still being shown and are influencing contemporary filmmakers. These men were more than just directors. With many of their films, they were responsible for almost everything: writing, casting, choosing locations, handling the camera, directing, editing, and financing.

Directing and editing are probably the most crucial phases of filmmaking. Today most directors control the acting and supervise the photography, carried out by skilled technicians who work with such problems as lighting, camera angles, and focusing, as well as the motion of the camera itself (some sequences use a highly mobile camera, while others use a fixed camera). Among the resources available to directors making choices about the use of the camera are the kinds of shots that may eventually be edited together. A **shot** is a single exposure of the camera without a break. Some of the most important kinds of shots follow:

Establishing shot: Usually a distant shot establishes important locations or figures in the action.

Close-up: An important object, such as the face of a character, fills the screen.

Long shot: The camera is far distant from the most important characters, objects, or scenes.

Medium shot: What the camera focuses on is neither up close nor far distant. There can be medium close-ups and medium long shots, too.

Following shot: The camera keeps a moving figure in the frame, usually keeping pace with the figure.

Point-of-view shot: The camera records what the character must be seeing; when the camera moves, it implies that the character's gaze moves.

Tracking shot: A shot in which the camera moves forward, backward, or sidewise.

Crane shot: The camera is on a crane or movable platform and moves upward or downward.

Handheld shot: The camera is carried, sometimes on a special harness, by the camera operator.

Recessional shot: The camera focuses on figures and objects moving away, as in Figure 12-10. A **processional shot** focuses on figures and objects moving toward the camera.

When you see films, you probably see all these shots many times. Add to these specific kinds of shots the variables of camera angles, types of camera lenses, variations in lighting, and variations in approach to sound, and you can see that the technical resources of the director are enormous. The addition of script and actors enriches the director's range of choices so that they become almost dizzying.

The editor puts the shots in order after the filming is finished. This selective process is highly complex and of supreme importance, for the structuring of the shots forms the film. The alternatives are often vast, and if the film is to achieve an artistic goal—insight into its subject matter—the shot succession must be creatively accomplished. The editor trims the shots to an appropriate length, then joins them with other shots to create the final film. Edited sequences sometimes shot far apart in time and place are organized into a unity. Films are rarely shot sequentially, and only a part of the total footage is shown in a film. The old saying of the bit-part actor—"I was lost on the cutting-room floor"—attests to the fact that sometimes interesting footage is omitted.

FIGURE 12-2
Medium interior shot from *Tokyo*
Story **(1953), by Yasujirō Ozu.** Ozu is
considered one of the finest Japanese
directors. *Tokyo Story* tells of older
parents visiting their children in
postwar Tokyo. The older generation
realizes it has no place in the new
Japan, as their children are too busy
to spend time with them.

©Shochiku/Kobal/REX/Shutterstock

In a relatively short time, the choice and editing of shots have become almost a kind of language. The parents on the left of the medium shot from Yasujiro's *Tokyo Story* (Figure 12-2) seem an essential part of the family because the physical space is so limited, but the irony is that later shots show them very much separated emotionally and psychologically from their ungrateful, busy children.

It helps to know the resources of the editor, who cuts the film to create the relationships between takes. The way these cuts are related is at the core of the director's distinctive style. Some of the most familiar of the director's and editor's choices follow:

Continuity cut: shots edited to produce a sense of narrative continuity, following the action stage by stage. The editor can also use a discontinuity cut to break up the narrative continuity for effect.

Jump cut: sometimes just called a "cut"; moves abruptly from one shot to the next, with no preparation and often with a shock

Cut-in: an immediate move from a wide shot to a very close shot of the same scene; the editor may "cut out," as well

Cross-cutting: alternating shots of two or more distinct actions occurring in different places (but often at the same time)

Dissolve: one scene disappearing slowly while the next scene appears as if beneath it

Fade: includes fade-in (a dark screen growing brighter to reveal the shot) and fade-out (the screen darkens, effectively ending the shot)

Wipe: transition between shots, with a line moving across or through the screen separating one shot from the next

Graphic match: joining two shots that have similar composition, color, or scene

Montage sequence: a sequence of images dramatically connected but physically disconnected

Shot, reverse shot: a pair of shots in which the first shot shows a character looking at something; reverse shot shows what the character sees

Our responses to film depend on the choices that directors and editors make regarding shots and editing almost as much as on the nature of the narrative and the appeal of the actors. In a relatively short time, film editing has become a kind of language—a language of imagery with close to universal significance.

When the editing is handled well, it can be profoundly effective, because it is impossible in real-life experience to achieve what the editor achieves. By eliminating the irrelevant, good editing accents the relevant. The *montage*—dramatically connected but physically disconnected images—can be made without a word of dialogue.

PERCEPTION KEY Editing

1. Study a film such as *The Bourne Identity* and identify at least three kinds of shots mentioned in the text. Find a point-of-view shot, a tracking shot, or a handheld shot. Which is most dramatic?
2. In such a film as *The Bourne Identity*, establish the effect on the viewer of shots that last a long time as opposed to a rapid succession of very short shots. Which of these two techniques contributes more to the participative experience of the film?
3. Find at least one jump cut and comment on the editor's decision to use it. How shocking or jarring is the cut? Is it effective in context?
4. Which continuity cuts does the editor of the film you have studied contribute most to your understanding of the film?

THE PARTICIPATIVE EXPERIENCE AND FILM

Our participation with film is often virtually involuntary. For one thing, most of us know exactly what it means to lose our sense of place and time in a movie. This loss seems to be achieved rapidly in all but the most awkwardly conceived films.

Cinematic realism makes it easy for us to identify with actors who represent our values (a kind of participation). For instance, in *Forrest Gump* (1994), Tom Hanks plays what seems to be, on the surface, a mentally defective person. But Gump is more than that—he is good at heart and positive in his thinking. He is a character in whom cunning—not just intelligence—has been removed, and in him the viewers see their lost innocence. It would be very doubtful that anyone in the audience consciously identified with Gump, but it was clear from the reception of the film that something in him resonated with the audience and was, in the final analysis, both appealing and cheering. Gump is an unlikely hero primarily because he is trusting, innocent, and good-hearted. When the audience participates with that film, it is in part because the audience members see in Gump something of what they would like to see in themselves.

It may be that we naturally identify with heroes in films, as we do in books. The characters played by extremely charismatic actors, like Jennifer Lopez or Matt Damon, almost always appeal to some aspect of our personalities, even if sometimes that aspect is frightening. Such may be the source, for instance, of the appeal of Hannibal Lecter in *The Silence of the Lambs* (1991) (Figure 12-3), in which Anthony Hopkins not only appears as a cannibal but actually gets away with it, identifying his former doctor as his next victim, whose liver he plans to eat with some "fava beans and a nice Chianti."

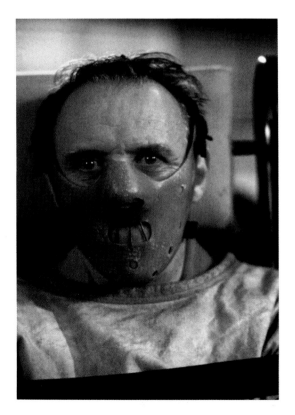

FIGURE 12-3
Anthony Hopkins as Hannibal Lecter in *The Silence of the Lambs* (1991).

©Orion/Kobal/REX/Shutterstock

There are two kinds of participative experiences with film. One is not principally filmic in nature and is represented by a kind of self-indulgence that depends on self-justifying fantasies. We imagine ourselves as James Bond, for example, and ignore the interrelationship of the major elements of the film. The other kind of participation evolves from an acute awareness of the details and their interrelationships. This second kind of participative experience means much more to us ultimately because it is significantly informative: We understand the content by means of the form.

THE FILM IMAGE

The starting point of film is the moving image. Just as still photographs and paintings can move us profoundly by their organization of visual elements, so can such images when they are set to motion. Indeed, many experts insist that no artistic medium ever created has the power to move us as deeply as the medium of moving images. They base their claim not just on the mass audiences who have been profoundly stirred but also on the fact that the moving images of the film are similar to the moving images we perceive in life. We rarely perceive static images, except when viewing such things as paintings or photographs. Watching a film closely can help us perceive much more intensely the visual worth of many of the images we experience outside film. Charlie Chaplin is evoked in someone walking in a jaunty, jumpy fashion with his feet turned out. There is a very long tracking shot in *Weekend* (1967), by Jean-Luc Godard, of a road piled up with wrecked or stalled cars. The camera glides along, nervelessly imaging the gridlock with fires and smoke and seemingly endless corpses scattered here and there along the roadsides—unattended. The stalled and living motorists are obsessed with getting to their vacation resorts. The horns honk and honk. The unbelievable elongation of the procession and the utter grotesqueness of the scenes evoke black humor at its extreme. If in reality we have to face anything even remotely similar, the intensity of our vision inevitably will be heightened if we have seen *Weekend*.

EXPERIENCING Still Frames and Photography

Study Figures 12-1 through 12-8. How would you evaluate these stills with reference to tightness of composition? For example, do the details and parts interrelate so that any change would disrupt the unity of the totality? Compare with Figure 2-2.

The still from *The Lady from Shanghai* (1947) in Figure 12-4 is carefully composed, a classic Hollywood close-up of Rita Hayworth, who plays Elsa Bannister. Orson Welles directed and acted in what has become a highly regarded example of film noir (dark film), a genre that usually involves crime and violence and is shot in sometimes threatening black and white. The emphasis on darkness reflects the attitude of the characters toward society, which is portrayed as ruthless, deceitful, and profoundly dangerous. Rita Hayworth is a "trophy wife" of Arthur Bannister, a strange, crippled criminal lawyer. His partner, George Grisby, has apparently concocted a scheme to kill Bannister while appearing to have been murdered himself. The complexity of the plot is standard in film noir, and in *The Lady from Shanghai* Orson Welles plays Michael O'Hara, an Irish sailor who, despite his better judgment, signs up on Bannister's yacht as an able seaman to pilot the boat through the Panama Canal to San Francisco. Grisby convinces O'Hara to pretend to murder him but never hints at his true motives. O'Hara follows through, but the situation becomes complicated by Grisby's murder and O'Hara's arrest. Because he had signed a confession, he is put on trial and Bannister defends him, without thinking he could get him off. O'Hara breaks out of the courthouse and is followed by Elsa, who hides him in Chinatown. O'Hara is drugged by Elsa's Chinese friends and, when he wakes, realizes that Elsa has killed Grisby and originally intended to murder Bannister and pin the crime on O'Hara. The film ends with a dramatic encounter in a hall of mirrors funhouse, where nothing is what it seems to be. The 1940s film noir classics reflect a social unrest and unease in the face of dramatic change. The old order, so to speak, had given over to a new and unknown reality, all reflected in stark black and white. The close-up of Elsa reveals both the attraction of beauty and the potential for evil and destruction.

FIGURE 12-4
The Lady from Shanghai (1947). This still from the film shows the use of strong light and dark shadow to intensify the allure and potential danger of Elsa Bannister (Rita Hayworth), who is the mysterious lady from Shanghai. This chiaroscuro style distinguishes the entire film.

Source: Columbia Pictures

Movement in motion pictures is caused by the physiological limitations of the eye. It cannot perceive the black line between frames when they move rapidly. All it sees is the succession of frames minus the lines that divide them, for the eye cannot perceive separate images or frames that move faster than one-thirtieth of a second. The images are usually projected at a speed of twenty-four frames per second, and the persistence of vision merges them. This is the "language" of the camera.

Because of this language, many filmmakers, both early and contemporary, attempt to design each individual frame as carefully as they might a photograph. (See "Photography and Painting: The Pictorialists" in Chapter 11.) Jean Renoir, the famous French filmmaker and son of painter Pierre-Auguste, sometimes composed frames like a tightly unified painting, as in *The Grand Illusion* (1936) and *The Rules of the Game* (1939). Sergei Eisenstein also framed many of his images especially carefully, notably in *Battleship Potemkin* (1925). David Lean, who directed *Brief Encounter* (1945), *Bridge on the River Kwai* (1957), *Lawrence of Arabia* (1962, rereleased 1988), *Dr. Zhivago* (1965), and *Ryan's Daughter* (1970), also paid close attention to the composition of individual frames.

Sam Worthington is Jake Sully in *Avatar* (Figure 12-5) and, despite being a spy whose avatar is gathering intel that would find the Na'vi weakness, falls in love with Neytiri. He ultimately joins the Na'vi and his brain is placed in his avatar permanently. In the still we see the tenderness in Neytiri and the strength in

FIGURE 12-5
Avatar **(2009).** A close-up shot from
the film, which was written and
directed by James Cameron, with
Zoe Saldana as Neytiri and Sam
Worthington as Jake Sully.

©Twentieth Century-Fox Film Corporation/
Kobal/REX/Shutterstock

Jake's avatar. Their relationship is emphasized by their overlapping figures and
their isolation from the blurred figures in the background. By contrast, Figure 12-6
from *Citizen Kane* shows the emptiness of the relationship of Charles Foster Kane
and his wife, Emily, who seem almost unaware of each other. The angle of the
shot emphasizes their separation. The cluttered details in the background are
in sharp focus, reminding us that physical objects are of utmost importance in
Kane's life.

FIGURE 12-6
Citizen Kane **(1941).** Kane (Orson
Welles) and his first wife, Emily
(Ruth Warrick), near the end of
their marriage, are seen in a shot
that emphasizes the distance
between them both physically and
emotionally. Placing the camera so
far below the table produced an
unsettling moment in the film.

©RKO/Kobal/REX/Shutterstock

Avatar is available as a regular film, but it was heavily advertised and projected in 3-D. Three-dimensional films have been a promise for more than a decade, but very few have been effective for more than the occasional shock value of objects flying at the viewer. *Avatar*, because of its setting in a hyperreal landscape and its flying mythical creatures, is more effective than most 3-D films. So far, it seems to be the most successful of such films.

For some directors, the still frames of the film must be as exactly composed as a painting. The theory is that if the individual moments of the film are each as perfect as can be, the total film will be a cumulative perfection. This seems to be the case only for some films. In films that have long, meditative sequences, such as Orson Welles's *Citizen Kane* (1941) or Ingmar Bergman's *Cries and Whispers* (1972), or sequences in which characters or images are relatively unmoving for significant periods of time, such as Robert Redford's *A River Runs Through It* (1994), the carefully composed still image may be significant. Nevertheless, no matter how powerful, most stills from fine films will reveal very little of the significance of the entire film all by themselves: It is their sequential movement that brings out their effectiveness. However, the still frame and the individual shot are the building blocks of film. Controlling the techniques that produce and interrelate these blocks is the first job of the film artist.

Camera Point of View

The motion in the motion picture can come from numerous sources. The actors can move toward, away from, or across the field of camera vision. When something moves toward the camera, it moves with astonishing speed, as we all know from watching the images of a moving locomotive (the favorite vehicle for this technique so far) rush at us and then "catapult over our heads." The effect of the catapult is noteworthy because it is a unique characteristic of the film medium.

People move before us the way they move before the camera, but the camera (or cameras) can achieve visual things that the unaided eye cannot: showing the same moving action from a number of points of view simultaneously, for instance, or showing it from a camera angle the eye cannot achieve. The realistic qualities of a film can be threatened, however, by being too sensational, with a profusion of shots that would be impossible in a real-life situation. Although such virtuoso effects can dazzle us at first, the feeling of being dazzled can degenerate into being dazed.

Another way the film portrays motion is by the movement or tracking of the camera. In a sequence in John Huston's *The Misfits* (1961), cowboys are rounding up wild mustangs to sell for dog food, and some amazing scenes were filmed with the camera mounted on a pickup truck chasing fast-running horses. The motion in these scenes is overwhelming because Huston combines two kinds of rapid motion—of trucks and of horses. Moreover, the motion is further increased because of the narrow focus of the camera and the limited boundary of the screen. The recorded action excludes vision that might tend to distract or to dilute the motion we are permitted to see. Much the same effect was achieved in the buffalo run in *Dances with Wolves* (1990) thirty years later. The screen in motion pictures always constrains our vision, even when we imagine the space beyond the screen that we do not see, as when a character moves off the filmed space. Eliminating the space beyond the images recorded by the camera circumscribes and fixes our attention. And such attention enhances the rapidity and intensity of the moving images.

A final basic way film can achieve motion is by means of the camera lens. Even when the camera is fixed in place, a lens that affords a much wider, narrower, larger, or smaller field of vision than the eye normally supplies will give the illusion of motion, since we instinctively feel the urge to be in the physical position that would supply that field of vision. Zoom lenses, which change their focal length along a smooth range—thus moving images gradually closer or farther away—are even more effective for suggesting motion. One favorite shot is that of a figure walking or moving in some fashion, which looks, at first, as if it were a medium shot but which is actually revealed as a long shot when the zoom is reversed. Since our own eyes cannot imitate the action of the zoom lens, the effect can be quite dramatic when used creatively. It is something like the effect that slow motion or stop motion has on us. It interrupts our perceptions of something—something that had seemed perfectly natural—in a way that makes us aware of the film medium itself.

PERCEPTION KEY Camera Vision

1. Directors frequently examine a scene with a viewfinder that "frames" the scene before their eyes. Make or find a simple frame (or use your hands to create a "frame") and examine the visual world about you. To what extent can you frame it to make it more interesting?
2. Using the frame technique, move your eyes and the frame simultaneously to alter the field of vision. Can you make any movements that the camera cannot? Do you become aware of any movements the camera can make that you cannot?
3. If the camera is the principal tool of filmmaking, do directors give up artistic control when they have cinematographers operate the machines? Does your experimenting in the questions above suggest there may be a camera "language" that directors should be controlling themselves? Given your experience with film and cameras, how might camera language be described?
4. Using a video camera, experiment with shooting the same visual information with the lens wide-angled, and then at different stages of zoom until you reach the end of your lens's zoom range. Review the product and comment on the way the camera treats visual space.

Sometimes technique can take over a film by becoming the most interesting aspect of the cinematic experience. The Academy Award winner *2001: A Space Odyssey* (1968), *Star Wars* (1977–2017), *Close Encounters of the Third Kind* (1977), *ET* (1982), and the seven *Star Trek* films of the 1970s and 1980s have similar themes, concentrating on space, the future, and fantastic situations. All include shots of marvelous technical achievements, such as the images of the computer-guided cameras that follow the space vehicles of Luke Skywalker and Han Solo in the dramatic conclusion of the original *Star Wars* (Figure 12-7). But some critics have argued that these technical achievements were ends rather than means to artistic revelation.

FIGURE 12-7
Star Wars: The Force Awakens **(2015).**
In the film, George Lucas used a
number of powerful special effects,
as in this threatening attack with a
light saber.

©Photo 12/Alamy

PERCEPTION KEY Technique and Film

1. Are the technical triumphs of films such as *Star Wars* used as means or ends? If they are the ends, then are they the subject matter? What kind of problem does such a possibility raise for our appreciation of the film?
2. In *Tom Jones* (1963), a technique called the "double take" was introduced. After searching for his wallet everywhere, Tom turns and looks at the audience and asks whether we have seen his wallet. Is this technique a gimmick or artistically justifiable? Could you make a defensible judgment about this without seeing the film?

VIOLENCE AND FILM

Because it is so easy to shoot a scene in various ways, a good director is constantly choosing the shot that he or she hopes has the most meaning within the total structure of the film. When Luis Buñuel briefly shows us the razoring of a woman's eyeball in *Un Chien Andalou* (1928) (it is really a slaughtered cow's eyeball), he is counting on our personal horror at actually seeing such an act, but the scene is artistically justifiable because Buñuel carefully integrated the scene into the total structure. Unfortunately, many films show sheer violence without any attempt to inform—for example, *Nightmare on Elm Street* (1985) and its many sequels, the Arnold Schwarzenegger film *Predator* (1988), and similar films. *Kill Bill* (2003, 2004), both volumes, as well as *A History of Violence* (2005) move in a somewhat different direction, in that they are not specifically horror films despite their depiction of violence. These have been nominated for a number of awards in recognition of their seriousness.

A film that was ahead of its time in portraying violence, *Reservoir Dogs* (1992), won Quentin Tarantino the respect of movie critics and the movie public. Tarantino followed up with *Pulp Fiction* (1994), three related tales set in Los Angeles and

FIGURE 12-8
Jamie Foxx in *Django Unchained*
(2009). Quentin Tarantino has made
violence central to his work. His films
have also been widely praised.

©Columbia/The Weinstein Company/Kobal/
REX/Shutterstock

reminiscent of the pulp fiction novels of Dashiell Hammett. While somewhat cartoonish in places, and laced with unexpected comedic moments, the film was nominated for several awards, among them the Palme d'Or at Cannes. *Django Unchained* (Figure 12-8) continued Tarantino's commitment to artful violence.

Clever directors can easily shock their audiences. But the more complex responses, some of which are as difficult to control as they are to attain, are the aim of the enduring filmmakers. When Ingmar Bergman shows us the rape scene in *The Virgin Spring* (1959), he does not saturate us with horror. And the murder of the rapists by the girl's father is preceded by an elaborate purification ritual that relates the violence and horror to profound meaning. In any art, control of audience response is vital. We can become emotionally saturated just as easily as we can become bored. The result is indifference.

PERCEPTION KEY Violence and Film

1. Many groups condemn violent films of the kind described as slasher films or films that gratuitously portray torture and gore. Do you agree with these groups? Do you feel that violent films affect viewers' behavior? How do they affect you? Is it possible to participate with a violent film?

2. Critics point to the fact that many of Shakespeare's plays—and the plays of his contemporaries—were often bloody and violent. They also say that violence in Shakespeare's plays is revelatory because it reveals the significance of the morality of his age. Do you feel that modern violent films are revelatory of the morality of our age?

3. Of the violent films you have seen, which one is certainly a work of art? Is violence the subject matter of that film? In what ways is the film revelatory?

SOUND

Al Jolson's *The Jazz Singer* (1927) introduced sound, although not everyone welcomed it. Sergei Eisenstein feared, as did many others, that sound might kill the artistic integrity of film because, with sound, no one would work with the images that create a film language and film would once again become subservient to drama. Eisenstein knew that images in motion could sustain the kind of dramatic tension that was once thought to be limited to the stage. This is a point of consummate importance. First of all, a film is images in motion. Great filmmakers may exploit sound and other elements, but they will never make them the basic ingredients of the film.

Sound in film involves much more than the addition of dialogue to the visual track. Music had long been a supplement of the silent films, and special portfolios of piano and organ music were available to the accompanist who played in the local theater while coordinating the music with the film. These portfolios indicated the kind of feelings that could be produced by merging special music with scenes, such as chase, love, or suspense. D. W. Griffith's *The Birth of a Nation* features a "rescue" charge by the Ku Klux Klan, which was cut to the dynamics of Richard Wagner's *Die Walküre.* Francis Ford Coppola may have had that in mind when he made the incredible helicopter battle scene in *Apocalypse Now* (1979) to Wagner's "Ride of the Valkyries." *Apocalypse Now,* a film about the Vietnam War, uses sound in exceptionally effective ways, especially in scenes such as the skyrocket fireworks battle deep in the jungle. But perhaps the most powerful cinematic sound produced so far occurs in the opening scenes of *Saving Private Ryan* (1998), directed by Steven Spielberg—the storming of the Normandy beach on D-day, June 6, 1944 (Figure 12-9).

Surround sound may intensify our experience of film. Not only do we expect to hear dialogue, but we also expect to hear the sounds we associate with the action on screen, whether it is the quiet chirping of crickets in a country scene in *Sounder*

FIGURE 12-9
Saving Private Ryan (1998). The opening scene of Steven Spielberg's film depicts American soldiers storming Omaha Beach during World War II.

©Universal/Kobal/REX/Shutterstock

(1972) or the dropping of bombs from a low-flying Japanese Zero in *Empire of the Sun* (1987). Subtle uses of sound sometimes prepare us for action that is yet to come, such as when in *Rain Man* (1989) we see Dustin Hoffman and Tom Cruise walking toward a convertible, but we hear the dialogue and road sounds from the next shot, when they are driving down the highway. That editing technique might have been very unsettling in the 1930s, but filmmakers have had eighty years to get our sensibilities accustomed to such disjunctions.

A famous disjunction occurs in the beginning of *2001: A Space Odyssey* (1968) when, watching images of one tribe of apes warring with another tribe of apes in prehistoric times, we hear the rich modern harmonies of Richard Strauss's dramatic tone poem *Also Sprach Zarathustra*. The music suggests one very sophisticated mode of development inherent in the future of these primates—whom we see in the first phases of discovering how to use tools. They already show potential for creating high art. Eventually the sound and imagery coincide when the scene changes to 2001, with scientists on the moon discovering a monolithic structure identical to one the apes had found on Earth.

PERCEPTION KEY Sight and Sound

1. In the next film you see, compare the power of the visuals with the power of the sound. Is there a reasonable balance between the two? Which one produces a more intense experience in you?
2. With Dolby sound systems in many movie houses, the use of sound is sometimes overwhelming. Which film of those you have recently seen has the most intense and powerful sound? Does it mesh well with the narrative line of the film? Why?
3. View an important film and turn off its sound for a period of time. Study the images you see and comment on their ability to hold your attention. Then turn on the sound and comment on how your experience of the film is altered. Go beyond the simple addition of dialogue. Try the experiment with a foreign film that has English subtitles.
4. View the same film and block the visual image by turning your back to it. Concentrate on the sound. To what extent is the experience of the film incomplete? How would you rate the relationship of sound to the visual images?

IMAGE AND ACTION

Most contemporary film is a marriage of sight and sound. Yet we must not forget that film is a medium in which the moving image—the action—is preeminent, as in Federico Fellini's *8½* (1963). The title refers to Fellini's own career, ostensibly about himself and his making a new film after seven and a half previous films. *8½* is about the artistic process. Guido, played by Marcello Mastroianni, brings a group of people to a location to make a film (Figure 12-10).

The film centers on Guido's loss of creative direction, his psychological problems related to religion, sex, and his need to dominate women. As he convalesces from his breakdown, he brings people together to make a film, but he has no clear sense of what he wants to do, no coherent story to tell. *8½* seems to mimic Fellini's situation so carefully that it is difficult to know whether Fellini planned out the film or

FIGURE 12-10
Federico Fellini's 8½ (1963).
Gianni di Venanzo's extraordinary recessional shot, showing Guido (Marcello Mastroianni) meeting his mistress, Carla (Sandra Milo), at the spa where he has gone to refresh his creative spirit.

Courtesy Everett Collection

not. He has said, "I appeared to have it all worked out in my head, but it was not like that. For three months I continued working on the basis of a complete production, in the hope that meanwhile my ideas would sort themselves out. Fifty times I nearly gave up."[1] And yet, most of the film is described in a single letter to Brunello Rondi (a writer of the screenplay), written long before the start of production.

The film is episodic, with memorable dream and nightmare sequences, some of which are almost hallucinatory. Such scenes focus on the inward quest of the film: Guido's search for the cause of his creative block so that he can resolve it. By putting himself in the center of an artistic tempest, he mirrors his own psychological confusion in order to bring it under control. Indeed, he seems intent on creating artistic tension by bringing both his wife and his mistress to the location of the film.

The film abandons continuous narrative structure in favor of episodic streams of consciousness in the sequences that reveal the inner workings of Guido's mind. In a way, they may also reveal the inner workings of the creative mind if we assume that Fellini projected his own anxieties into the film. *8½* is revelatory of the psychic turmoil of creativity.

The computer has altered the possibilities of action in modern films, from *Star Wars* to Alejandro Iñárritu's *The Revenant* (2015), which is set in 1823 and is about a group of white trappers in Indian country in the far west. It is based on a semi-autobiographical story of Hugh Glass, who, surviving the attack by a mother bear and the abandonment by his hunting team, somehow managed to return to civilization. The subject matter of the film is in part about the indestructibility of the determined individual, but it is also about the power of nature in an almost endless landscape.

---

[1]John Kobal, *The Top 100 Movies* (New York: New American Library, 1988).

FIGURE 12-11
The Revenant **(2015).** In this powerful shot from Alejandro G. Iñárritu's film, Hugh Glass (Leonardo Di Caprio) is attacked by a mother bear. This is an example of modern technology at work in film. The bear was enacted by a man in a large "suit," which was converted into a bear by the computer.

Source: 20th Century Fox

The bear attack (Figure 12-11), which is the most memorable scene in the film, pits the extraordinary power of nature against man's attempts to tame it. In essence, the computer manipulation makes it possible to portray that struggle with a sense of reality—essentially taming it by technology.

CINEMATIC STRUCTURE

Michael Cimino's portrayal of three hometown men, Mike, Steve, and Nick, who fight together in Vietnam, *The Deer Hunter* (1978), has serious structural problems because the film takes place in three radically different environments, and it is not always clear how they are related. Yet it won several Academy Awards and has been proclaimed one of the great antiwar films. Cimino took great risks by dividing the film into three large sections: sequences of life in Clairton, Pennsylvania, with a Russian Orthodox wedding and a last hunting expedition for deer; sequences of the three men fighting in Vietnam, then as war prisoners playing Russian roulette to the amusement of their guards; and sequences afterward in Clairton, where only one of the three men, Mike, played by Robert DeNiro, is able to live effectively. He sets out to get Steven, played by John Savage, who lost his legs and an arm, to return from the wheelchair ward of the VA hospital to his wife. Then he returns to Vietnam to find his best friend, Nick, played by Christopher Walken, a heroin addict still in Saigon, playing Russian roulette for hardened Vietnamese gamblers. Russian roulette was not an actual part of the Vietnam experience, but Cimino made it a metaphor for the senselessness of war.

Cimino relied in part on the model of Dante's *Divine Comedy,* also divided into three sections—Hell, Purgatory, and Paradise. In *The Deer Hunter,* the rivers of molten metal in the steel mills and, more obviously, the war scenes suggest the ghastliness of Hell. The extensive and ecstatic scenes in the Russian Orthodox church suggest Paradise, while life in Clairton represents an in-between, a kind of Purgatory. In one of the most stirring episodes, when he is back in Saigon during the American evacuation, looking for Nick, Mike is shown standing up in a small boat, negotiating his way through the canals. The scene is a visual echo of Eugène Delacroix's *Dante and Virgil in Hell,* a famous nineteenth-century painting. For anyone who recognizes the allusion to Dante, Cimino's structural techniques become clearer, as do his views of war in general and of the Vietnam War in particular.

The function of photography in films such as *8½* and *The Deer Hunter* is sometimes difficult to assess. If we agree that the power of the moving image is central to the ultimate meaning of the motion picture, we can see that the most important structural qualities of any good film develop from the choices made in the editing stage. Sometimes different versions of a single action will be filmed; then the director and the editor decide which will be in the final mix after testing each version in relation to the overall structure.

The episodic structure of Ridley Scott's *Thelma & Louise* (1991) (Figure 12-12) lends itself to contrasting the interiors of a seamy Arkansas nightclub and a cheap motel with the magnificent open road and dramatic landscape of the Southwest. Louise, played by Susan Sarandon, and Thelma, played by Geena Davis, are on the run in Louise's 1956 Thunderbird convertible after Louise shoots and kills Harlan, who attempted to rape Thelma. Knowing their story will not be believed, they head for Mexico and freedom but never get there. Callie Khouri wrote the script for this feminist film and cast the women as deeply sympathetic outcasts and desperadoes— roles traditionally reserved for men. In one memorable scene, a truck driver hauling a gasoline rig harasses and makes lecherous faces at the women. The cross-cutting builds considerable tension, which is relieved, at first, when the women pull over as if they were interested in him. As the driver leaves his truck to walk toward them,

FIGURE 12-12
***Thelma & Louise* (1991).** Susan Sarandon and Geena Davis star in Ridley Scott's road-style film with a reversal—the people driving the Thunderbird are women, not men, racing away from the law.

©Pictorial Press Ltd/Alamy

they shoot his rig, and it explodes like an inferno. The editing in this film is quite conventional, but everyone who has seen it is very likely to remember this scene, the exceptional power of which depends on the use of cross-cutting.

The editor's work gives meaning to the film just as surely as the scriptwriter's and the photographer's. Observe, for instance, the final scenes in Eisenstein's *Battleship Potemkin*. The *Potemkin* is steaming to a confrontation with the Russian fleet. Eisenstein rapidly cuts from inside the ship to outside: showing a view of powerfully moving engine pistons, then the ship cutting deeply into the water, then rapidly back and forth, showing anxiety-ridden faces, all designed to raise the emotional pitch of anyone watching the movie. This kind of cutting or montage was used by Alfred Hitchcock in the shower murder scene of the 1960 horror thriller *Psycho*. He demonstrated that the technique could be used to increase tension and terror, even though no explicit murderous actions were shown on screen. Ironically, the scene was so powerful that its star, Janet Leigh, avoided showers as much as possible, always preferring the bath.

CINEMATIC DETAILS

We cannot completely translate films into language. We can only approximate a translation by describing the connections—emotional, narrative, symbolic, or whatever—implied by the sequence of images. Within the structural segments of any film, we will see how the details fill out the form of the film. When we watch the overturning coffin in Bergman's *Wild Strawberries* (1957), for example, we are surprised to find that the figure in the coffin has the same face as Professor Borg, the protagonist, who is himself a witness to what we see. Borg is face to face with his own death. That the details in this scene have special meaning seems clear, yet we cannot completely articulate their significance. The meaning is embodied in the moving images. The scene has a strong tension and impact, and yet it is apparent that the full meaning of this moment depends on the context of the whole film in which it appears. The relation of detail to structure exists in every art, of course, but that relation in its nuances often may more easily be missed in our experiences of the film. For one thing, we are not accustomed to permitting images to build their own meanings apart from the meanings we already associate with them. Second, we do not always observe the way one movement, one image, or one gesture will mean something in one context and an entirely different thing in another context. Third, moving images generally are more difficult to remember than still images and thus it is more difficult to become aware of their connections.

The filmmaker must control contexts, especially with reference to detail. In Eric Rohmer's film *Claire's Knee* (1970), a totally absurd gesture—caressing the knee of an indifferent and relatively insensitive young woman—becomes the fundamental focus of the film. This gesture is loaded with meaning throughout the entire film, but loaded only for the main masculine character and us. The young woman is unaware that her knee holds such power over the man. Although the gesture is absurd, in a way it is plausible, for such fixations can occur in anyone. But this film is not concerned solely with plausibility; it is mainly concerned with this detail in a cinematic structure that reveals what is unclear in real-life experience—the complexities of some kinds of obsessions. And this is done primarily through skillful photography and editing rather than through spoken narrative.

A highly successful film functions like any other work of art. To achieve the status of art, a film must have a structural integrity that, for some narrative films approaches that of theater or written fiction. The coherence of the structure will reveal the subject matter and ultimately permit the film, through the development of details, to transform the subject matter and become revelatory in that it will reveal its significance. We go to great films to be moved emotionally and to gain insight into their content. Structure and cinematic details move together to achieve such a state.

PERCEPTION KEY Cinematic Detail

1. Watch a silent film such as the Academy Award–winning *The Artist* (2011). Enumerate the most important details. If a gesture is repeated, does it accumulate significance? If so, why? Does the absence of dialogue increase the importance of visual detail?
2. Examine a few recent films for their use of visual details. Do they function in making the cinematic structure more coherent? Be specific. Did you find any film in which detail plays no significant role?
3. Examine a single scene in a recent film. Analyze the use of detail. In a carefully made film, the details will relate organically to the overall structure. How carefully made does the scene you have analyzed seem to be?

THE CONTEXT OF FILM HISTORY

All meanings, linguistic or nonlinguistic, exist within some kind of context. Most first-rate films exist in many contexts simultaneously, and it is our job as sensitive viewers to be able to decide which are the most important. Film, like every art, has a history, and this history is one of the more significant contexts in which every film takes place. To make that historical context fruitful in our filmic experiences, we must do more than just read about that history: We must accumulate a historical sense of film by seeing films that have been important in the development of the medium. Most of us have a rich personal backlog in film; we have seen a great many films, some of which are memorable and many of which have been influenced by landmark films.

Furthermore, film exists in a context that is meaningful for the life work of a director and, in turn, for us. When we talk about the films of Orson Welles, Ingmar Bergman, or Federico Fellini, we are talking about the achievements of artists just as much as when we talk about the achievements of Rembrandt, Vermeer, or van Gogh. Today we watch carefully for films by Steven Spielberg, Francis Ford Coppola, Woody Allen, Oliver Stone, Joel and Ethan Coen, Pedro Almodóvar, Martin Scorsese, Alejandro Iñárritu, Spike Lee, Jane Campion, Quentin Tarantino, and Lina Wertmuller—to name only a few of the most active current directors—because their work has shown a steady development and because they, in relation to the history of the film, possess a vision that is transforming the medium. In other words, these directors are altering the history of film in significant ways. In turn, we should be interested in knowing what they are doing because they are providing new contexts for increasing our understanding of film.

Our concerns in this book have not been exclusively with one or another kind of context, although we have assumed that the internal context of a work of art is necessarily of first importance. But no work can be properly understood without resorting to external contextual examination. To understand the content of a work of art, we must understand something about the subject matter, and the subject matter is always embedded in some external context. Even such a simple act as a gesture may need explanation. For example, in Greece, to put the palm of your hand in the face of someone is considered insulting. If we do not know that and are watching a film involving Greece that includes the gesture, we may be completely misled. A visual image, a contemporary gesture, even a colloquial expression will sometimes show up in a film and need explication in order to be fully understood. Just as we sometimes have to look up a word in a dictionary—which exists outside a poem, for instance—we sometimes have to look outside a film for explanations. Even Terence Young's James Bond thriller movies need such explication, although we rarely think about that. If we failed to understand the political assumptions underlying such films, we would not fully understand what was going on.

TWO GREAT FILMS: *THE GODFATHER* AND *CASABLANCA*

Francis Ford Coppola's *The Godfather* (Figure 12-13), produced in 1972, is based on Mario Puzo's novel about Vito Corleone, an Italian immigrant fleeing from Sicilian Mafia violence. He eventually became a don of a huge crime family in New York City. The film details the gradual involvement of Michael Corleone, played by Al Pacino,

FIGURE 12-13
The Godfather (1972). Marlon Brando plays Don Vito Corleone, the Godfather, conferring with a wedding guest asking for an important favor at the beginning of Francis Ford Coppola's film.

in his father's criminal activities during the years from 1945 to 1959. His father, Vito, played by Marlon Brando, suffers the loss of Sonny, an older son, and barely survives an assassination attempt. As Michael becomes more and more a central figure in his family's "business," he grows more frightening and more alienated from those around him until, as Godfather, it seems he becomes totally evil.

Although some critics complained that the film glorified the Mafia, almost all have praised its technical mastery. A sequel, *The Godfather: Part II,* was produced in 1974 and, although not as tightly constructed as the first film, fleshes out the experience of Michael as he slowly develops into a mob boss. Both films center on the ambiguities involved in the conversion of the poverty-ridden Vito into a wealthy and successful gangster and Michael's conversion from innocence to heartless criminality.

The Godfather films both engage our sympathy with Michael and increasingly horrify us with many of his actions. We admire Michael's personal valor and his respect for father, family, and friends. But we also see the corruption and violence that are the bases of his power. Inevitably we have to work out for ourselves the ambiguities that Coppola sets out.

The Narrative Structure of The Godfather *Films*

The narrative structure of most films supplies the framework on which the filmmaker builds the artistry of the shots and sound. An overemphasis on the artistry, however, can distract a viewer from the narrative, whereas a great film avoids allowing technique to dominate a story. Such is the case with *The Godfather* and *The Godfather: Part II,* we believe, because the artistry produces a cinematic lushness that helps tell the story.

The first film begins with Michael Corleone, as a returning war hero in 1945, refusing to be part of his father's criminal empire. The immediate family enjoys the spoils of criminal life—big cars, a large house in a guarded compound, family celebrations, and lavish weddings. Although Michael's brothers are active members of the crime family, they respect his wishes to remain apart.

In a dispute over whether to add drug-running to the business of gambling, prostitution, extortion, and labor racketeering, Vito is gunned down, but not killed. Michael comes to the aid of his father and so begins his career in the Mafia. It takes him only a short time to rise to the position of Godfather when Vito is too infirm to continue. When he marries Kay, played by Diane Keaton, Michael explains that the family will be totally legitimate in five years. She believes him, but the audience already knows better. It is no surprise that seven years later the family is more powerful and ruthless than ever.

In a disturbing and deeply ironic sequence, Michael acts as godfather in the church baptism of his nephew at the same time his lieutenants are murdering the men who head the five rival crime families. Coppola jump-cuts back and forth from shots of Michael in the church promising to renounce the work of the devil to shots of his men turning the streets of New York into a bloodbath. This perversion of the sacrament of baptism illustrates the depths to which Michael has sunk.

In the second film, as the family grows in power, Michael moves to Tahoe, gaining control of casino gambling in Nevada. He corrupts a senator, who even while demanding kickbacks expresses contempt for Italians. When the senator is compromised by killing a prostitute, however, he cooperates fully with the Corleones. The point is made again and again that without such corrupt officials, the Mafia would be significantly less powerful.

Michael survives an assassination attempt made possible by his brother Fredo's collusion with another gangster who is Michael's nemesis. At first, Michael does nothing but refuse to talk to Fredo, but when their mother dies, he has Fredo murdered. Meanwhile, Kay has left him, and those who were close to him, except his stepbrother, Tom Hagen (Robert Duvall), have been driven away or murdered. The last images we have of Michael show him alone in his compound, staring into a darkened room. We see how far he has fallen since his early idealism.

Coppola's Images

Coppola chooses his frames with great care, and many would make interesting still photographs. He balances his figures carefully, especially in the quieter scenes, subtly using asymmetry to accent movement. Sometimes he uses harsh lighting that radiates from the center of the shot, focusing attention and creating tension. He rarely cuts rapidly from one shot to another but depends on conventional establishing shots—such as showing a car arriving at a church, a hospital, a home—before showing us shots of their interiors. This conventionality intensifies our sense of the period of the 1940s and 1950s, since most films of that period relied on just such techniques.

Darkness dominates, and interiors often have a tunnel-like quality, suggesting passages to the underworld. Rooms in which Michael and others conduct their business usually have only one source of light, and the resulting high contrast is disorienting. Bright outdoor scenes are often marked by barren snow or winds driving fallen leaves. The seasons of fall and winter predominate, suggesting loneliness and death.

Coppola's Use of Sound

The music in *The Godfather* helps Coppola evoke the mood of the time the film covers. Coppola used his own father, Carmine Coppola, as a composer of some of the music. There are some snatches of Italian hill music from small villages near Amalfi, but sentimental dance music from the big band period of the 1940s and 1950s predominates.

An ingenious and effective use of sound occurs in the baptism/murder scene discussed earlier. Coppola keeps the sounds of the church scene—the priest reciting the Latin liturgy, the organ music, the baby crying—on the soundtrack even when he cuts to the murders being carried out. This accomplishes two important functions: It reinforces the idea that these two scenes are actually occurring simultaneously, and it underscores the hypocrisy of Michael's pious behavior in church. Because such techniques are used sparingly, their usage in this scene works with great power.

The Power of The Godfather

Those critics who felt the film glorified the Mafia seem not to have taken into account the fated quality of Michael. He begins like Oedipus—running away from his fate. He does not want to join the Mafia, but when his father is almost killed, his instincts push him toward assuming the role of Godfather. The process of self-destruction consumes him as if it were completely out of his control. Moreover, despite their power and wealth, Michael and the Corleones seem to have a good time only at weddings, and even then the Godfather is doing business in the back room. Everyone in the family suffers. No one can come and go in freedom. Everyone lives in an armed camp. All the elements of the film reinforce that view. The houses are opulent, but vulnerable to machine guns. The cars are expensive, but they blow up. Surely such a life is not a glory.

In shaping the film in a way that helps us see Mafia life as neither glamorous nor desirable, Coppola forces us to examine our popular culture—one that seems often to venerate criminals like Bonnie and Clyde, Jesse James, Billy the Kid, and John Dillinger. At the same time, Coppola's refusal to treat his characters as simply loathsome, his acknowledgment that they are in some sense victims as well as victimizers, creates an ambiguity that makes his films an impressive achievement.

PERCEPTION KEY *The Godfather*

1. Watch *The Godfather* on a large screen if possible. Examine the ways in which the pleasing quality of the visuals alters depending on what is being filmed. Are the violent moments treated with any less visual care than the lyrical moments? What happens on screen when the images are unbalanced or skewed enough to make you feel uncomfortable?
2. *The Godfather* is sometimes ironic, as when church music is played while gangsters are murdered. How many such moments can you find in the film in which irony is achieved through the musical choices?
3. To what extent does *The Godfather* "lionize" the criminal enterprise of the Mafia? Does the film lure the viewer into accepting as positive the values of the mob? What does the film do to reveal the moral failures of the mob? Why is there so much reference to religion in the film?
4. *The Godfather* was produced almost fifty years ago, when the Mafia was a serious power in the United States. If you take into account the social circumstances surrounding the film, would you say that today—with most organized crime bosses in prison—our reactions to this film would make it more or less difficult to romanticize the Mafia? Are you tempted to romanticize these criminals?
5. Is the structure of *The Godfather* episodic, tragic, or comic? Do we experience the feelings of fear and pity? What feelings are engendered by the film? What revelatory experience did you have from watching the film?

Casablanca (1942), a film often cited as an iconic classic, was not expected to be a great success. Plans for the film began in January 1942, during World War II. France had surrendered to the Germans after only a few weeks in 1940; London was being bombed; the entire British Expeditionary Force was stranded on the beaches of Normandy at Dunkirk and saved by English sailors and citizens powering small boats. The United States was split between supporting Hitler and decrying against him. It took the attack by Japan on Hawaii's Pearl Harbor to bring the United States into the war against Japan and the Nazis. Before the film was released, the U.S. Army invaded North Africa, which gave the film more significance and hastened it into theaters. That is the historical context of *Casablanca*. It was a time when the United States had wakened from a political coma and victory was uncertain.

FIGURE 12-14
Rick, Captain Renault, Victor Laszlo, and Ilsa Lund meet at Rick's Place. Rick and Ilsa had been lovers the year before, and the scene is tense.

©Moviestore collection Ltd/Alamy

Before reading any further, view Michael Curtiz's *Casablanca* (1942) in the currently available restored print. Once you have done that, consider this analysis.

Rick meets Victor Laszlo and Ilsa Lund, but he is not happy. He had loved Ilsa and is bitter because she "stood him up" in Paris when the Germans marched in. Ilsa has come to Casablanca with her husband, Victor, without knowing she would meet Rick (Figure 12-14). Captain Renault shrewdly puzzles out the relationship between them. Renault is a Vichy-French officer who will not arrest Laszlo—as the Germans wish him to. At this time, the colony in northern Africa was governed by the so-called Free French, a limited arrangement the Nazis had set up in return for France's surrender in June 1940. The Vichy government collaborated with the Germans, and in Casablanca everyone must behave carefully. The purpose of the shot is to establish everyone's relationship in terms of politics, character, and emotion.

The artistic context of *Casablanca* is that of the typical chiaroscuro film noir style of black and white with exquisitely framed and composed shots. But instead of being a film noir murder mystery, it is a film noir political mystery with an exceptionally strong romantic core. At first, audiences were surprised, possibly because its genre was mixed. But soon enough it became a major success and won Academy Awards for Best Picture and Best Director.

The political context involves Rick Blaine (Humphrey Bogart), a club owner in North Africa in a Free French colony. He begins as an anti-hero, saying, "I don't stick my neck out for nobody." But his background includes anti-Nazi activity in Ethiopia and Spain. In addition, Victor Laszlo (Paul Henreid) shows up in Rick's Place and is recognized as an international leader of the resistance to Germany. Laszlo arrives in Casablanca to get letters of transit that will permit him to fly to neutral Portugal and from there to America.

FIGURE 12-15
Rick (Humphrey Bogart), who stopped drinking when the Germans marched into Paris, is heartbroken by seeing Ilsa (Ingrid Bergman) with her husband. He is still in love with her and "drowns" himself with alcohol. The tight shot is profoundly dark, in tune with Rick's feelings.

Source: Warner Brothers

The context of romance involves Rick and Ilsa Lund (Ingrid Bergman), who meet in 1940, weeks before the Germans march into Paris. They have an affair and vow to leave Paris together. But before she fell in love with Rick, Ilsa had been told that her husband, Victor Laszlo, had died in a German concentration camp. However, when she and Rick were to leave Paris, she discovered Victor was alive and as a result she left Rick standing alone at the last train out of Paris, breaking his heart.

More than a year later they meet again in Casablanca. Rick, who was destroyed emotionally by her leaving him, sees her and says, "Of all the gin joints, in all the towns, in all the world, she walks into mine" (Figure 12-15).

continued

Ilsa has Sam (Dooley Wilson) play her and Rick's favorite song, "As Time Goes By" (Figure 12-16), thus setting up a painful memory, and a flashback portrays Rick and Ilsa's short love affair in Paris. Among the many famous quotations from the film, it is in Paris where Rick first admires Ilsa and says, "Here's looking at you, kid." Much of the flashback film footage of German armies on the move is authentic, showing that as early as January 1942 people in the United States knew what was really happening in Europe. They also knew about concentration camps.

The role music plays in *Casablanca* may be surprising, but the premise is that Rick is running a nightclub, and the club has its own orchestra as well as entertainers who play music, sing songs, and dance. Max Steiner was the composer for the film, but he based his work on some of the most memorable music in the club, "As Time Goes By," and "La Marseillaise," the French national anthem. The background music hints at those melodies while providing the usual mood changers typical of feature films.

One of the most powerful and moving moments of the film is when the German officers enter Rick's club and eventually rise to sing a famous German song, "Watch on the Rhine." Victor Laszlo cannot sit, listening to it, and rises and tells Rick's orchestra to play "La Marseillaise" (Figure 12-17). The leader of the orchestra looks to Rick, who nods his head, and the entire audience in the club rises to sing the French national anthem, drowning out the German officers. This scene is the dramatic crisis of the film because the German commandant, Major Strasser, closes down the club and begins pursuing Victor Laszlo with a seriousness he has not shown before. The music is indeed powerful. It has been pointed out that with only three American major actors in the film (Bogart, Dooley, and Joy Paige), the rest of the actors were primarily refugees. Many of them stood with the music playing and cried honest tears for their own circumstances. Today, seventy-five years later, the issues of war, fascism, and tragic romance are as relevant as they were when *Casablanca* was made.

The latter part of the film centers on the letters of transit, taken from two murdered German couriers and passed on to Rick to keep for Ugarte (Peter Lorre), who is captured and killed. Soon Victor Laszlo learns that Rick has the letters, and Ilsa tries to get Rick to give them to her. He refuses, and in a dramatic scene she pulls a gun on him but does not shoot. It is left vague but implied that she breaks down and confesses her love for him, and they apparently make love one last time. They agree to give Victor one of the letters of transit and then they will go off together.

FIGURE 12-16

Ilsa tells Sam (Dooley Wilson) to play "As Time Goes By." She says, "Play it, Sam." The song brings back the pain Rick felt in Paris. It was "their song." Sam knows the pain the song will cause, but he plays it, anyway, because he cannot refuse Ilsa. This moment is one of the key musical instances in which the film makes an emotional appeal to the audience.

Source: Warner Brothers

FIGURE 12-17

Victor Laszlo leads the orchestra in singing "La Marseillaise," the French national anthem, drowning out the Nazis singing "Watch on the Rhine."

Source: Warner Brothers

Major Strasser (Conrad Veidt) appears to stop Victor from getting on the plane and draws his gun on Rick after Rick tells him to drop the phone; Rick shoots Strasser, with Captain Renault (Claude Rains) watching. As Victor and Ilsa's plane is in the air on its way to Lisbon and then to the United States, the French police arrive and Renault, surprisingly, tells them Strasser has been shot and that they should "round up the usual suspects" (Figure 12-18).

Ilsa expects that the deal she made with Rick would send Victor off alone and that she and Rick would be together. But at the airport, Rick changes things. He knows Ilsa belongs with her husband and that if she stays she will regret it, "Maybe not now, but much later on" (Figure 12-19). This scene is almost a cliché, but the point was that in December of 1942 Germany controlled virtually all of Europe and had millions in concentration camps where genocide was the protocol. When *Casablanca* was made, there was absolutely no certainty that the Nazis would be defeated. Rick's act of sacrifice and his experience with Victor Lazslo and Ilsa Lund—giving them the letters of transit—meant that he was no longer a bystander in the worldwide struggle against fascism. Rick, who said he would stick his neck out for no one, ends by having lost his club and risked everything for a cause. Ultimately, the film establishes its moral center in Rick.

The film ends with Renault and Rick deciding they should leave Casablanca for Brazzaville, another Free French settlement, until things cooled down. In a film full of famous quotations, Rick says, walking away with Renault, "Louie, I think this is the beginning of a beautiful friendship."

FIGURE 12-18
Captain Renault orders his policemen "to round up the usual suspects," one of the most memorable lines in *Casablanca*.

Source: Warner Brothers

FIGURE 12-19
Rick tells Ilsa that she must go with her husband. Even though they both love each other, Rick sacrifices his love so that she can be with her husband, doing the work of the Resistance that will defeat Germany.

Source: Warner Brothers

PERCEPTION KEY Focus on Michael Curtiz's *Casablanca*

1. Examine the control Curtiz uses over lighting in the film. How does he intensify the emotional content of specific scenes?
2. Review the historical situation of the early years of World War II. What had happened in Europe that made this film seem important to an American audience?
3. Film noir was a technique Curtiz had mastered in earlier films, all focused on crime and the terror it engendered in society. How effective was the film noir technique in portraying the political circumstances in this film?
4. Comment on the relationships of men and women in this film. What does Curtiz's care in developing their characters reveal about how men regard women? Is his focus limited to the way in which men and women related to each other in the 1940s, or is what he observes true today?
5. The setting of the film is North Africa, in a French colony. The colony was governed by the Vichy French, not the Germans. Research the Vichy government in the 1940s. What does the film reveal about how that government functioned?
6. Ilsa accuses Rick—when he is drinking heavily—of feeling sorry for himself. What does she mean by this, and what is your view? Is he reacting badly?
7. Rick is portrayed as an anti-hero—one who would not act to save others. He will not "stick his neck out." What was the U.S. position on joining the war effort during the time of the film in early 1941, before Pearl Harbor caused the nation to declare war? Is Rick a symbol?
8. Comment on the artistic quality of the shots in the film. What kinds of shots—long, short, medium, and so on—seem to be most successful? How does the artistic quality of the shots help reveal the content of the film?
9. Given the seriousness of the world war, does the mix of politics and romance cheapen the issues and values developed in the film, or does it enrich them?

EXPERIMENTATION

In the early days of film, complex technical problems were at the forefront—lighting, zooming, montage, and the like. Most of these problems now have answers, thanks especially to early filmmakers such as Griffith and Eisenstein. Today the problems center on what to do with these answers. For example, Andy Warhol, primarily a painter and sculptor, did some interesting work in raising questions about film, especially about the limits of realism, for realism is often praised in films. But when Warhol put a figure in front of a camera to sleep for a full eight hours, we got the message: We want a transformation of reality that gives us insight into reality, not reality itself. The difference is important because it is the difference between reality and art. Except when unconscious or dreaming, we have reality in front of us all the time. We have art much less frequently. Realistic art is a selection of elements that convey the illusion of reality. When we see Warhol's almost direct transcription of reality on film, we understand that selecting—through directing and editing—is crucial to film art. The power of most striking films is often their ability to condense experience—to take a year, for example, and portray it in ninety minutes. This condensation is what Marcel Proust, one of the greatest of novelists, expected from the novel:

Every emotion is multiplied ten-fold, into which this book comes to disturb us as might a dream, but a dream more lucid, and of a more lasting impression, than those which come to us in sleep; why, then, for a space of an hour he sets free within us all the joys and sorrows in the world, a few of which, only, we should have to spend years of our actual life in getting to know, and the keenest, the most intense of which would never have been revealed to us because the slow course of their development stops our perception of them. It is the same in life; the heart changes . . . but we learn of it only from reading or by imagination; in reality its alteration . . . is so gradual that . . . we are spared the actual sensation of change.[2]

Some films address the question of the portrayal of reality. Antonioni's *Blow Up* (1966), for example, has the thread of a narrative holding it together: a possible murder and the efforts of a magazine photographer, through the medium of his own enlargements, to confirm the reality of that murder. But anyone who saw the film might assume that the continuity of the narrative was not necessarily the most important part of the film. Much of the meaning seems to come out of what were essentially disconnected moments: an odd party, some strange driving around London, and some extraordinary tennis played without a ball. What seemed most important, perhaps, was the role of the film itself in suggesting certain realities. In a sense, the murder was a reality only after the film uncovered it. Is it possible that Antonioni is saying something similar about the reality that surrounds the very film he is creating? There is a reality, but where? Is *Blow Up* more concerned with the film images as reality than it is with reality outside the film? If you see this fascinating film, be sure you ask that puzzling question.

Some more-extreme experimenters remove the narrative entirely and simply present successions of images, almost in the manner of a nightmare or a drug experience. Sometimes the images are abstract, nothing more than visual patterns, as with abstract painting. Some use familiar images, but modify them with unexpected time-lapse photography and distortions of color and sound. Among the more successful films of this kind are *Koyaanisqatsi* (1983) and *Brooklyn Bridge* (1994).

Animated Film

The public generally is convinced that film, like literature and drama, must have plots and characters. Thus, even filmic cartoons are rarely abstract, although they are not photographs but drawings. Such animated films as *Pinocchio* (1940), *Fantasia* (1940), and *Dumbo* (1941) have yielded to enormously successful later films such as *The Yellow Submarine* (1968), *Beauty and the Beast* (1993), *The Lion King* (1994), *Toy Story* (1995), *Pocahontas* (1995), and *Shrek* (2004).

Computer-generated images have long replaced the hand-drawn figures that characterized the earliest animations. The computer image permits lifelike movement, facial expression, and stylized figures that speak an international emotional language. *Zootopia* (Figure 12-20) not only earned more than a billion dollars in release but also won the Academy Award for best animated feature film.

---

[2]Marcel Proust, *Swann's Way*, trans. C. K. Scott Moncrieff (New York: Modern Library, 1928), p. 119.

It may be unreasonable to consider animated films as experimental, and it is certainly unreasonable to think of them as children's films, since adult audiences have made them successful. What they seem to offer an audience is a realistic approach to fantasy that has all the elements of the traditional narrative film. This may also be true of animated films using clay figures and puppets for actors. These have had a narrower audience than cartoon and computer animations and have been restricted to film festivals, which is where most experimental films are presented.

PERCEPTION KEY Make a Film

The easy availability of video recorders makes it possible for you to make a digital film. With a video camera, you may need to rerecord on a computer, reorganizing your visual material to take advantage of the various shot and editing techniques.

1. Develop a short narrative plan for your shots. After shooting, edit your shots into a meaningful sequence.
2. Instead of a narrative plan, choose a musical composition that is especially interesting to you and then fuse moving images with the music.
3. Short of making a film, try some editing by finding and clipping from twenty to thirty "stills" from magazines, brochures, newspapers, or other sources. Choose stills you believe may have some coherence and then arrange them in such a way as to make a meaningful sequence. How are your stills affected by rearrangement? This project might be more interesting if you use a PowerPoint presentation. Then add a soundtrack to heighten interest by clarifying the meaning of the sequence.

Summary

Cinema is a complex and challenging art because of the necessary and often difficult collaboration required among many people, especially the director, scriptwriter, actors, photographer, and editor. The range of possible subject matters is exceptionally extensive for cinema. The resources of the director in choosing shots and the imagination of the editor in joining shots provide the primary control over the material. Such choices translate into emotional responses evoked from the audience. The point of view that can be achieved with the camera is similar to that of the unaided human eye, but because of technical refinements, such as the wide-angle zoom lens and moving multiple cameras, the dramatic effect of vision can be greatly intensified. Because it is easy to block out everything irrelevant to the film in a dark theater, our participative experiences with cinema tend to be especially strong and much longer, of course, than with other visual arts. The temptation to identify with a given actor or situation in a film may distort the participative experience by blocking our perception of the form of the film, thus causing us to miss the content. The combination of sound, both dialogue and music (or sound effects), with the moving image helps engage our participation. Cinema is the most popular of our modern arts.

Photo: Kira Perov. Courtesy Bill Viola Studio

Chapter 13

TELEVISION AND VIDEO ART

THE EVOLUTION OF TELEVISION

Television, the most widely used artistic medium in contemporary culture, grew out of the radio broadcasts of the early decades of the twentieth century and developed in part from the traditions of drama and film. Because it was a product of a commercial culture, and because the Federal Communications Commission and governmental agencies that oversaw its early development insisted on its goals being devoted more to entertainment than to education, television has been shaped by the needs of advertisers. This was not inevitable but a decision made by politicians in the United States. Television developed differently in the United Kingdom and other nations; but now, more than eighty years after the widespread introduction of television programming, the model established by the United States has become the norm.

Television was originally ignored by filmmakers because the inherent limitations of the medium held them back. Standard-definition television images are projected at thirty frames per second, instead of twenty-four, in order to overcome the limitations of the low-resolution image itself. The pixels in a video screen do not admit the range of contrast and the level of detail and resolution that are common to the continuous imagery of film. The interior of the cathode-ray tube has 525 vertical by 740 horizontal lines of pixels (a pixel is a group of green, red, and blue light-emitting phosphors), and because of technical limitations, the actual screen size is close to 480 by 740 pixels.

Today the use of digital projection and digital cameras has made some of those limitations less significant. Current television screens are large enough to create home theaters. High-definition broadcast standards have closed the gap between television and film to a considerable extent. High-definition flat screens can contain 1,080 vertical by 1,920 horizontal pixels, permitting vastly improved details from both broadcast television and DVDs.

> **PERCEPTION KEY** Television and Cinema
>
> 1. To what extent does watching a film on television make it more difficult to have a participatory experience as compared to watching the same film in a theater? Does the size of the moving image determine or limit your participatory experience? Is the absence of a large audience a contributing factor?
> 2. What kinds of shots dominate television programming: close-ups, midrange shots, long shots? Are there any visual techniques used in television that are not used in film?
> 3. The video screen has less tonal range than film and less ability to represent detail. How do television programs try to accommodate these limitations? How pronounced are the differences in visual quality between television and film?

THE SUBJECT MATTER OF TELEVISION AND VIDEO ART

The moving image is as much the subject matter of television and video art as it is of film. The power of the image to excite a viewer, combined with music and sound, is more and more becoming an intense experience as the technology of the medium develops. Surround sound, large projection screens and LCDs, and the development of digital high definition have transformed the "small box" into an overwhelming and encompassing television experience that can produce almost the same kind of participation that we experience in a movie theater.

The subject matter of a given television program can range from the social interaction of characters on programs such as *Seinfeld* (1990–1998), *Friends* (NBC, 1994–2004), and NCIS (CBS, 2003–present) (Figure 13-1) all the way to the political and historical issues revealed in *Roots* (ABC, 1977) and *Holocaust* (NBC, 1978). Programming can be realistic or surrealistic, animated or with living actors, but in all cases the power of the moving image is as important in television as in cinema.

Video art is, however, the antithesis of commercial entertainment television. Because broadcast television centers on the needs of advertisers and depends on reaching specific demographics, it has become slick and predictable. There is little room for experimentation in commercial television, but the opposite is true for video art. Artists such as Nam June Paik and Bill Viola are distinct in that their work has pioneered the use of video terminals, video imagery and sound, and video projection as fundamental to the purposes of the video artist.

Instead of a single image to arrest our attention, Nam June Paik often uses simultaneous multiple video monitors with different images whose intense movement is rarely linear and sequential, as in conventional broadcast television. His images appear and disappear rapidly, sometimes so rapidly that it is difficult to know exactly what they are. Paik has inspired numerous contemporary artists who work

FIGURE 13-1
NCIS, Naval Crime Investigation Service.
Set in Washington, D.C., this long-running series has been popular since 2003.

Photo: Monty Brinton/CBS. ©2009 CBS Broadcasting Inc. All Rights Reserved/Courtesy of Everett Collection

with and interact with monitors to achieve various effects. Bill Viola's work is often composed of multiple projected images using slow motion and low-volume sound. His work is hypnotic and so profoundly anticommercial that it forces us to look at the combination of visual and aural imagery in completely new ways. Video art surprises us and teaches us patience at the same time.

Just as television programs and films can be experienced on computer screens, cell phones, and tablets, the same is true for video art because it is an international movement. The Internet permits us to see the work of a great many leading video artists from around the world at our convenience.

COMMERCIAL TELEVISION

For more than half a century in the United States, a few major networks—National Broadcasting Corporation, Columbia Broadcasting System, American Broadcasting Company, Public Broadcasting System, and Fox Entertainment—dominated commercial television. In the United Kingdom, the British Broadcasting Corporation was the primary source of commercial television. Similar patterns existed in other nations. Since 2000, however, the spread of cable service has enlarged the sources of programming and has begun a major shift in the habits of viewers, who now have a much greater range of choices among hundreds of channels. Today cable service is threatened by innovation because the habits of viewers are constantly changing.

The Television Series

Studying the content of early situation comedies reveals much about the social structure of the family and the larger community. Early comedies were often ethnic in content: *The Goldbergs* (CBS, 1949–1955) portrayed a caring Jewish family in New York City. The show ended when the family "moved" to the suburbs. *The Life of Riley* (NBC, 1953–1958) starred William Bendix as a riveter in a comedy about an Irish working-class family in Los Angeles. *Amos and Andy* (CBS, 1951–1953), which moved from radio, was set in Harlem, but because of complaints about black stereotypes, it was soon dropped by the network. Yet it had been a popular program even among some African Americans. These early shows, including *The Honeymooners* (NBC, 1952–1956, specials in 1970), with Jackie Gleason, usually portrayed urban working-class families facing some of the same everyday problems as did the audience.

All in the Family (1971–1979) (Figure 13-2) was something different from the ethnic comedies. Archie Bunker was the model of the unaware bigot, prejudiced against Jews, blacks, and foreigners. At the time, the politically incorrect language was shocking on mainstream television. But the show was considered one of the most important comedies of its era. The subjects it tackled—racism, homosexuality, feminism, the Vietnam War, abortion, rape, impotence, cancer, religion, and more—became part of the national conversation. Because the Bunkers had their daughter, Gloria, and her husband, Michael, living with them, the show offered a contrast between the war years generation and the Baby Boomers, who saw the world with a different lens.

FIGURE 13-2
All in the Family. In a typical scene from the series, Archie Bunker (Carroll O'Connor) spars with his neighbor, George Jefferson (Sherman Hemsley).

©Zuma Press, Inc./Alamy

The Structure of the Self-Contained Episode

The early television series programs were self-contained half- or one-hour narratives that had a beginning, a middle, and an end. The episodes of each program were broken by commercial interruption, so the writers made sure you wanted to see what happened next by creating cliff-hangers. But each episode was complete in itself. Because there was no background preparation needed, the viewer could see the episodes in any order and be fully satisfied. Until late in the 1980s, that was the standard for a series. In the popular western series *Bonanza* (NBC, 1959–1973), the characters generally remained the same, the situations were familiar and appropriate to the locale, and the sense of completion at the end of each episode was satisfying, as it is, for instance, in most films.

The pattern was constant in most genres of dramas. Recent crime dramas, *Law and Order* (NBC, 1990–2010), *CSI* (CBS, 2000–2015), and each of their "branded" versions, follow the same pattern. Each of these successful series depends on a formula. *Law and Order,* the most successful show of its kind, relies on interpreting versions of recent crimes ("ripped from the headlines"). There is a clear-cut division between the police, who investigate a crime, and the prosecutors, who take the case to court. *CSI* (Figure 13-3) in its several versions usually follows two separate killings in each episode and spends a great deal of time in the lab, analyzing fingerprints and other forensic details. So far, these have held the attention of mass audiences. But the structure of these shows is predictable, and each episode is, for the most part, complete so that no one who comes to any episode needs to be "brought up to speed" in order to appreciate the action.

The important thing about the usual series episode on television is that it is self-contained. It does not need preparation in advance, nor does it need explanation. It is a "one-off" each time the program airs. What do not change—usually—are the characters, the locale, and the time when the program airs.

FIGURE 13-3
CSI, Crime Scene Investigation.
Elizabeth Shue and Ted Danson
have "a meeting of the minds" from
an episode of one of the longest-
running police procedural programs.

Photo by Michael Yarish/©CBS/Courtesy
Everett Collection

The Television Serial

One type of program with which commercial television has set itself apart from
the standard production film is the serial. Whereas the standard production film is
about 120 minutes long, a television serial production can be open-ended. Soap operas, daytime television's adaptation of radio's ongoing series, are broadcast at the
same hour each weekday. Viewers can begin with any episode and be entertained,
even though each episode has only a minor resolution. Early television soap operas
such as *Another World* (NBC, 1964–1999), *The Secret Storm* (CBS, 1954–1974), and
Search for Tomorrow (CBS, 1951–1986) were continuing stories focusing on personal
problems involving money, sex, and questionable behavior in settings reflecting the
current community. In Spanish-language programming, *telenovelas* do the same.

FIGURE 13-4

Roots. In this scene from Alex Haley's television miniseries, the most widely watched drama of its time, Kunta Kinte (LeVar Burton) represents Haley's ancestor as he is brought in chains from Africa.

Courtesy Everett Collection

In a sense, the structure of the soap opera contributed to television's development of the distinctive serial structure that remains one of the greatest strengths of the medium. Robert J. Thompson has said, "The series is, indeed, broadcasting's unique aesthetic contribution to Western art."[1] The British Broadcasting Corporation can be said to have begun the development of the serial show with historical epics such as the hugely popular open-ended *Upstairs, Downstairs* (BBC, 1971–1975) and twelve-part *I, Claudius* (BBC, 1976), both of which are now available from download sources and on DVD.

Roots: The Triumph of an American Family

The first important serial program in the United States was *Rich Man, Poor Man* (ABC, 1976), a twelve-episode adaptation of a novel by Irwin Shaw. But the power of the serial was made most evident by the production of *Roots* (ABC, 1977), which was seen by 130 million viewers, the largest audience of any television series (Figure 13-4). More than 85 percent of all television households were tuned to one or more of the episodes.

The subtitle of the serial, *The Triumph of an American Family,* focused the public's attention on family and family values. Alex Haley's novel represented itself as a search for roots, for the ancestors who shaped himself and his family. African American slaves were ripped from their native soil, and the meager records of their travel to the West did not include information about their families. But Haley showed how, by his persistence, he was able to press far enough to find his original progenitor, Kunta Kinte, in Africa.

Roots, which lasted twelve hours, explored the moral issues relative to slavery as well as racism and the damage it does. The network was uneasy about the production

[1]Quoted in Glen Creeber, *Serial Television* (London: British Film Institute, 2004), p. 6.

and feared it might not be popular, which is the primary reason the twelve episodes were shown on successive nights. The opening scenes of the program, not in Haley's novel, show white actor Ed Asner, then a popular television figure, as a conscience-stricken slave boat captain. This was intended to make the unpleasantness of the reality of slavery more tolerable to a white audience. The network executives were, as we know now, wrong to worry, because the series captured the attention of the mass of American television viewers. Never had so many people watched one program. Never had so many Americans faced questions related to the institution of slavery in America and what it meant to those who were enslaved. *Roots* changed the way many people thought about African Americans, and it changed the way most Americans thought about television as merely entertainment.

Home Box Office: *The Sopranos*   From 1999 to 2007, in eighty-six episodes, David Chase's epic portrait of Tony Soprano and his family riveted HBO cable viewers. Unlike all other shows in the gangster style, *The Sopranos* (Figure 13-5) portrayed Tony as a fragile, haunted man seeing a psychiatrist. His dysfunctional family attracted much more attention than any normal Mafia activities would ordinarily have done. Because of the show's quirkiness, the major networks, ABC, CBS, and Fox, rejected the series. Because HBO was a subscription service, and not available on the airwaves, *The Sopranos* had the advantage of being able to use language characteristic of mob characters, an advantage that made the series achieve more credibility.

The Sopranos's narrative line was extended throughout the six-season run of the show. The standard episodic self-contained structure was abandoned early on and, as a result, HBO established new expectations on the part of its audience. *The Sopranos* was

FIGURE 13-5
The Sopranos. Paulie Walnuts (Tony Sirico) and Tony Soprano (James Gandolfini) in front of their meeting place, Centanni's Meat Market. Paulie is getting a suntan.

Source: HBO

FIGURE 13-6

The Wire. In this scene from the final season of the series, Marlo Stanfield (Jamie Hector) and Felicia "Snoop" Pearson (Felicia Pearson) are young drug lords whose irrational violence alarms their older criminal counterparts, whose own behavior was murderous enough.

Source: HBO

the first major extended serial to change the way in which viewers received their dramatic entertainment. In 1999 that was completely new to television, but today it is common for viewers to wait before watching all the episodes of a given season. The term "bingeing" was applied to viewers who watched the first thirteen episodes of a Netflix release of *House of Cards,* a study of British politics, all at a marathon single sitting.

HBO has produced several extended series since *The Sopranos,* including *Deadwood* (2004–2006), *Boardwalk Empire* (2010–2014), and *Game of Thrones* (2011–present). None of these, however, rises to the artistic level of its finest production, *The Wire* (2002–2008).

Home Box Office: *The Wire* While *The Sopranos* portrayed the life of a Mafia family, another crime drama aimed at portraying the city of Baltimore as a way of demonstrating that all the segments of a community are interwoven. David Simon, formerly a reporter for a Baltimore newspaper, and Ed Burns, a former homicide detective, are responsible for creating the drama, drawing on their personal experience. *The Wire* is about the frustrations of a police unit that tries to use wiretapping to track the progress of street criminals deep in the drug trade (Figure 13-6). Their successes and failures are the primary material of the drama.

The Wire won many awards over its five seasons, although it never won an Emmy. Critics have described the drama as perhaps the best ever produced for television. Its success depended on a gritty realism that often introduced uncomfortable material. The drama focused on six segments of the community: the law, with police, both black and white, using sometimes illegal techniques in response to frustration; the street drug trade, largely dominated by young black men; the port of Baltimore, with its illegal immigration schemes and other criminal activity, run essentially by white union workers; the politicians of the city, all with their own compromises, both black and white; the public school system, which houses some of the criminals

FIGURE 13-7
The Wire. Omar Little (Michael
Kenneth Williams), an avenging
spirit, intends to wreak vengeance on
Marlo and Snoop, who have killed his
lover and his close friend.

Source: HBO

for a while; and the newspapers, whose news coverage turns out not always to be
honestly produced.

The bleakness of the portrait of the city is a call to action. The real mayor of Baltimore
approved the project and gave considerable support for its production in the face of a
possibly damaging view of the city partly because cities like Baltimore all face the same
range of problems. Seeing these problems for what they are helps to clarify the true
values that all such cities must recognize. A true portrait is a first step in restitution.

Michael K. Williams, who plays Omar Little (Figure 13-7)—a gun-wielding thief
who specializes in robbing criminals, who cannot go to the police—stated in an interview that "what *The Wire* is, is an American story, an American social problem.
There's a Wire in every . . . city." Not every city is willing to face the truth. Omar Little
is gay, dangerous, but living by a rigid code of his own design. He was in many of the
sixty episodes. The NAACP presented him an award for his acting in *The Wire.*

The drama appeared, like *The Sopranos,* on Home Box Office. Numerous websites
detail the episodes and provide information on each character in the drama as well as
on the critical reception of the drama. The extent of the drama, which is serial rather
than episodic, is much greater than what could be achieved in a feature film. The
complexity of the issues that face the law, the horror of criminal life in the streets,
and the machinations of high-level politicians facing the same problems most large
American cities face needed an extensive and far-reaching drama perfectly suited to
television.

Three Emmy Winners

In recent years most of the television programs that have won the Primetime
Emmy Award for Outstanding Drama Series have been serial in nature rather than
self-contained single programs.

FIGURE 13-8
Downton Abbey. Mr. Carson, the butler, and Lady Mary Crawley try out their new gramophone. The introduction of new technology—electricity, the telephone, and radio—added to the appeal of the series.

Nick Briggs/©Carnival Films for Masterpiece/ PBS/Courtesy Everett Collection

By its third season, the British serial drama *Downton Abbey* (PBS, 2010–2015) (Figure 13-8) had become one of the most watched television programs in the world. Almost the diametrical opposite of *The Sopranos* and *The Wire*, it presents a historical period in England in which the language is formal by comparison and the manners impeccable. What we see is the upheaval of the lives of the British aristocracy in the wake of historical forces that cannot be ignored or stemmed.

The first season began with a major historical event, the sinking of the *Titanic* in 1912. Down with the ship went Patrick Crawley, the young heir to Downton Abbey. The result is that, much to the dismay of the Dowager Countess Violet Crawley, the great house will now go to the Earl of Grantham's distant cousin, Matthew Crawley, a person unknown to the family. Young Matthew enters as a middle-class solicitor (lawyer) with little interest in the ways of the aristocracy. But soon he finds himself in love with his distant cousin, Lady Mary Crawley, beginning a long and complicated love interest that becomes one of the major centers of the drama for three seasons. Lord Grantham and his wife, Cora, Countess of Grantham, have three daughters, and therefore the question of marriage is as important in this drama as in any Jane Austen novel.

In the aftermath of the attacks on the World Trade Center in 2001, and the resultant war in the Middle East, a number of television shows have centered their action on terrorism and the war in Iraq. *Homeland* (Showtime, 2011–present) (Figure 13-9), with Claire Danes as Carrie Mathison and Mandy Patinkin as Saul Berenson, both of the CIA, has been a durable and timely excursion into the Arab world as it has suffered war and devastation and has brought the threat of terror to Europe and the West. One of the twists in the show is that Carrie Mathison is bipolar and needs to be on lithium to function normally. As a result, she sometimes cracks up and behaves uncontrollably. Some critics have seen this as a reflection of the West's response to the threats of terrorism. The show won the Emmy for best drama in 2012.

Game of Thrones (2011–present) (Figure 13-10) won the Emmy for best drama in 2015 and 2016. The show is based on the book by George R. R. Martin. It is a fantasy historical program that seems to represents medieval society in a northern European wintry landscape featuring an immense ice wall keeping out the barbarians and whitewalkers. From the beginning, *Game of Thrones* features incredible cruelty, torture, murders, deceit, sexual depravity, and the kind of vicious world that only a cable provider like HBO could make available. The story lines are so dense and complex that there is a discussion and partial synopsis after every episode.

FIGURE 13-9
Homeland. Carrie Mathison (Claire Danes) talks with a contact in season five.

©Showtime Networks/Photofest

FIGURE 13-10
Game of Thrones. Cersei, now the Queen of the Seven Kingdoms, seated on the Iron Throne at the end of season six.

Source: HBO

Yet this show has the dimensions of epic literature and production values that are, at the minimum, astonishing. "The Battle of the Bastards," episode 60, is bloody and immense in scope. Even though it is fantasy, the effort was made to replicate the destruction of superior Roman troops at the battle of Cannae (216 BCE) by Hannibal, the Carthaginian general who enclosed the Romans and suffered them their greatest defeat in a legendary battle. *Game of Thrones* also alludes to Shakespeare's historical plays, which revealed the deception and cunning that attended the courts of kings. Unlike Shakespeare, however, the show uses dragon eggs that are a gift in episode 1 and become full-blown flying warriors in episode 60.

FOCUS ON **The Americans**

The Americans (FX, 2013–present) is a sleeper of a serial drama—in several senses. For one thing, it took a while for the series to catch on to the public and build an audience. But by the second season critics were calling it the best series on television. It is a sleeper in another sense: The major characters, Elizabeth (Keri Russell) and Philip Jennings (Matthew Rhys), are a sleeper cell of Russian spies living in Washington, D.C., as ordinary Americans (Figure 13-11). Such an arrangement might seem improbable except for the fact that the series is based on actual sleeper cells discovered in Massachusetts in 2005. There may be more.

Both Elizabeth and Philip were trained scrupulously in Russia before being placed in suburban America. They knew American customs and were warned never to speak anything but English, even to other Russian agents. As a result they appear totally ordinary, having dinner with friends and raising two children, Paige (Holly Taylor) and Henry (Kiedrich Sellati). They have to answer to their controls, Claudia (Margot Martindale) and Gabriel (Frank Langella) (Figure 13-12). But these controls constantly refer back to a superior power, the Center, which makes sometimes unreasonable demands on Elizabeth and Philip. In this sense, the characters have a license to kill and a demand to be improvisational, but at root they are pawns of the system.

From the first episode, Philip finds America remarkable and alluring. When he and Elizabeth arrive in their first motel room, Philip is astonished to find a working air conditioner. We think for a while that he may have his head turned, but Elizabeth is staunch and later even reports to Claudia that Philip may be unreliable. As a result, in a later episode, Philip is kidnapped and beaten to make him confess he is a spy. But his kidnappers are Russian agents testing him, and he realizes what Elizabeth has done. It shakes their relationship for an episode or two.

Elizabeth and Philip have an arranged marriage that changes and develops as the series progresses. They gradually begin to love one another and they wish well for their children. However, as Paige in season five begins to realize that her parents are not just travel agents, but also spies, she becomes involved and Philip fears for her (Figure 13-13). He wants her not to be a spy like him, but Gabriel, who acts as a grandfather figure to them, implies that he is unable to help him if the Center wishes her to be one of them (Figure 13-14). As it is, Elizabeth seems eager for Paige to be permitted to follow their path if she wishes.

Such tensions abound through the first five years of the serial. We see problems in episode one that show up in the fifth season. Allusions to Abraham Lincoln are frequent early and late, with comparisons to the current president, Ronald Reagan. The time period is that of the 1980s.

FIGURE 13-11
Keri Russell as Elizabeth Jennings and Matthew Rhys as Philip Jennings. They live in a modest home with period cars (mostly Oldsmobiles) and appear to live a normal life as owners of a travel agency. Their cover permits them to travel frequently on their operations and sometimes stay over for periods of time.

Source: FX

FIGURE 13-12
Frank Langella as Gabriel and Margot Martindale as Claudia in a late episode of *The Americans*. Just as Gabriel is concerned and sensitive, Claudia is hardnosed and determined.

Source: FX

When Ronald Reagan was shot in March 1981, the Russian handlers feared that the blame would be put on Russia. The Secretary of State, Alexander Haig, without the actual authority, took over the White House and seemed to be staging a coup. Gabriel thought he would order a nuclear strike against Russia. The tensions among the Russians led Philip and Elizabeth to unearth munitions and weapons designed to kill the Secretary of State—and they came close to being caught. In that incident Elizabeth shot a policeman who had stopped their vehicle. The killings are often done by Elizabeth and are sometimes almost wanton.

Another source of tension early in the series is the arrival of Stan Beeman (Noah Emmerich), an FBI man assigned to counterterrorism who moves in next door to Elizabeth and Philip. Throughout the seasons Stan and Philip become friends and the two families interact with dinners and events. Stan's son, Will, and Paige become romantically close, making Philip and Elizabeth so concerned that they forbid her to see him (Figure 13-15). In season five they explain the risks she would be taking with all of their futures. Paige also moves slightly apart from her parents by joining a church and being baptized. This detail in season three has curious developments when Philip uses religion and prayer to dupe a young girl whom he needs in order to gain access to her father's top secret papers.

Both Elizabeth and Philip are expected to use sex to achieve their ends. Both have sex with people from whom they seek vital information. Early in the series that is not a major emotional issue, but as they grow more and more loving toward each other it begins to arouse deep feelings, even jealousy. In the process of their making sexual connections, Philip and Elizabeth usually wear disguises that include often fanciful wigs. In some cases they sustain their extra relationships over long periods of time.

The abrupt scene shifts from one sexual relationship—which constitutes, in essence, a specific spying operation—to another are often jarring and demand continuing attention from one episode to another. The effect is to keep the viewer off guard, which is a metaphor for the operatives who keep the FBI off guard.

The style of the show is marked by flashbacks to childhood in Russia, during very hard times. For example, Philip's father was a guard in a prison camp, and not a nice man. Elizabeth remembers a fatherless childhood with a mother who somehow avoided being the prey of a powerful government figure.

The Americans provides its audience with an introduction to the values and problems of a recent historical era, the era of the Cold War and its thawing in the 1980s. The threat of nuclear war was in the air. The changes in Russian government after the death of its leader, Leonid Brezhnev, in late 1982 led to changes in American policies. Russia was fighting in Afghanistan, and the United States had recently been defeated in Vietnam. *The Americans* explores problems with Russian actions and, from Philip and Elizabeth's point of view, problems with what American authorities were doing.

The Americans has developed into a kind of time capsule recording a nervous period in international affairs, told from the point of view of people who were operatives on the ground trying to shape the direction of history. *The Americans* is not just an intense spy story but also a historical analysis that is revelatory of a period in international politics that shaped the world as we know it today.

FIGURE 13-15

Elizabeth and Philip explain to Paige how she might reveal their true identity if she continues to have Will as her boyfriend. Will is the son of the FBI agent next door. Elizabeth is giving Paige a way to hold her fingers to help her keep her secret even if she is in a romantic situation with Will.

Source: FX

PERCEPTION KEY Focus on *The Americans*

1. To what extent does *The Americans* contribute to your education? To what extent is the appeal of the series linked to what you learn from it about the late years of the Cold War between Russia and America?
2. A great deal of attention is paid to the composition of individual frames of the drama. Comment on the quality of individual images and on the nature of the pacing of the drama. To what audience do you feel this series has the most appeal?
3. How accurate do you think the portrayal of society is in *The Americans*? What dramatic qualities lead you to think it accurate or inaccurate?
4. Some critics have complained about the sudden violence and cold-blooded killing on the part of Elizabeth. Do you agree? Do you find that the series deserves the warnings that begin each segment?
5. How would you compare *The Americans* with another historical serial drama such as *Homeland, Mad Men,* or *Downton Abbey*?

VIDEO ART

Unlike commercial dramatic television, video art avoids a dramatic narrative line of the kind that involves points of tension, climax, or resolution. In this sense, most video art is the opposite of commercial dramatic television. Whereas television programming is often formulaic, predictable in structure, and designed to please a mass audience, video art is more experimental and radical in structure, which often results in its pleasing its audience in a very different way.

Video art dates from the early 1950s. Its most important early artist is Nam June Paik (1932–2006), whose work opened many avenues of experimentation and inspired an entire generation of video artists. Paik's *Video Flag* (1986) is a large installation approximately six feet high by twelve feet wide, with eighty-four video monitors with two channels of information constantly changing, at a speed that makes it difficult to identify the specific images on each monitor. The effect is hypnotic and strange, but viewers are usually captured by the imagery and the dynamism of the several patterns that alternate in the monitors. Paik experimented widely with video monitors, combining them, in one case, to produce cello music, played by Charlotte Moorman, a musician and performance artist. In another installation, *Arc Double Face* (1985), he produced a large doorway composed of monitors with three separate video channels showing simultaneously.

Peter Campus (b. 1937) has been a seminal figure in video art. His *Three Transitions* (1973) at New York's Museum of Modern Art is a five-minute video of three transformations of his own image. The first shows himself projected on a paper partition. He stands dressed in a yellow sport coat facing the partition. Slowly we see a knife coming through from the other side of the partition and sticking out through his back. Slowly the knife slices down through his back, and then we see the partition sliced apart as his hand seems to reach through both the partition and his back to make room for his head and body coming through. The effect is uncanny. The second of the transitions shows him rubbing his face, and as he rubs we see another face showing through, as if his face were layers and each time he rubs he shows another layer. In the last transition we see him holding a large photograph of himself, which he sets afire. The fire takes a long time to eat away at the photograph, eventually but slowly burning his own moving image. Campus specializes in mysterious video experiences in which his educational background, experimental psychology, comes into play.

Some of the work of the video artists mentioned here can be viewed on YouTube, Vimeo, and other video sites online. For instance, Janine Antoni's *Tear* (2008) (Figure 13-16) can be seen on YouTube. Antoni is a performance artist and sculptor who walks a tightrope in her video *Touch* (2002), also viewable online. As in most modern video art, the pacing and rhythms are very slow, especially compared to the rapid-cut commercial television programs. Antoni has said that the slow movement of video art has the purpose of engaging all the senses, but, curiously, the slow pacing sometimes becomes hypnotic so that one participates with the work on a very different level even as compared with looking at a painting.

The Swiss artist Pipilotti Rist was given the entire New Museum in New York to mount her latest show, *Pixel Forest* (2016) (Figure 13-17). Rist has been involved in video art for some years. Her show *Ever Is Over All* (1997) was said by Peter Schjeldahl to blur the boundaries of art and entertainment. It was shown at the Museum of Modern Art in the atrium, where she projected sharply contrasting videos on adjacent walls. It can be seen online. In 2016 *Pixel Forest* filled the second, third, and fourth floors of the New Museum of New York. In some rooms the museum provided second-hand (sanitized) beds for those who wished to lie down and feel surrounded by the videos. For the month of January 2017, Rist's video *Open My Glade (Flatten)* (2000–2017) was shown every evening in Times Square from 11:57

FIGURE 13-16
Janine Antoni, *Tear*, 2008. Lead, steel
4,182-pound, 33-inch-diameter
wrecking ball. 11 × 11-foot HD video
projection with surround sound. Janine
Antoni is a sculptor who works in
video. She uses both in *Tear*.

©Janine Antoni; courtesy of the artist and
Luhring Augustine, New York

FIGURE 13-17
Pipilotti Rist, *Pixel Forest***. 2016. The
New Museum of New York.** For her
second installation in New York, the
Swiss artist Pipilotti Rist had three
floors of the New Museum for her
work. She projected videos on walls,
ceilings, and floors. In several rooms
she had beds for viewers to lie down
as they experienced the show.

©Leanza/Epa/REX/Shutterstock

FIGURE 13-18
The Feast of Trimalchio (2009–2010),
AES+F Group. Multichannel HD video
installation (9-, 3-, and 1-channel
versions), series of pictures, series
of portfolios with photographs and
drawings.

©2017 AES+F/Artists Rights Society (ARS),
New York

to midnight. For thirty years her work has been influential in forming the video aesthetic.

Video art is international and growing. The Russian group known as AES+F Group, composed of four artists, Tatiana Arzamasova, Lev Evzovich, Evgeny Svyatsky, and Vladimir Fridkes, formed in 1987 and have shown in several important exhibitions, such as the Venice Biennale. In 2009 they showed their video composition *The Feast of Trimalchio* (Figure 13-18) at the Sydney Biennale in Australia. *The Feast of Trimalchio* figures in a Roman novel by Petronius Arbiter called *The Satyricon* and it became a symbol for wasteful opulence and orgiastic entertainment. The AES+F Group have used their imagery to satirize for today what Petronius satirized for ancient Rome. They set their figures in a modern luxury hotel on a fantasy island as a protest against the rampant commercialism of modern Russia.

Doug Aitken mounted a gigantic video projection on the outside walls of the Museum of Modern Art in New York City in 2007 (Figure 13-19). *Sleepwalkers* consists of five thirteen-minute narratives of people of different social classes going to work at different nighttime jobs. The evening projections were slightly altered with each presentation. He said about his work,

> I wanted to create very separate characters and explore their connections almost through movement and place. The characters are as diverse as possible and, as these stories come closer and closer together, you see the shared lines, the connections.[2]

Aitken has been working in the medium of video for some time and won the International Prize at the Venice Biennale in 1999 for *Electric Earth*.

Another remarkable installation that moved from the Getty Museum in Los Angeles to the National Gallery of Art in London is *The Passions* (2000–2002), a study of the uncontrollable human emotions that Viola sees as the passions that

---

[2]Quoted in Ellen Wulfhorst, "Sleepwalks" Exhibit Projected on NY's MOMA, Reuters, January 19, 2007.

FIGURE 13-19
Doug Aitken's *Sleepwalkers*. Aitken's projections on the walls of the New York Museum of Modern Art in 2007 attracted a considerable crowd and critical responses from the media.

©Nicole Bengiveno/The New York Times/Redux

EXPERIENCING Jacopo Pontormo and Bill Viola: *The Visitation*

The most celebrated video artist working today is Bill Viola (b. 1951), whose work has been exhibited internationally with great acclaim. He is steeped in the tradition of the old master painters, especially those of the fourteenth and fifteenth centuries in northern Europe and Italy. His techniques vary, but one of the most effective is the slow-motion work that makes it possible to observe every action in great detail. He uses high-definition video where available and achieves effects that recall great paintings. His work is meditative and deeply thoughtful. *The Greeting* (1995) (Figure 13-20) is a projection in heroic size of three women standing in a cityscape reminiscent of a Renaissance painting. Indeed, the work was inspired by Jacopo Pontormo's *The Visitation* (1578) (Figure 13-21), a sixteenth-century painting on panel in an Italian Church.

FIGURE 13-20
Bill Viola, *The Greeting*. 1995. Video/sound installation projected some four times life size. The movement of the figures, which is very, very slow, is extraordinary to watch in part because we can examine every moment with the same intensity as our examination of a painting—which *The Greeting* in many ways resembles.

Photo: Kira Perov. Courtesy Bill Viola Studio

The Pontormo is a religious painting. The woman in violet blue in the center is Mary and the woman in green and orange is her cousin Elizabeth. They both have halos over their head. Mary tells Elizabeth she is pregnant (with Jesus) and Elizabeth tells Mary she is pregnant (with John the Baptist). This is a major historic moment (which Pontormo often painted). Examine the Pontormo for its structure and its organization of colors. The two figures in the background are witnesses, one very young, one older. Examine how Viola selects three women and poses them in a similar position, but with the young witness in the middle, looking on.

Pontormo's moment was of great cultural importance in 1578 and Viola borrows Pontormo to make an important statement as well. We see it as a greeting of happy women, but with Pontormo's painting as an echo, this moment takes on a significant spiritual value. Our age does not see the same values that the late sixteenth century saw, but we, too, as Viola reminds us in so much of his work, have moments of spiritual insight and when one thinks about it, the greeting of any two people resonates spiritually as a meeting of minds, a connection of friends, a sense of human joy.

In *The Greeting*, the wind blows softly, moving the women's draped clothing. Except for the wind, the projection is almost soundless, the action pointedly slow but ultimately fascinating. The resources of slow-motion video are greater than we would have thought before seeing these images. Viola's techniques produce a totally new means of participation with the images, and our sense of time and space seems altered in a manner that is revelatory of both the sensa of the work and the human content of greeting and joy.

After examining these two works, search online for a video of Bill Viola's *The Greeting*. How do you see the relationship between Viola and Pontormo's work? What has Viola done to help echo the spiritual significance of Pontormo's painting? What is different about your experience of Pontormo's painting and Viola's video art?

FIGURE 13-21
Jacopo Pontormo (1494–1556), *The Visitation* c. 1528, oil on panel, 79.5 × 61.5 inches. Carmignano, Pieve di San Michele Arcangelo.

©Remo Bardazzi/Electa/Mondadori Portfolio/Getty Images

great artists of the past alluded to in their work. *The Quintet of the Astonished* (2000) (Figure 13-22), one of several video installations in the series *The Passions,* was projected on a flat-screen monitor, revealing the wide range of emotions that these figures were capable of. The original footage was shot at 300 frames per second but then exhibited at the standard television speed of 30 frames per second. At times, it looks as if the figures are not moving at all, but eventually the viewer sees that the expressions on the faces change slowly and the detail by which they alter is extremely observable, as it would not be at normal speed. *The Passions* consists of several different installations, all exploring varieties of emotional expression.

Fire Woman, available online, is an image of a woman standing in front of a wall of fire (Figure 13-23). Slowly, she falls forward into a deep pool of water, and the image is revealed to be a reflection. Bill Viola's work is informed by classical artists and by his own commitment to a religious sensibility. A practicing Buddhist, he is deeply influenced by Zen Buddhism. A sense of peace informs his work and his humanistic spirituality. In his comments about his work, he often observes the religious impulse as it has been expressed by the artists of the Renaissance whom he admires, and as it has informed his awareness of spirituality in his own life.

FIGURE 13-22
Bill Viola, *The Quintet of the Astonished*.
2000. Video/sound installation,
rear projected on a screen mounted
on a wall. The work is a study in the
expression of feelings.

Photo: Kira Perov. Courtesy Bill Viola Studio

FIGURE 13-23
Bill Viola, *Fire Woman*. 2005. Color video
freestanding LCD panel. This installation
is part of a series involving air, earth, fire,
and water, designed for a production of
Richard Wagner's opera *Tristan and Isolde*
performed at the Opéra National de Paris
in 2005.

Photo: Kira Perov. Courtesy Bill Viola Studio

PERCEPTION KEY Bill Viola and Other Video Artists

Most of us do not live near an installation by Bill Viola or other video artists, but there is a great deal of video art online, including some of Viola's. This Perception Key relies on your having the opportunity to see some of the important online sites.

1. The James Cohan Gallery website contains a good deal of information about Bill Viola and his work. It includes video excerpts of him talking about what he does, and it includes video still samples of his work. Do you find the noncommercial approach he takes to art satisfying or unsatisfying? What do you feel Viola expects of his audience?
2. You can see a still from Viola's installation called *City of Man* (1989), composed of three projections, at the Guggenheim Museum in New York. In this installation, the images move with speed. The three images are very different and together form a triptych. Which can you interpret best? Which seems most threatening? What seems to be the visual message of this installation? How do you think the alternation of images on and off would affect your concentration on the imagery?
3. Sample video art by going online to the websites of the following artists: Bill Viola, David Hall, and Tine Louise Kortermand. Which work of art seems most interesting and most successful? What qualities do you find revealing in the piece you most admire? In which is the participative experience most intense? In which work is it easiest to interpret the content?
4. Video art is still in its infancy. If you have access to a video camera and a video monitor, try making a short piece of video art that avoids the techniques and clichés of commercial television. How do your friends react to it? Describe the techniques you relied upon to make your work distinct.

SUMMARY

Television is the most widely available artistic medium in our culture. The widespread accessibility of video cameras and video monitors has brought television to a new position as a medium available to numerous artists, both professional and amateur. Television's technical limitations, those of resolution and screen size, have made it distinct from film, but new technical developments are improving the quality of its imagery and its sound. Commercial television dramas have evolved their own structures, with episodic programs following a formulaic pattern of crisis points followed by commercial interruption. The British Broadcasting Corporation helped begin a novel development that distinguishes television from the commercial film: the open-ended serial, which avoids crisis-point interruption and permits the medium to explore richer resources of narrative. Video art is, by way of contrast, completely anticommercial. It avoids narrative structures and alters our sense of time and expectation. Because it is in its infancy, the possibilities of video art are unlike those of any other medium.

Source: Metropolitan Museum of Art,
Harris Brisbane Dick Fund, 1939

Chapter 14

IS IT ART OR SOMETHING LIKE IT?

ART AND ARTLIKE

In Chapter 2, we argued that a work of art is a form-content. The form of a work of art is more than just an organization of media. Artistic form clarifies, gives us insight into some subject matter (something important in our world). A work of art is revelatory of values. Conversely, an *artlike* work is not revelatory. It has form but lacks a form-content. But what is revelatory to one person might not be to another. What is revelatory to one culture might not be to another. As time passes, a work that was originally not understood as art may become art for both critics and the public—cave paintings, for example.

It is highly unlikely that the cave painters and their society thought of their works as art. If one argues that art is entirely in the eye of the beholder, then it is useless to try to distinguish art from the artlike. But we do not agree that art is *entirely* in the eye of the beholder. And we think it is of paramount importance to be able to distinguish art from the artlike. To fail to do so leaves us in chaotic confusion, without any standards.

It is surely important to keep the boundaries between art and the artlike flexible, and the artlike should not be blindly disparaged. Undoubtedly, there are many artlike works—much propaganda, *pornography*, and shock art, for example—that

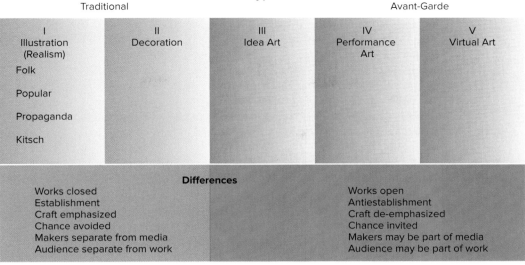

General Guidelines for Types of "Artlike" Creations

Traditional				Avant-Garde
I Illustration (Realism)	II Decoration	III Idea Art	IV Performance Art	V Virtual Art
Folk Popular Propaganda Kitsch				

Differences

Works closed	Works open
Establishment	Antiestablishment
Craft emphasized	Craft de-emphasized
Chance avoided	Chance invited
Makers separate from media	Makers may be part of media
Audience separate from work	Audience may be part of work

may deserve condemnation. But to denigrate the artlike in order to praise art is critical snobbery. For the most part, the artlike plays a very civilizing role, as does, for instance, the often marvelous beauty of crafts. To be unaware, however, of the differences between art and the artlike or to be confused about them weakens our perceptive abilities. This is especially true in our time, for we are inundated with myriad works that are labeled art, often on no better grounds than that the maker says so.

Concepts (beliefs) govern percepts to some extent. Confused concepts lead to confused perceptions. The fundamental and common feature that is shared by art and the artlike is the crafting—the skilled structuring of some medium. The fundamental feature that separates art from the artlike is the revelatory power of that crafting, the form-content, the clarification of some subject matter. But we may disagree about whether a particular work has revelatory power. The borderline between art and the artlike can be very tenuous. In any case, our judgments should always be understood as debatable.

We shall classify and briefly describe some of the basic types of the artlike. We will use examples mainly from the visual field, not only because that field usually cannot be shut out but also because that field seems to be the most saturated with what appears to be art. Our classifications will not be exhaustive, for the various manifestations of the artlike, especially in recent years, appear endless. Nor will our classifications be exclusive, for many kinds of the artlike mix with others. For example, folk art may be decoration and usually is a popular art.

We shall briefly analyze five fundamental types of works that often are on or near the boundary of art: illustration, decoration, idea art, performance art, and virtual art (see the chart "General Guidelines for Types of 'Artlike' Creations"). This schema omits, especially with respect to the avant-garde, other types and many species. However, our schema provides a reasonable semblance of organization to a very broad and confusing range of phenomena that rarely has been addressed. The schema, furthermore, highlights the most important issues. The division between the traditional and the avant-garde points up the powerful shift in the "new art" trends beginning with Dada during World War I. The avant-garde seems to exist in every art tradition, but never has it been so radicalized as in our time. That is one reason the art of our time is so extraordinarily interesting from a theoretical perspective. We flock to exhibitions and hear, "What is going on here? This is art? You've got to be kidding!" Those who are conservative in approaching the avant-garde should remember this caution by the late Jean Dubuffet, the painter-sculptor: "The characteristic property of an inventive art is that it bears no resemblance to art as it is generally recognized and in consequence . . . does not seem like art at all."

Avant-garde works can be revelatory—they can be art, of course. But they do it in different ways from traditional art, as is indicated by the listing under "Differences" on the chart. The key: Does the work give us insight? This typology is one way of classifying works that are not revelatory, but that does not mean they cannot have useful and distinctive functions. The basic function of decoration, for example, is the enhancement of something else, making it more interesting and pleasing. The basic function of idea art is to make us think about art. Every work should be judged by its unique merits. We should be in a much better position now than before the study of this text to make distinctions, however tentative, between art and the artlike. It can be a fascinating and illuminating study.

CONCEPTION KEY Theories

Our theory of art as revelatory, as giving insight into values, may appear to be mired in a tradition that cannot account for the amazing developments of the avant-garde. Is the theory inadequate? As you proceed with this chapter, ask yourself whether the distinction between art and artlike is valid. How about useful? If not, what theory would you propose? Or would you be inclined to dismiss theories altogether?

ILLUSTRATION

Realism

An *illustration* is almost always realistic; that is, the images closely resemble some object or event. Because of this sharing of realistic features, the following are grouped under "Illustration" in the chart: folk art, popular art, propaganda, and kitsch.

The structure of an illustration portrays, presents, or depicts some object or event as the subject matter. We have no difficulty recognizing that wax figures in a museum are meant to represent famous people. But do realistic portrayals give us something more than presentation? Some significant interpretation? If we are correct in thinking not, then the forms of these wax figures only present their subject matter. They do not interpret their subject matter, which is to say they lack content or artistic meaning. Such forms—providing their portrayals are realistic—produce illustration. They are not artistic forms. They are not form-content.

PERCEPTION KEY *Woman with a Purse*

Is Figure 14-1 a photograph of a real woman? An illustration? A work of art?

FIGURE 14-1
Duane Hanson, *Woman with a Purse.*
1974. This is one of a group of
life-size, totally realistic fiberglass
"counterfeits" of real people. They
represent a sculptural trompe l'oeil
that blurs the line between art and
life.

Art: ©Estate of Duane Hanson/Licensed
by VAGA, New York, NY. Photo: ©AKG
London

The following experience happened to one of the authors:

> On entering a large room in the basement gallery of the Wallraf-Richartz Museum in Cologne, Germany, I noticed a woman standing by a large pillar staring at an abstract painting by Frank Stella. She seemed to be having an exceptionally intense participative experience with the Stella. After a few participative experiences of my own with the Stella and some other paintings in that room, I was amazed to find the lady still entranced. My curiosity was aroused. Summoning courage, I moved very close to find that the "woman" was in fact a sculpture—the *trompe l'oeil* was almost unbelievable, becoming recognizable only within a few feet. Very few visitors in that gallery made my amusing discovery. And when they did, they too were amazed and amused, but no one's attention was held on this lady very long. Any concentrated attention was given to the technical details of the figure. Was the hair real? Were those real fingernails? We decided they were. The form of the sculpture seemed to be less than artistic, apparently revealing nothing about women or anything else, except for exceptional craftsmanship. The late Duane Hanson's *Woman with a Purse* is so extraordinarily realistic that it is a "substitute," a duplicate of the real thing. Is *Woman with a Purse* an example of art or the artlike? We will return to this question later in this chapter.

Folk Art

There is no universally accepted definition of ***folk art***. Most experts agree, however, that folk art is outside fine art or what we simply have been calling art. Unfortunately, the experts offer little agreement about why.

Folk artists usually are both self-taught and trained to some extent in a nonprofessional tradition. Although not trained by "fine artists," folk artists sometimes are directly influenced by the fine-art tradition, as in the case of Henri Rousseau, who was entranced by the works of Picasso. Folk art is never aristocratic or dictated by the fashions of the artistic establishment, and it is rarely fostered by patrons. Folk art is an expression of the folkways of the "plain society," the average person. Folk art generally is commonsensical, direct, naive, and earthy. The craft or skill that produces these things is often of the highest order.

The snapshot aesthetic of photography is, in a sense, folk art because even before Kodak's Brownie Camera was introduced in 1900 people had been taking photographs without any training about composition or balance and content. The snapshot is an unmeditated "instant" image valued usually as a record of a person or a place and not as a work of art. Richard Estes's *Baby Doll Lounge* (Figure 14-2) is not a photograph. This very large oil painting may be a copy of a photograph that, if we saw it, we would consider a snapshot. It shows a simple street scene with a car close to its center, but without the Baby Doll Lounge, which, according to the title, is the subject of the original photo. Estes is not a folk painter. He is highly skilled and well trained. The photograph is an accurate rendering of the snapshot (therefore also the scene). Is this painting art or artlike?

FIGURE 14-2
Richard Estes, *Baby Doll Lounge*. 1978. Oil on canvas, 3 × 5 feet. Estes, who painted in oils, created a style that emulated photography but tried to outdo it.

©Richard Estes, courtesy Marlborough Gallery, New York. Photo: ©Christie's Images Ltd - Artothek

Henri Rousseau painted seriously from age forty-nine, when he retired on a small pension from the customs house to paint full time. He studied paintings in French museums and made every effort to paint in the most realistic style of the day. He was sometimes the butt of ironic comments that overpraised his work, but instead of taking offense, he seems to have accepted such comments as sincere. Picasso gave a dinner in his honor in 1908, two years before Rousseau died, and some commentators feel Picasso may have been mildly ironic in his praise. Rousseau painted animals he had seen only in zoos or in dioramas in natural history museums, and sometimes he painted animals together that could never have shared the same space. His sense of perspective was lacking throughout his career, and his approach to painting was marked by odd habits, such as painting all one color first, then bringing in the next color, and so on. However, his lack of skill came at a time in art history when Surrealism was under way, and his particular unrealities began to seem symbolic and significant in ways that a realistic painting, such as Estes's *Baby Doll Lounge,* could not. This is especially true of *The Sleeping Gypsy* (Figure 14-3), which improbably places a strange-looking lion next to a gypsy whose position is so uncertain as to suggest that he or she may roll out of the painting. Rousseau's intention was to make the painting totally realistic, but the result is more schematic and suggestive than realistic.

PERCEPTION KEY Richard Estes and Henry Rousseau

1. Which painting exhibits more skill? Is it skill that determines which of these paintings is more artlike?
2. How important is accuracy of representation to deciding whether a painting is art?
3. Which painting is more useful as an illustration?

FIGURE 14-3
Henri Rousseau, *The Sleeping Gypsy*.
1897. Oil on canvas, 51 × 79 inches.
Rousseau was a customs agent
during the day but a painter in his
free time. Although without training
in art, he became one of the most
original figures in modern art.

©The Museum of Modern Art/Licensed by
SCALA/Art Resource, NY

4. Does translating a snapshot into an oil painting make a work of art? Does the painting make the snapshot a work of art? How does this painting affect your valuation of photography as an art form?
5. What does *Baby Doll Lounge* reveal as a painting that it would not reveal as a photograph?
6. In each painting, decide what the subject matter is. Then decide whether the form transforms the subject matter and creates content. Which painting has more-interesting content? Why?

Popular Art

Popular art—a very imprecise category—encompasses contemporary works enjoyed by the masses. The masses love Norman Rockwell, dismiss Mondrian, and are puzzled by Picasso. In music Shostakovich and John Cage sometimes mystify the general public. But lovers of Beethoven string quartets often find it difficult to love heavy metal rock bands and rap music. The reverse is true, as well. The distinction between fine art and popular art does not always hold people back from enjoying both, but it seems to be rare.

The term "Pop" derives from Richard Hamilton's painting *Just what is it that makes today's homes so different so appealing?* (1956), of a nude muscle-builder holding a gigantic lollypop in a cluttered living room with a nude woman on a sofa wearing a lampshade for a hat. In the 1960s and 1970s, Pop Art was at the edge of the avant-garde, startling to the masses. But as usually happens, time makes the avant-garde less controversial, and in this case the style quickly became popular. The realistic showings of mundane objects were easily comprehended. Here was an

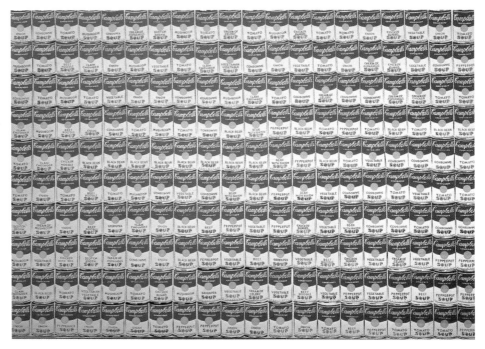

FIGURE 14-4
Andy Warhol, *200 Campbell's Soup Cans*. 1962. Acrylic on canvas, 72 × 100 inches. The leader of the Pop Art movement, Warhol became famous for signing cans of Campbell's soup and fabricating individual cans of Campbell's soup. For a time, the soup can became an identifier of Pop Art.

©2017 The Andy Warhol Foundation for the Visual Arts, Inc./Artists Rights Society (ARS), New York. Photo: ©The Andy Warhol Foundation Inc./Trademarks, Campbell Soup Company

art people could understand without snobbish critics. We see the tomato soup cans in supermarkets. Andy Warhol helps us look at them as objects worthy of notice (Figure 14-4), especially their blatant repetitive colors, shapes, stacking, and simplicity. For the masses, we have an art that seems to be revelatory.

PERCEPTION KEY Pop Art

1. Is Warhol's painting revelatory? If so, about what?
2. Go back to the discussion of Duane Hanson's work. If you decide that the Warhol work is art, then can you make a convincing argument that *Woman with a Purse* helps us really *see* ordinary people and thus also is a work of art? These are controversial questions.

PERCEPTION KEY Norman Rockwell's *Freedom from Want*

Next to Andrew Wyeth, Rockwell is probably the most popular and beloved American painter. A very modest man, Rockwell always insisted that he was only an illustrator. He frequently worked from photographs. Does the folksy piety appear sentimental in *Freedom from Want* (Figure 14-5)? Is the scene superficial? Does the scene stir your imagination? Does the painting make any demand on you? Enhance your sensitivity to anything? Enlarge your experience? Is *Freedom from Want* art or illustration? Despite his popularity, Rockwell is almost universally described as an illustrator by the experts. They claim that his works are composed of pictorial clichés. Do you agree? Who anoints the experts?

FIGURE 14-5
Norman Rockwell, *Freedom from Want*. 1943. Oil on canvas, 45¾ × 35½ inches. An iconic representation of the American family during World War II, this image was parodied in the film *American Gangster*, with Denzel Washington at the head of the table.

Professional work can be much more realistic than folk art. Professional technical training usually is a prerequisite for achieving the goal of very accurate representation, as anyone who has tried pictorial imitation can attest. Professionals who are realists are better at representation than folk painters, as Richard Estes's *Baby Doll Lounge* demonstrates. Realistic painting done by professionals is one of the most popular kinds of painting, for it requires little or no training or effort to enjoy. Often, very realistic paintings are illustrations, examples of the artlike. Sometimes, however, realistic painters not only imitate objects and events but also interpret what they imitate, crossing the line from illustration to art.

PERCEPTION KEY Estes and Rockwell

1. Does the sharp-focus realism (known as "photo-realism" because it is based on photography) of *Baby Doll Lounge* make it an illustration?
2. Note the reflections in the store windows. Do we ever see reflections quite like that? If not, then can one reasonably argue that by means of such transformation Estes heightens our awareness of such "things as they are" in the cityscape?
3. Do you think that Norman Rockwell worked from a photograph to paint *Freedom from Want*? Is cutting off the heads on each side of the painting typical of photographs of scenes such as this? How impressive is Rockwell's artistic technique? Does his technique make this a work of art?
4. In terms of realism, how realistic is this portrait of a family sitting down to a happy Thanksgiving Day meal? Is it possible that this is more of a fantasy than a reality? Is it possible that this painting might serve as propaganda for family values? How would that affect its value as a work of art?
5. Compare Richard Estes's *Baby Doll Lounge* with Norman Rockwell's *Freedom from Want*. Which seems more representative of the world in which you live? Which transforms its subject matter more? Which has a richer content?

Baby Doll Lounge, in our opinion, is a work of art. Estes worked from a series of photographs, shifting them around in order to portray interesting relationships of abstract shapes as well as the illusion of realism. Thus, the buildings in the left background are reflected in the glass in the right foreground, helping—along with the bright curving line on the dark roof of the building slightly left of center—to tie the innumerable rectangles together. A geometrical order has been subtly imposed on a very disorderly scene. Estes has retained so much realistic detail, totally unlike Mondrian in *Broadway Boogie Woogie* (see Figure 4-10), that initially we might think we are looking at a photograph. Yet, with a second look, it becomes apparent that this cannot be a photograph of an actual scene, for such a complete underlying geometry does not occur in city scenes. Moreover, people are totally absent, a possible but unlikely condition. An anxious, pervasive silence emanates from this painting. Despite the realism, there is a dreamy unreality. Take an early Sunday morning stroll in a large city, with the dwellers still asleep, and see if you do not perceive more because of Estes.

The line between realistic painting that is illustration and realistic painting that is art is particularly difficult to draw with respect to the paintings of Andrew Wyeth, hailed as the "people's painter" and arguably the most popular American painter of all time. His father, N. C. Wyeth, was a gifted professional illustrator, and he rigorously trained his son in the fundamentals of drawing and painting. Wyeth was also carefully trained in the use of tempera, his favorite medium, by the professional painter Peter Hurd, a brother-in-law. So although a nonacademic and although trained mainly "in the family," Wyeth's training was professional. Wyeth is not a folk painter.

Among the great majority of critics, Wyeth is not highly appreciated, although there are outstanding exceptions, such as Thomas Hoving, former director of the Metropolitan Museum of Art. Wyeth is not even mentioned, let alone discussed, in Mahonri Young's *American Realists*. Clement Greenberg, one of the most respected

FIGURE 14-6
Andrew Wyeth, *Christina's World*.
**1948. Tempera on gessoed panel,
32¼ × 47¾ inches.** Wyeth was
probably America's most popular
artist of the second half of the
twentieth century. This is his most
famous painting.

critics of recent times, asserted that realistic works such as Wyeth's are out of date and "result in second-hand, second-rate paintings." In 1987 an exhibition of Wyeth's work was held at the National Gallery of Art in Washington, D.C. Some critics demurred: Wyeth makes superficial pictures that look like "the world as it is," except tidied up and sentimentalized. They claim that Wyeth is a fine illustrator, like his father, but that the National Gallery of Art should be used for exhibitions of art, not illustrations. Notice again, incidentally, the relevance of the question: What is art?

Wyeth's most beloved and famous painting is *Christina's World* (Figure 14-6). He tells us,

> When I painted it in 1948, *Christina's World* hung all summer in my house in Maine and nobody particularly reacted to it. I thought is this one ever a flat tire. Now I get at least a letter a week from all over the world, usually wanting to know what she's doing. Actually there isn't any definite story. The way this tempera happened, I was in an upstairs room in the Olson house and saw Christina crawling in the field. Later, I went down on the road and made a pencil drawing of the house, but I never went down into the field. You see, my memory was more of a reality than the thing itself. I didn't put Christina in till the very end. I worked on the hill for months, that brown grass, and kept thinking about her in her pink dress like a faded lobster shell I might find on the beach, crumpled. Finally I got up enough courage to say to her, "Would you mind if I made a drawing of you sitting outside?" and drew her crippled arms and hands. Finally, I was so shy about posing her, I got my wife Betsy to pose for her figure. Then it came time to lay in Christina's figure against that planet I'd created for all those weeks. I put this pink tone on her shoulder— and it almost blew me cross the room.[1]

---

[1]Wanda M. Corn, *The Art of Andrew Wyeth* (Greenwich, Conn.: New York Graphic Society, 1964), p. 38.

1. Does Wyeth's statement strike you as describing the crafting of an illustrator or the "crafting-creating" of an artist? But is such a question relevant to distinguishing illustration from art? Is not *what is made* the issue, not the *making* (see Chapter 2)?
2. Would you describe the painting as sentimental (see Chapter 11)? Could it be that sometimes critics tag works as sentimental because of snobbery?
3. Is this a pretty painting? If so, is such a description derogatory?
4. Is *Christina's World* illustration or art? Until you see the original in the museum, keep your judgment more tentative than usual.

Propaganda

The purpose of **propaganda** art is to persuade us to believe a specific message, not to have an artistic experience. No species of the artlike is as realistically illustrative as propaganda because mass persuasion requires the easy access of realism. The essence of propaganda is to spread political pride in nation, ethnicity, political commitment, or national purpose. Propaganda is created and spread by institutions of some sort, whether secular, political, or religious. These institutions are bent on persuading people to their cause by means of their message.

EXPERIENCING Propaganda Art

When we consider a Fascist poster such as Anselmo Ballester's huge poster *A Noi! (To Us!)* (Figure 14-7) we find it easy to resist the appeal, particularly as we know that Fascism resulted in a terrifying war in which upwards of 20 million people died. Once the historical situation is understood, even as technically good a poster as Ballester's is not likely to persuade any of us today. In the case of this poster, the message is "dressed up" for us with a beautiful young woman who has accepted the propaganda message and is now trying to get us to join her. The art itself is like the frosting on a cake, but in this case we know the cake is fatal.

This striking poster portrays a young woman giving the Fascist salute. She is caught up in what appear to be flowing flaglike billows of cloth. Their designs echo the then current art nouveau style in green and red, the colors of the Italian Fascist flag referenced below her right arm. Slightly grayed out, the heroic Roman arch and images of the ancient Roman SPQR legion remind the viewer of the once great military power of the Roman empire. One purpose of the poster was to boost morale and encourage enrollment in the military before World War II. But the more important purpose was to encourage young people to take pride in being Italian Fascists.

Fascism began in Italy on October 29, 1922, when Mussolini became prime minister. The cry at the base of the poster, *A Noi! (To Us)*, is a succinct way of praising the Fascist movement and at the same time saying, "Italy first." "To us" means that now Italy is for Italian Fascists and that people other than "us" come second.

When we examine this poster we see an idealized portrait of a woman whose expression not only is determined but tells us that she has a purpose in life, a sense of destiny. Most propaganda posters in the period before World War II (and during it) concentrated on the government's having preached to the people again and again that they were not ordinary folks, but folks who participated in a national destiny aimed at making them great. In this poster the allusions to the Roman empire blatantly declare a rebirth of Roman power.

Nazi Germany flooded Europe with posters of heroic SS men and saluting soldiers praising Hitler, all in realistic detail. The same was true in China during the rule of Mao Tse-Tung. Even today, huge posters of Mao stand in public places. Abstract art was condemned in Nazi Germany as decadent because it could not be turned into good propaganda for the system. The problem with propaganda art is not that it is realistic but that it is limited. Its message is primarily political, not primarily artistic.

In the case of *A Noi!* we see a realistic portrayal with dramatic swirling colors. The technique of the artist is remarkable and we would expect the result to have been effective in shaping the opinion of those who viewed it in its original setting. That is partly because the artist, Anselmo Ballester (1897–1974), was the most famous designer of posters for hundreds of films shown in Italy from the period of the silent film to the great era of the 1930s and 1940s. His gift was interpreting the drama of films in a visual form. He does the same for the Fascist movement in Italy.

1. At first glance, would you recognize Ballester's poster as propaganda art? Would a viewer need to be Italian to recognize this poster as propaganda? Is the poster any less propagandistic now than it was in the 1930s?
2. What propaganda art have you seen? Which government produced it? How effective is it?
3. Some propaganda artifacts are not so easily dismissed. Try to see either *Triumph of the Will* (1936) or *Olympia* (1938), by Leni Riefenstahl (1902–2003), a popular actress and film director who worked for Hitler. The camera work is extraordinarily imaginative. These films glorify Nazism. Can these films be considered art?
4. Compare Ballester's poster with Peter Blume's painting *The Eternal City* (see Figure 1-3), which was not designed to be propaganda but nevertheless presents an anti-Fascist message of a monstrous Mussolini and his Blackshirts beating people. In what ways are Blume's artistic choices much different than Ballester's? Are there any similarities?

FIGURE 14-7
Anselmo Ballester, *To Us!*, Italian Fascist propaganda poster (ca. 1930), lithograph, 55 × 78.5 inches.

©DeAgostini/Getty Images

FOCUS ON **Kitsch**

Kitsch refers to works that realistically depict easily identifiable objects and events in a pretentiously vulgar, awkward, sentimental, and often obscene manner. Kitsch triggers disgust at worst and stock emotions at best, trivializing rather than enriching our understanding of the subject matter. The crafting of kitsch is sometimes striking, but kitsch is the epitome of bad taste.

Of course, it is also true that kitsch is a matter of taste. There is no adequate definition of kitsch other than to cite the critic Clement Greenberg, who called kitsch vulgar and popular with great mass appeal. He might have been thinking of the paintings, sometimes on velvet, of girls with huge pitying eyes, of performances of Elvis Presley imitators, and cheap reproductions of paintings in the form of souvenir key chains and

continued

mouse pads. But he was also thinking about the work of painters such as William-Adolphe Bouguereau (1825–1905), whose technique and craftsmanship are impeccable but whose paintings are to some extent empty yet very appealing.

Bouguereau is often cited as producing kitsch, which means paintings that appeal to the masses in part because they are easy to respond to and their skill in presentation implies that they must be important. They are completely without irony because they obviously expect to be taken seriously. They are designed to awaken in the viewer a sense of sweetness, pity, and sentimentality. Critics describe kitsch as pretentious, demanding from the viewer responses that the work itself really does not earn. Kitsch is work that says, "I am very impressive, so I must be very important." In looking at Bouguereau's *Cupid and Psyche* (Figure 14-8), what response do you feel it asks you to give to it? What is its importance?

Yet, no matter what one might say about *Cupid and Psyche* as an example of bad taste, there is a wide audience that finds it quite delightful. Who can resist the cherubic pair and their childlike affection for each other? Who can say that there might not be room for such appreciation, even if the painting does not have the same kind of aesthetic value as, say, Manet's *A Bar at the Folies-Bergère* (see Figure 4-16)?

Jeff Koons's sculpture *Michael Jackson and Bubbles* (Figure 14-9) portrays a garishly dressed Michael Jackson with his chimpanzee Bubbles. This sculpture, which was produced in an edition of three in a workshop in Germany, has been described as "tacky" kitsch primarily because it seems to be in such bad taste. Yet, one of the copies sold for more than $5 million, and the other two are in museums in San Francisco and Los Angeles.

FIGURE 14-8
William-Adolphe Bouguereau, *Cupid and Psyche as Children*. 1890. Oil on Canvas, 27⅞ × 47 inches. Private Collection.

©Christie's Images/Bridgeman Images

FIGURE 14-9
Jeff Koons (b. 1955), *Michael Jackson and Bubbles*. 1988. Porcelain, 42 × 70½ × 32½ inches (106.7 × 179.1 × 82.6 cm). San Francisco Museum of Modern Art. Purchased through the Marian and Bernard Messenger Fund and restricted funds.

©Jeff Koons

Koons presented sculptures of vacuum cleaners, basketballs, inflatable toys, and other everyday items with such seriousness as to attempt to convince his audience that they were high art. Late in his career he even made essentially pornographic representations of himself and his wife, a former porn star. In the case of Bouguereau, there may have been no conscious intention to produce kitsch, but Koons certainly knew the traditions of kitsch and seems to have been intentionally producing it with a sense of irony and awareness. He seems to have been challenging his audience to appreciate the work not as kitsch, but because it is kitsch and that the audience knows it is kitsch. Bouguereau's audience, by contrast, would appreciate his work without an awareness that it is considered kitsch by respected art critics.

What all this demonstrates is that kitsch is a complex issue in art. Because it is essentially a description that relies on a theory of taste, we must keep in mind that taste is highly individual. Yet, we must also recognize that one develops a taste in the arts by studying them and expanding one's experience of the arts. A person with a wide experience of music or painting will develop a different sense of taste than a person who has only a meager experience.

Kitsch has been around for centuries, especially since the 1700s, but now it seems to have invaded every aspect of our society. Bad taste greets us everywhere—tasteless advertisements, silly sitcoms and soap operas, vile music, superficial novels, pornographic images, and on and on. Where, except in virgin nature, is kitsch completely absent? According to Milan Kundera, "The brotherhood of man on earth will be possible only on the base of kitsch." Jacques Sternberg says, "It's long ago taken over the world. If Martians were to take a look at the world they might rename it kitsch." Are these overstatements? As you think about this, take a hard look at the world around you.

PERCEPTION KEY Kitsch

1. Do you agree that there is something such as good taste and bad taste in the arts? What are the problems in making any judgment about someone's taste? Are you aware of your own taste in the arts? Is it changing, or is it static?
2. Why might it be reasonable to describe a person who calls Bouguereau's painting kitsch as an art snob?
3. What is the form-content of Bouguereau's painting? What is the form-content of Koons's sculpture? To what extent does either work reveal important values?
4. What does it mean to say that either of these works is ironic? Does irony elevate their value as a work of art? Is either of these, in your estimation, a true work of art?

DECORATION

The instinct to decorate objects seems to have begun very early. We know of few cultures that do not decorate their tools, their garments, their weapons, and sometimes themselves. The impulse seems to derive from a desire to have something beautiful to sustain their attention. The concept of beauty is not discussed in art circles today as it was even a hundred years ago. For our discussion of the arts, beauty is implied, but as we aim for insight and revelatory values in art, we can see that beauty is only one quality of significant art. Much modern art, such as Duane Hansen's life-size figures, tends to ignore the idea of beauty. ***Decoration*** seems to be a universal need.

Decorated objects are often very beautiful, but they do not necessarily inform us of anything deeper than the fact that beauty is a human requirement, especially of developed cultures, producing pleasure. From the Egyptians, to the Greeks, Christians, and Muslims, the urge to decorate religious places, objects, and garments is universal.

Among the most astounding examples of decoration are the illuminated pages of the Book of Kells, a manuscript book containing the four gospels of the New Testament. With almost 300 folio pages of script and illumination, this book is one of the great treasures of the Trinity College Library in Dublin, Ireland. It was created by monks in Ireland in the late eighth or early ninth century and apparently buried for safekeeping during a Viking raid. Each illuminated page, such as the Chi-Rho page (Figure 14-10) took sometimes more than a year to complete. The level of detail on this page is such that strong magnification is needed to see all the animals, people, vegetation, and trees that cover almost every surface. The Greek letters Chi-Rho

FIGURE 14-10
The Chi-Rho page from the Book of Kells (ca. 800 CE), Trinity College, Dublin.

©PHAS/Universal Images Group/
Rex/Shutterstock

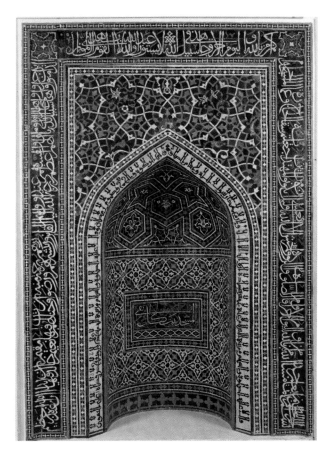

FIGURE 14-11
Mihrab (1354–1355), Iran, Isfahan.
Mosaic of polychrome-glazed cut tiles
on stonepaste body; set into mortar,
1,135⅙ × 113¹¹⁄₁₆ inches.

Source: Metropolitan Museum of Art, Harris
Brisbane Dick Fund, 1939

are the first two letters in Christ's name, and the page is illuminated not just to be beautiful but to be a form of appreciation to the idea of God. Anything less detailed might be an insufficient form of worship.

Because Islamic practice generally rules out art that represents animals or people, the decorative arts in Islam are dominant. As in the instance of the great Alhambra in Granada, Spain, buildings are often decorated lavishly with tiles, including writing that echoes the Quran or the sayings of Mohammed in the Kadith (a book of his observations). Beautiful temple lamps, vases, wall hangings, rugs, furniture, garments, and everyday kitchen materials offer extraordinary examples of the Islamic impulse to create art. The fourteenth-century Mihrab from the Madrasa of Imami (Figure 14-11) is described as a prayer nook. It usually forms part of a wall facing Mecca in a mosque, but this example is from a school in Iran. The structure is faced with tiles that contain writing. The text across the top of the doorway is "Said [the Prophet] (on him be blessing and peace): . . . witness that there is no God save Allah and that Muhammad is his Apostle and the Blessed Imam, and in legal almsgiving, and in the pilgrimage, and in the fast of Ramadan, and he said, on him be blessing and peace" [Met Museum]. The function of the decoration is to venerate God while at the same time pleasing the worshipers in the mosque.

The mid- and late nineteenth century in England produced a wide range of artful decoration when William Morris (1834–1896), poet, painter, designer, and proprietor of the Kelmscott Press, gave a major lecture called "The Decorative Arts." Morris was close friends with Dante Gabriel Rossetti and most of the other Pre-Raphaelite Brotherhood of painters and writers. Morris began to create tapestries, rugs, and wallpaper with distinctive designs usually based on natural forms of trees, flowers, birds, and other animals. His influences were distinctly medieval, with a strong interest in Arthurian legend. While not as intensely detailed as the Chi-Rho page, his works covered every space and featured remarkably vivid colors. His wallpapers were much sought after. One of his most revered designs, Jasmine (Figure 14-12), features floral images in a pattern that is more exploratory than simply repetitive, yet it is a distinctive image, subtle, warming, with a constant suggestion of nature.

A more modern form of decorative arts is often unwanted and uncelebrated because it is produced anonymously in public spaces, yet a few graffiti artists have become recognized in the last twenty-five years. Keith Haring, Robert McGee, and Jean-Michel Basquiat are the best known because they moved their work into galleries where it could be bought. But most graffiti artists work anonymously and scorn the official art world (Figure 14-13). Their mission is to leave a mark, much like

FIGURE 14-12
William Morris, Jasmine, 1872.
Block-printed wallpaper, 21 7/16 ×
22 1/2 inches.

Source: The Metropolitan Museum of Art.
Purchase, Edward C. Moore Jr. Gift, 1923.
Accession Number 23.163.4j

FIGURE 14-13
**Anonymous, wall graffiti, circa 2009.
London, South Bank.** The South Bank
Arts Center on the Thames River
preserves a space for graffiti artists.
This segment of a heavily painted
wall is typical of the mix of lettering,
forms, and color of the South Bank
graffiti.

©Lee A. Jacobus

some of the paintings in the caves in France and the markings found on stone walls
in the American Southwest. The urge of such artists is satisfied by making a statement, even if some of the time the statement involves defacing important buildings
or illegally painting subway cars, train cars, and commercial trucks. Currently, mobile electronic devices, such as tablets and phones, have apps that permit them to
make graffiti wallpaper and graffiti designs, demonstrating the public interest in
this form of expression.

PERCEPTION KEY Decoration

1. Is the Chi-Rho page in the Book of Kells a work of art? If so, describe your participation with it and your understanding of its form-content.
2. What do you see as the relationship between William Morris's wallpaper, Jasmine,
   and abstract art? Is Jasmine abstract?
3. What do you see as the relationship between decorative arts and beauty? Which
   paintings in this book are most beautiful in your opinion? Are they related to decorative arts?
4. Do you consider the graffiti to be a work of art? If so, what should be its title?
5. Should the Mihrab be considered architecture or sculpture? Describe the sources
   of artistic pleasure it is designed to produce.
6. What are the revelatory qualities of any of these pieces? What values do you understand better for your participation with these works?
7. What does the fact that you can download graffiti to use as wallpaper on your computer tell you about its decorative values?

IDEA ART

Idea art began with the Dadaists around 1916. Although never dominant, idea art has survived by spawning "isms"— *Duchampism*, Conceptualism, Lettrism, New Dadaism, to name just a few—with little consensus about an umbrella name that indicates a common denominator. Idea art raises questions about the presuppositions of traditional art and the art establishment—that is, the traditional artists, critics, philosophers of art, historians, museum keepers, textbook writers, and everyone involved with the understanding, preservation, restoration, selling, and buying of traditional art. Sometimes this questioning is hostile, as with the Dadaists. Sometimes it is humorous, as with Marcel Duchamp. And sometimes it is more of an intellectual game, as with many of the conceptual artists. We will limit our discussion to these three species.

Dada

The infantile sound of "dada," chosen for its meaninglessness, became the battle cry of a group of disenchanted young artists who fled their countries during World War I and met, mainly by chance, in Zurich, Switzerland, in 1916. Led by the poet Hugo Ball, they assembled at the Cabaret Voltaire. In their view, humanity had forsaken reason—utterly. The mission of *Dadaism* was to shock a crazed world with expressions of outrageous nonsense, negating every traditional value.

During those years the Dadaists for the most part tried to make works that were not art, at least in the traditional sense, for such art was part of civilization. They usually succeeded, but sometimes they made art in spite of themselves. The influence of the Dadaists on succeeding styles—such as surrealist, abstract, environmental, Pop, performance, body, shock, outsider, and conceptual art—has been enormous. Picabia announced:

> Dada itself wants nothing, nothing, nothing, it's doing something so that the public can say: "We understand nothing, nothing, nothing." The Dadaists are nothing, nothing, nothing—certainly they will come to nothing, nothing, nothing.
> Francis Picabia
> Who knows nothing, nothing, nothing.

But there is a dilemma: To express nothing is something. Picabia dropped ink on paper, and the resulting form is mainly one of chance, one of the earliest examples of a technique later to be exploited by artists such as Jackson Pollock. Picabia's inkdrops all had important titles, such as *The Blessed Virgin*, but they were visually indecipherble.

Idea art does not mix or embody its ideas in the medium. Rather, the medium is used to suggest ideas. Medium and ideas are experienced as separate. In turn, idea art tends increasingly to depend on language for its communication. And in recent years, idea art has even generated a species called Lettrism, or word art—see, for example, *Keith Arnatt Is an Artist* (Figure 14-14).

KEITH ARNATT IS AN ARTIST

FIGURE 14-14
Keith Arnatt, *Keith Arnatt Is an Artist*.
1972. Wall inscription exhibited in
1972 at the Tate Gallery in London.
Letters on a wall constitute the
entire work of art, including the
ideas behind the words.

©2017 Artists Rights Society (ARS),
New York/DACS, London. Photo: ©Tate,
London 2017

> ## PERCEPTION KEY Keith Arnatt
>
> 1. Why would the curators of the highly respected Tate Gallery in London include such a work, especially one that requires such a large space?

Duchamp and His Legacy

Dada, the earliest species of idea art, is characterized by its anger at our so-called civilization. Although Duchamp cooperated with the Dadaists, his work and the work of those who followed his style (a widespread influence) are more anti-art and anti-establishment than anti-civilization. Duchamp's work is usually characterized by humor.

> ## PERCEPTION KEY *L.H.O.O.Q.*
>
> 1. Is *L.H.O.O.Q.* (Figure 14-15) an example of idea art?
> 2. Is *L.H.O.O.Q.* a work of art?

L.H.O.O.Q. is hardly anti-civilization, but it is surely anti-art and anti-establishment, funny rather than angry. It is a hilarious comment on the tendency to glorify certain works beyond their artistic value. To desecrate one of the most famous paintings of the Western world was surely a great idea if you wanted to taunt the art establishment. And ideas gather. Sexual ambiguity, part of both Leonardo's and

FIGURE 14-15
Marcel Duchamp, *L.H.O.O.Q.* **1919.**
Drawing, 7¾ × 4⅛ inches. Private
collection. In several different
ways, Duchamp commits an act
of desecration of the *Mona Lisa*,
perhaps the most famous painting
in the West.

©Association Marcel Duchamp/ADAGP,
Paris/Artists Rights Society (ARS), New
York 2017. Photo: ©Cameraphoto Arte,
Venice/Art Resource, NY

Duchamp's legends, is evident in Leonardo's *Mona Lisa* (see Figure 1-5). By penciling in a mustache and beard, Duchamp accents the masculine. By adding the title, he accents the feminine. *L.H.O.O.Q.* is an obscene pun, reading phonetically in French, "Elle a chaud au cul" ("She has a hot ass").

Conceptual Art

Conceptual art became a movement in the 1960s, led by Sol LeWitt, Jenny Holzer, Carl Andre, Christo, Robert Morris, Walter De Maria, Keith Arnatt, Terry Atkinson, Michael Baldwin, David Bainbridge, and Joseph Kosuth. There was a strategy behind the movement: Bring the audience into direct contact with the creative concepts of the artist. LeWitt claimed that "a work of art may be understood as a conductor from the artist's mind to the viewer's," and the less material used the better. The world is so overloaded with traditional art that most museums stash the bulk of their collections in storage bins. Now if we can get along without the material object, then the spaces of museums will not be jammed with this new art, and it will need no conservation, restoration, or any of the other expensive paraphernalia necessitated by the material work of art. Conceptual art floats free from material limitations; can occur anywhere, like a poem; and often costs practically nothing.

FIGURE 14-16
Christo and Jeanne-Claude, *Wrapped Reichstag*. 1971–1995, Berlin.

©Regis Bossu/Sygma/Getty Images

In recent years LeWitt modified his early Conceptualism. In an exhibition in 2001 involving a whole floor of the Whitney Museum in New York City, a vast array of color fields, mainly within large geometrical shapes, blazed out from the walls. LeWitt provided exact detailed blueprints to guide a dozen or so crafts-people. LeWitt did none of the work and very little supervising. He provided the ideas—the rest could be done by anyone with a little skill. The creativity is in the conceptual process that produced the blueprints. The crafting is completely secondary.

Christo and Jeanne-Claude have produced huge public projects such as *Wrapped Reichstag* (Figure 14-16), in which they wrapped a sprawling government building in Berlin. They have financed their projects directly through the sale of drawings, collages, and scale models of their work. When they erected *Running Fence* in Sonoma and Marin Counties in Northern California in 1975, they constructed an eighteen-foot-high canvas fence that stretched for 24.5 miles across the prop-erties of forty-nine farmers, all of whom gave permission for the project. After fourteen days, it was dismantled. The farmers kept the materials on their land if they wanted them. The effect was striking, as can be seen from a YouTube video discussing the project in which those who worked on it report on their memories. *Wrapped Reichstag,* a much later project than *Running Fence,* made Berlin a desti-nation for international art lovers because such a complete transformation of a major building such as this was a surprise. The mystery of the project was part of its appeal.

Christo has said of other projects that the wrapped object itself is not necessarily the art object, but that the entire environment in which the object appears is essen-tial to the aesthetic experience. In this sense, projects of this sort are conceptual. They are impermanent, lasting only a matter of days, and they are based on ideas.

CONCEPTION KEY Conceptual Art

1. Some conceptual artists assert that their work raises, for the first time, truly basic questions about the nature of art. Do you agree?
2. Is idea art, in general, art or artlike? More specifically, in general, is Dada art or artlike? Duchampism? Conceptual art?

PERFORMANCE ART

Unlike conceptual art, *performance art* (as distinct from the traditional performing arts) brings back physicality, stressing material things as much as or more than it does concepts. There are innumerable kinds of performances, but generally they tend to be site-specific, the site being either constructed or simply found. There rarely is a stage in the traditional style. But performances, as the name suggests, are related to drama. They clearly differ, however, especially from traditional drama, because usually there is no logical or sustained narrative, and perhaps no narrative at all. Sometimes there is an effort to allow for the expression of the subconscious, as in Surrealism. Sometimes provocative anti-establishment social and political views are expressed. Generally, however, performances are about the values of the disinherited, the outsiders.

Chance is an essential element of the form, which is to say the form is open. The factor of chance may weaken the crafting, for crafting is ordering, and chance is likely to be disordering in a performance situation. Interaction between artist and audience is often encouraged. According to the performance artist Barbara Smith, "I turn to question the audience to see if their experiences might enlighten mine and break the isolation of my experience, to see if my Performance puts them into the same dilemma." The performance is an open event, full of suggestive potentialities rather than a self-contained whole, determined and final.

Visual effects are usually strongly emphasized in a performance, often involving expressive movements of the body, bringing performance close to dance. In early performances, language was generally limited. In recent performances, however, language has often come to the fore. Thus, Taylor Woodrow, a British performer, and two collaborators covered themselves with spray paint, attached themselves to separate painted canvases by means of harnesses, stood there for about six hours, and talked with the curious.

Karen Finley (Figure 14-17) became famous for a performance work called *We Keep Our Victims Ready*, a piece that anatomized aspects of American society in 1990, when the feminist movement was strong and when many efforts were being made to censor artists whose work was critical of American culture. Typical of many performance pieces, Finley used nudity, profanity, and an alarming attack on heterosexual white males, who, in her view, controlled society. In one section of her piece, she stripped to her panties and smeared chocolate over her body in an effort to represent what she felt was a woman's battered self-image resulting in a sense of disgust at her own body. It was no surprise that she was one of four performance artists whose work was denied support from the National Endowment for the Arts despite huge audiences and what became a national tour of her work.

FIGURE 14-17
Karen Finley, a performance
artist, uses her own body to make
statements, often covering herself
with various food products or other
substances, such as feathers.

©Rick Mackler/Zumapress/Newscom

Ordinarily performance art does not repeat itself, nor does it produce a tour. But the resultant uproar from the powerful politicians in the community essentially guaranteed a widespread audience for Finley and has led to continued success. Like all performance art, *We Keep Our Victims Ready* was designed to be memorable and sometimes shocking. Because there are no rules for performance art and usually no way to buy it, the experience is what counts; and whether it is art may depend on whether you agree with the performer, who says it is art. For us, ultimately, the question is whether the experience informs through its form.

PERCEPTION KEY Performance Art

1. Does the fact that there are no rules to performance art affect our view of whether we can legitimately consider it art? One critic says that performance art is art because the performer says so. How valid is that argument?
2. If you were to strip down and cover yourself with chocolate, would you then be an artist?
3. William Pope.L, wearing only shorts and shoes, chained himself for six hours to an ATM in protest against capitalism, conversing with passersby all the while. Under what conditions might that constitute performance art?
4. Were you to attempt performance art, what would your strategies be? What would you do as a performer? Would it be obvious that your performance was art?

VIRTUAL ART

Virtual art is based on computer technology, often producing a mixture of the imaginary and the real. For example, imagine a world in which sculptures act in unpredictable ways: taking on different shapes and colors, stiffening or dancing, talking back or ignoring you, or maybe just dissolving. At a very sophisticated computer laboratory at Boston University, a team of artists and computer craftspeople have created a fascinating installation called *Spiritual Ruins*. One dons a pair of 3-D goggles and grabs a wand. On a large screen, a computer projects a vast three-dimensional space into which we appear to be plunged. Sensors pick up and react to the speed and angle of the wand. With this magical instrument, we swoop and soar like a bird over an imaginary, or virtual, park of sculpture. We are in the scene, part of the work. We have little idea of what the wand will discover next. We may feel anxiety and confrontation, recalling bumping into hostile strangers in the streets. Or the happenings may be peaceful, even pastoral. Embedded microchips may play sculptures like musical instruments. Or sometimes the space around a sculpture may resound with the sounds of nature. Exact repetition never seems to occur. Obviously we are in an imaginary world, and yet because of our activity it also seems real. Our participation is highly playful.

The most popular form of virtual art is video games, which are played by hundreds of millions of people around the world. Video games have a reasonable claim to being today's most popular form of entertainment. Books have been written about video art, and the Smithsonian's American Art Museum hosted an exhibition beginning in March 2012 called The Art of Video Games, which lasted almost seven months. In 2013 the Museum of Modern Art announced that it is collecting video games, acquiring forty titles such as *Pac-Man*, *Tetris*, *Myst*, *SimCity*, and *Minecraft*. The museum's curators agree that video games are art, but they also insist that they are valued for their design. Many of the games involve elaborate fantasy-world art, such as *Oddworld: Stranger's Wrath*; *Shin Megami Tensei: Digital Devil Saga*; and *Elder Scrolls IV: Oblivion*. While the earliest games needed no narrative, many modern games have attracted film writers and novelists to supply the narratives and characters used in games such as *Fatal Frame II: Crimson Butterfly*; *Alone in the Dark: The New Nightmare*; and the *Legend of Zelda*.

Violent or antisocial games, such as *Halo 4* and *Call of Duty: Black Ops II* (Figure 14-18), as well as *Brothers in Arms* and the several *Grand Theft Auto* games, have created a fear that they contribute to antisocial behavior in some players. Defenders of these games point to developing quick wits, quick reactions, and judgment under pressure as being advantageous. Very few defenders or attackers comment on the artistic qualities of the virtual landscapes, realistic characters, or colorful interiors.

PERCEPTION KEY Video Games

1. If you feel video games are a form of art, how would you defend them against those who feel they are merely artlike?
2. Which video game of those you are familiar with has the best video art? What distinguishes it from inferior games?

FIGURE 14-18
Call of Duty: Black Ops II. 2012. Video
game, Activision.

Source: Activision Blizzard

3. How legitimate is it to compare narrative video games with narrative cinema production? How does the use of violence in cinema compare with the use of violence
   in video games?
4. Many people praise a work of art for its realism. Is video game art better when it
   is realistic? Or is realism a nonessential criterion for video game art? What are the
   essential qualities that made video game art satisfying to you?
5. Comment on the artistic values of *Call of Duty: Black Ops II*.

SUMMARY

Artlike works share many basic features with art, unlike works of non-art. But the
artlike lacks a revealed subject matter, a content that brings fresh meaning into our
lives. The artlike can be attention-holding, as with illustration; or fitting, as with
decoration; or beautiful, as with craftwork; or thought-provoking, as with idea art;
or attention-grabbing, as with performance art; or fantasy-absorbing, as with virtual
art. Art may have these features also, but what "works" fundamentally in a work
of art is revelation. Because it lacks revelatory power, the artlike generally does not
lend itself to sustained participation (see Chapter 2). Yet what sustains participation
varies from person to person. Dogmatic judgments about what is art and what is
artlike are counterproductive. We hope that our approach provides a stimulus for
open-minded but guided discussions.

Chapter 15

THE INTERRELATIONSHIPS OF THE ARTS

Close ties among the arts occur because artists share a special purpose: the revelation of values. Furthermore, every artist must use some medium, some kind of "stuff" that can be formed to communicate that revelation (content) about something (subject matter). All artists share some elements of media, and this sharing encourages their interaction. For example, painters, sculptors, and architects use color, line, and texture. Sculptors and architects work with the density of materials. Rhythm is basic to the composer, choreographer, and poet. Words are elemental for the poet, novelist, dramatist, and composer of songs and operas. Images are basic to the painter, filmmaker, videographer, and photographer. Artists constitute a commonwealth—they share the same end and similar means.

APPROPRIATION

Artistic *appropriation* occurs when (1) artists combine their basic medium with the medium of another art or arts but (2) keep their basic medium clearly dominant. For example, music is the basic medium for composers of opera. The staging may include architecture, painting, and sculpture. The language of the drama may include poetry. The dance, so dependent on music, is often incorporated in opera, and sometimes in contemporary opera so are photography and even film. Yet music almost always dominates in opera. We may listen to Beethoven's *Fidelio* or Bizet's

Carmen time after time, yet it is hard to imagine anyone reading the *librettos* over and over again. Although essential to opera, the drama, along with the staging, rarely dominates the music. Often the librettos by themselves are downright silly. Nevertheless, drama and the other appropriated arts generally enhance the feelings interpreted by the music.

PERCEPTION KEY Opera

Attend an opera or watch a video of an opera by Puccini, perhaps *La Bohème*.

1. Read the libretto. Is it interesting enough to achieve participation, as with a good poem or novel? Would you want to read it again?
2. Have you experienced any opera in which the drama dominates the music? Wagner claimed that in *The Ring* he wedded music and drama (as well as other arts) so closely that neither dominates the *Gesamtkunstwerk* (complete artwork). Read the libretto of one of the four operas that constitute *The Ring*, and then go to or listen to the opera. Do you agree with Wagner's claim?
3. Go to Verdi's *Otello*, one of his last operas, or watch a video. Shakespeare's drama is of the highest order, although much of it is lost, not only in the very condensed libretto but also in the translation into Italian. Does either the music or the drama dominate? Or is there a synthesis?

Except for opera, architecture is the art that appropriates the most. Its centering of space makes room for the placement of sculpture, painting, and photography; the reading of poetry; and the performance of drama, music, and dance. The sheer size of architecture tends to make it prevail over any of the incorporated arts, the container prevailing over the contents.

PERCEPTION KEY Architecture

1. Visit a church, synagogue, or mosque near you. What other arts are "included" in the structure? Are the arts decorations or works of sculpture, painting, or music? How appropriate are those works to the function and appearance of the building?
2. Do you know of any works of architecture that are completely free of the other arts and would seem to resist the incorporation of the other arts? Any buildings that are pure, so to speak?

INTERPRETATION

When a work of art takes another work of art as its subject matter, the former is an *interpretation* of the latter. Thus, Zeffirelli's film *Romeo and Juliet* takes Shakespeare's drama for its subject matter. The film interprets the play. It is fascinating to observe how the contents—the meanings—differ because of the different media. We will analyze a few interesting examples. Bring to mind other examples as you read the text.

Film Interprets Literature: Howards End

E. M. Forster's novel *Howards End* (1910) was made into a remarkable film in 1992 (Figures 15-1 and 15-2) by producer Ismail Merchant and director James Ivory. Ruth Prawer Jhabvala wrote the screenplay. The film stars Anthony Hopkins and Emma Thompson, who, along with Jhabvala, won an Academy Award. The film was nominated as best picture, and its third Academy Award went to the design direction of Luciana Arrighi and Ian Whittaker.

The team of Merchant-Ivory, producer and director, has become distinguished for period films set in the late nineteenth century and early twentieth century. Part of the reputation won by Merchant-Ivory films is due to their detailed designs. Thus, in a Merchant-Ivory film one expects to see Edwardian costumes meticulously reproduced, period interiors with prints and paintings, authentic architecture, both interior and exterior, and details sumptuously photographed so that the colors are rich and saturated and the atmosphere appropriately reflecting the era just before and after 1900.

All of that is true of the production of *Howards End*. But the subtlety of the interplay of the arts in the film is intensified because of the subtlety of the interplay of the arts in the novel. Forster wrote his novel in a way that emulates contemporary drama, at least in part. His scenes are dramatically conceived, with characters acting in carefully described settings, speaking in ways that suggest the stage. Moreover, Forster's special interest in music and the role culture in general plays in the lives of his characters makes the novel especially challenging for interpretation by moving images.

The film follows Forster's story faithfully. Three families at the center of the story stand in contrast: the Schlegel sisters, Margaret and Helen; a rich businessman, Henry Wilcox, his frail wife, Ruth, and their superficial, conventional children; and a poor, young, unhappily married bank clerk, Leonard Bast, whom the Schlegel

FIGURE 15-1

Anthony Hopkins and Emma Thompson in *Howards End*. Henry Wilcox (Hopkins) and Margaret Schlegel (Thompson), now married, react to bad news.

Source: Sony Pictures Classics

FIGURE 15-2
**Emma Thompson and Helena
Bonham Carter in *Howards End*.**
Margaret Schlegel (Thompson) tries
to understand her sister Helen's
(Bonham Carter) motives in helping
Leonard Bast.

sisters befriend. Margaret and Helen are idealistic and cultured. The Wilcoxes, except for Ruth, are uncultured snobs. When Ruth dies, Henry proposes to and is accepted by Margaret. Her sister, Helen, who detests Henry, is devastated by this marriage and turns to Leonard Bast. The story becomes a tangle of opposites and, because of the stupidity of Henry's son Charles, turns tragic. In the end, thanks to the moral strength of Margaret, reconciliation becomes possible.

Read the novel first, and then see the film. In one scene early in the novel, some of the protagonists are in Queen's Hall in London listening to Beethoven's Fifth Symphony. Here is Forster's wonderful description:

> It will be generally admitted that Beethoven's Fifth Symphony is the most sublime noise that has ever penetrated into the ear of man. All sorts and conditions are satisfied by it. Whether you are like Mrs. Munt, and tap surreptitiously when the tunes come—of course, not so as to disturb the others; or like Helen, who can see heroes and shipwrecks in the music's flood; or like Margaret, who can only see the music; or like Tibby, who is profoundly versed in counterpoint, and holds the full score open on his knee; or like their cousin, Fräulein Mosebach, who remembers all the time that Beethoven is "echt Deutsch" [pure German]; or like Fräulein Mosebach's young man, who can remember nothing but Fräulein Mosebach: in any case, the passion of your life becomes more vivid, and you are bound to admit that such a noise is cheap at two shillings.

Now that is a passage surely worth recording. But how could you get it into a film unless by a "voiceover," an awkward technique in this context? Observe how this scene is portrayed in the film. Also observe in the film the awkward drawn-out scenes of Leonard Bast pursuing Helen in the rain (she inadvertently had taken his umbrella when leaving the concert hall). One keeps wondering why the soaking Leonard does not simply run and catch up with Helen. In the novel, these events are much more smoothly handled. In such portrayals, written language has the advantage.

Conversely, the film captures something in 1992 that the novel could not have achieved in its own time—the sense of loss for an elegant way of life in the period before World War I. The moving images create nostalgia for a past totally unrecoverable. Nostalgia for that past is, of course, also created by Forster's fine prose, but not with the power of moving images. Coming back to the novel after its interpretation by the film surely makes our participation more complete.

PERCEPTION KEY *Howards End*

1. Do the filmic presentations of Margaret Schlegel and Henry Wilcox "ring true" to Forster's characterizations? If not, what are the deficiencies?
2. Is the background music effective?
3. What kind or kinds of cinematic cuts are used in the film: jump cuts? Continuity cuts? Fades? How effective are the cuts?
4. In which work, the novel or the film, are the social issues of greater importance? Which puts more stress on the class distinctions between the Basts and both the Schlegels and the Wilcoxes? Which seems to have a stronger social message?
5. How does the film—by supplying the images your imagination can only invent in reading the novel—affect your understanding of the lives of the Schlegels, Wilcoxes, and Basts?
6. Is it better to see the film first or to read the novel first? What informs your decision?

Music Interprets Drama: The Marriage of Figaro

Perhaps in the age of Wolfgang Amadeus Mozart (1756–1791), the opera performed a function for literature somewhat equivalent to what the film does today. Opera—in combining music, drama, sets, and sometimes dance—was held in highest esteem in Europe in the eighteenth century. And despite the increasing competition from film and musical comedy, opera is still performed to large audiences in theaters and larger audiences on television. Among the world's greatest operas, few are more popular than Mozart's *The Marriage of Figaro* (1786), written when Mozart was only thirty.

Mozart's opera interprets the French play *The Marriage of Figaro* (1784), by Pierre Augustin de Beaumarchais, a highly successful playwright friendly with Madame Pompadour, mistress of Louis XVI at the time of the American Revolution. Beaumarchais began as an ordinary citizen, bought his way into the aristocracy, survived the French Revolution, went into exile, and later died in France. His plays were the product of, yet comically critical of, the aristocracy. *The Marriage of Figaro*, written in 1780, was held back by censors as an attack on the government. Eventually produced to great acclaim, it was seditious enough for later commentators to claim that it was an essential ingredient in fomenting the French Revolution of 1789.

Mozart, with Lorenzo Da Ponte, who wrote the libretto, remained generally faithful to the play, although changing some names and the occupations of some characters. They reduced the opera from Beaumarchais's five acts to four, although the entire opera is three hours long.

In brief, it is the story of Figaro, servant to Count Almaviva, and his intention of marrying the countess's maid Susanna. The count has given up the feudal tradition, which would have permitted him to sleep with Susanna first, before her husband. However, he regrets his decision because he has fallen in love with Susanna and now tries to seduce her. When his wife, the countess, young and still in love with him, discovers his plans, she throws in with Figaro and Susanna to thwart him. Cherubino, a very young man—sung by a female soprano—feels the first stirrings of love and desires both the countess and Susanna in turn. He is a page in the count's employ, and when his intentions are discovered, he is sent into the army. One of the greatest *arias* in the opera is "Non più andrai" ("From now on, no more gallivanting"), which Figaro sings to Cherubino, telling him that his amorous escapades are now over. The nine-page aria is derived from part of a single speech of Beaumarchais's Figaro:

> No more hanging around all day with the girls, no more cream buns and custard tarts, no more charades and blind-man's-bluff; just good soldiers, by God: weatherbeaten and ragged-assed, weighed down with their muskets, right face, left face, forward march.[1]

Mozart's treatment of the speech demonstrates one of the resources of opera as opposed to straight drama. In the drama, it would be very difficult to expand Figaro's speech to intensify its emotional content, but in the opera the speech or parts of it can be repeated frequently and with pleasure, since the music that underpins the words is delightful to hear and rehear. Mozart's opera changes the emotional content of the play because it intensifies feelings associated with key moments in the action.

The aria contains a very simple musical figure that has nonetheless great power in the listening. Just as Mozart is able to repeat parts of the dialogue, he is able to repeat notes, passages, and patterns. The pattern repeated most conspicuously is that of the arpeggio, a chord whose notes are played in quick succession instead of simultaneously. The passage of three chords in the key of C expresses a lifting feeling of exuberance (Figure 15-3). Mozart's genius was marked by a way of finding the simplest, yet most unexpected, solutions to musical problems. The arpeggio is practiced by almost every student of a musical instrument, yet it is thought of as something appropriate to practice rather than performance. Thus, Mozart's usage comes as a surprise.

del - le bel - le tur-ban-do il ri - po - so,
Such di - ver - sions are done with and o - ver,

The essence of the arpeggio in the eighteenth century was constant repetition, and in using that pattern, Mozart finds yet another way to repeat elements to

FIGURE 15-3
An arpeggio from "Non più andrai" ("From now on, no more gallivanting"), from the end of act 1 of *The Marriage of Figaro*. Figaro sings a farewell aria to Cherubino, who has been sent to the army because of his skirt chasing. It can be heard on YouTube.

[1]Pierre Augustin de Beaumarchais, *The Marriage of Figaro*, trans. Bernard Sahlins. (Chicago: Ivan R. Dee, 1994), p. 29.

intensify the emotional effects of the music. The listener hears the passage, is captured, yet hardly knows why it is as impressive and as memorable as it is. There are ways of doing similar things in drama—repeating gestures, for example—but there are very few ways of repeating elements in such close proximity as the arpeggio does without risking boredom.

The plot of the opera, like that of the play, is based on thwarting the plans of the count with the use of disguise and mix-ups. Characters are hidden in bedrooms, thus overhearing conversations they should not hear. They leap from bedroom windows, hide in closets, and generally create a comic confusion. The much older Marcellina and her lawyer, Bartolo, introduce the complication of a breach of promise suit between her and Figaro just as Figaro is about to marry. The count uses it to his advantage while he can, but the difficulty is resolved in a marvelously comic way: Marcellina sees a birthmark on Figaro and realizes he is her son and the son of Bartolo, with whom she had an affair. That finally clears the way for Figaro and Susanna, who, once they have shamed the count into attending to the countess, can marry.

Mozart's musical resources include techniques that cannot easily be duplicated in straight drama. For example, his extended use of duets, quartets, and sextets, in which characters interact and sing together, would be impossible in the original drama. The libretto gave Mozart a chance to have one character sing a passage while another filled in with an aside. Thus, there are moments when one character sings what he thinks others want him to say, while another character sings his or her inner thoughts, specifically designed for the audience to hear. Mozart reveals the duplicity of characters by having them sing one passage "publicly" while revealing their secret motives "privately."

The force of the quartets and the sextets in *The Marriage of Figaro* is enormous, adding wonderfully to the comic effect that this opera always achieves. Their musical force, in terms of sheer beauty and subtle complexity, is one of the hallmarks of the opera. In the play, it would be impossible to have six characters speaking simultaneously, but with the characters singing, such a situation becomes quite possible.

The resources that Mozart had in orchestration helped him achieve effects that the stage could not produce. The horns, for example, are sometimes used for the purpose of poking fun at the pretentious count, who is a hunter. The discords found in some of the early arias resolve themselves in later arias when the countess smooths them out, as in the opening aria in act 2: "Porgi Amor" ("Pour forth, O Love"). The capacity of the music to emulate the emotional condition of the characters is a further resource that permits Mozart to emphasize tension, as when dissonant chords seem to stab the air to reflect the anxiety of the count. Further, the capacity to bring the music quite low (pianissimo) and then contrast it with brilliant loud passages (fortissimo) adds a dimension of feeling that the play can barely even suggest.

Mozart's *The Marriage of Figaro* also has been successful because of its political message, which is essentially democratic. The opera presents us with a delightful character, Figaro, a barber become a servant, who is level-headed, somewhat innocent of the evil ways of the world, and smart when he needs to be. He loves Susanna, who is much more worldly-wise than he but who is also a thoughtful, intelligent young woman. In contrast, the count is an unsympathetic man who resents the fact that his servant, Figaro, can have what he himself wants but cannot possess. The count is outwitted by his servant and his wife at almost every turn. The countess is a sympathetic character. She loves her husband, knows he wants to be unfaithful, but plays along with Susanna and Figaro in a scheme involving assignations and disguises in order to shame him into doing the right thing. The audiences of the late 1700s loved the play because they reveled in the amusing way that Figaro manipulates his aristocratic master. Beaumarchais's play was as clear about this as the opera. Mozart's interpretation of the play (his subject matter) reveals such a breadth and depth of feeling that now the opera is far more appreciated than the play.

PERCEPTION KEY **Beaumarchais's and Mozart's *The Marriage of Figaro***

Read Beaumarchais's play and Da Ponte's libretto, and see or listen to Mozart's opera. Several videos are available of the Beaumarchais play as well as of Mozart's opera. The Deutsche Grammophon version of the opera, with Dietrich Fischer-Dieskau as the count, is excellent and has English subtitles. Listening to the opera while following the libretto is also of great value. Listen for the use of individual instruments, such as the clarinets on the off-beat, the power of horns and drums, and the repetition of phrases. Pay attention especially to the finale, with its power, simplicity, and matchless humor.

1. Compare the clarity of the development of character in both play and opera. What differences in feelings do the respective works produce?
2. Is character or plot foremost in Beaumarchais's work? Which is foremost in Mozart's?
3. Suppose you knew nothing about the drama and listened only to the music. Would your participation be significantly weakened?

Painting Interprets Poetry: The Starry Night

The visual qualities of poetry sometimes inspire or anticipate painting. One interesting example is that of Vincent van Gogh's most famous painting, *The Starry Night* (Figure 15-4). Van Gogh was a tormented man whose slide into insanity has been chronicled in letters, biographies, romantic novels, and films. His painting of a tortured night sky is filled with dynamic swirls and rich colors, portraying a night that is intensely threatening. He wrote, "Exaggerate the essential and leave the obvious vague."

In 1888 van Gogh wrote to his sister praising the work of Walt Whitman. He assured her that their brother Theo had Whitman's poetry, which was available to him in 1886. He commented on some lines of Whitman that suggested to him "under the starlit vault of Heaven a something which after all can only be called God—and eternity in its place above this world." On December 23 (or 24), 1888, van Gogh experienced a mental episode and cut off part of his ear. He was then admitted to a mental hospital, where he reported that he had spent a great deal of time contemplating the night sky and painting a number of canvases, which he described to his brother. Among them was *The Starry Night*.

Scholars such as Mark Van Doren, Hope B. Werness, and Jean Schwind have noted numerous similarities between Walt Whitman and Vincent van Gogh. They

FIGURE 15-4
Vincent van Gogh, *The Starry Night*.
1889. Oil on canvas, 29 × 36¼
inches (73.7 × 92.1 cm). Museum
of Modern Art, New York. Acquired
through the Lillie P. Bliss Bequest.
Van Gogh's most famous painting
represents the view outside the
window of his sanitarium room—
painted in daylight as a night scene.

©The Museum of Modern Art, NY/Scala/Art
Resource, NY

noted that Whitman's ecstatic verse complements some of the energy of van Gogh's painting. The very title of van Gogh's painting appears in *Leaves of Grass*:

FROM NOON TO STARRY NIGHT

Thou orb aloft full-dazzling! thou hot October noon!
Flooding with sheeny light the gray beach sand,
The sibilant near sea with vistas far and foam,
And tawny streaks and shades and spreading blue;
O sun of noon refulgent! my special word to thee.

> (Walt Whitman,1819–1892, Leaves of Grass Book
> XXXII,"From Noon to Starry Night." Project Gutenburg.)

A passage from Whitman that Hope Werness[2] sees as closely connected with *The Starry Night* is also cited by other commentators on Whitman and van Gogh:

Hurrying with the modern crowd as eager and fickle as any,
Hot toward one I hate, ready in my madness to knife him,
Solitary at midnight in my back yard, my thoughts gone from me a long while,
Walking the old hills of Judaea with the beautiful gentle God by my side,
Speeding through space, speeding through heaven and the stars,

---

[2]Werness, Hope B. "Whitman and Van Gogh: Starry Nights and Other Similarities." *Walt Whitman Quarterly Review* 2 (Spring 1985), 35-41.

Speeding amid the seven satellites and the broad ring, and the
diameter of eighty thousand miles,
Speeding with tail'd meteors, throwing fire-balls like the rest,
Carrying the crescent child that carries its own full mother in its belly,
Storming, enjoying, planning, loving, cautioning,
Backing and filling, appearing and disappearing,
I tread day and night such roads.
I visit the orchards of spheres and look at the product,
And look at quintillions ripen'd and look at quintillions green.

(Walt Whitman, 1819–1892, *Leaves of Grass Book III,*
"Song of Myself." Project Gutenburg.)

The reference to the "crescent child that carries its own full mother in its belly" has
been seen as clarifying the portrait of the crescent moon involved in the noon sun
in the right upper corner of the painting. In addition, van Gogh may have felt a sympathetic strain in Whitman's poetry and in his character. Whitman's expression,
"ready in my madness," may have helped van Gogh experience his own mental
condition as related to art, not just insanity.

PERCEPTION KEY **Vincent van Gogh's *The Starry Night* and
Walt Whitman**

1. In what ways do the samples from Walt Whitman's *Leaves of Grass* echo the details
   or the structure of *The Starry Night*?
2. Which details in *The Starry Night* suggest a connection with Whitman's "tail'd meteors" and "fire-balls"?
3. Some critics have felt that the imagery of *The Starry Night* somehow expresses
   emotions allied with mental states of high anxiety and possibly mental instability.
   Why might they feel this way?
4. Don McLean wrote music and lyrics for a song inspired by van Gogh's painting.
   The lyrics and music for "Vincent (Starry Starry Night)" can be heard on YouTube:
   Search Don McLean Starry Starry Night. What effect does the addition of music
   have on your appreciation of van Gogh's painting? In what ways does it enrich your
   understanding of the painting?
5. Try writing your own song or your own poem as an interpretation of van Gogh's
   painting.

Sculpture Interprets Poetry: Apollo and Daphne

The Roman poet Ovid (43 BCE–17 CE) has inspired artists even into modern times.
His masterpiece, *The Metamorphoses,* includes a large number of myths that were of
interest to his own time and that have inspired readers of all ages. The title implies
changes, virtually all kinds of changes imaginable in the natural and divine worlds.
The sense that the world of Roman deities intersected with humankind had its
Greek counterpart in Homer, whose heroes often had to deal with the interference
of the gods in their lives. Ovid inspired Shakespeare in literature, Botticelli in painting, and perhaps most impressively the sculptor Gian Lorenzo Bernini (1598–1680).

Bernini's technique as a sculptor was without peer in his era. His purposes were
quite different from those of most modern sculptors in that he was not particularly

interested in "truth to materials." If anything, he was more interested in showing how he could defy his materials and make marble, for example, appear to be flesh in motion.

Apollo and Daphne (1622–1625) represents a section of *The Metamorphoses* in which the god Apollo falls in love with the nymph Daphne (Figure 15-5). Cupid had previously hit Apollo's heart with an arrow to inflame him, while he hit Daphne with an arrow designed to make her reject love entirely. Cupid did this in revenge for Apollo's having killed the Python with a bow and arrow. Apollo woos Daphne fruitlessly, she resists, and he attempts to rape her. As she flees from him, she pleads with her father, the river god Peneius, to rescue her, and he turns her into a laurel tree just as Apollo reaches his prey. Here is the moment in Ovid:

> The god by grace of hope, the girl, despair,
> Still kept their increasing pace until his lips
> Breathed at her shoulder; and almost spent,
> The girl saw waves of a familiar river,
> Her father's home, and in a trembling voice
> Called, "Father, if your waters still hold charms
> To save your daughter, cover with green earth
> This body I wear too well," and as she spoke
> A soaring drowsiness possessed her; growing
> In earth she stood, white thighs embraced by climbing
> Bark, her white arms branches, her fair head swaying
> In a cloud of leaves; all that was Daphne bowed
> In the stirring of the wind, the glittering green
> Leaf twined within her hair and she was laurel.

FIGURE 15-5
Gian Lorenzo Bernini, *Apollo and Daphne*. 1622–1625. Marble, 8 feet high. Galleria Borghese, Rome. The sculpture portrays Ovid's story of Apollo's foiled attempt to rape the nymph Daphne.

©Scala/Art Resource, NY

EXPERIENCING Bernini's *Apollo and Daphne* and Ovid's *The Metamorphoses*

1. If you had not read Ovid's *The Metamorphoses*, what would you believe to be the subject matter of Bernini's *Apollo and Daphne*? Do you believe it is a less interesting work if you do not know Ovid?

One obvious issue in looking at this sculpture and considering Ovid's treatment of Apollo and Daphne is that today very few people will have read Ovid before seeing the sculpture. In the era in which Bernini created the work, he expected it to be seen primarily by well-educated people, and in the seventeenth century, most educated people would have been steeped in Ovid from a young age. Consequently, Bernini worked in a classical tradition that he could easily rely on to inform his audience.

Today that classical tradition is essentially gone. Few people, comparatively, read Roman poets, yet the people who see this sculpture in the Galleria Borghese in Rome respond powerfully to it, even without knowing the story it portrays. Standing before this work, one is immediately struck by its size, eight feet high, with the figures fully life-size. The incredible skill of the sculptor is apparent in the ways in which the fingers of Daphne are becoming the leaves of the plant that now bears her name—she is metamorphosing before our eyes, even if we do not know the reference to Ovid's *The Metamorphoses*. The question aesthetically is how much difference does our knowledge of the source text for the sculpture make for our responses to and participation with the sculpture? The interesting thing about knowledge is that once one has it, one cannot "unhave" it. Is it possible to set apart enough of our knowledge of Ovid to look at the sculpture the way we might look at a sculpture by Henry Moore or David Smith? Without knowledge of Ovid, one would see figures in action impressively represented in marble, mixed with important but perhaps baffling vegetation. Visitors to the sculpture seem genuinely awed by its brilliance, and just being told that it portrays a moment in Ovid hardly alters their response to the work. Only when they read Ovid and reflect on the relationship of text to sculpture do they find their responses altered.

2. What does Bernini add to your responses to Ovid's poetry? What is the value of a sculptural representation of a poetic action? What are the benefits to your appreciation of either Bernini or Ovid?

3. Bernini's sculpture is famous for its virtuoso perfection of carving. Yet in this work, "truth to materials" is largely bypassed. Does that fact diminish the effectiveness of the work?

Ovid portrays the moment of metamorphosis as a moment of drowsiness as Daphne becomes rooted and sprouts leaves. It is this instant that Bernini has chosen, an instant during which we can see the normal human form of Apollo, while Daphne's thighs are almost enclosed in bark, her hair and hands growing leaves. The details of this sculpture, whose figures are life-size, are extraordinary. In the Galleria Borghese in Rome, one can walk around the sculpture and examine it up close. The moment of change is so astonishingly wrought, one virtually forgets that it is a sculpture. Bernini has converted the poem into a moment of drama through the medium of sculpture.

Certainly Bernini's sculpture is an "illustration" of a specific moment in *The Metamorphoses*, but it goes beyond illustration. Bernini has brought the moment into a three-dimensional space, with the illusion of the wind blowing Apollo's garments and with the pattern of swooping lines producing a sense of motion. From almost any angle, this is an arresting interpretation, even for those who do not recognize the reference to Ovid.

Drama Interprets Painting

One of the remarkable connections in the arts is the musical theater piece *Sunday in the Park with George* (1984) (Figure 15-6), the Pulitzer Prize–winning play that interpreted George Seurat's (1859–1891) painting *A Sunday Afternoon on the Island of la Grande Jatte* (1884).

The theater interpretation centered on an imaginative biography of Seurat, who was famous for his pointilistic painting style, in which he painted using tiny points of paint that the eye merges so as to perceive an image of people, animals, and things. Seurat's figures in the painting are quite static, posed as if waiting to be photographed. He said he had in mind a Greek bas-relief in the Parthenon that showed a procession of ordinary Greek citizens. At the time he painted the picture, he was known for his general democratic ideals. The island of the Grande Jatte was a favorite place for Parisians to "hang out" in the warm weather. It was where people of many stations of life would socialize. The theater interpretation ends each act with a *tableau vivant* that re-creates the painting.

The first act of the play is set in 1884 Paris, with Jake Gyllenhaal portraying Seurat in a vain effort to save his love for Dot, his mistress. But she rejects him because she feels they do not belong together. The second act is set in 1984—or the present—in which Gyllenhaal plays Seurat's grandson and Ashford plays his grandmother. Modern critics have seen the play as a commentary on the democracy of the modern world.

FIGURE 15-6
Sunday in the Park with George
(1984), by Stephen Sondheim and James Lapine. Jake Gyllenhaal and Annaleigh Ashford appeared in the 2017 revival of the play.

©Sara Krulwich/The New York Times/ Redux

FOCUS ON Photography Interprets Fiction

Although a great many classic paintings were stimulated by narratives, such as Bible stories, Homeric epics, and Ovidian romances, the modern tradition of visual art interpreting fiction has been limited to illustration. Illustrations in novels usually provided visual information to help the reader imagine what the characters look like and what the setting of the novel contributes to the experience of reading. The traditional novelist usually provided plenty of description to help the reader. However, in recent years the profusion of cinema and television interpretations of novels, both historical and contemporary, has led writers to provide fewer descriptive passages to help the reader visualize the scenes. The cinema and television images have substituted for the traditional illustrations because people know what England, France, Ireland, Asia, and Africa look like, and the actors playing the roles of Heathcliff, Anne Elliot, Cleopatra, Hamlet, Macbeth, Jane Eyre, Anna Karenina, and many more have provided indelible images that make book illustration superfluous.

Jeff Wall, a Canadian photographer, is known for his careful preparation of the scenes that he photographs. For example, he spent almost two years putting together the materials for his photograph of *After "Invisible Man" by Ralph Ellison, the Prologue* (Figure 15-7). Ralph Ellison's novel *Invisible Man* (1952) concerns a character known only as the invisible man. The invisible man is a young African American who realizes, in the 1940s, that he is invisible to the general American public. He explains in the prologue to his story that after beating a white man who insulted him, he relents, realizing that the man probably never even saw him. As an African American, he realizes that he has no status in the community, no real place in his own country because of the power of racism. Ellison's novel, widely considered the best American novel of the mid-twentieth century, exposes the depth of racism and how it distorts those who are its victims.

Jeff Wall concentrates on a single moment in the book—in the prologue, in which the invisible man explains how he has tried to make himself visible to his community.

FIGURE 15-7
Jeff Wall, *After "Invisible Man" by Ralph Ellison, the Prologue.* **1999–2000. Museum of Modern Art 1999–2000, printed 2001. Silver dye bleach transparency; aluminum light box, 5 feet 8½ inches × 8 feet 2¾ inches (174 × 250.5 cm).** The invisible man sits in his underground room where even all the lighting he has assembled cannot make him visible to the community of which he is an important part.

Courtesy of the artist

Without light I am not only invisible, but formless as well; and to be unaware of one's form is to live a death. I myself after existing some twenty years, did not become alive until I discovered my invisibility.

That is why I fight my battle with Monopolated Light & Power. The deeper reason, I mean: It allows me to feel my vital aliveness. I also fight them for taking so much of my money before I learned to protect myself. In my hole in the basement there are exactly 1,369 lights. I've wired the entire ceiling, every inch of it. And not with fluorescent bulbs, but with the older, more-expensive-to-operate kind, the filament type. An act of sabotage, you know. I've already begun to wire the wall. A junk man I know, a man of vision, has supplied me with wire and sockets. Nothing, storm or flood, must get in the way of our need for light and ever more and brighter light. The truth is the light and the light is the truth.

continued

Jeff Wall has done what the invisible man has done. He has installed 1,369 filament lights in the space he has constructed to replicate the basement that the invisible man refers to as his "hole." It is his safe place, where he can go to write down the story that is the novel *Invisible Man*. Critics at the Museum of Modern Art contend that Wall has completely rewritten the rules for illustrating fiction by his efforts at making us come close to feeling what the invisible man's lighted place means to him. Illustrators usually select moments and aspects of the fiction's description, but Wall tries to include everything in the basement, even beyond the text's detail. Photography is celebrated often for its ability to document reality; Wall uses photography to document unreality, the only partly described basement room. In this sense, the photograph is hyper-real and thereby reveals the values in the novel in a new way.

PERCEPTION KEY Photography Interprets Fiction

1. The Museum of Modern Art says that Wall's approach to illustrating fiction essentially reinvents the entire idea of illustration. To what extent do you agree or disagree? Could the same be said of *Sunday in the Park with George*?
2. Wall's photograph does not have all the bulbs lighted. In fact, he has chosen to light only some of the bulbs in order to improve the lighting for his photograph. Is that decision a defect in his effort to interpret the novel, or is it the very thing that makes his interpretation more dramatic and more likely to produce a response in the viewer? Comment on the formal qualities of the photograph, the organization of visual elements, the control of color, the position of the figure of the invisible man. How strong is this photograph?
3. After reading *Invisible Man* (if you have the opportunity), what do you feel the photograph adds to your understanding of Ellison's character and his situation?

Architecture Interprets Dance: National Nederlanden Building

In what may be one of the most extraordinary interactions between the arts, the celebrated National Nederlanden Building in Prague, Czech Republic, by the modernist architect Frank Gehry, seems to have almost replicated a duet between Ginger Rogers and Fred Astaire. The building in Prague has been called "Ginger and Fred" since it was finished in 1996 (Figure 15-8). It has also been called "the dancing building," but everyone who has commented on the structure points to its rhythms, particularly the windows, which are on different levels throughout the exterior. The building definitely reflects the postures of Ginger Rogers and Fred Astaire as they appeared in nine extraordinary films from 1933 to 1939 (Figure 15-9). Gehry is known for taking considerable chances in the design of buildings (such as the Guggenheim Museum Bilbao; see Figures 6-24 to 6-26). The result of his effort in generally staid Prague has been a controversial success largely because of its connection with Rogers and Astaire's image as dancers.

Painting Interprets Dance and Music: The Dance and Music

Henri Matisse (1869–1954) was commissioned to paint *The Dance* and *Music* (both 1910) by Sergei Shchukin, a wealthy Russian businessman in Moscow who had

FIGURE 15-8
Frank Gehry, National Nederlanden Building, Prague. 1992–1996. Widely known as "Ginger and Fred," the building's design was inspired by the dancers Ginger Rogers and Fred Astaire, whose filmed dance scenes are internationally respected.

©Don Klumpp/The Image Bank/Getty Images

FIGURE 15-9
Ginger Rogers and Fred Astaire in one of their nine films together. Their configuration closely resembles the form of the building in Prague known as "Ginger and Fred."

©RKO Radio Pictures/Photofest

been a longtime patron. The works were murals for a monumental staircase and, since the Russian Revolution of 1917, have been at the Hermitage in Saint Petersburg. In Matisse's time, Shchukin entertained lavishly, and his guests were sophisticated, well-traveled, beautifully clothed patrons of the arts who went regularly to the ballet, opera, and lavish orchestral concerts. Matisse made his work stand in stark contrast to the aristocratic world of his potential viewers.

According to Matisse, *The Dance* (Figure 15-10) was derived originally from observation of local men and women dancing on the beach in a fishing village in southern France, where Matisse lived for a short time. Their *sardana* was a stylized and staid traditional circle dance, but in the Matisse the energy and joy are wild. *The Dance* interprets the idea of dance rather than any particular dance. Moreover, it is clear that Matisse reaches into the earliest history of dance, portraying naked women and a man dancing with abandon on a green mound against a dark blue sky. Their sense of movement is implied in the gesture of each leg, the posture of each figure, and the instability of pose. The figures have been described as primitive, but their hairdos suggest that they might be contemporary dancers returning to nature and dancing in accord with an instinctual sense of motion.

Music is similarly primitive, with a fiddler and a pipes player (who look as if they were borrowed from a Picasso painting) and three singers sitting on a mound of earth against a dark blue sky (Figure 15-11). They are painted in the same flat reddish tones as the dancers, and it seems as if they are playing and singing the music that the dancers are themselves hearing. Again, the approach to the art of music is as basic as the approach to the art of dance, except that a violin, of course, would not exist in a primitive society. The violin represents the strings, and the pipes represent the woodwinds of the modern orchestra, whereas the other musicians use the most basic of instruments, the human voice. The figures are placed linearly, as if they were notes on a staff, a musical phrase with three rising tones and one falling

FIGURE 15-10
Henri Matisse, *The Dance*. 1910.
Decorative panel, oil on canvas, 102¼
× 125½ inches. The Hermitage, St.
Petersburg. Painted for a Russian
businessman, this hymn to the idea
of dance has become an iconographic
symbol of the power of dance.

©2017 Succession H. Matisse /Artists Rights
Society (ARS), New York. Photograph ©The
State Hermitage Museum, St. Petersburg/
photo by Vladimir Terebenin

FIGURE 15-11
Henri Matisse, *Music*. 1910.
Decorative panel, oil on canvas, 102¼
× 153 inches. The Hermitage, St.
Petersburg. This painting hangs near
Matisse's *The Dance* in the Hermitage.
The five figures are placed as if they
were notes on a music staff.

©2017 Succession H. Matisse /Artists Rights
Society (ARS), New York. Photograph
©The State Hermitage Museum, St.
Petersburg/photo by Vladimir Terebenin

tone (perhaps C A B C G). Music is interpreted as belonging to a later period than
that of the dance.

The two panels, *The Dance* and *Music,* seem designed to work together to imply
an ideal for each art. Instead of interpreting a specific artistic moment, Matisse appears to be striving to interpret the essential nature of both arts.

PERCEPTION KEY Painting and the Interpretation of *The Dance* and *Music*

1. Must these paintings—which are close in size—be hung near each other for both to achieve their complete effect? If they are hung next to each other, do their titles need to be evident for the viewer to respond fully to them?
2. What qualities of *The Dance* make you feel that kinetic motion is somehow present in the painting? What is dancelike here?
3. What does Matisse do to make *Music* somehow congruent with our ideas of music? Which shapes within the painting most suggest music?
4. Suppose the figures and the setting were painted more realistically. How would that stylistic change affect our perception of the essential nature of dance and music?
5. Does participating with these paintings and reflecting on their achievement help you understand and, in turn, enjoy dance and music?

It is fitting to close this chapter with questions arising from a film and an opera that take as their subject matter the same source: Thomas Mann's famous short story *Death in Venice,* published in 1911. Luchino Visconti's 1971 film interprets the story in one way; Benjamin Britten's 1973 opera interprets the story in a significantly different way. Both, however, are faithful to the story. The difference in media has much to do with why the two interpretations of Mann's story are so different despite their basically common subject matter.

EXPERIENCING *Death in Venice*: Three Versions

Read Thomas Mann's *Death in Venice*. This is a haunting tale—one of the greatest short stories of the twentieth century—of a very disciplined, famous writer who, in his fifties, is physically and mentally exhausted. Gustav von Aschenbach seeks rest by means of a vacation, eventually going to Venice. On the beach there, he becomes obsessed with the beauty of a boy. Despite Aschenbach's knowledge of a spreading epidemic of cholera, he remains, and being afraid the boy will be taken away, withholds information about the epidemic from the boy's mother. Casting aside restraint and shame, Aschenbach even attempts, with the help of a barber, to appear youthful again. Yet Aschenbach, a master of language, never speaks to the boy, nor can he find words to articulate the origins of his obsession and love. Collapsing in his chair with a heart attack, he dies as he watches the boy walking off into the sea. Try to see Visconti's film, starring Dirk Bogarde. And listen to Britten's opera with the libretto by Myfanwy Piper, as recorded by London Records, New York City, and starring Peter Pears.

1. Which of these three versions do you find most interesting? Why?
2. Does the film reveal insights about Aschenbach (and ourselves) that are missed in the short story? Does the opera reveal insights that escape both the short story and the film? Be specific. What are the special powers and limitations of these three media?
3. In both the short story and the opera, the opening scene has Aschenbach walking by a cemetery in a suburb of Munich. The film opens, however, with shots of

continued

Aschenbach entering Venice in a gondola. Why do you think Visconti did not use Mann's opening? Why, on the other hand, did Britten use Mann's opening?

4. In the opera, unlike the film, the dance plays a major role. Why?

5. The hold of a boy over a mature, sophisticated man such as Aschenbach may seem at first highly improbable and contrived. How does Mann make this improbability seem plausible? Visconti? Britten?

6. Is Britten able to articulate the hidden deeper feelings of Aschenbach more vividly than Mann or Visconti? If so, how? What can music do that these other two media cannot do in this respect? Note Aschenbach's thought in the novella: "Language could but extol, not reproduce, the beauties of the sense." Note also that Visconti often uses the music of Gustav Mahler to help give us insight into the depths of Aschenbach's character. Does this music, as it meshes with the moving images, do so as effectively as Britten's music?

7. Do these three works complement one another? After seeing the film or listening to the opera, does the short story become richer for you? If so, explain.

8. In the short story, Socrates tells Phaedrus, "For beauty, my Phaedrus, beauty alone, is lovely and visible at once. For, mark you, it is the sole aspect of the spiritual which we can perceive through our senses, or bear so to perceive." But in the opera, Socrates asks, "Does beauty lead to wisdom, Phaedrus?" Socrates answers his own question: "Yes, but through the senses . . . and senses lead to passion . . . and passion to the abyss." Why do you think Britten made such a drastic change in emphasis?

9. What insights into our lives are brought to us by these works? For example, do you have a better understanding of the tragedy of beauty and of the connection between beauty and death? Again, do we have an archetype?

SUMMARY

The arts closely interrelate because artists have the same purpose: the revelation of values. They also must use some medium that can be formed to communicate that revelation, and all artists use some elements of media. Furthermore, in the forming of their media, artists use the same principles of composition. Thus, interaction among the arts is easily accomplished. The arts mix in many ways. Appropriation occurs when an artist combines his or her medium with the medium of another art or arts but keeps the basic medium clearly dominant. Interpretation occurs when an artist uses another work of art as the subject matter. Artists constitute a commonwealth—sharing the same end and using similar means.

©Lee A. Jacobus

Chapter 16

THE INTERRELATIONSHIPS OF THE HUMANITIES

THE HUMANITIES AND THE SCIENCES

In the opening pages of Chapter 1 we defined the humanities as that broad range of creative activities and studies that are usually contrasted with mathematics and the advanced sciences, mainly because in the humanities strictly objective or scientific standards typically do not dominate.

Most college and university catalogs contain a grouping of courses called "the humanities." First, studies such as literature, the visual arts, music, history, *philosophy*, and *theology* are almost invariably included. Second, studies such as psychology, anthropology, sociology, political science, economics, business administration, and education may or may not be included. Third, studies such as physics, chemistry, biology, mathematics, and engineering are never included. The reason the last group is excluded is obvious—strict scientific or objective standards are clearly applicable. With the second group, these standards are not always so clearly applicable. There is uncertainty about whether they belong with the sciences or the humanities. For example, most psychologists who experiment with animals apply the scientific method as rigorously as any biologist. But there are also psychologists—C. G. Jung, for instance—who speculate about such phenomena as the "collective unconscious" and the role of myth (see Chapter 8). Those psychologists belong in the humanities.

Rigorous objective standards may be applied in any of the humanities. Thus, painting can be approached as a science—by the historian of medieval painting, for example, who measures, as precisely as any engineer, the evolving sizes of halos. On the other hand, the beauty of mathematics—its economy and elegance of proof—can excite the lover of mathematics as much as, if not more than, painting. Edna St. Vincent Millay proclaimed that "Euclid alone has looked on beauty bare." And so the separation of the humanities and the sciences should not be observed rigidly. The separation is useful mainly because it indicates the dominance or the subordinance of the strict scientific method in the various disciplines.

THE ARTS AND THE OTHER HUMANITIES

Artists are humanists. But artists differ from the other humanists because they create works that reveal values. Artists are sensitive to the important concerns of their societies. That is their subject matter in the broadest sense. They create artistic forms that clarify these values. The other humanists—such as historians, philosophers, and theologians—reflect upon, rather than reveal, values. They study values as given, as they find them. They try to describe and explain values—their causes and consequences. Furthermore, they may judge these values as good or bad. Thus, like artists, they try to clarify values, but they do this by means of analysis (see Chapter 3) rather than artistic revelation.

Artists may contribute to other humanists by revealing values and informing them through their media of the nature and importance of those values. This is the help that the artists give to the other humanists. Suppose a historian is trying to understand the bombing of Guernica by the Fascists in the Spanish Civil War. Suppose he or she has explored all factual resources. Even then, something very important may be left out: a vivid awareness of the suffering of the noncombatants. To gain insight into that pain, Picasso's *Guernica* (see Figure 1-4) may be very helpful. The same may be said of Francisco Goya's painting *May 3, 1808* (see Figure 2-3), showing the execution of prisoners of war. Art can provide an emotional understanding that data and information cannot.

Other humanists, such as critics and sociologists, may aid artists by their study of values. For example, we have concerned ourselves in some detail with criticism—the description, interpretation, and evaluation of works of art. Criticism is a humanistic discipline because it usually studies values—those revealed in works of art—without strictly applying scientific or objective standards. Good critics aid our understanding of works of art. We become more sensitively aware of the revealed values. This

> **CONCEPTION KEY** **Other Humanists and Artists**
>
> 1. What is the relationship between Picasso's painting *Guernica* and the historical event it portrays? Was Picasso making a statement that can be thought of as contributing to history?
> 2. Picasso painted a night bombing, but the actual bombing occurred in daylight. Why the change? As you think about this, remember that the artist transforms in order to inform.

EXPERIENCING The Humanities and Students of Medicine

Study the following report by Joann Loviglio for the Associated Press, published March 20, 2007.

Modern medicine provides doctors with an array of sophisticated machines that collect and present data about their patients, but the human eye is an invaluable yet often underappreciated diagnostic tool.

To address that, a new collaboration of Jefferson Medical College and the Pennsylvania Academy of the Fine Arts has been created to teach aspiring doctors to closely observe, describe and interpret the subtlest details with the eye of an artist.

The art-and-medicine program kicked off its first workshop Friday with a group of 18 white-coated medical students visiting the academy's museum and a dynamic representation of their chosen profession: Thomas Eakins's masterwork *The Gross Clinic,* which depicts an operation in progress.

The first- and second-year med students heard how to take a "visual inventory"—paying attention to overall elements of the painting, like texture and brightness, and specifics such as body language and facial expressions.

Besides the two-hour Visual Perception workshop, others slated for the 2007–2008 school year are Accuracy and Perception, Hand-Eye Coordination, Art in Healing, and Sculpture and Surgery. The courses are a mix of demonstrations, lectures and hands-on art lessons.

A 2001 study in the *Journal of the American Medical Association* found that medical students in a similar Yale University program acquired more astute observational skills than their colleagues who didn't take the courses. In addition to assessing a patient's well-being during an office visit, finely honed visual abilities can also allow doctors to spot subtle changes in a patient's X-rays over time, for example.

Increasingly, medical schools nationwide are incorporating humanities courses to their curricula.

According to the Association of American Medical Colleges, 89 of the country's 125 medical schools have humanities as an educational element included in a required course, and 66 have it as an elective. (There's overlap because some schools have both.) The figures include all humanities, not just visual arts, spokeswoman Nicole Buckley said. Other humanities studies in medical schools include literature, performing arts, and music.

FIGURE 16-1

Thomas Eakins, *Portrait of Dr. Samuel D. Gross (The Gross Clinic).* 1875. Oil on canvas, 8 feet × 6 feet 6 inches. Philadelphia Museum of Art. *The Gross Clinic* honors Samuel D. Gross, Philadelphia's most famous surgeon. He stands ready to comment on the surgery being performed on a nameless man's thigh. Eakins has caught Gross in a moment confident of great success. Many of the figures in the painting were known to his audience, and Eakins himself is portrayed in the upper right, in the shadows. Critics have claimed this is one of the greatest nineteenth-century American paintings.

continued

1. Eakins's *The Gross Clinic* portrays Samuel D. Gross, a famous surgeon, supervising an operation on a man's left thigh (Figure 16-1). Judging from the expressions on the faces of those involved in the operation, what might a medical student learn about the values that most interested the painter?
2. It seems clear that painting can be important to medical students' education in the humanities. What does this painting reveal about the nature of surgery in 1875?
3. What values does Thomas Eakins's *The Gross Clinic* reveal that could have an impact on students of medicine?
4. How might historians of medicine interpret Eakins's *The Gross Clinic*?
5. What might a medical student learn from this painting that could make the student a better doctor?

deeper understanding brings us into closer rapport with artists, and such rapport helps sustain their confidence in their work.

Artists reveal values; the other humanists study values. That does not mean, of course, that artists may not study values but that such study is subordinated to revealing values in an artistic form that attracts our participation.

VALUES

A value is something we care about, something that matters. A value is an object of an interest. The term "object," however, should be understood as including events or states of affairs. Positive values are those objects of interest that satisfy us or give us pleasure, such as good health. Negative values are those objects of interest that dissatisfy us or give us pain, such as bad health.

When the term "value" is used alone, it usually refers to positive values only, but it may also include negative values. In our value decisions, we generally seek to obtain positive values and avoid negative values. But except for the very young child, these decisions usually involve highly complex activities. To have a tooth pulled is painful, a negative value, but doing so leads to the possibility of better health, a positive value. *Intrinsic values* involve the feelings—such as pleasure and pain—we have of some value activity, such as enjoying good food or experiencing nausea from overeating. *Extrinsic values* are the means to intrinsic values, such as making the money that pays for the food. *Intrinsic-extrinsic values* not only evoke immediate feelings but also are means to further values, such as the enjoyable food that leads to future good health.

Values, we propose, involve a valuer and something that excites an interest in the valuer. *Subjectivist theories of value* claim, however, that it is the interest that projects the value on something. The painting, for example, is positively valuable only because it satisfies the interest of someone. If no one is around to project interest, then it is not a valuable object. Value is entirely relative to the valuer. *Objectivist theories of value* claim, conversely, that it is the object that excites the interest. The painting is positively valuable even if no one has any interest in it. Value is in the object independently of any subject. Jane is beautiful even if no one is aware of her beauty.

The *relational theory of value*—which is the one we have been presupposing throughout this book—claims that value emerges from the relation between an interest and an object. A good painting that is satisfying no one's interest at the moment nevertheless possesses potential value. A good painting possesses properties that under proper conditions are likely to stimulate the interest of a valuer. The subjectivist would say that this painting has no value whatsoever until someone projects value on it. The objectivist would say that this painting has actualized value inherent in it whether anyone enjoys it or not. The relationalist would say that this painting has potential value, that when it is experienced under proper conditions, a sensitive, informed participant will actualize the potential value. To describe a painting as "good" is a recognition that the painting has positive potential value. For the relationalist, value is realized only when objects with potential value connect with the interests of someone.

Values are usually studied with reference to the interaction of various kinds of potential value with human interests. For example, criticism tends to focus on the intrinsic values of works of art; economics focuses on commodities as basically extrinsic values; and *ethics* focuses on intrinsic-extrinsic values as they relate to moral standards.

Values that are described scientifically as they are found we shall call *value facts*. Values that are set forth as norms or ideals or what ought to be we shall call *normative values*. Smoking cigarettes is, for some people, a source of satisfaction, both physically and socially. The value facts known about smoking cigarettes tell us that they damage one's lungs and ultimately cause heart attacks and several forms of cancer. Smoking cigarettes conjures a conflict between the intrinsic value of satisfaction and the extrinsic value of early, painful death. Normative values tell us what our behavior should be. An ideal position on the smoking of cigarettes would tell us that good health in the future is to be preferred to pleasant satisfaction in the present.

The arts and the other humanities may clarify our normative value decisions, thus clarifying what ought to be and what we ought to do. We are beings who must constantly choose among various value possibilities. Paradoxically, even not choosing is often a choice. The humanities can help by revealing consequences of value choices that scientists do not consider. The other humanists help by clarifying consequences of value choices that escape both artists and scientists. For example, the historian or sociologist might trace the consequences of value choices in past societies. Moreover, the other humanists—especially philosophers—can take account of the entire value field, including the relationships between factual and normative values.

CONCEPTION KEY Value Decisions

1. You may have made a judgment about whether or not to smoke cigarettes. Was there any evidence—other than the scientific—that was relevant to your decision? Explain.
2. Reflect about the works of art we have discussed in this book. Which of them clarified value possibilities for you in a way that might influence your value decisions? If so, how? Be as specific as possible. Do some arts seem more relevant than others in this respect? If so, why?
3. Do you think that political leaders are more likely to make wise decisions if they are sensitive to the arts? Back up your answer with reference to specific leaders.
4. Is there is any correlation between a flourishing state of the arts and a democracy? A tyranny? Back up your answers with reference to specific leaders.

Factual values can be verified experimentally, put through the tests of the scientific method. Normative values are verified experientially, put through the tests of good or bad consequences. Satisfaction, for ourselves and the others involved, is an experiential test that the normative values we chose in a given instance were probably right. Suffering, for ourselves and the others involved, is an experiential test that the normative values we chose were probably wrong. Experiential testing of normative values involves not only the immediacy of experience but also the consequences that follow. Science can also point out these consequences, of course, but science cannot make them so forcefully clear and present as the arts, thus so thoroughly understandable.

The arts are closely related to the other humanities, especially history, philosophy, and theology. In conclusion, we shall give only a brief sketch of these relationships, for they are very complex and require extensive analyses that we can only suggest.

FOCUS ON **The Arts and History, the Arts and Philosophy, the Arts and Theology**

The Arts and History

Historians try to discover the what and the why of the past. They need as many relevant facts as possible in order to describe and explain the events that happened. Often they may be able to use the scientific method in their gathering and verification of facts. But in attempting to give as full an explanation as possible as to why some of the events they are tracing happened, they function as humanists, for here they need understanding of the normative values or ideals of the society they are studying. Among their main resources are works of art. Often such works will reveal people's hopes and fears—their views of birth and death, blessing and disaster, victory and disgrace, endurance and decline, themselves and God, fate and what ought to be. Only with the understanding of such values can history become something more than a catalog of events.

In one of his most famous sonnets, John Milton immortalized a moment in 1655 by reference to history and the horrors of a single event. In "On the Late Massacre in Piedmont," Milton refers to a mass killing in a religious war in northern Italy carried out by the Catholic Duke of Savoy. He attacked a Protestant group called Waldensians, who had lived in the region peacefully for almost 200 years. The slaughter took place on April 24, 1655, close to Easter.

ON THE LATE MASSACRE IN PIEDMONT

Avenge, O Lord, thy slaughtered saints, whose bones
    Lie scattered on the Alpine mountains cold;
    Even them who kept thy truth so pure of old,

When all our fathers worshiped stocks and stones,
Forget not: in thy book record their groans
    Who were thy sheep, and in their ancient fold
    Slain by the bloody Piedmontese, that rolled
Mother with infant down the rocks. Their moans
The vales redoubled to the hills, and they
    To heaven. Their martyred blood and ashes sow

O'er all the Italian fields, where still doth sway
    The triple Tyrant; that from these may grow
    A hundredfold, who, having learnt thy way,
    Early may fly the Babylonian *woe*.

[Note: "The triple Tyrant" refers to the pope, who wore a three-sectioned tiara; "the Babylonian woe" is Milton's reference to the Catholic Church.]

Milton's role in this historical event was as a representative of the British Protestant government, drafting and sending an official protest to the Duke of Savoy. Milton's poem was designed for his immediate English audience and ultimately for us. His detail and his metaphors reveal the significance, to him, of this terrible massacre of people, like sheep, who were unaware that the Duke's soldiers had come to kill them or convert them.

The Arts and Philosophy

Philosophy is, among other things, an attempt to give reasoned answers to fundamental questions that, because of their generality, are not treated by any of the more specialized disciplines. Ethics, *aesthetics*, and metaphysics (or speculative philosophy), three of the main divisions of philosophy, are closely related to the arts. Ethics is often the inquiry into the presuppositions or principles operative in our moral judgments and the study of norms or standards for value decisions. If we are correct, an ethic dealing with norms that fails to take advantage of the insights of the arts is inadequate. John Dewey even argued that

> Art is more moral than moralities. For the latter either are, or tend to become, consecrations of the status quo, reflections of custom, reenforcements of the established order. The moral prophets of humanity have always been poets even though they spoke in free verse or by parable.[1]

Sarah Norcliffe Cleghorn (1876–1959) was a friend of Robert Frost and a Vermonter most of her life. She was also an activist and deeply concerned with social issues. The New England in which she lived was filled with mills like those Lewis Hine photographed in North Carolina (Figure 16-2), producing the clothing and necessaries

FIGURE 16-2
Lewis Hine (1874–1940), *Rhodes Mfg. Co., Lincolnton, NC. Spinner. A moment's glimpse of the outer world. Said she was 10 years old. Been working over a year. Location: Lincolnton, North Carolina.* (Hine's title). 1908. National Archives.

©Lewis Hine/The Image Works

---

[1]John Dewey, *Art as Experience* (New York: Minton, Balch, 1934), p. 348.

continued

of much of the nation. Young children worked regularly in those mills, especially up in the top floors, where there was less room for adults to stand upright. The wealthy men who owned the mills worked the laborers intensely while they sometimes enjoyed their recreations. Cleghorn's poem, published in 1916, has no title because it is a quatrain from a longer poem, but it has been widely quoted as it is here:

> The golf links lie so near the mill
> That almost every day
> The laboring children can look out
> And see the men at play.

For Cleghorn, the irony of men at play while children work, like the girl looking out the window in Hine's photograph, was an ethical issue. The labor system of the day saw no problem with what she described, but she wrote this poem in protest.

Throughout this book we have been elaborating an aesthetics, or philosophy of art. We have been attempting to account to some extent for the whole range of the phenomena of art—the creative process, the work of art, the experience of the work of art, criticism, and the role of art in society. On occasion we have avoided restricting our analysis to any single area within that group, considering the interrelationships of these areas. And on other occasions we have tried to make explicit the basic assumptions of some of the restricted studies. These are typical functions of the aesthetician, or philosopher of art. For example, much of our time has been spent doing criticism—analyzing and appraising particular works of art. But at other times, as in Chapter 3, we have tried to make explicit the presuppositions or principles of criticism. Critics, of course, may do this themselves, but then they are functioning more as philosophers than as critics. Furthermore, we have also reflected on how criticism influences artists, participants, and society. This, too, is a function of the philosopher.

The Arts and Theology

Theology involves the study of the sacred. As indicated in Chapter 1, the humanities in the medieval period were studies about humans, whereas theology and related studies were studies about God. But in present times, theology, usually broadly conceived, is placed with the humanities. Moreover, for many religious people today, ultimate values or the values of the sacred are not necessarily ensconced in another world "up there." In any case, some works of art—the masterpieces—reveal ultimate values in ways that are relevant to contemporary life. For many artists, art is an avenue to the sacred.

The great cathedrals of the Middle Ages in Europe were often decorated with stone carvings around the portals (doorways). We know the identities of many of the figures on, for example, Chartres Cathedral. Most of them are recognizable as saints or apostles; some are gargoyles and apocryphal figures. However, the one in Figure 16-3 is known only as a crowned woman with a halo holding a book. The sculpture represented here is a twentieth-century copy, which is

FIGURE 16-3

The crowned woman with a halo holding a book on the left portal of the west facade of Chartres Cathedral.

©Lee A. Jacobus

why it is so clear-featured. The original is in the crypt. But we see that the urge to decorate the church with sculpture may have included the representation of local people of high standing, either in terms of aristocratic influence or special high moral reputation. This figure is represented as holy, as queenly, and as scholarly. The medieval valuation of religious experience produced innumerable such examples of sacred art. This is a case of appropriation, in which the structure uses sculpture to complete its mission.

The Jesuit priest Gerard Manley Hopkins (1844–1889) wrote some of the best religious poetry of his time. He did not publish while he lived, and wrote relatively little, but his work has been considered of the first order of Victorian poetry. His theology included an appreciation of the value of sensory experience. His poem "Pied Beauty," published in 1918, praises God for the beauty perceptible in the natural world, especially in animals and objects whose markings may seem to imply that they are imperfect.

PIED BEAUTY

Glory be to God for dappled things—
    For skies of couple-color as a brinded cow;
      For rose-moles all in stipple upon trout that swim;
Fresh-firecoal chestnut-falls, finches' wings;
    Landscape plotted and pieced—fold, fallow, and plough;
      And áll trádes, their gear and tackle and trim.

All things counter, original, spare, strange;
    Whatever is fickle, freckled (who knows how?)
      With swift, slow; sweet, sour; adazzle, dim;
He fathers-forth whose beauty is past change:
                          Praise him.

Hopkins reflects on the whole of experience by his meditation on the "thisness" of physical experience through the senses that leads him to a deeper understanding of the spiritual qualities of beauty, which he connects directly to God. Hopkins destroyed his early poetry and stopped writing for many years because he thought writing poetry was inappropriate to his calling as a theologian. But his studies of the early church theologian Duns Scotus (1265/66–1308), who promoted the concept of "thisness," freed Hopkins to begin writing again. Scotus's concept of "thisness" gave Hopkins permission to write about the physical world, as he does in "Pied Beauty." Hopkins takes pleasure in sensual experience in the fashion of most observant poets.

CONCEPTION KEY   Ethics and the Arts

1. Reflect on the works of art we have discussed in this book. Which ones do you think might have the most relevance to an ethicist? Why?
2. How does the sculpture of the crowned woman with a halo holding a book seem to represent the sacred and the ethical?
3. What seem to be the ethical issues that concern Lewis Hine?
4. What seem to be the ethical issues that concern Sarah Norcliffe Cleghorn?
5. How do Hine's photograph and Cleghorn's poem contribute to a humanist's understanding of values?
6. In what ways are Hine's photograph and Cleghorn's poem revelatory? Do they transform their subject matter?

SUMMARY

The arts and the other humanities are distinguished from the sciences because in the former, generally, strictly objective or scientific standards are irrelevant. In turn, the arts are distinguished from the other humanities because in the arts values are revealed, whereas in the other humanities values are studied. Furthermore, in the arts perception dominates, whereas in the other humanities conception dominates.

In our discussion about values, we distinguish between (1) intrinsic values—activities involving immediacy of feeling, positive or negative; (2) extrinsic values—activities that are means to intrinsic values; and (3) intrinsic-extrinsic values—activities that not only are means to intrinsic values but also involve significant immediacy of feeling. A value is something we care about, something that matters. The theory of value presupposed in this book has been relational; that is, value emerges from the relation between a human interest and an object or event. Value is not merely subjective—projected by human interest on some object or event—nor is value merely objective—valuable independently of any subject. Values that are described scientifically are value facts. Values set forth as norms or ideals or what ought to be are normative values. The arts and the other humanities often have normative relevance: by clarifying what ought to be and thus what we ought to do.

Finally, the arts are closely related to the other humanities, especially history, philosophy, and theology. The arts help reveal the normative values of past cultures to the historian. Philosophers attempt to answer questions about values, especially in the fields of ethics, aesthetics, and metaphysics. Some of the most useful insights about value phenomena for the philosopher come from artists. Theology involves the study of religions, and religions are grounded in ultimate concern for values. No human artifacts reveal ultimate values more powerfully to the theologian than works of art.

GLOSSARY

A

A-B-A In music, a three-part structure that consists of an opening section, a contrasting second section, and a return to the first section.

Abstract, or nonrepresentational, painting Painting that has the sensuous as its subject matter.

Acrylic In painting, pigment bound by a synthetic plastic substance, allowing it to dry much faster than oils.

Adagio A musical term denoting a slow and graceful tempo.

Aerial perspective The portrayal of distance in painting by means of dimming light and atmosphere. See *perspective*.

Aesthetics Philosophy of art: the study of the creative process, the work of art, the aesthetic experience, principles of criticism, and the role of art in society.

Agnosticism Belief that one cannot know for sure whether God exists.

Aleatory Dependent on chance.

Allegory An image, a figure, or a term that symbolizes a specific hidden meaning.

Allegretto A musical term denoting a lively tempo but one slower than allegro.

Allegro A musical term denoting a lively and brisk tempo.

Alliteration In literature, the repetition of consonant sounds in two or more neighboring words or syllables.

Ambiguity Uncertain meaning, a situation in which several meanings are implied. Sometimes implies contradictory meanings.

Anapest A poetic metrical foot of three syllables, the first two being short and the last being long.

Andante A musical term denoting a leisurely tempo.

Appropriation In the arts, the act of combining the artist's basic medium with the medium of another art or arts but keeping the basic medium clearly dominant. See *synthesis* and *interpretation*.

Arabesque A classical ballet pose in which the body is supported on one leg, and the other leg is extended behind with the knee straight.

Arcade In architecture, a series of arches side by side and supported by columns or piers.

Arch In architecture, a structural system in which space is spanned by a curved member supported by two legs.

Archetype An idea or behavioral pattern, often formed in prehistoric times, that becomes a part of the unconscious psyche of a people. The archetype is embedded in the "collective unconscious," a term from Jungian psychology that has been associated by Jung with myth. In the arts, the archetype is usually expressed as a narrative pattern, such as the quest for personal identity. See *myth*.

Architrave In post-and-lintel architecture, the lintel or lowermost part of an entablature, resting directly on the capitals of the columns.

Arena Theater A stage arrangement in which the stage is surrounded on all sides by seats.

Aria An elaborate solo song used primarily in operas, oratorios, and cantatas.

Art Deco In the visual arts, a style prevalent between 1915 and 1940.

Art Nouveau A style of architecture characterized by lively serpentine curves and organic growth.

Artistic form The organization of a medium that clarifies or reveals a subject matter. See *content, decorative form, subject matter,* and *work of art*.

Artlike Works that possess some characteristics of works of art but lack revelatory power.

Assemblage The technique of sculpture, such as welding, whereby preformed pieces are attached. See *modeling*.

Assonance A sound structure employing a similarity among vowels but not consonants.

Atonal Music without a dominant key.

Auteur The author or primary maker of the total film, usually the director.

Avant-garde The "advance guard"—innovators who break sharply with traditional conventions and styles.

Axis line An imaginary line—generated by a visible line **or** lines—that helps determine the direction of the eye in any of the visual arts.

Axis mundi A vertically placed pole used by some primitive peoples to center their world.

B

Baroque The style dominant in the visual arts in seventeenth-century Europe following the Renaissance, characterized by vivid colors, dramatic light, curvilinear heavy lines, elaborate ornamentation, bold scale, and strong expression of emotion. Music is the only other art of that time that can be accurately described as Baroque. See *Rococo*.

Beauty An arrangement that is pleasing.

Binder The adhering agent for the various media of painting.

Blank verse Poetry with rhythm but not rhyme.

Buttress In architecture, a structure built on a wall, vault, or an arch for reinforcing support.

C

Cadence In music, the harmonic sequence that closes a phrase.

Cantilever In architecture, a projecting beam or structure supported at only one end, which is anchored to a pier or wall.

Carving Shaping by cutting, chipping, hewing, etc.

Casting The process of making a sculpture or other object by pouring liquid material into a mold and allowing it to harden.

Catharsis The cleansing or purification of the emotions and, in turn, a spiritual release and renewal.

Centered space A site—natural or human-made—that organizes other places around it.

Character In drama, the agents and their purpose.

Chiaroscuro Technique in painting that combines and contrasts light and shade.

Chord Three or more notes played at the same time.

Cinematic motif In film, a visual image that is repeated either in identical form or in variation.

Cinematography The way the film camera tells a story.

Classical style In Greek art, the style of the fifth century BCE. More generally, the term "Classical" sometimes refers to the ancient art of Greece and Rome. Also, it sometimes refers to an art that is based on rational principles and deliberate composition. The lowercase term "classic" can mean excellence, whatever the period or style.

Closed line In painting, hard and sharp line. See *line*.

Coda Tonal passage or section that ends a musical composition.

Collage A work made by pasting bits of paper or other material onto a flat surface.

Collective unconscious Jung's phrase for the universality of myths among cultures, some of which had no contact.

Color The property of reflecting light of a particular wavelength.

Color value Shading, the degree of lightness or darkness of a hue.

Comedy A form of drama that is usually light in subject matter and ends happily but that is not necessarily void of seriousness.

Complementary colors Colors that lie opposite each other on the color wheel.

Composition The organization of the elements. See *design*.

Computer art Works using the computer as the medium.

Conception Thinking that focuses on concepts or ideas. See *perception*.

Conceptual art Works that bring the audience into direct contact with the creative concepts of the artist; a de-emphasis on the medium.

Conceptual metaphor A comparison that evokes ideas.

Configurational center A place of special value, a place to dwell.

Connotation Use of language to suggest ideas and/or emotional coloration in addition to the explicit or denoted meaning. "Brothers and sisters" denotes relatives, but the words may also connote people united in a common effort or struggle, as in the "International Brotherhood of Teamsters" or the expression "Sisterhood is powerful." See *denotation*.

Consonance When two or more tones sounded simultaneously are pleasing to the ear. See *dissonance*.

Content Subject matter detached by means of artistic form from its accidental or insignificant aspects and thus clarified and made more meaningful. See *subject matter*.

Cool color A color that is recessive, such as blue, green, and black.

Cornice The horizontal molding projecting along the top of a building.

Counterpoint In music, two or more melodies, themes, or motifs played in opposition to each other at the same time.

Craft Skilled making.

Craftwork The product of craft, usually utilitarian and beautiful.

Crescendo A gradual increase in loudness.

Criticism The analysis and evaluation of works of art.

Cross-referencing Memory of a similar work that enriches a participative experience.

Crosscutting In film, alternation between two separate actions that are occurring at the same time.

D

Dadaism A movement begun during World War I in Europe that was anti-everything; a precursor of shock art and Duchampism.

Decoration An artlike element added to enhance or adorn something else.

Decorative form The organization of a medium that pleases, distracts, or entertains but does not inform about values. See *artistic form*.

Denotation The direct, explicit meaning or reference of a word or words. See *connotation*.

Denouement The section of a drama in which events are brought to a conclusion.

Descriptive criticism The description of the subject matter and/or form of a work of art.

Design The overall plan of a work before implementation. See *composition*.

Detail Elements of structure; in painting, a small part.

Detail relationships Significant relationships between or among details. See *structural relationships*.

Diction In literature, drama, and film, the choice of words with special care for their expressiveness.

Dissolve In film, the slow ending of a scene.

Dissonance When two or more tones sounded simultaneously are unpleasant to the ear. See *consonance*.

Documentarists Photographers who document the present to preserve a record of it as it disappears.

Duchampism School of art that produced works that are anti-art and anti-establishment but are funny rather than angry. See *Dadaism*.

Dynamics In music, the loudness and softness of the sound.

E

Earth sculpture Sculpture that makes the earth the medium, site, and subject matter.

Earth-dominating architecture Buildings that "rule over" the earth.

Earth-resting architecture Buildings that accent neither the earth nor the sky, using the earth as a platform with the sky as a background.

Earth-rooted architecture Buildings that bring out with special force the earth and its symbolism. See *sky-oriented architecture*.

Eclecticism A combination of several different styles in a work.

Editing In film, the process by which the footage is cut, the best version of each scene chosen, and these versions joined together for optimum effect. See *montage*.

Elements The basic components of a medium. See *media*.

Elements of drama (Aristotle's) Plot, character, thought, diction, spectacle, and music. See entries under individual elements.

Embodiment The meshing of medium and meaning in a work of art.

Emotion Strong sensations felt as related to a specific and apparent stimulus. See *passion* and *mood*.

Epic A lengthy narrative poem, usually episodic, with heroic action and great cultural scope.

Epicureanism The belief that happiness is based on pleasure.

Episodic narrative A story composed of separate incidents (or episodes) tied loosely together. See *organic narrative*.

Ethics The inquiry into the presuppositions or principles operative in our moral judgments. Ethics is a branch of philosophy.

Evaluative criticism Judgment of the merits of a work of art.

Expressionism School of art in which the work emphasizes the artist's feelings or state of mind.

Extrinsic value The means to intrinsic values or to further, higher values. See *intrinsic value*.

F

f/64 Group A group of photographers whose name derives from the small aperture, *f*/64, which ensures that the foreground, middle ground, and background will all be in sharp focus.

Fantasia A musical composition in which the "free flight of fancy" prevails over conventional structures such as the sonata form.

Figure of speech Language used to heighten effect, especially by comparison.

Flaw in character (hamartia) In drama, the prominent weakness of character that leads to a tragic end.

Flying buttress An arch that springs from below the roof of a Gothic cathedral, carrying the thrust above and across a side aisle.

Folk art Work produced outside the professional tradition.

Form-content The embodiment of the meaning of a work of art in the form.

Forte A musical term denoting loud.

Framing The photographic technique whereby important parts of figures or objects in a scene are cut off by the edges of the photograph.

Fresco A wall painting. Wet fresco involves pigment applied to wet plaster. Dry fresco involves pigment applied to a dry wall. Wet fresco generally is much more enduring than dry fresco.

Frieze Low-relief sculpture running high and horizontally on a wall of a building.

Fugue A musical composition in which a theme, or motive, is announced and developed contrapuntally in strict order. See *counterpoint*.

G

Genre Kind or type.

Genre painting Subjects or scenes drawn from everyday life portrayed realistically.

Gouache A watercolor medium with gum added.

Greek cross A cross with equal vertical and horizontal arms. See *Latin cross*.

H

Happenings Very impromptu performances, often involving the audience. See *shock art*.

Harmony The sounding of notes simultaneously.

Hearer One who hears music without careful attention to details or structure. See *listener*.

High-relief sculpture Sculpture with a background plane from which the projections are relatively large.

Historical criticism The description, interpretation, or evaluation of works of art with reference to their historical precedents.

Hue The name of a color. See *saturation*.

Humanities Broad areas of human creativity and analysis essentially involved with values and generally not using strictly objective or scientific methods.

I

Iambic pentameter Type of poetic meter. An iamb is a metrical unit, or foot, of two syllables, the first unaccented and the second accented. Pentameter is a five-foot line. See *sonnet*.

Idea art Works in which ideas or concepts dominate the medium, challenging traditional presuppositions about art, especially embodiment. In an extreme phase, ideas are presented in diagram or description rather than in execution. See *embodiment*.

Illumination Hand-drawn decoration or illustration in a manuscript.

Illustration Image that closely resembles an object or event.

Imagery Use of language to represent objects and events with strong appeal to the senses, especially the visual.

Impasto The painting technique of heavily applying pigment so as to create a three-dimensional surface.

Impressionist school The famous school of art that flourished between 1870 and 1905, especially in France. Impressionists' approach to painting was dominated by a concentration on the impression light made on the surfaces of things.

Improvisation Music or other performance produced on the spur of the moment.

Inorganic color In painting, flat color, appears laid on the object depicted. See *organic color*.

Intaglio A printmaking process in which ink is transferred from the grooves of a metal plate to paper by extreme pressure.

Intentional fallacy In criticism, the assumption that what the artists say they intended to do outweighs what they in fact did.

Interpretation In the arts, the act of using another work of art as subject matter. See *appropriation* and *synthesis*.

Interpretive criticism Explication of the content of a work of art.

Intrinsic value The immediate given worth or value of an object or activity. See *extrinsic value*.

Irony A literary device that says one thing but means another. Dramatic irony plays on the audience's capacity to perceive the difference between what the characters expect and what they will get.

K

Key A system of tones based on and named after a given tone—the tonic.

Kitsch Works that realistically depict objects and events in a pretentious, vulgar manner.

L

Labanotation A system of writing down dance movements.

Largo A musical term denoting a broad, very slow, stately tempo (also called lento).

Latin cross A cross in which the vertical arm is longer than the horizontal arm, through whose midpoint it passes. Chartres and many other European cathedrals are based on a recumbent Latin cross. See *Greek cross*.

Legato A musical term indicating that a passage should be played smoothly and without a break between the tones.

Leitmotif In music, a leading theme.

Libretto The text of an opera.

Line A continuous marking made by a moving point on a surface. The basic building block of visual design.

Linear perspective The creation of the illusion of distance in a two-dimensional work by means of converging lines. In one-point linear perspective, developed in the fifteenth century, all parallel lines in a given visual field converge at a single vanishing point on the horizon. See *perspective*.

Listener One who listens to music with careful attention to details and structure. See *hearer*.

Living space The feeling of the comfortable positioning of things in the environment that promotes both liberty of movement and paths as directives.

Low-relief sculpture Sculpture with a background plane from which the projections are relatively small.

Lyric A poem, usually brief and personal, with an emphasis on feelings or states of mind as part of the subject matter. Lyric songs use lyric poems.

M

Machine sculpture Sculpture that reveals the machine and/or its powers.

Madrigal In music, a secular song usually for two or three unaccompanied voices.

Mass In sculpture, three-dimensional form suggesting bulk, weight, and density.

Media The materials out of which works of art are made. These elements either have an inherent order, such as colors, or permit an imposed order, such as words; these orders, in turn, are organizable by form. Singular, *medium*. See *elements*.

Melodic line A vague melody without a clear beginning, middle, and end.

Melodrama In theater, a genre characterized by stereotyped characters, implausible plots, and emphasis on spectacle.

Melody A group of notes having a perceivable beginning, middle, and end. See *theme*.

Metaphor An implied comparison between different things. See *simile*.

Middle Ages The centuries roughly between the dissolution of the Roman Empire (ca. 500) and the Renaissance (fifteenth century).

Mixed media The combination of two or more artistic media in the same work.

Mobile A constructed structure whose components have been connected at the joints to move by force of wind or motor.

Modeling The technique of building up a sculpture piece by piece with some malleable material. See *assemblage*.

Moderato A musical term instructing the player to be neither fast nor slow in tempo.

Modern art The bewildering variety of styles that developed after World War II, characterized by the tendency to reject traditionally accepted styles, emphasizing originality and experimentation, often with new technologies.

Modern dance A form of concert dancing relying on emotional use of the body, as opposed to formalized or conventional movement, and stressing emotion, passion, mood, and states of mind.

Montage The joining of physically different but usually psychologically related scenes. See *editing*.

Mood A feeling that arises from no specific or apparent stimulus.

Motive In music, a brief but intelligible and self-contained unit, usually a fragment of a melody or theme.

Myth Ancient stories rooted in primitive experience, usually of unknown authorship, ostensibly based on historical events of great consequence.

▍ N ▍

Narrative A story told to an audience.

Narrator The teller of a story.

Negative space In sculpture, any empty or open space.

Neo-classical A return in the late eighteenth and early nineteenth centuries, in reaction to the Baroque and the Rococo, to the Classical styles of ancient Greece and Rome, characterized by reserved emotions. See *Romanticism*.

New Comedy Subject matter centered on the foibles of social manners and mores. Usually quite polished in style, with bright wit and incisive humor.

Nocturne In music, a pensive, dreamy composition, usually for piano.

Normative values Values set forth as norms or ideals, what "ought to be."

▍ O ▍

Objective correlative An object, representation, or image that evokes in the audience the emotion the artist wishes to express.

Objectivist theory of value Value is in the object or event itself independently of any subject or interest. See *relational* **and** *subjectivist theory of value*.

Ode A ceremonious lyric poem.

Oil painting Artwork in which the medium is pigment mixed with linseed oil, varnish, and turpentine.

Old Comedy Subject matter centered on ridiculous and/or highly exaggerated situations. Usually raucous, earthy, and satirical.

Onomatopoeia The use of words whose sounds suggest their meaning.

Open line In painting, soft and blurry line. See *closed line*.

Organic color In painting, color that appears deep, as if coming out of an object depicted. See *inorganic color*.

Organic narrative A story composed of separable incidents that relate to one another in tightly coherent ways, usually causally and chronologically. See *episodic narrative*.

▍ P ▍

Panning In film, the moving of the camera without pause.

Paradox An apparent contradiction that, upon reflection, may seem reasonable.

Participative experience Letting something initiate and control everything that comes into awareness—thinking from.

Pas de deux A dance for two dancers.

Pas de trois A dance for three dancers.

Passion Emotions elevated to great intensity.

Pediment The triangular space formed by roof jointure in a Greek temple or a building on the Greek model.

Perception Awareness of something stimulating our sense organs.

Perceptual metaphor A comparison that evokes images.

Performance art Generally site-specific events often performed with little detailed planning and leaving much to chance; audience participation may ensue. See *shock art*.

Perspective In painting, the illusion of depth.

Philosophy The discipline that attempts to give reasoned answers to questions that—because of their generality—are not treated by any of the more specialized disciplines. Philosophy is the systematic examination of our fundamental beliefs.

Piano   A musical term instructing the player to be soft, or quiet, in volume.

Pictorial space   The illusory space in a painting that seems to recede into depth from the picture plane (the "window effect").

Pictorialists   Photographers who use realistic paintings as models for their photographs. See *straight photography*.

Picture plane   The flat surface of a painting, comparable to the glass of a framed picture behind which the picture recedes in depth.

Pigment   For painting, the coloring agent.

Plot   The sequence of actions or events in literature and drama.

Polyphony   In music, two or more melodic lines sounded together.

Pop Art   Art that realistically depicts and sometimes incorporates mass-produced articles, especially the familiar objects of everyday life.

Popular art   Contemporary works enjoyed by the masses.

Pornography   Works made to sexually arouse.

Post-and-lintel   In architecture, a structural system in which the horizontal pieces (lintels) are upheld by vertical columns (posts). Also called post-and-beam.

Presentational immediacy   The awareness of something that is presented in its entirety with an "all-at-onceness."

Presto   A musical term signifying a rapid tempo.

Pretext   The underlying narrative of the dance.

Primary colors   Red, yellow, and blue. See *secondary colors*.

Print   An image created from a master wooden block, stone, plate, or screen, usually on paper. Many impressions can be made from the same surface.

Processional shot   The camera focuses on figures and objects moving toward the camera.

Propaganda   Political persuasion.

Proportion   Size relationships between parts of a whole.

Proscenium   The arch, or "picture frame," stage of traditional theater that sets apart the actors from the audience.

Protagonist   The chief character in drama and literature.

❚ Q ❚

Quest narrative   In literature, a story that revolves around the search by the hero for an object, prize, or person who is hidden or removed. This typically involves considerable travel and wandering on the part of the hero.

Quoins   Large squared stones, often roughly cut, that accent the corners of a building.

❚ R ❚

Realism   The portrayal of objects and events in a highly representational manner. An important style of painting around 1840–1860.

Recessional shot   The camera focuses on distant figures while leaving foreground figures somewhat blurred, used typically when the distant figure is leaving.

Recitative   Sung dialogue in opera, cantata, and oratorio.

Recognition   In drama, the moment of truth, often the climax.

Region   In painting, a large part. See *detail*.

Regional relationships   Significant relationships between regions. See *structural relationships*.

Relational theory of value   Value emerges from the relation between a human interest and an object or event. See *objectivist* **and** *subjectivist theory of value*.

Relief   With sculpture, projection from a background.

Renaissance   The period in Europe from the fifteenth through sixteenth century with a renewed interest in ancient Greek and Roman civilizations. See *Classical style*.

Representational   Descriptive of portrayals that closely resemble objects and events.

Representational painting   Painting that has specific objects or events as its primary subject matter. See *abstract painting*.

Requiem   A mass for the dead.

Reversal   In drama, when the protagonist's fortunes turn from good to bad.

Rhyme   A sound structure coupling words that sound alike.

Rhythm   The relationship, of either time or space, between recurring elements of a composition.

Ritardando   In music, a decrease in tempo.

Rococo   The style of the visual arts dominant in Europe during the first three-quarters of the eighteenth century, characterized by light curvilinear forms, pastel colors, ornate and small-scale decoration, the playful and lighthearted. Rococo music is lighter than Baroque. See *Baroque*.

Romanticism   Style of the nineteenth century that in reaction to Neo-classicism denies that humanity is essentially rational and the measure of all things, characterized by intense colors, open line, strong expression of feeling, complex organizations, and often heroic subject matter.

Rondo   A form of musical composition employing a return to an initial theme after the presentation of each new theme—for example, A-B-A-C-A-D-A.

Rubato   A style of musical performance in which the performer takes liberties with the rhythm of the piece.

S

Satire   Literature that ridicules people or institutions.

Saturation   The purity, vividness, or intensity of a hue.

Scherzo   A musical term implying playfulness or fun. The word literally means "joke."

Sciences   Disciplines that for the most part use strictly objective methods and standards.

Sculpture in the round   Sculpture freed from any background plane.

Secondary colors   Green, orange, and violet. See *primary colors*.

Sensa   The qualities of objects or events that stimulate our sense organs, especially the eyes. See *sensuous*.

Sensuous   In painting, the color field as composed by sensa. See *abstract painting*.

Sentimentality   Oversimplification and cheapening of emotional responses to complex subject matter.

Setting   In literature, drama, opera, dance, and film, the time and place in which the work of art occurs. The setting is established mainly by means of description in literature and spectacle in drama, opera, dance, and film.

Shape   The outlines and contours of an object.

Shock art   Attention-grabbing works intended to shock or repel, which usually fail to hold attention.

Shot   In film, a continuous length of film exposed in the camera without a break.

Simile   An explicit comparison between different things, using comparative words such as "like."

Sky-oriented architecture   Buildings that bring out with special emphasis the sky and its symbolism. See *earth-resting, earth-rooted,* and *earth-dominating architecture*.

Soliloquy   An extended speech by a character alone with the audience.

Sonata form   In music, a movement with three major sections—exposition, development, and recapitulation—often followed by a coda.

Sonnet   A poem of fourteen lines, with fixed rhyming patterns, typically in iambic pentameter. See *iambic pentameter*.

Space   A hollow volume available for occupation by shapes, and the effect of the positioned interrelationships of these shapes.

Space sculpture   Sculpture that emphasizes spatial relationships and thus tends to de-emphasize the density of its materials.

Spectacle   The visual setting of a drama.

Spectator experience   Thinking at something. See *participative experience*.

Staccato   In music, the technique of playing so that individual notes are short and separated from each other by sharp accents.

State of mind   An attitude or orientation of mind that is relatively enduring.

Stereotype   A very predictable character. See *type character*.

Stoicism   The curbing of desire to cope with the inevitability of pain.

Straight photography   Style that aims for excellence in photographic techniques independent of painting. See *pictorialists*.

Structural relationships   Significant relationships between or among details to the totality.

Structure   Overall organization of a work.

Style   The identifying features—characteristics of form—of a work or group of works that identify it with an artist, group of artists, era, or culture.

Subject matter   What the work of art "is about"; some value *before* artistic clarification. See *content*.

Subjectivist theory of value   Value is projected by human interest on some object or event. See *objectivist* and *relational theory of value*.

Sunken-relief sculpture   Sculpture made by carving grooves of various depths into the surface planes of the sculptural material, the surface plane remaining perceptually distinct.

Surface relief   Sculpture with a flat surface plane as the basic organizing plane of the composition, but with no clear perceptual distinction perceivable between the depths behind the surface plane and the projections in front.

Surrealism   A painting style of the 1920s and 1930s that emphasizes dreamlike and fantastic imagery.

Symbol   Something perceptible that stands for something more abstract.

Symmetry   A feature of design in which two halves of a composition on either side of a central vertical axis are more or less of the same size, shape, and placement.

Synthesis   In the arts, the more or less equal combination of the media of two or more arts. See *appropriation* and *interpretation*.

T

Tactility   Touch sensations, both inward and outward.

Tempera   In painting, pigment bound by egg yolk.

Tempo   The speed at which a composition is played.

Tertiary colors   Colors produced by mixing the primary and secondary colors.

Texture   The surface "feel" of a material, such as "smooth" bronze or "rough" concrete.

Theatricality   Exaggeration and artificiality.

Theme   In music, a melody or motive of considerable importance because of later repetition or development. In other arts, a theme is a main idea or general topic.

Theme   In music, a melody or motive of considerable importance because of later repetition or development. In other arts, a theme is a main idea or general topic.

Theology   The study of the sacred.

Thought   The ideas expressed in works of art. Also, the thinking that explains the motivations and actions of the characters in a story.

Timbre   A quality given a musical tone by the overtones that distinguish musical instruments from each other.

Tone   A sound that has a definite frequency.

Tragedy   Drama that portrays a serious subject matter and ends unhappily.

Tragicomedy   Drama that includes, more or less equally, characteristics of both tragedy and comedy.

Transept   The crossing arm of a church structured like a Latin cross. See *Latin cross*.

Truth to materials   Respect for the distinctive characteristics of an artistic medium.

Twelve-tone technique   A twentieth-century atonal structuring of music—no tonic or most important tone—developed especially by Schoenberg.

Tympanum   The space above an entranceway to a building, often containing sculpture.

Type character   A predictable character. See *stereotype*.

I V I

Value facts   Values described scientifically. See *normative values*.

Values   Objects and events that we care about, that have great importance. Also, with regard to color, value refers to the lightness or darkness of a hue.

Vanishing point   In linear perspective, the point on the horizon where parallel lines appear to converge.

Virtual art   Computer-created, imaginary, three-dimensional scenes in which the participant is involved interactively.

Virtuoso   The display of impressive technique or skill by an artist.

I W I

Warm color   A color that is aggressive, such as red and yellow.

Watercolor   For painting, pigment bound by a water-soluble adhesive, such as gum arabic.

Work of art   An artifact that informs about values by means of artistic form. See *artistic form*.

INDEX

Viola, Bill, 331–332
  City of Man, 351
  The Greeting, 348–349, 348*f*
  The Passions, 347–349
  The Quintet of the Astonished, 349, 350*f*
violence, and film, 310–311
The Virgin Spring (Bergman), 311
virtual art, 376–377
virtuoso, 269
Visconti, Luchino, *Death in Venice,*
  395–396
Vishneva, Diana, 271, 271*f*
The Visitation (Pontormo), 348–349, 349*f*
visual powers, and painting,
  58–59
Vulture and Child in Sudan (Carter), 29–30,
  29*f*

I W I

Wagner, Richard
  Die Walküre, 312
  Ring of the Niebelungs, 264, 379
Waiting for Godot (Beckett), 221
Wall, Jeff, *After "Invisible Man" by Ralph
  Ellison, the Prologue,* 391–392, 391*f*
Wallis, Henry, 86–88
  The Death of Chatterton, 86*f,* 88
Wall Street, New York (Strand),
  287, 287*f*
Wang Chang-Ling, "So-Fei Gathering
  Flowers," 186–187
Wang Qingsong, *Can I Cooperate with You?,*
  296–297, 296*f*

Wang Yuanqi, *Landscape after Wu Zhen,* 65,
  66, 67*f,* 72, 73
Warhol, Andy, 280, 326
  Marilyn Monroe series, 65
  200 Campbell's Soup Cans, 358, 358*f*
watercolor, 64, 73
Waterhouse, John, *La Belle Dame Sans
  Merci,* 179, 180*f*
Weekend (Godard), 305
Weems, Carrie Mae, *Untitled (Man
  smoking),* 294, 294*f,* 298
Weiss, Peter, *Marat/Sade,* 222
We Keep Our Victims Ready (Finley),
  374–375
Welles, Orson, *Citizen Kane,*
  306–307
Wesselman, Tom, *Great American Nude,*
  36*f,* 40, 69, 73
Weston, Edward, 29
  Nude, 284, 284*f*
West Side Story, 273, 273*f*
"When I have fears . . ." (Keats),
  178–179
Whiteman, Paul, 248
Whitman, Walt, 385–387
  From Noon to Starry Night, 386–387
Wilde, Oscar, *The Importance of Being
  Earnest,* 198–199, 201
Wild Strawberries (Bergman), 317
Williams, Michael Kenneth, 339, 339*f*
Williams, Tennessee, *The Glass Menagerie,*
  199
Willis, Wallace, 235
The Wire, 338–339, 338*f,* 339*f*

Woman I (de Kooning), 70, 71*f,* 73, 75, 80
Woman with a Purse (Hanson), 355,
  355*f,* 358
Woodrow, Taylor, 374
word art, 370, 371*f*
works of art. *See also* artistic form; content;
  participation; subject matter
  basic terms, 19
  detail, regional and structural
    relationships, 46–48
  overview, 17–41
works of art, identifying, 18
  conceptually, 18
  perceptually, 18–19
Wrapped Reichstag (Christo and Jeanne-
  Claude), 373, 373*f*
Wright, Frank Lloyd, 128
  Kaufmann house (Fallingwater), 135,
    135*f,* 145
  Solomon R. Guggenheim Museum, 128,
    129*f,* 130*f,* 138, 145, 147
Wyeth, Andrew, 360
  Christina's World, 360–362, 361*f*
Wyeth, N. C., 360

I Y I

Yeats, William Butler, "The Lake Isle of
  Innisfree," 50
Youth (Conrad), 184

I Z I

Zootopia, 327–328, 329*f*